Chaos and Conspiracy

The Framing of the McBrearty Family

Gerard Cunningham

Gill & Macmillan

Gill & Macmillan Ltd
Hume Avenue, Park West, Dublin 12
with associated companies throughout the world
www.gillmacmillan.ie

978 07171 4571 3

Type design by Make Communication
Print origination by Carole Lynch
Printed in the UK by CPI Mackays, Chatham ME5 8TD

This book is typeset in Linotype Minion and Neue Helvetica.

The paper used in this book comes from the wood pulp of
managed forests. For every tree felled, at least one tree is
planted, thereby renewing natural resources.

A CIP catalogue record for this book is available
from the British Library.

5 4 3 2 1

To Mam and Dad
and
To Catherine

'There are always two ways of looking at these things:
There's the chaos theory and there's the conspiracy theory.'
—PAUL McDERMOTT SC, TRIBUNAL BARRISTER
DAY 481, 12 JULY 2006

'Many journalists have fallen for the conspiracy theory of government.
I do assure you that they would produce more accurate work if they adhered to the cock-up theory.'
—SIR BERNARD INGHAM

Contents

Acknowledgments

There are many people I need to thank for making this book possible. First off, on a general note, I would like to acknowledge all those people in Dublin and Donegal who asked me when I was going to write the book, and nagged me to keep at it when I felt the task would never end.

My colleagues in Press Association sat through the weeks and months of evidence with me, and kept me sane on those occasions when I needed to check with someone else that the outlandish evidence I was listening to wasn't my ears playing tricks on me. I hope you all realise how much I appreciated your patience, good humour and company.

Vincent Browne and the production team at RTÉ's *Tonight with Vincent Browne* were able to see both the humour in the daily evidence emerging at the tribunal, and the serious issues behind it.

My wife Catherine patiently proofread several drafts as the book evolved, and her suggestions and criticisms were always coherent and to the point. When I became too immersed in the details, she pulled me back from the brink and kept my eye on the big picture. This would be a much lesser work without her support and input.

The staff at the Morris tribunal frequently went beyond the call of duty when I needed to check a detail, from something as routine as how to spell the name of a witness to the importance of sometimes apparently trivial pieces of evidence. Likewise my thanks to the staff in the Garda Liaison Office at the tribunal, and Gwen Malone Stenographers, who saved my skin more than once when I needed to double-check a quote or get a copy of the day's transcript for RTÉ.

I had the good fortune to meet many people from what is usually described as the extended McBrearty family in the press, who are in fact several families. To the Quinns, Brollys, Peoples, McConnells, McBreartys, Crossans and others, my thanks for sharing your stories and at times, your remarkable courage. To the many other witnesses, both Gardaí and civilians, who took the time to talk to me and often gave me insight into the background behind their evidence, my thanks also.

Finally, I would like to thank the good folks at Gill & Macmillan, in particular publishing director Fergal Tobin and managing editor Deirdre Rennison Kunz, without whom this book would never have seen the light of day.

To all those I've omitted to mention by name, my apologies. Without your help, this book would not have been possible.

GERARD CUNNINGHAM
KILDARE
FEBRUARY 2009

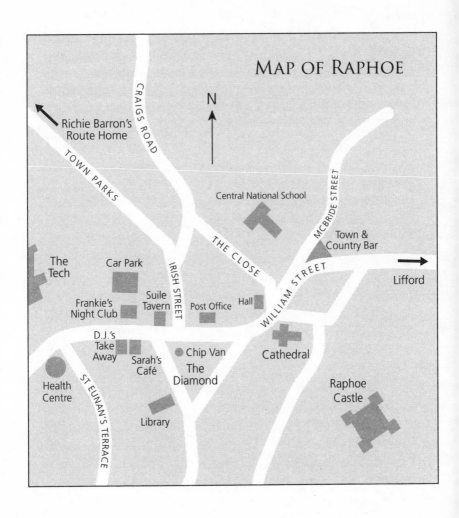

MAP OF RAPHOE

N

Richie Barron's Route Home

CRAIGS ROAD

TOWN PARKS

Central National School

MCBRIDE STREET

Town & Country Bar

THE CLOSE

The Tech

Car Park

IRISH STREET

WILLIAM STREET

Lifford

Frankie's Night Club

Suile Tavern

Post Office

Hall

D.J.'s Take Away

Sarah's Café

Chip Van

The Diamond

Cathedral

Health Centre

ST EUNAN'S TERRACE

Library

Raphoe Castle

Quotations in this book have been taken from direct evidence given to the Morris tribunal, statements made to the original Garda investigation and the Carty investigation, and interviews with tribunal investigators. In some cases quotations have been edited for readability. Conversations have been reconstructed based on contemporary notes and statements, and evidence given at the tribunal.

Prologue
The Death of Richie Barron

Richie Barron may have been on the ground already when the vehicle hit him, sitting down for a rest as he tried to make his way home, tired and drunk. Whether he was standing or not, the vehicle struck the back of his head, above his left ear, with tremendous force. He lost consciousness instantly.

What followed was simple and cruel physics. Some of the force from the forward momentum of the car transferred itself to Richie's head. The deadly blow, probably from a flat object like a bumper or a fixed wing mirror, crushed the back of his skull like an eggshell, breaking the bone into more than twenty pieces. On the surface, it cut a 3.5 cm gash above his ear.

Some of the kinetic energy which had transferred to Richie's head was dissipated when it caused the back of his head to fracture into pieces, but much of it still remained. The force caused his head to jerk round violently, and the sudden wrenching caused one of his neck bones to fracture. As his head turned, thrown forward by the blow, it was propelled through the air, dragging his body after, travelling in an arc.

Richie Barron hit the road head first, as immense force propelled him to the ground. The rough tarmac gashed his forehead and face, leaving a Y-shaped scar, the tail about 10 cm and the forks each about 4 cm in length. Part of the skin was stretched and torn off by the force of the landing. This tearing away of flesh as it comes into contact with a rough road surface is a typical feature of road traffic accidents.

The power of the blow did further damage to Richie below the skin. The rough road surface scratched itself into the front of his skull, leaving several scuff marks and two small fractures in the hard bone. In the fraction of a second of impact, immense pressure built up along the surface of his skull, until his head cracked.

The main crack began roughly in the centre of his forehead, and the remaining force in Richie's body travelled along the crack. It extended downwards until it reached his jaw, where it ended. Somehow, the forces also caused his upper denture to break into three pieces. One of these lodged in his throat.

The crack also travelled upwards over the top of Richie's head until it met one of the eggshell fractures he had suffered an instant before from the initial blow to the back of his head. At that point, the force of the crack dissipated along the pre-existing fissure, so that it ended in a T-junction with the first fracture.

Remarkably, Richie Barron seems to have suffered few other injuries from the violent collision. He had deep grazes along the back of his right hand, wrist and index finger, and abrasions on the knuckles of his left hand. The skin at the top of his left little finger was torn and hanging, exposing the tip of the bone. State pathologist Professor Marie Cassidy examined the photographs from Richie Barron's autopsy several years later for the Morris tribunal. She said the hand wounds were what she would expect to see in the victim of a traffic collision, rather than defensive wounds.

Richie lay on the road, unconscious. His brain had sustained massive damage, and his airway began to fill with blood, some of which reached his lungs and stomach. He had probably lost consciousness within seconds due to the massive trauma he suffered.

When he was found, Richie Barron was lying on his back, and his legs were crossed below the knees. A Garda sergeant later speculated that the driver of the hit and run vehicle might have turned Richie over to check his condition. Seeing the open wound on his face, the driver might have panicked and fled the scene.

However, the pathologists who gave evidence at the tribunal could not give a firm opinion on how Richie came to lie on his back. There were too many factors: the speed of the vehicle, the angle of impact, Richie's exact position at the moment he was struck. With so much raw force in a vehicle impact, there was no predicting where or how a human body might land.

Lee Parker was the first person to arrive at the scene at 12.54 a.m. 'As I came near to Matt McBride's house at Townparks, Raphoe, I saw a man lying on the road,' Lee remembered. 'He was lying on the left-hand side of the road as you go up the hill.'

Lee noticed 'a serious amount of thick blood around his head on the road. 'I saw no glass or debris or dirt or anything on the road. All I saw was Richie and the blood. It hadn't rained for about half an hour but the road was damp.

'I didn't get out of the car at all. I drove on the few yards to McBride's gate and parked. I ran in and knocked on the door.'

Rita McBride opened the window to see what the noise was about.

'Ring for an ambulance and the guards, Richie Barron is lying on the road and the blood is pouring out of him,' Lee told her.

Rita told her daughter Alison to call the ambulance, and asked her other daughter Hilary to phone Richie's son Stephen, before going outside to see if she could help.

By the time Lee Parker got back to Richie, others had arrived at the scene. Sean Duffy, the butcher, was heading into town. He first thought Richie might be asleep, and shook him. Edward Johnston was on his way home from the town, and pulled over too.

Sean Duffy and Edward Johnston both noticed the wound on Richie's forehead. Duffy felt Richie's neck for a pulse, but found none.

When Lee arrived back from telling the McBrides to call an ambulance, Sean Duffy told him he had found no pulse, and Richie was cold. Lee could see that Richie hadn't been moved from when he originally found him.

Duffy left shortly after, and drove into town, where he told Stephen McCullagh—who ran the Suile Tavern—what had happened. From there, the news spread around the town. Edward Johnston stayed at the scene until much later, after the Gardaí arrived, and he spoke to them.

Rita McBride came out to see if she could help, and saw Richie Barron. She touched his face and spoke to him, but got no reply.

Richie's son Stephen Barron arrived. Rita McBride spoke to him, and Stephen asked her daughter Hilary to fetch a blanket. She did as he asked and gave the blanket to Stephen, who covered his father with it.

They waited for the ambulance and the Guards.

Chapter 1

Where Were the Guards?

The McBrides dialled 999. The emergency services put her through to the ambulance first. They then contacted the Guards.

Kevin Monaghan, an ambulance driver, received the call to go to Raphoe at around 1 a.m. on 14 October 1996. He was told to go to Raphoe to a traffic accident. He told his colleague Leonard Diver, who asked him to double-check if the address was Townparks, Raphoe, or Townparks, Convoy. He double-checked and verified the address was Raphoe.

When Monaghan arrived, he saw a number of people standing around Richie Barron. There was a lot of blood, and 'it looked to us like a hit and run,' he remembered. He got the stretcher from the ambulance, as it was a 'turn and burn'. It was necessary to get the victim to hospital as quickly as possible. Barron had a serious head injury and if still alive would be in shock. There were no Guards at the scene when the ambulance left.

At 1.05 a.m., Garda Patrick Boyce was working at Alpha, the Garda communications centre in Letterkenny. He logged a phone call from the McBrides that a man was injured at Townparks, Raphoe.

Using Foxtrot, the Garda mobile radio communications system, Boyce tried to contact Garda Padraig Mulligan, who was on duty in Raphoe, but couldn't raise the Garda. At 1.08 a.m. he contacted Lifford Garda station.

Garda PJ McDermott was the station orderly in Lifford. Also on duty were Garda John Birney and Garda James McDwyer, on mobile patrol in a Garda car. McDermott was about to go on his meal break when the call came through.

Lifford is a twenty-four-hour station, there is always a Garda on duty there. Because McDermott was about to go on his forty-five-minute meal break, the two Gardaí on patrol, James McDwyer and John Birney, had returned to the station. They would remain there until he finished his meal break, then resume their patrol.

McDermott later claimed that Garda Boyce in the Alpha communications centre was sure the address was Townparks, but was unsure if it was in Raphoe or Convoy. McDermott said he knew a Mrs McBride who lived in Townparks, Convoy, so they decided it must be Convoy, not Raphoe.

The truth was simpler. McDermott was about to take his meal break. If he sent the Lifford patrol car to Raphoe, there would be no one left to keep the station open, and he would have to forego his meal. The Lifford car was due in Raphoe in an hour's time when the nightclub emptied, and McDwyer and Birney knew that if they went to the accident, they'd miss their tea break in the station too. It was simpler to give Alpha the brush-off.

Faced with the need to explain the delayed response to the 999 call, the Lifford Guards concocted the story of confusion between Townparks, Convoy, and Townparks, Raphoe. However, the lie was uncovered when the Morris tribunal checked it out, and discovered that Gardaí in Ballybofey had no record of a call from Alpha reporting an accident in Convoy, indicating that Garda Boyce had been quite sure it was Townparks, Raphoe.

When the McBrides called Alpha a second time, telling Boyce that the ambulance was already there, and asking where the Guards were, Boyce called the Lifford Guards and ordered them to get to Raphoe. Boyce never logged the second call. The Alpha correspondence log only records the first 999 call at 1.05 a.m. The next entry is not until 2.15 a.m., when Alpha got the news that Richie Barron was pronounced dead at Letterkenny hospital.

When Boyce made the second call, ordering the Lifford Guards to get to Raphoe, McDermott had gone home for his meal, and Birney and McDwyer were enjoying a break and a cup of tea upstairs. Birney and McDwyer couldn't leave the station unattended. They telephoned McDermott at home, told him to get back down to the station, and left for Raphoe as soon as he got back.

The squad car eventually left Lifford for Raphoe, around 1.20 a.m. according to Birney's statement at the time. Ambulance driver Eamon Monaghan believed he arrived at the scene between 1.20 a.m. and 1.25 a.m. Garda McDwyer recorded their time of arrival at the scene as 1.34 a.m. By then Monaghan was driving the ambulance back to Letterkenny, while Leonard Diver attempted CPR on Richie Barron.

The drive from Lifford to Raphoe takes less than ten minutes. An immediate response could have meant the squad car would have arrived in Raphoe by 1.15 or 1.20 a.m. It is possible the ambulance would still have beaten the Garda car to Raphoe. But if the Gardaí had arrived before the ambulance, they could have accurately recorded the position in which Richie was found.

The emergency medical team, led by Dr Hamad Zuhari, was waiting in Casualty, and tried to resuscitate Richie Barron when the ambulance arrived, but there was no sign of life. Richie Barron was pronounced dead on arrival at 1.50 a.m.

Back at Alpha, Boyce was told at 2.15 a.m. that Richie Barron was dead. Boyce did not notify the acting district officer of the accident that night. Asked at the tribunal why he didn't contact a superintendent, he answered, 'You might get a quick transfer.'

'The practice is not to call them in the middle of the night in relation to traffic accidents,' Garda Boyce said. 'There were three members at the scene and they were dealing with it.'

'I think it was Superintendent Fitzgerald on call that night, but I'm not sure,' he said. In fact Fitzgerald was on annual leave that day, and Milford District Superintendent Frank Fitzpatrick was the acting district officer that weekend.

Boyce went off duty at 6 a.m. In the five hours since the 999 call, he had notified no one except the Guards at Lifford station of the fatality.

———

There was one Guard on duty in Raphoe that night.

Garda Padraig Mulligan went on duty at 8 p.m. on Sunday 13 October 1996, but he had no patrol car available to him. The Lifford car was in the garage for repairs, and so the Lifford Guards had the use of the Raphoe car. Mulligan took care of some paperwork in the station, then walked a foot patrol around the town. Around 9 p.m. he stopped Lee Parker and checked his license and car insurance. At about 10.30 he spoke to Robert Stephen Barnett, who was sitting in his car in the Diamond, the market square in the centre of the town.

Around 11.20 p.m. Mulligan's friend, off duty Garda John O'Dowd, called in to the station. 'I was glad to see him,' Mulligan remembered. 'I'd been on my own all weekend.'

O'Dowd later told tribunal investigators that they decided to go for a spin in O'Dowd's new car. They ended up in a pub in Lifford, and had a pint each. Mulligan ordered a pint of Smithwicks ale.

Lifford Garda James Connolly was off duty that night and at around 10.30 p.m., he decided to go for a drink in Daly's pub in Lifford. He got there around 11 p.m. 'At a particular stage, I can't be absolutely sure but it was some time around 11.30 p.m. or maybe even midnight or later I recall seeing Garda Padraig Mulligan and Garda John O'Dowd standing at the bar ordering a drink,' he would later tell the Carty team. 'I could see them from where I was standing in the lounge.'

Connolly said Mulligan was facing towards him, and O'Dowd had his back to him, as he spotted them in the bar from where he was standing in the lounge, perhaps twenty feet away. In his statement to the Carty team on 28 April 2000, Connolly said he thought the two Guards were gone when he left Daly's at 1 a.m., although he did not see them leave.

Mulligan admitted at the Morris tribunal that he had been drinking while on duty. 'About 1 a.m. we left, went back into his car and went back to Raphoe through Ballindrait.' He left his walkie-talkie switched off in O'Dowd's car while he was in the pub. He did not hear any talk on the Foxtrot radio on the way back to Raphoe.

Back in Raphoe, they pulled up in the Diamond. There was a fight outside Frank McBrearty's nightclub, the Parting Glass. The fight broke up when Mulligan told them to stop. 'They were from Northern Ireland,' Mulligan remembered. When the fight dispersed, Mulligan and O'Dowd headed back to the Diamond. Mulligan saw an ambulance, and as they pulled up at the Suile Tavern, Stephen McCullagh flagged them down.

'Padraig, did you hear about the accident?' McCullagh asked. 'Richie Barron was knocked down up at Townparks.'

'Just as he was talking to me, the Lifford patrol car pulled up alongside,' Mulligan recalled. Birney and McDwyer had finally arrived in Raphoe. Mulligan took some brief details from Stephen McCullagh, and the two cars drove up to the spot where Richie Barron had been found.

Garda Padraig Mulligan was now the officer in charge at the scene. 'Beyond McBride's house, I saw fourteen or fifteen people standing,' Mulligan explained. There were several cars parked nearby. John O'Dowd drove past the scene, turned his car, and left the lights on facing the scene.

'I got out before it had turned,' Garda Mulligan said. '[O'Dowd] shone his light back towards Raphoe, on the area where the blood was. The accident would be my area, so I would be investigating the accident. I spoke to Lee Parker. He said he was driving home and he saw a body lying on the road . . . He recognised it was Richie Barron. He thought maybe he was drunk, but then he saw the blood. He went in to McBride's and rang the ambulance.'

The four Guards examined the area and spoke to the crowd which had gathered.

McDwyer saw a mass of blood about two feet in circumference lying three feet from the side of the road, and examining the area he found a piece of flesh about five feet away. 'I wasn't sure what it was,' he recalled. 'I touched it with my pen, I saw there was hair on it so I knew it was skin.' McDwyer explained he did not touch anything with his hands, as that was a job for the scenes of crime examiner.

McDwyer made a mental note of the position of the piece of skin tissue and a pool of blood, but did not take notes at the time. He did not discuss it afterwards with the scenes of crime examiner, who made a sketch recording the location of a piece of skin tissue found at the scene the next day.

When a call came through from Letterkenny hospital that Richie Barron was dead, the Guards discussed what to do.

It was late at night. It was raining. It was dark. It was cold. It looked like a straightforward hit and run traffic accident. Mulligan, Birney and McDwyer decided to go to Letterkenny hospital to collect and preserve Richie Barron's clothing.

Chief Superintendent Michael McCarthy was called as an expert witness on traffic accident investigations at the Morris tribunal. His criticism of the Gardaí at the scene pulled no punches. A Garda at a road traffic accident should seek to help the injured, and preserve the accident site for forensic investigation, he noted.

'The primary responsibility was to preserve the scene. Anything that came after that was secondary,' McCarthy reported. The Chief Superintendent criticised the failure to preserve the spot where Richie Barron was found, minimise traffic disruption, and preserve the pool of blood. There was an onus on the Guards at the scene to call in a forensic team. 'You had a scene with a substantial amount of blood,' he emphasised. 'Preservation of the scene should have taken place.'

In addition, statements from witnesses at the scene should have been taken 'there and then' while memories were fresh. Instead, the man who discovered Richie Barron, Lee Parker, was not contacted to make a statement until five days later. It was also five days before any vehicles known to have been in the area the night Richie Barron died were forensically examined.

————

O'Dowd wasn't officially on duty that night. While the other Guards examined the scene, he had made himself busy, checking the tractors in the McBrides' shed to see if the engines were still warm, he later told investigators. Oddly, he remembered three tractors, while Nora McBride said there was only one vehicle in the shed that night. O'Dowd then drove towards Manorcunningham, to check on a local farmer who had a reputation for driving without insurance, and might therefore have left the scene of an accident. At some point, he came across Eamon Strain.

Eamon Strain was interviewed several times about what he saw the night Barron died, although the first time was not until 9 November 1997, thirteen months after the event. He and his girlfriend Anne Toye went to a film in Letterkenny that night, and afterwards he dropped her home. After he dropped her off, Eamon drove down the road to his own home.

'As I had just turned right the lights of a car came on behind me,' he remembered. 'I assumed it was the Guards and I stopped. The car behind me then reversed a short distance for about three or four yards. The head-lights were still on. The car then came forward again to where it was parked originally. I was looking at this car moving in the mirror. I then saw the door of this car open and a man in the driver's seat appeared to be looking for something. This man then got out of his car and came up to the passenger door of my van.'

The man opened the passenger door and leaned inside the van, resting his knee on the passenger seat. 'Don't be afraid. We're investigating a hit and run,' he said. 'There was a poor ould cunt knocked down.'

The man—Eamon assumed he was a Garda although he wasn't in uniform—spoke for about five minutes, and Eamon drove off. He was about forty-five years old, clean-shaven, with short sandy hair. Eamon felt uneasy during the encounter. The Garda used crude language, unusual for a member of the force, and had not asked his name or asked to see any identification.

The following morning, when he heard Highland Radio report that Richie Barron had died in a hit and run at 12.30 a.m., Eamon Strain calculated that he had been stopped about fifteen minutes later, at 12.45 a.m. Strain was not approached to make a statement to anyone about this man for a year. On 9 November 1997, he made a statement about the incident to Detective Garda Alphie McHale.

He was interviewed again on 7 October 1999 by Detective Sergeant James Fox, a member of the Carty team. Fox noted first that Eamon could not remember what time the incident happened, but said he arrived home at 2 a.m., and he was stopped about twenty minutes drive from home. This would mean he was stopped around 1.45 a.m., not 12.45 a.m. However, Eamon also said that he was stopped around the time the radio report said Richie Barron died, that is around 12.45 a.m.

In the Carty interview, Eamon gave a fuller account of the night. The film finished around 10.45 p.m., then he and his girlfriend went to a Letterkenny pub to meet some friends. Eamon didn't drink, but Anne did. They were about an hour in the pub, which would indicate they left at 11.45 p.m. He drove Anne home, and they sat in the car talking for less than thirty minutes. That would mean he was stopped around 12.35 a.m.

On 17 April 2000, Eamon made a statement to Detective Garda Thomas Flynn. He again said he was stopped 'fifteen minutes after the time mentioned on the radio'. He arrived home twenty minutes later or so, at 1.15 a.m. to 1.20 a.m. He said he had mentioned it to Anne Toye later, and she had told her mother, who in turn 'mentioned it to a Guard on BSE duty' about a week later.

Anne Toye confirmed Eamon's account in interviews with the Carty team in 1999. Her mother Madge Toye confirmed in 2000 that she reported the incident to a Garda a week or so later at a checkpoint in Lifford. She gave the Garda her phone number, but he never got back to her to take a statement. She added that over a year later two Gardaí called to the house and asked Patrick, her husband, about the incident.

When the incident room on the Barron case received the information from the Garda at the BSE checkpoint—a week after Richie Barron's death—that a Garda had stopped someone the night Richie Barron died, John O'Dowd remembered the incident. 'That was me,' he told the case conference. However, O'Dowd's memory was at odds with Eamon Strain's. O'Dowd remembered stopped a car containing 'Eamon Strain and a Toye girl'. He also said he stopped the car at 1.45 a.m., not 12.45 a.m. He said he had gone up the road to check on an uninsured farmer, and when he saw their car, decided to talk to them in case they had seen anything.

O'Dowd was told to follow up on the report by the conference, but did nothing. When he did provide a statement on the encounter, it was so much at odds with what Eamon Strain said, the tribunal described it as 'a complete invention'.

'It is difficult to understand why, if Garda O'Dowd had nothing to hide, he told so many lies about his behaviour that evening,' Justice Morris wrote.

———

Back at the scene, Mulligan felt it would not have been possible to get a scenes of crime examiner because of the late hour. 'There's no man on call out,' he explained. 'There wasn't a simple roster to call a man out.' The Garda said he had since lost his notes of the accident. 'I was never asked to provide a sketch. I was never asked to provide details of what I saw.'

Mulligan accepted responsibility for not asking around Raphoe that night what cars were in town. 'At the time I didn't think of doing that,' he said. 'It should have been done.' Mulligan added that the system had now changed, today the scene would be preserved, he would have support available to examine it. Extra people would be available in order to preserve the scene, and technical people would be brought in at daylight. Notification would be sent to senior management to take over the investigation.

Standard operating procedure is to contact the district superintendent in the event of a serious accident. However, Superintendent John Fitzgerald was not contacted until the morning and told that Richie Barron was dead.

Mulligan believed it was up to Alpha, the communications centre in Letterkenny, to contact the superintendent at the time. He assumed Communications would have called his superintendent. 'If it was now I would ring myself or demand he was contacted.'

'I would never think to ring the superintendent,' he said. 'I don't think he'd have liked a phone call at that time of the morning.'

When the Gardaí arrived at Letterkenny hospital, Mulligan spoke to a staff nurse, and to Dr Zuhari, before meeting Richie's son Stephen. However, he did not view Richie Barron's remains or arrange to have his clothing removed. There were grieving family members present, and he didn't want to intrude. Instead, he told a hospital porter to secure Barron's clothing, it would be collected later. The Gardaí left the hospital and returned to Raphoe without collecting Richie's clothes, the stated reason for their trip to the hospital.

There was one final oddity that night. At 3.50 a.m., someone in Raphoe Garda station telephoned John O'Dowd at his home. Padraig Mulligan was the Garda on duty, and he said he didn't make the call. O'Dowd said he didn't remember receiving it. The call took place around the time the three on-duty Gardaí arrived back in Raphoe. When they got there, they met Patrick 'Packie' Gallagher. He had been in a fight earlier, and was looking for 'Garda protection' and a lift home.

The Gardaí told Packie they were busy, but to head away from the town and they would take care of the town. Packie asked them if they were investigating the accident, and said his brother Paul 'Gazza' Gallagher had been drinking and speeding. They asked Packie if he knew anything about the accident, but there was nothing more he could tell them. The call at 3.50 a.m. may have been Padraig Mulligan telling O'Dowd what Packie had said, a lead to follow up. Or Mulligan might just have called O'Dowd to tell him Richie Barron had died.

When he learned of the death of Richie Barron the following morning, Superintendent John Fitzgerald asked Inspector Jim Gallagher to prepare a report on Garda behaviour at the scene. Gallagher eventually concluded he could not 'see the reason for three officers to have to travel to the hospital' leaving the scene unpreserved.

Inspector Gallagher's report was not completed until the following spring, and was forwarded to Donegal Division Chief Superintendent Denis Fitzpatrick by Superintendent Kevin Lennon on 6 March 1997, a month after Lennon was transferred in as district officer to Letterkenny. Superintendent John Fitzgerald had transferred out of the division the previous month.

Even before writing his report, Judge Morris was critical of the Gardaí for leaving the scene for the hospital. 'There could have been young people in town driving a car with a broken windscreen or a broken headlamp that would have solved the whole thing,' he said. 'I think the public has a right to know why was any investigation not carried on at that time. Is anybody accepting that it should have been done? Is anybody accepting responsibility that it wasn't done?' he asked Garda James McDwyer.

'We did everything we possibly could given the circumstances,' Garda McDwyer said. 'No one ever asked me ever why I didn't preserve the scene. Subsequently four years later, after it came into the spotlight, then I was asked.'

Meanwhile at Alpha, Garda Boyce noted an anonymous male caller at 3.45 a.m. reporting that Paul 'Gazza' Gallagher had been driving around Raphoe in a Renault 9 and was very drunk. He passed the information to Sergeant Joe Hannigan to follow up. At 6.25 a.m. a second caller, this time a woman, said a Renault car had come down the Mongorry Road to Raphoe at about 1 a.m., and had failed to stop at the Diamond junction. The caller identified the driver as Gazza Gallagher. This time, according to the log in Letterkenny, Boyce passed the information to Detective Sergeant Sylvie Henry.

Chapter 2
A Deficit of Information

At 6 a.m., Garda PJ Boyce went off duty at Alpha, handing over to Garda Joseph McManus. McManus did up the Form C9 paperwork for a hit and run report on Richie Barron, and at 7.45 a.m., he called District Superintendent John Fitzgerald and told him there was a road death.

Superintendent John Fitzgerald retired from An Garda Síochána in December 2004 after completing forty years in the force. In 1996 he was an experienced officer with thirty-two years of service and a wide range of knowledge as Detective Garda, Detective Sergeant and Detective Inspector. He headed the Crime Unit in Sligo for a number of years, and was a member of the Divisional Investigation Teams in Sligo/Leitrim and Donegal. On 9 March 1992, Fitzgerald was appointed District Officer of Letterkenny Garda district.

Fitzgerald reeled off a list of questions. Who was the scenes of crime officer? Had the scene been preserved? Were there any suspects? Had a Garda travelled to Letterkenny General Hospital to preserve evidence? He wasn't happy with what he heard. He ordered the scene preserved immediately, and an investigation begun.

Fitzgerald was not on duty that morning. He had been on annual leave since the previous Thursday, 10 October, and was not due back at work until the following day, Tuesday. He was called 'as a matter of courtesy'. He was unable to discover if Superintendent Frank Fitzpatrick of Milford, the acting district officer over the weekend for Letterkenny, had been informed. McManus wasn't sure.

'The scene was an absolute disaster, I'm not going to go into that,' Fitzgerald recalled wryly at the Morris tribunal. He ordered McManus to contact Garda Niall Coady, a scenes of crime officer stationed in Castlefin, and Sergeant Joe Hannigan, the sergeant in Raphoe.

On Monday morning at 9 a.m., Inspector Jim Gallagher was scheduled to take over as acting district officer. Since there was only an hour or so left until Gallagher took over, Fitzgerald didn't bother calling Fitzpatrick, his substitute while he was on leave. Instead, he rang Inspector Gallagher and told him to take overall charge of the case as acting district officer.

John McGinley and Jim Gallagher were the uniformed inspectors in the district. Letterkenny was one of five districts in the Donegal Division, and the border county was also allocated a detective 'border superintendent', with responsibility for coordinating subversive intelligence throughout the division and liaison with the RUC in Northern Ireland. One week into the investigation, on Monday 21 October 1996, Superintendent Joe Shelly would take up this post, based in Letterkenny, and would play a prominent role in the subsequent investigation. Although not on duty, he'd arrived some days earlier to arrange accommodation in his new posting. Coincidentally, Inspector Jim Gallagher is a brother-in-law of Superintendent Shelly.

After he spoke to Gallagher, Superintendent Fitzgerald called Inspector John McGinley and told him to 'look after things on the ground, and make sure everything was covered'. McGinley was scheduled to attend the District Court in Lifford that morning, but he assured the superintendent he'd get to Raphoe as soon as that was out of the way. An experienced detective, McGinley had served in Drogheda, Co. Louth, and at the Bridewell in Dublin, as well as in several Donegal stations during his twenty-four-year career.

When Fitzgerald spoke to the designated scenes of crime officer, Garda Niall Coady, he learned that Coady already knew about the accident. While Fitzgerald was phoning the inspectors, Garda McManus at Alpha had contacted Coady, and Coady was waiting to be relieved at Castlefin station before going to the scene.

At the Morris tribunal years later, Jim Gallagher explained how he discovered an old diary in his attic while searching for revision notes for his son, who was preparing for the Leaving Certificate examinations. His entry for the 14 October 1996 read:

'At 9.10 a.m. received phone call from Superintendent Fitzgerald, there was a fatal hit and run accident in Raphoe, in which a 55 year old man Richard Barron received fatal injuries. He indicated that I should act as district officer. At 10.10 a.m. Detective Sergeant Henry informed me that he had viewed the body and was not totally convinced this man had died from a traffic accident, as he appeared to have defence injuries to his hands. I went to the morgue and viewed the body. Deceased had severe head injuries, deceased had also injuries to both hands . . . Pathologist indicates that the injuries were consistent with being struck with a blunt instrument and didn't rule out a traffic accident.'

———

Garda Niall Coady began duty as station orderly in Castlefin at 6 a.m. on the morning of Monday 14 October 1996.

Coady had completed a scenes of crime course that year, and was very keen about his new responsibilities. When he found out there had been a fatality, he began phoning around to find out if the scene had been preserved. He rang Lifford Garda station, but found out the Gardaí who had answered the 999 call had gone off duty.

As Coady was making his calls, Superintendent John Fitzgerald rang him and ordered him to attend the scene in Raphoe. As soon as relief arrived, Coady left immediately for Raphoe in his private car with his scenes of crime kit, collecting Garda James Connolly in Lifford first. They arrived in Raphoe at about 9.10 a.m.

As Coady arrived at the scene, he saw about half a dozen people standing around. He was told the road had been swept. One local man would later explain how he had helped clean the 'thick-looking blood with white pieces through it' at the scene of the accident 'because of the children walking past the scene'. Coady told people to move back, so he could cordon off the area.

'I certainly was perturbed by the fact that the scene had been contaminated,' he said later. 'It left me in a difficult situation. I was also annoyed that the road had been swept.' The road was lightly discoloured by blood but 'it wouldn't have been obvious to the naked eye without close examination'. Mattie McBride showed Coady the spot where Richie Barron was found, as did Lee Parker when he arrived later.

Coady was told Richie Barron was found lying with one leg outstretched, the other bent under him. The tail of his coat was turned up under his torso, so that he was lying on the bottom of his coat. Coady took measurements and drew a sketch map. Garda Kevin O'Malley took photographs of the area. When Inspector John McGinley and Sergeant Brendan Roache arrived, they too examined the area.

On the sketch, Coady noted a 'hair strand and skin lifted at scene'. It will never be known for sure if this is the same piece of skin Garda James McDwyer saw the previous night. Coady agreed with the tribunal chairman that passing traffic or a sweep with a yard brush could account for a piece of skin being embedded in the road when he discovered it the next morning.

The skin sample, labelled NC9, was handed over to a forensic laboratory in Dublin along with other exhibits three days later, on Thursday 17 October. The forensic report prepared by Dr Liam Fleury refers to Sample NC9 as simply a 'strand of hair found at scene'.

'A long time afterwards, I'm not sure when, I learned that a Garda had stated that he had observed skin tissue at the scene. I did not observe any skin tissue,' Coady wrote in a statement on 10 June 2003. Giving evidence at the tribunal in July 2004, he said the strand of hair and skin labelled NC9 were 'more or less the same dimensions' as those on a sketch Garda

McDwyer drew of the piece of flesh he had discovered and left untouched at the scene the night before.

State pathologist Prof. Marie Cassidy would explain to the Morris tribunal years later that skin left on the roadway due to the force of impact is often a vital clue in identifying a death as due to a road collision.

'He had to be moving across the road at some speed,' the forensic pathologist explained. 'Therefore, even if he were hit on the back of the head with a weapon, that couldn't produce enough force to move his head across the ground with such force as to tear out a piece of skin and put this grooving on his skull.'

In his report Mr Justice Morris described the failure to preserve the piece of skin as soon as Garda McDwyer found it as 'a disgraceful neglect of duty'.

Scenes of crime examiner Coady searched the area thoroughly, both the road and the gulleys by the side. He also put on his wet gear and went through the water drain in case any evidence had washed in there and could still be recovered from the dirt and muck. He then sorted through the loose leaves and twigs he had recovered from the murky water to see if anything useful could be found. It was a fruitless search.

―――

Sergeant Brendan Roache worked in the Traffic Corps in Letterkenny. Superintendent Fitzgerald told him to 'round up some traffic men' to investigate a road traffic accident, and go to Raphoe.

Niall Coady was already in Raphoe when Roache arrived. He had found red, blue and white paint embedded in the road, but could not tell if it was old or new. There was no other evidence that he could see at the scene. They searched up to 500 yards from the scene, checking the road and ditches, looking for any evidence, and took photographs. There wasn't much point. Any evidence had either been washed away by the night's rain, or cleaned up the next morning.

After two hours at the scene, Roache went to examine a stolen car found in a nearby town, then returned to the scene in Raphoe.

By the time Detective Sergeant Joseph Sylvester 'Sylvie' Henry got to the scene, Niall Coady and the two inspectors for the Letterkenny district, Jim Gallagher and John McGinley, were already there.

Henry was one of the most experienced detectives in Letterkenny. He joined An Garda Síochána in 1974, and was promoted to the rank of sergeant in 1982. He became a detective sergeant in 1986.

'It was annoying us that whatever hope there was of finding something there, all hope was gone,' said Henry.

Henry thought it was around 10.30 a.m. that morning that he visited the morgue in Letterkenny to inspect Richie Barron's body, along with Detective Garda PJ Keating and mortuary technician Eamon McNulty. McNulty and Henry put on surgical gloves, to avoid contaminating evidence. Henry was concerned about Barron's injuries. There were cuts on the dead man's hands, which he thought looked like defensive wounds.

'I assisted Sergeant Henry in doing a thorough examination of the body,' McNulty said later. Apart from the head and hand wounds, he did not notice any other marks. Henry said he did not touch the body. However, he went to see Inspector Gallagher after he had finished in the hospital. An hour later, Henry and Keating returned to the mortuary along with Gallagher. Henry pointed out the wounds on Richie Barron's hands. 'I didn't touch the body because it was a crime scene and hadn't been evaluated by a scenes of crime officer,' Gallagher said.

———

While the Guards were investigating in Raphoe, a stolen and damaged car was found some miles away. Inspector Jim Gallagher went there with Sylvie Henry. The car was eventually eliminated from inquiries. The damage to the car would have indicated more extensive injuries to Richie Barron. The only way it could be the car would be if it had hit Richie Barron and later crashed. 'We couldn't rule it out so we took it in,' Gallagher said.

Inspector John McGinley was not aware the scenes of crime examiner found a piece of skin at the scene. 'I understood whatever hairs were found, there may have been minute pieces of skin attached. I wasn't aware that there was any substantial piece of skin found,' he told Michael Buckley, a solicitor representing Garda James McDwyer at the tribunal. 'If Garda Coady had found any substantial piece of skin or flesh I'm sure he would have averred to it. There was a difficulty insofar as the scene wasn't preserved. There was a loss of evidence, there was a deficit of information.'

Garda Connolly was relieved at the scene by Sergeant Joe Hannigan at 12.10 p.m. By 2.15 p.m. in the afternoon, Coady had finished, and he left to travel to Letterkenny hospital.

———

All Young Frank McBrearty ever wanted out of life was to build his own home to raise his young family. On Monday 14 October 1996, he was working on the house outside Raphoe along with electrician Damien

McDaid when Inspector Jim Gallagher and Detective Sergeant Sylvie Henry called up sometime between 3 and 4 p.m. Young Frank spotted his father in the car with the two Gardaí.

The day before, Frank had played a game of football with Frankie's United, a local soccer team sponsored by the family business. Before cattle dealer Richie Barron's death, Young Frank weighed twelve stone, and had played soccer at junior level. He also boxed in Ulster and Irish championships, and represented his local athletic club at national level. He hoped to play soccer semi-professionally at some stage.

Frank had gone to work at his father's nightclub, the Parting Glass, on Sunday evening. He arrived at about 8.30 p.m. There was a lot to do, sorting out staff, checking there was sufficient stock, checking the toilets were clean, the nitty gritty of running a successful nightclub. Frank was his father's 'eyes and ears', he told the tribunal, making sure everything went well.

The doors opened at 10 p.m., and things were brisk. October isn't the busiest time of year, so the McBreartys encouraged patrons by offering free admission for the first hour. Old Frank spent most of the night by the door. His son moved around, keeping an eye on the nightclub and the adjoining bar, the Tudor Lounge, also owned by the family.

Young Frank took pride in his work. 'I know everything goes on in the nightclub,' he told tribunal lawyer Paul McDermott. 'I'm in that business since I'm ten years old.'

Monday was Young Frank's day off. He didn't go near Raphoe because if his father saw him he'd find work for him. When the detectives arrived, Young Frank was building a house on the outskirts of the town. He had four children, the youngest barely two months old, and they were living in rented accommodation in Letterkenny. 'It was my dream to build my own house the way I wanted it,' he remembered at the tribunal. He wanted the new house finished by Christmas, and had spent the day checking with workers and buying electrical materials.

Inspector Gallagher and Detective Sergeant Henry wanted to know if anyone was put out of the nightclub around the time Richie Barron died, roughly between 12.30 and 1 a.m. Frank told them that Paul 'Gazza' Gallagher was ejected from the disco at about that time. Gallagher had 'hit a boy with a bottle the week before', and was 'giving a girl hassle'. When the bouncers told McBrearty, he went to Gazza and told him he could walk out or be thrown out. Gallagher walked.

Shortly after Gazza was shifted, a fight broke out between two men, part of a group from Northern Ireland. The pair were ejected, and Young Frank, the nightclub bouncers, and some of the other Northerners moved outside to calm them down.

About ten people were at the entrance to the car park, keeping the feuding Northerners separated, when local electrical contractor Damien

McDaid came down from the car park driving at speed. Old Frank McBrearty banged on the side of McDaid's van and 'told him to cop himself on'.

After the disco finished, Young Frank asked one of the staff to fetch a burger for him from a nearby chip shop while they closed up the premises, and headed home around 3 a.m. in the morning.

———

Dr David Barry, a consultant pathologist with the North Western Health Board based in Letterkenny General Hospital, carried out the postmortem at 3.30 p.m. on Monday 14 October. Before he began, he spoke to Inspector McGinley, who asked him to 'keep an open mind'.

Dr Barry said it could not be determined with certainty whether Richie Barron's injuries were as a result of an assault or because of an impact with a car. His final report, completed the following year, would state simply that Richie Barron 'died of head injuries.'

The pathologist said Gardaí told him that it was a death as a result of a hit and run, but he was also told to keep an open mind and form his own conclusions. At the Morris tribunal he told counsel for the Garda Commissioner he was the first person to raise the possibility of an assault.

'He suggested that the injury [to Richie Barron's forehead] would be consistent with being struck with a blunt instrument,' Inspector McGinley wrote later. Present at the autopsy along with McGinley were Garda Kevin O'Malley, who took photographs, Garda Padraig Mulligan, who had formally identified the body, Garda Niall Coady, the scenes of crime officer, and Detective Garda Michael Jennings.

Coady took tissue and other samples. He could not remember if O'Malley was told which photographs to take by Dr Barry.

Coady said that Inspector McGinley spoke with Dr Barry at the postmortem, but no one said anything to him which indicated that Richie Barron died by any means other than a road traffic collision. At a Garda conference following the post-mortem, Richie Barron's death was also treated as a collision.

However, having considered the evidence from Dr Barry and others, the Morris tribunal concluded that 'the preponderance of evidence suggests that Dr Barry told the senior officer present, who was Inspector John McGinley, that it was possible or probable that an assault was involved.'

Searches of the area were carried out during the week, during which an aluminium pipe and several pieces of timber were recovered. All these items were sent to the forensic science laboratory in Dublin. Coady was not briefed on autopsy results, but he learned that the searches on his exhibits yielded nothing, apart from the blood on the road, which matched Richie Barron's blood type.

In the weeks that followed, searches were also carried out between the spot where Richie Barron was found and Frankie's nightclub. Coady also examined several cars in Raphoe as possible hit and run vehicles. These inquiries turned up nothing.

Back in Raphoe on that first day, four statements were taken from witnesses. The local sergeant, Joe Hannigan, had already spoken to Old Frank McBrearty in his pub. The nightclub owner told the sergeant he'd seen Richie outside the Suile Tavern a little after midnight when he was walking his son Andy to his car. Manny Hegarty was in Frank McBrearty's pub when Hannigan visited. He told Hannigan how he'd been in a fight with Richie Barron in the Suile Tavern the night before.

Rodney Gibson worked as a barman in the Central Hotel. When Sergeant Hannigan visited him at his work, Gibson told him that Richie Barron was in the hotel at 9 p.m., and had two pints of Harp lager in the space of thirty to forty-five minutes.

Meanwhile, Sidney Vance, who had been in the Suile Tavern, told Detective Garda Pat Flynn he saw the fight between Manny and Richie, but 'they didn't get any serious slaps on each other'. Vance left the Suile Tavern after midnight to go to Frankie's, but left again after a quarter hour to go home. He saw Richie ahead of him as he headed up Irish Row, and decided to turn back. Sidney was the last person to see Richie Barron alive.

Sitting in Raphoe Garda station, Padraig Mulligan wrote up an initial report on the case, although he did not mention that he went to a pub with John O'Dowd while he was supposed to be on duty. In fact, he didn't mention O'Dowd at all, beginning his narrative at the point where Birney and McDwyer arrived from Lifford and met him in the Diamond.

———

Whatever reservations Dr Barry might have expressed, the Gardaí said they left the autopsy believing Richie Barron died in a hit and run traffic collision.

'There was no suspicion of foul play in my mind,' Inspector McGinley said. 'At that stage we were actively pursuing vehicles that may have been involved.'

'I believed it was a traffic accident but there was no guarantee,' he added, but qualified this by saying, 'It was still early days. At that point there was still relatively little known.'

Inspector Jim Gallagher set up a conference on the case after the autopsy. He remembered that Inspector John McGinley reported Dr Barry's findings that 'it was a blunt instrument that caused the injuries to Mr Barron, and he said that in the context of a traffic accident'.

'What John McGinley was conveying to me was that these injuries were caused by a blunt instrument, and that was a car,' Inspector Gallagher recalled. 'Certainly homicide or assault didn't enter into the equation.'

Gallagher's journal entry for that day reads: 'Pathologist indicates that the injuries were consistent with being struck with a blunt instrument and didn't rule out a traffic accident', which seems to give a different emphasis to the two possibilities.

Whatever the emphasis, it seems both possibilities were still being considered on Monday evening. Despite this, no one thought to contact the State pathologist. The scene was left unprotected. Barron's remains were released to his family.

Inspector Gallagher also remembered that Coady spoke at the case conference about paint, hair and follicles he had removed at the scene. Sergeant Joe Hannigan spoke about Richie Barron's background.

Detective Sergeant Sylvie Henry and Inspector Gallagher told the meeting that Paul 'Gazza' Gallagher was evicted from McBrearty's nightclub, the Parting Glass, the night before. Sergeant Roache was told to look for Gallagher's car.

————

In the days and weeks that followed Richie Barron's death, teams of Gardaí from the Letterkenny district went to Raphoe to take statements from many of the people who were in the town that night, building a picture of his movements on his last day.

The weekend had begun with good news for Richie. His daughter Geraldine had given birth to a baby boy, her first child, in Altnagelvin hospital on Friday. Around 5 p.m. on Sunday 13 October 1996 Nora Barron went to visit her new grandson in Derry along with her in-laws. Nora asked Richie if he wanted to come, but he told her he'd leave it until Monday or Tuesday; the hospital would be too crowded with visitors on Sunday. Richie stayed home, and that evening walked into town. He left his home for the last time at around 6 p.m. that evening. He arrived in the Diamond, the market square at the centre of the town, at 6.30 p.m.

It appears Richie went to the Central Hotel first, and spent the evening visiting several of the pubs in the Diamond. He was spotted at various times in the Diamond bar, and in the Tír Chonaill bar. Sometime between 10 and 10.30 p.m., he headed to the Town & Country, a pub run by Mark Quinn.

One witness, Geoffrey Dolan, was interviewed by Detective Garda Pat Flynn three days later. He arrived in the Town & Country pub at 10.40 p.m., where he had made plans to meet up with Michael Peoples and his wife Charlotte. Geoffrey and Michael sat at the bar chatting. Charlotte sat at a table chatting with some friends.

Richie Barron appeared to be fairly drunk. As Mark McConnell passed, he said something. Geoffrey Dolan heard later that it started because Richie said something about Mark's goatee beard.

'There was a bit of pulling and pushing at the end of the bar, not a fight or anything, just a bit of scuffling,' Geoffrey Dolan remembered. 'Mark just told him to go away.'

The row, such as it was, seems to have been over within moments. It seems to have started when Richie spotted Mark McConnell coming out of the toilets. 'Look at that excuse for a McBrearty,' Richie said to Richard McBrearty, who was sitting talking with him at the bar. Mark McConnell's mother is a sister of Old Frank McBrearty, and Richard is Mark's cousin.

Mark overheard the comment. 'Who's an excuse?' he asked. 'Have you got a problem?'

'I said you're a poor excuse for a McBrearty,' said Richie.

'Sit down, you old pensioner,' Mark laughed. 'I'm not a McBrearty, I'm a McConnell. Catch yourself on, go home to your bed.'

Mark Quinn, the bar owner, was on the spot almost immediately. 'Mark, your name's up in the pool room,' he told McConnell.

At the same time, Richard McBrearty put his hand on Richie Barron and held him back. Roisin McConnell stood in front of her husband, along with Mark Quinn.

Richie wasn't impressed. 'I'll kill you, you bastard,' he shouted as Mark walked away. Customers held him back as he tried to remove his jacket. 'Let me at him,' he demanded.

Mark McConnell headed into the pool room. Back in the bar, Richie calmed down, and went back to his drink.

Martin Quigley, the barman, saw the argument, but before he could do anything, his boss Mark Quinn was already calming things down.

Charlotte Peoples said the argument 'was over before it started'. Her husband Michael said it was 'just a slanging match'.

'I was a bit annoyed, but no way angry,' was Mark McConnell's verdict. 'After a couple of minutes I didn't even think about it again.'

It was the last time Mark McConnell saw Richie Barron. Although he was in and out of the pool room during the night, the cattle-dealer had left before Mark next emerged.

Shortly after the row in the Town & Country, Richie left the pub and went to the Suile Tavern. The pub door was already closed, but barman Declan McCullagh heard the knock and let Richie in. Richie was 'drunk, but not legless, I've seen him worse,' Declan recalled. Richie ordered a small whiskey, and sat chatting to Phonsie Crawford.

John 'Manny' Hegarty, a horse and cattle dealer like Richie, approached and asked about some money he said Richie owed him. The row over the disputed debt came to blows. Richie caught Manny a blow on his forehead, cutting him, before Eugene Gamble got between the two men. McCullagh the barman held Richie back. Annoyed, Richie went to leave, but Phonsie Crawford told him to sit and finish his drink. Richie sat quietly, saying nothing while Manny persisted in asking about the old debt. 'I checked Manny a good few times to keep quiet and he eventually shut up when I told him to get out or shut up,' McCullagh remembered.

Richie Barron left the Suile Tavern sometime after midnight. Declan McCullagh offered to arrange a taxi or a lift for him, but Richie refused, saying 'No, I'll walk it.'

The old market square in Raphoe, although known as the Diamond, is actually a triangle. The northern side of the triangle runs east–west, and the other two sides converge at the southern end of the Diamond. The Suile Tavern is in the northwest corner of the triangle. Heading west past Frankie's nightclub and the local vocational school (the 'Tech' or technical school) is Meetinghouse Street, and the next town of Convoy. On the eastern side of the Diamond, William Street leads away to the north and east.

Roughly halfway between the Suile Tavern at the west end and the Town & Country bar past the east end, bisecting the northern axis of the triangle, Irish Row heads due north out of the town. McGranaghan's pub and shop are located at the corners of Irish Row and the Diamond. Richie headed for Irish Row and home.

When Richie left the Suile Tavern sometime after midnight, he'd been drinking since 6.30 p.m., and was the worse for wear. Several people saw Richie as he made his way from the Suile Tavern to Irish Row.

Old Frank McBrearty saw Richie around midnight leaning against the window sill outside the Suile Tavern as Frank escorted his son Andy and Andy's girlfriend to their car. 'How's it going, Richie?' he asked. 'Just middling,' was the answer.

Mark Bogle remembered leaving the Town & Country sometime between midnight and 12.30 a.m. He saw Richie lighting a cigarette by McGranaghan's shop at the corner of Irish Row.

Lee Parker was sitting in a car chatting with some friends. He saw Richie between 12.15 a.m. and 12.30 a.m., 'staggering' towards McGranaghan's.

Roberta Browne saw Richie at the corner of McGranaghan's between 12.30 a.m. and 12.35 a.m. The time stayed with her because her father had gone home ahead of her, and she was aware of the lateness of the hour. As she passed Richie, he tugged her jacket and asked was she going dancing, and did she have enough money. The odd question stuck in her mind. When she looked back a moment later, Richie had disappeared around the corner.

David Parke was sitting in a car by the petrol pumps in the Diamond. He saw Richie heading round the corner at McGranaghan's. Richie was holding the wall to support himself. David thought this might have been as late as 12.45 a.m.

Sidney Vance left the Suile Tavern sometime after midnight, and went to Frankie's. After ten or fifteen minutes though, he decided to go home. He left the nightclub and headed to Irish Row. As he made his way up Irish Row towards the Mongorry Road, he saw Richie up ahead. Sidney changed his mind and decided to head back to Frankie's again.

At first, Sidney told Gardaí he turned back to Frankie's because he had to go to the toilets. At the tribunal, he said Richie was walking slower than he was. Sidney, who was eighteen at the time, did not want to catch up to Richie, and have to talk to him. He had seen the fight between Richie and Manny Hegarty earlier in the Suile Tavern, and probably was worried in case he got drawn into a row with the curmudgeon.

When Sidney Vance saw Richie, he was perhaps 200 metres from the spot where he was found lying on the road. Sidney is the last person known to have seen Richie until Lee Parker saw him lying on the road, just short of 12.55 a.m.

In his first statement to Detective Patrick Flynn the best time Sidney Vance could put on it was that it was 'near one o'clock'.

On the first anniversary of Richie Barron's death, presumably under similar conditions, Superintendent Kevin Lennon arranged for a Garda to walk 'in a drunken fashion' up Irish Row and the Mongorry Road to the point where Richie was found. The journey took seven and a half minutes. If this is an accurate time, and Richie left the Diamond between 12.30 a.m. and 12.35 a.m., as most witnesses remember, then Richie arrived at the spot where he was found at between 12.37 a.m. and 12.42 a.m.

Richie Barron's watch stopped at 12.38 a.m. His wife Nora later told detectives that Richie always kept the correct time. However, tribunal barrister Peter Charleton sc noted this could be a 'total coincidence', as watchmaker George Patton was able to restart the timepiece simply by winding it. 'There was no apparent damage,' the watchmaker told the tribunal.

After Frank McBrearty saw Richie Barron outside the Suile Tavern, he took his son Andy to his car. Andy had been drinking, and was in no condition to drive. Frank made sure his son got into the passenger seat, and he got into the back himself. Andy's girlfriend drove the car as far as the Dispensary at the western end of town, then Frank got out and walked back to his nightclub, the Parting Glass, picking up bottles and glasses on the road as he did so. Andy's girlfriend drove him home.

There was a disco in the Parting Glass. Shortly after Old Frank McBrearty got back, he saw his son Young Frank ejecting someone, and asked what was going on. Young Frank told him that the culprit, Paul 'Gazza' Gallagher, was barred because he'd been in a fight the week before.

Gardaí were still piecing together much of the story of Richie Barron's movements on Monday evening. Only a handful of statements had been taken by that stage. Following the conference that evening, Superintendent Fitzgerald was briefed by Inspector John McGinley about the post-mortem results. Fitzgerald's memory is that McGinley told him the pathologist was not in a position to say Richie Barron's injuries were as a result of a road traffic collision. However, McGinley said he didn't think at the time that Richie Barron died as a result of anything other than a collision.

Later that evening, the Barron family collected Richie's remains. Richie's brother Vincent Barron said he was told by a morgue assistant that his brother's injuries were not consistent with a car collision. At the wake house later that night, the talk was about how Richie had died.

Chapter 3

The Talk at the Wake House

A blunt instrument could have caused the wounds to Richie Barron. That's what Superintendent John Fitzgerald remembered Inspector McGinley telling him on the morning of Tuesday 15 October.

Superintendent Fitzgerald spoke to Dr Barry later on Tuesday. The pathologist told him he could not say definitively that Richie Barron had died as a result of a road traffic collision. At this stage though, Fitzgerald still did not feel it was necessary to contact the State pathologist Professor John Harbison and get a definitive answer. 'In my mind it was a road traffic accident,' he remembered.

After the hectic activity on Monday, policing in north Donegal slipped back into its normal routine. Niall Coady reported for duty as usual in Castlefin at 6 a.m. that morning. A blanket had been placed over Richie Barron to keep him warm when he was found on the roadside, and Coady collected it from Letterkenny hospital later that day in case it contained trace evidence. He spent much of the day in Ballybofey, collecting evidence at the scene of a break-in in Dunnion's Café. Someone had broken in through the back window at the toilets, stolen cash, and emptied the slot machines. Coady managed to recover palm and finger prints on the washbasin. They were upside-down, most likely left by the thief as he balanced himself on his way in. There was also a stolen car to see to. Meanwhile, Sergeant Brendan Roache spent most of Tuesday looking for Gazza Gallagher's car, a cream-coloured Renault 9 banger with registration number 880IH.

Superintendent Fitzgerald asked Inspector Jim Gallagher to produce an urgent report on Garda procedures at the scene of Richie Barron's death. He wanted to know why the Guards had been late arriving at the scene, and why the scene wasn't preserved overnight. The superintendent compiled a list of eleven questions. It would be four months before Inspector Gallagher returned the completed report to Fitzgerald's successor in Letterkenny, Superintendent Kevin Lennon.

Superintendent Fitzgerald said he had been told by his superior, Chief Superintendent Denis Fitzpatrick, to assign the compilation of the report on Garda procedures to Inspector Gallagher, but 'not to allow it to over-shadow the investigation'.

In February 1997, Superintendent Kevin Lennon succeeded Superintendent Fitzgerald as Letterkenny district officer. In March 1997, Lennon wrote to Chief Superintendent Fitzpatrick describing as 'grievous negligence' the failure of the Gardaí on the spot to preserve the scene, with all three of them going to Letterkenny hospital.

'In my view, this amounts to neglect of duty by the members concerned, and warrants investigation under Garda disciplinary procedures,' Lennon wrote.

A few more statements were added to the Barron case file on Tuesday. Jacqueline Hunter told Sergeant Hannigan she saw Richie heading into town as she returned from church service between 5.30 p.m. and 6 p.m. Eugene Gamble told Hannigan that he let Richie Barron into the Suile Tavern after midnight, and gave him a whiskey. Richie and Manny Hegarty argued, and he separated them. Richie finished his drink, and left the bar between 12.20 a.m. and 12.25 a.m.

David Parke told Garda Padraig Mulligan he saw Richie turning up Irish Row at 12.30 a.m. Sean Duffy made a statement to Detective Garda Pat Flynn describing how he saw Richie Barron lying on the road as he drove to Raphoe just after 1 a.m.

Just before 6 p.m. in the evening, Garda Philip Collins took a statement from Martin Quigley, the barman in the Town & Country. He said Richie Barron arrived around 10 p.m., and had about four whiskies and a pint of Harp lager. He saw Richie and Mark McConnell arguing between 11.15 p.m. and 11.30 p.m. Bar owner Mark Quinn told them to stop and they did. Quigley didn't want to get his boss in trouble for keeping a late house. The legal closing time was 11 p.m., but the bar was still open well after 1 a.m. He told the Guard he left the pub at 12.30 a.m.

Inspector John McGinley recalled that by Tuesday evening, the investigators had very few leads, and 'it was decided to have a conference on Wednesday to examine the case'.

'At conference on Tuesday evening it was known that [Richie Barron] had a row in a pub,' McGinley said. 'It was obviously something that would have to be explored.' Oddly, the much more serious row with Manny Hegarty, which actually came to blows, didn't feature. It was the brief exchange of words with Mark McConnell the Gardaí were interested in.

'Dr Barry's findings would be a factor too. He didn't conclusively say it was a traffic accident,' McGinley added.

It was not until Tuesday, when the statement was taken from Sean Duffy, the second person to arrive at the scene, that the investigators knew for sure that Richie Barron was found lying on his back. This was unusual for hit and run victims, who are normally found lying face down. 'When all the facts were known from the witnesses at the scene, it opened the possibility that it may have been more than a traffic accident,' John McGinley told the tribunal.

Meanwhile, Richie Barron's wake entered its second night. Friends and neighbours, among them Old Frank McBrearty and his wife Rosalind, paid their last respects. At the wake house, the mourners speculated on the unusual cut on Richie's forehead. It didn't look like the kind of thing to be expected in a car collision. Richie had been in a fight with Mark McConnell the night he died, it was said, and there was a history of bad blood between younger members of the Barron, McBrearty and McConnell families.

Pat Doherty was among the mourners. He had worked in Scotland with Richie Barron in his younger days. Pat's son William was with him. Some people were saying it was a hit and run, others that it was murder. Pat Doherty spoke to Richie's brother Vincent Barron about the rumours. Vincent told him he'd asked the Gardaí about it, but they hadn't said much. William Doherty was a good friend of Stephen Barron, Richie's son. Stephen remembered Vincent saying that someone at the hospital had said there was 'something suspicious about the death'. Stephen also heard someone say 'Snodgrass had something to do with your father'. Mark McConnell was known locally as Snodgrass, a nickname given to him because he played guitar with a Derry rock band of the same name.

'It didn't really register with me. I didn't really take it on,' Stephen recalled.

William Doherty phoned Garda John O'Dowd and told him what was being said at the wake. Doherty later said he first heard the rumour when he stopped in a shop in Raphoe earlier in the day. He claimed he wasn't sure how much credibility to give to the rumour that Richie Barron was murdered, but he decided to pass it on anyway. 'People were putting one and one together and getting three,' is how he explained it.

Whether Doherty presented the information as a tip-off that Richie Barron had been murdered or as information about a misguided rumour that should be set straight, it is obvious from O'Dowd's actions following the phone call how he interpreted Doherty's information.

O'Dowd took the phone call from Doherty around 9.45 p.m. on Tuesday evening. O'Dowd immediately tried to call his district officer, Superintendent Fitzgerald, at Letterkenny station but couldn't reach him.

He then called Chief Superintendent Denis Fitzpatrick at home and told him about the rumour and the source of his information. O'Dowd recalled that the information from Doherty was that 'the talk about it up in the wake house is that it was supposed to be a murder and that Mark McConnell and one of the McBreartys was involved'.

After he spoke to Chief Superintendent Fitzpatrick, O'Dowd then called Sergeant Joe Hannigan. O'Dowd's phone records show the telephone calls to the station, Chief Fitzpatrick and Hannigan that night. He did not tell Hannigan where the information had come from.

O'Dowd was excited at the information. In his excitement, the tribunal decided, he exaggerated what he'd been told. The rumour became firm information from a reliable source.

William Doherty was well known to Garda John O'Dowd. They had first met three months earlier on 9 July 1996, when Doherty was arrested on suspicion he was involved in a kidnapping. Doherty remembered the date of the kidnapping, 3 July 1996, as it was his twenty-fourth birthday. Because he remembered the date, he also remembered where he was that day. He was released after Detective Garda Michael Jennings verified his alibi.

A few weeks after the kidnapping arrest, O'Dowd stopped Doherty again, this time for driving without insurance, vehicle tax or a driving license. 'As a result of stopping him,' O'Dowd explained later, 'he contacted me shortly after this at my work in Raphoe and he wanted to meet me. The basis was that he had something useful to tell me.' O'Dowd claimed that Doherty said the IRA wanted him to join up, and he offered to do so in the role of informer in return for getting off on his traffic offences.

Doherty had already been convicted of dangerous driving in 1990, and had also been convicted of assault charges and drunk and disorderly behaviour the same year. He was convicted of speeding and driving without a safety belt in 1995, and was facing a court appearance on an assault charge when O'Dowd stopped him in 1996. 'Any time I drank I always seemed to get into trouble,' he reflected ruefully at the tribunal.

What happened when John O'Dowd stopped William Doherty some time after he had been arrested is disputed. Each man claimed the other made the first approach, offering a deal to provide information on local crime if there were no charges. O'Dowd claimed Doherty went on to provide information, both on subversive and 'ordinary' crime. Doherty said this was nonsense. He said the only information he ever provided to Gardaí on crime was when he told them the rumour that Richie Barron was assaulted, the name of a possible hit and run suspect, and that Noel McBride, a friend of his, had stolen a television aerial from the 'Tech', the local vocational school in Raphoe.

O'Dowd said that after the traffic stop, Doherty offered to provide information on the IRA, and named several men believed by Gardaí to be members of the organisation. O'Dowd claimed that in the following months, Doherty provided him with several pieces of information about the IRA, as well as information on local drug dealers and other 'Crime Ordinary'. The Raphoe Garda said he had approached Chief Superintendent Denis Fitzpatrick about his new source, and the Chief told him to submit any information on confidential C77 forms, sent directly to Crime & Security, the Garda intelligence and counter-terrorism branch at Phoenix Park headquarters.

'I brought this to the attention of my Chief Superintendent at the time, Chief Superintendent Fitzpatrick, and he directed me that I should meet this fellow and see what he had to offer,' O'Dowd recalled.

'Initially, he provided me with information in relation to crime locally and in the general area. We mounted an operation in September in relation to drugs coming into the town. The information came from him.'

As a result of the operation, the Guards arrested a man in a Raphoe pub, who was carrying 'about eighty' ecstasy tablets. 'There was other stuff that he told me about in relation to local fellows that would be in the drug scene and a lot of petty stuff initially,' O'Dowd added.

'I used to pick him up along the road. He'd ring me and he'd say he'd be in touch at such and such a place on occasion. A lot of the times he did come up to my house or I brought him there for a discussion.'

Kevin Lennon, then the district superintendent in Buncrana, had a reputation as an experienced man in dealing with counter-terrorism. He had received specialised training from the FBI and MI5, and scored several spectacular successes in the early 1990s, foiling IRA attacks on RUC/British Army border checkpoints by the Donegal cells of the Provisional IRA. Fitzpatrick had been particularly impressed when in January 1994, wearing a woolly hat and disguised as a tramp, he watched as Gardaí intercepted a shipment of home-made explosives heading for the border. The operation was masterminded by Lennon, then an inspector. But what Fitzpatrick didn't know was that the 'IRA courier', Adrienne McGlinchey, was not an IRA member. The operation, and Lennon's other successes, were charades stage-managed by the ambitious officer to promote his career.

Fitzpatrick told O'Dowd to liaise with Lennon on anything he got from Doherty. The Provos did not look kindly on traitors, so it was vital to protect his identity. Only Fitzpatrick, Lennon, and O'Dowd would know that Doherty was providing information.

O'Dowd did not record the results of all the meetings with Doherty, but when he did he used Form C77, a secret Garda document used to submit intelligence to headquarters. The original and one copy are sent to headquarters. The second copy is sent to the Chief Superintendent and the Garda holds on to the third copy.

The only problem was, Doherty had little to offer by way of real intelligence. That wouldn't be a problem for very long, however. In a police force which devoted considerable resources to the fight against terrorism, there were considerable kudos to be gained for any officer who submitted c77s. The Morris tribunal concluded that the supposed intelligence in the c77 reports, much of it 'both false and dramatic', was a fiction. Justice Morris had 'no doubt whatsoever that Superintendent Lennon and Garda O'Dowd were involved in deliberately creating bogus c77s and they did this for the purposes of personal advancement'.

'Sometime after I initially met Chief Superintendent Fitzpatrick,' O'Dowd recalled, 'he asked me to work with Lennon and that was fine. That was around, I'd say the end of August, maybe September, he told me this.' Lennon, however, believed that he didn't get to meet Doherty until almost the end of the year.

'I'm very vague on it but, from the first meeting, I was happy that [Lennon] was happy with Doherty, if you know what I mean,' O'Dowd recalled. 'There was a general discussion about local people involved in the organisation and Doherty seemed to know all these people and I got the impression that Superintendent Lennon was happy enough to run with this fellow.'

When O'Dowd told Chief Superintendent Denis Fitzpatrick that he had information from William Doherty that Richie Barron was murdered, it was no ordinary call from a member of the public passing on information. Doherty was O'Dowd's man. This was a tip-off from a trusted source.

'The Chief told me to be in in the morning at a quarter past nine in the conference room, that was Wednesday morning,' O'Dowd recalled.

Immediately after the phone call to Chief Superintendent Fitzpatrick, the scene where Richie Barron's body was found in Raphoe was again preserved, at 11 p.m. on Tuesday night, although the initial scene preservation, from just after 9 a.m. on Monday morning until 2 p.m. that afternoon, had revealed little of value. This time, the search area was widened to include the surrounding fields. The second Garda search for the area focused largely on locating a murder weapon. The scene would be preserved until 2 p.m. on Thursday. Superintendent Fitzgerald didn't remember being told by Fitzpatrick that the Barron case was a possible murder until Wednesday morning, but agreed he was 'the most likely person to give the order' to preserve the scene for a second time. 'I'd have the muscle to do it. Denis Fitzpatrick would have the muscle to do it,' he observed.

Superintendent Fitzgerald said he was never told where the information came from. However, Chief Superintendent Fitzpatrick insisted, 'I told

John Fitzgerald who it was and who brought it in, that it was John O'Dowd gave the information and that it came from William Doherty. I have no doubt about that. I am quite clear that I gave that information to John Fitzgerald.'

Fitzgerald disagreed. 'That is not correct. The name Doherty was not conveyed to me until months later,' he told the tribunal. He also said he was not told the information had come through Garda O'Dowd.

'Mark my words, it is a murder,' Fitzpatrick told Fitzgerald. 'Mark McConnell and one of the McBreartys did it.'

————

The rumour would evolve over time. 'First of all it was Mark McConnell, then it was Mark McConnell and one of the McBreartys, then Mark McConnell and Frank McBrearty,' Detective Sergeant Sylvie Henry remembered. 'But when exactly each one came into it I'm not sure.' He felt it was not until after the conference on 22 October, one week after Richie Barron died, that Young Frank McBrearty's name came up. Mark's mother is a sister of Old Frank McBrearty, making Mark and Young Frank first cousins.

Mark McConnell was twenty-seven years old in 1996. He had married Roisin Quinn two years before, and they lived in Tullyvinney, just outside Raphoe, with their one-year-old son Dean. Mark worked as a painter/decorator but was unemployed at the time, although he got a bit of work as a part-time musician.

Mark went to the funeral of a friend on the morning of Sunday 13 October. When he got home, he watched some football on television, then Mark and Roisin called down to her mother, Anna Quinn, and her sister Edel Quinn, along with baby Dean. 'She called to visit at the home at about seven o'clock that evening,' Edel Quinn remembered. 'She stayed for a while, Mark had left her off and he went up to the Town & Country. I had at that time my boyfriend's car so I offered her a lift up and she said yes.'

After Mark left Roisin and Dean at his mother-in-law's, he parked his car in Sheep's Lane, and headed into the Town & Country. He planned to have a pint while Roisin and her mother chatted, then head home when Roisin came to collect him from the pub.

At 7.45 p.m. Roisin McConnell went from her mother's home to the Town & Country. Edel remembered she took Dean with her. Edel dropped Roisin off at 7.45 p.m., then headed to nearby Strabane with a neighbour to collect her boyfriend, Edward 'Ebby' Walsh. They got back to Raphoe between 8.30 p.m. and 9 p.m., and headed to Friel's Hotel.

Roisin had planned simply to collect Mark and head home, but she decided to have a drink first. 'Roisin came in to get Mark to go home and then just sat on,' her sister Katrina Brolly remembered. While the men talked among themselves and played pool, the women were busy arranging practical matters. Katrina Brolly's three children arrived, including her son, then almost thirteen years old. Babysitters had to be sorted out, so they arranged for the Brolly children to take young Dean McConnell up to the Brolly house. Roisin arranged to spend the night with Katrina. Mark would be too drunk to drive, and there was no point waking Dean if he was sleeping. Better to spend the night with her sister, and walk back into town in the morning to collect the car. Roisin told Mark of the plans during one of his forays out of the pool room.

Roisin's brother Paul Quinn and his wife Sue arrived in the Town & Country sometime between 9.20 p.m. and 9.45 p.m. They met up with Mark and Roisin McConnell and joined the party. Paul Quinn and Mark McConnell hung round the pool room for most of the night, playing doubles, while the women chatted. The few drinks was turning into a Quinn family gathering. Another Quinn brother, Gerard, and his wife Kay were also there. Gerard didn't know what time he arrived in the Town & Country. He'd been drinking since midday. He didn't remember much of the night, though he thought he played a few pool games with the Dolan family, who were also in the pub, celebrating a birthday. Mark, who usually dressed up in his trademark black clothes for a night out, was still dressed in the casual sweats and tracksuit pants he'd been wearing around the house, and took some gentle ribbing from the others over his dowdy appearance.

Geoffrey Dolan arrived in the Town & Country at about 10.40 p.m. He had made plans to meet up with Michael and Charlotte Peoples. Geoffrey and Michael sat at the bar chatting. Charlotte sat chatting with Roisin and her group. Charlotte is Roisin's first cousin. Geoffrey saw Richie Barron chatting with Richard McBrearty across the bar, and saw the row between Richie and Mark McConnell.

Meanwhile, around 11 p.m., Roisin's sister Edel Quinn and her boyfriend Ebby Walsh left Friel's Bar and headed to the Tudor Lounge, the McBreartys' lounge bar.

It was after midnight when Geoffrey Dolan and Michael Peoples left the Town & Country to get some cash. Michael was low on funds, and Geoffrey gave him a lift up to his home in St Eunan's Terrace to get his ATM bank card so they could pay into the disco at the Parting Glass and continue the session. The ATM withdrawal was recorded at 12.19 a.m. 'Probably the most precise time we have,' tribunal barrister Paul McDermott observed years later, as the lawyers tried to sort through different memories of who was where at what time that night.

After cashing up at the ATM, Michael and Geoffrey headed back to the Town & Country to pick up Charlotte. They headed to Frankie's. Geoffrey remembered Old Frank, Willie Logan and Frank's niece Christine McBrearty at the door when they arrived.

Edel Quinn and her friends were still drinking in the Tudor Lounge. Old Frank told his son Young Frank to let them into the nightclub for free. Edel thought it was about 12.30 a.m. when Young Frank brought them up to the nightclub.

Geoffrey Dolan wasn't impressed with the disco in Frankie's. He left Michael and Charlotte Peoples after a few minutes and went outside to his car. He pulled in behind Damien Gamble, who was parked outside the Tech. He got into Damien Gamble's car, and they sat chatting.

Back at the Town & Country, Sue Quinn asked the bar owner Mark Quinn to order a taxi home. It was getting late, coming up to 1 a.m., and Sue decided there was no point in paying to get into Frankie's nightclub for less than an hour.

At 12.50 a.m. Mark McConnell asked Mark Quinn for a pint. It was well past closing time, but Quinn was in a good mood, he'd been celebrating as much as working that night. His wife Donna was upstairs with his newborn son, Oliver. Quinn gave McConnell the late pint.

———

Geoffrey Dolan reckoned he was in Damien Gamble's car fifteen minutes when they spotted the fight. As far as he could tell there were two or three men involved, moving out on to the street in front of Frankie's. The three ran off towards St Eunan's Terrace. Curious, Damien reversed the car and followed them. As they headed up the Terrace, Geoffrey saw John O'Dowd in his car. A uniformed Garda, presumably Padraig Mulligan, was talking to the fighters, calming them down. That seemed to be the end of the entertainment, so they headed back to the Tech.

Ten minutes after he'd got a late pint, Mark McConnell asked for another drink. He'd had an accident, and spilled the last one. Quinn looked at the clock. It was 1 a.m. Enough was enough. He refused the drink. It was time to go. Martin Quigley, the barman, had just finished up and was leaving, planning on heading to Frankie's. He saw Mark McConnell asking his boss for another pint. He left quickly, as he didn't want to have to refuse a pint to a customer.

A little after 1 a.m. the taxi arrived. Taxi driver William Bogle thought it was between 1.05 a.m. and 1.10 a.m. when he knocked on the window of the Town & Country for Paul and Sue Quinn. Sue remembered Roisin and Mark McConnell were still there. So were Gerard and Kay Quinn, and the pub owner, Mark Quinn. Ursula Keaveney, the babysitter, remembered Paul and Sue Quinn arrived home between 1.25 a.m. and 1.30 a.m. The McConnells left shortly after Paul and Sue Quinn.

On their way from the Town & Country to the Parting Glass, Mark and Roisin met Stephen McCullagh outside the Suile Tavern. Mark asked Stephen if he was going to the Parting Glass; Stephen said he was heading home. Mark and Stephen chatted for a few minutes, then Mark and Roisin headed to Sarah's Café to order a takeaway.

Just after saying goodbye to Mark McConnell, Stephen McCullagh met Sean Duffy. The butcher told him the bad news from up the road, that he had found Richie Barron lying injured or dead on the road. Shortly after Duffy left, Stephen McCullagh saw his brother Declan, and flagged him down. They went up to see Richie Barron, and arrived just as the ambulance did. Stephen McCullagh helped the ambulance men with the stretcher, then returned to the town.

Back in town, Stephen McCullagh noticed Padraig Mulligan returning to the Diamond having sorted out the fight involving the three men who had run up from Frankie's nightclub up the Terrace. He waved down the Garda, and told him what he'd just heard. As Mulligan took in the details, the Lifford squad car arrived. Mulligan and John O'Dowd drove up to the scene along with the two Gardaí from Lifford.

———

Carmel Connolly and Philomena Laird were working the late shift in Sarah's Café when Mark and Roisin McConnell stopped in. They ordered chicken curry and fried rice, and said they'd come back and collect it after the disco finished. Mark went to the toilet, while Roisin chatted with another customer, Wilma Laird, who was there before her.

Meanwhile, as Michael and Charlotte Peoples left Frankie's, they met Michelle Scott. Michelle had just spoken to Sean Duffy, and he told her about Richie Barron. Michelle passed the news on to Charlotte.

Michelle noticed 'a scuffle' as she was going back to the disco. 'Frank Senior was standing in the middle of three or four fellows,' she recalled. Michelle told Willie Logan and Old Frank the news about Richie Barron, and Frank asked where she heard it. Half in shock by what she'd learned, Michelle was unable to remember at first who had told her. She went outside to check the news again, then remembered it was Sean Duffy.

When Geoffrey Dolan and Damien Gamble arrived back at the Tech after their sightseeing trip up St Eunan's Terrace to watch the fight, Geoffrey went back into his own car, and drove down to the front of the nightclub. Geoffrey was pulling the car out when he saw Mark and Roisin

McConnell heading into the nightclub. Geoffrey said hello, and Mark McConnell came over for a chat. Geoffrey mentioned the row with Richie Barron in the Town & Country. 'He's a wild man, isn't he?' Mark laughed. They stood and chatted for a few minutes, and Roisin went ahead into the nightclub alone.

As Mark left Geoffrey to head for the disco, Geoffrey saw Charlotte Peoples. She looked upset; Michelle Scott had told her about Richie Barron. Charlotte got into the front passenger seat of Geoffrey's car, and told Dolan to pick up Michael, who was walking towards the Diamond. Michael Peoples got into the back of the car. Geoffrey Dolan drove towards the Diamond, turned left at Irish Row, drove up past the old cinema, and headed to the scene. A crowd of people had gathered. There was nothing to be done. Geoffrey Dolan dropped the Peoples home, and stayed a while for a cup of tea, letting the night unwind. He got home around 2.20 a.m.

Meanwhile, back at the Parting Glass nightclub, Mark and Roisin McConnell joined Edel Quinn and Ebby Walsh inside the disco. They were there about fifteen minutes when Edel heard the news from Karen McBrearty about Richie, and told Roisin. 'She was a bit annoyed because Mark and Richie had some kind of an argument earlier,' Edel remembered. Roisin asked Edel to say nothing to Mark, because he'd had a row the last time he saw Richie.

'So then we decided that we would leave the disco, get Mark out,' Edel Quinn remembered. 'So we said to Mark that we were going. So the four of us left and as we were leaving Roisin stopped with Frank McBrearty Senior and asked him about Richie Barron.

'Mark had noticed something was going on, that she was with Frank Senior, and he went up and he asked what was going on. They told him that Richie Barron had been knocked down. But that night Frank McBrearty Senior had told us that he was still alive, that he wasn't dead.'

Edel remembered Mark was upset by the news. 'He just said trust him to have an argument with the man, that's the last time he'd seen him.'

Mark and Roisin McConnell left Frankie's with Edel Quinn and Ebby Walsh. They drove up to the McConnells' home in Tullyvinney to collect baby things for Dean.

On the way back, Mark and Roisin collected their curry order from Sarah's. Philomena Laird remembered it was after 2 a.m., because her friend Brenda Laird was there at the time, and Brenda had arrived at 2 a.m.

Edel and Ebby then dropped the McConnells off at the Brollys' house in St Eunan's Terrace.

Catherine 'Dolly' Eaton was babysitting for her daughter Charlotte and son-in-law Michael Peoples. She was wakened by the noise when they arrived home. Charlotte told her Richie Barron was hurt in a hit and run.

Dolly was upset. Richie was a good friend of hers. 'Her and Richie got on the best, they really did,' Charlotte remembered. 'They always had a natter whenever they met.'

Dolly phoned Letterkenny hospital to ask how Richie was doing. Richie was her second cousin, but she knew the hospital would only give out information to close relatives. She told the hospital she was Richie's aunt.

Later that night Mark McConnell would also call the hospital, when Roisin asked him to find out how Richie was doing. He too claimed to be a relative of Richie's, as he knew the hospital would not give out any information otherwise. He hung up after the hospital checked with Richie's family and found out there was no relative of the name Mark had given. No one was sure to believe Mark when he told them he'd tried to ring the hospital. He'd been reluctant to do so at first, and the telephone was in the hallway, so no one heard him make the call.

Chapter 4

We Should Call Harbo

Being told by his chief superintendent that Richie Barron was murdered had a huge impact on Superintendent John Fitzgerald.

The Letterkenny superintendent didn't remember getting a telephone call from the Chief on Tuesday night. His first memory was of Chief Superintendent Fitzpatrick calling him into his office on Wednesday morning to tell him the Barron case was a murder. Possibly the sequence of events was that on Tuesday night he was told it was a murder, and on Wednesday morning he was given further information, including the suspects' names.

'That has a huge impact, a statement as solid as that coming from a chief superintendent, looking at him and his body language that he believed this was the situation, and the definite way in which he said it,' Fitzgerald told the Morris tribunal.

'Thank you, I'll take it on board, we have to keep an open mind,' is the rather mundane response Fitzgerald said he made when given the startling news from his boss.

Fitzgerald didn't ask the Chief where he got his information. 'I assumed it was from Garda John O'Dowd or Superintendent Lennon. If it was from anyone else they would have come to me,' he said. Why only these two men would contact Fitzpatrick directly was never entirely clear from Fitzgerald's evidence. The only link between them was William Doherty, yet the superintendent said he was unaware of Doherty's existence at the time. It seems, however, that Fitzgerald became aware of a relationship between O'Dowd, Lennon and Fitzpatrick, bypassing the normal chain of command.

A meeting on the case was convened at Letterkenny garda station on Wednesday morning, 16 October 1996. Until then, by most accounts, Richie Barron's death hadn't looked like anything more than a routine if tragic traffic investigation, even if Dr Barry was ambiguous in his initial findings. The body had been released to the family for a traditional wake. The burial was scheduled for 11 a.m. that morning. In rural Ireland, funerals customarily take place on the third day after death. The Gardaí are reluctant to interfere with the rituals of mourning unless absolutely necessary.

Among those at the Wednesday morning meeting were Superintendent John Fitzgerald, Inspector John McGinley, Inspector Jim Gallagher, Detective Sergeant Sylvie Henry, Sergeant Joe Hannigan, Sergeant Brendan Roache, Garda John O'Dowd and Garda Tina Fowley. Up to thirty Guards in total attended the conference. Memories of what happened are vague, confused and contradictory.

Superintendent Fitzgerald said he did not share the Chief's information with the meeting. He wanted them to approach the case with an open mind, and reach their own conclusions based on the evidence. O'Dowd said that as soon as McGinley entered the room the inspector 'made a beeline' for him, whipped out a piece of paper, and asked him 'What's the story, John?'

'I met John McGinley there, Inspector McGinley,' O'Dowd recalled. 'There was a crowd gathered. There was the Chief, Superintendent Fitzgerald, John McGinley. As far as I remember Brendan Roache was there and I think Tina Fowley might have been there. . . . There was a meeting convened and I gave the same details of the information to John McGinley and he wrote it down on a piece of paper. The discussion went on about what should be done.'

McGinley said he never spoke to O'Dowd. 'It didn't happen,' was his simple response when asked about O'Dowd's account. He also said he was unaware that the Chief had phoned his Super the night before. 'The information that John Fitzgerald got, I didn't become aware of that for a considerable period,' he said. The Morris tribunal made no finding on whether the incident actually occurred.

The meeting began. Sergeant Brendan Roache remembered the mood in the room changed when O'Dowd said, 'There's more to it than meets the eye.' O'Dowd also said, 'We should call Harbo.' Roache said the senior officers, Fitzgerald, McGinley and Gallagher, did not ask O'Dowd what he meant by these cryptic remarks, but instead immediately left the room to contact the State pathologist, Professor John Harbison.

Tina Fowley remembered Fitzgerald looking at his watch and saying, 'Time is of the essence, we must see about this' as he left the room following O'Dowd's comment.

'I didn't say that,' Fitzgerald responded.

The junior ranks sat around discussing the logistics of stopping a burial. Tina Fowley suggested the coffin be kept above ground in the morgue at the hospital. The funeral could go ahead, they finally decided, but the grave would not be filled in, and could instead be covered temporarily with a plastic sheet or a wood panel.

McGinley said he did not ask Superintendent John Fitzgerald what he knew, or why he was calling Professor Harbison. 'He was the district officer. It was his call,' he said. 'He didn't tell me. That's the type of man he was.'

McGinley disagreed with Garda Tina Fowley and Sergeant Joe Hannigan about how senior officers left the conference. He said that in the first week there was 'no firm information' at the conference that Richie Barron was murdered. 'It was 22 October when the first firm information came in, in my view,' he recalled. The only information in the first week was the rumour 'but there was nothing attached to that'.

'They were away for a while, and there was a discussion of, if Dr Harbison came down, what would happen,' Detective Sergeant Henry remembered. 'What are we going to do? Are we going to allow the funeral Mass to go ahead?' He learned that medical reports were being faxed to Professor Harbison. 'Somebody may have come in looking for them. I'm not sure.'

Some, like Tina Fowley, remembered the meeting fizzling out as people drifted off. Others, like Detective Sergeant Henry, said there was a definite end when Fitzgerald returned and told them he was contacting Professor Harbison. Sergeant Roache remembered it ended with Inspector Gallagher telling everyone they would have to 'wait and see'.

Fitzgerald said he spoke with McGinley about Dr Barry's autopsy. 'How he died was in limbo. We didn't know how he died, at that stage, but I felt it was still a road traffic accident.' As a result of the doubt, Fitzgerald decided to contact Professor Harbison and sound out his opinion. The pathologist was giving evidence in the Four Courts in Dublin that day. Fitzgerald knew that McGinley had once worked in the Bridewell Garda station next to the Four Courts, and had him call his colleagues there and arrange for the pathologist to take a telephone call. The superintendent also arranged for McGinley to fax up a copy of Dr Barry's preliminary report to the pathologist at the Bridewell. Fitzgerald then telephoned the pathologist.

Ann Glennon Moynihan worked as a court inspector in the Bridewell Garda station. She remembered the call from Superintendent Fitzgerald. She had known the superintendent for years; he knew her parents in Sligo. He asked her to locate Professor Harbison 'as he required him very urgently. I remember Superintendent Fitzgerald saying something about he may have to stop a funeral taking place.'

The court inspector did not remember if she went to the Four Courts personally to get Professor Harbison, but she did remember he made a telephone call from the station, and received a fax message there.

Fitzgerald told tribunal investigator and Royal Canadian Mounted Police Chief Superintendent Brian Garvie that he didn't mention the word 'murder' to Professor Harbison. He didn't want to influence the pathologist's opinion any more than he did his own conference. He wanted an independent reaction to the report. 'I was very particular about not mentioning that. I was particular about it,' he insisted.

At the tribunal Professor Marie Cassidy said that a forensic pathologist reading Dr Barry's report would conclude it was a hit and run traffic collision. 'In my opinion it is highly unlikely that these injuries would result from an assault,' Professor Cassidy told the tribunal. 'In particular the injury to the right side of the forehead would be extremely unusual, given that an object would have to strike it with considerable force to produce grooves in the bone, and if so, there would be expected much more extensive fracturing at that site.

'There was also a lack of injuries which would be described as defensive type injuries; although there were injuries described to the hands, these were localised to the areas which were unclothed. My conclusion was that death was due to a head injury, and that would be consistent with having occurred due to a motor vehicle collision.'

Fitzgerald said the State pathologist told him travelling to Donegal would be a duplication of work already performed by the local pathologist, Dr David Barry. 'Professor Harbison's advice was to bury the body,' Fitzgerald recalled. The tribunal felt Harbison never said anything in such strong terms, simply because he was never asked to come to Donegal. At most, Fitzgerald asked him in vague terms for an opinion on Barry's report.

Because Harbison was not brought to Donegal, the Gardaí never had the benefit of a properly conducted forensic post-mortem examination. If they had, then they would have learned that Richie Barron was not murdered. It was another missed opportunity, described by Justice Morris as 'one of the most fundamental errors in the investigation'. Without a professional forensic pathologist's report, the Barron investigation was about to become a murder inquiry, without ever taking the basic step of establishing that a murder took place.

Superintendent Fitzgerald said at the tribunal that he still regarded Mr Barron's death as a hit and run, and kept an open mind even after the burial. Professor Harbison told the tribunal he did not remember being brought from the Four Courts to the Bridewell to speak to Superintendent Fitzgerald. He simply had no memory of the telephone call. However, he said it was 'rather unlikely' that he would refuse to go to a suspicious death if asked to do so. There were no circumstances under which he could refuse to respond to a call from the Gardaí to examine a body. 'As I perceive it, I must respond,' he told Mr Justice Frederick Morris.

It was not until six years later, on 6 July 2001, that the body of Richie Barron was exhumed as part of the Carty inquiry. As a result of the autopsy and examination of original post-mortem photographs, Professor Harbison decided Richie Barron's head injuries were 'more severe than the average cause of death by a fall or blow to the head'. The back of his skull had suffered 'enormous and gross damage' and was 'extensively shattered'. Because the pathologist was not called to Donegal in 1996, none of this information was available to the original investigation team.

In his initial report following the exhumation, Professor Harbison felt the frontal injury happened first, followed by the blow to the back as Richie Barron's head struck the ground. However, at the tribunal he said he was 'quite happy' to accept the alternative explanation of the British Home Office pathologist, Professor Helen Whitwell, and two other forensic pathologists—that Barron was struck on the back of his head and suffered the frontal injuries as he hit the ground—as an equally valid hypothesis. He persevered in his initial opinion that the first impact was at the front of Mr Barron's head, rather than the back, but said neither possibility could be excluded. However, all the pathologists agreed that the gross damage done to Richie Barron's head was as the result of a collision, not from a blow to the head from an assault.

Inspector Jim Gallagher recorded in his journal that the Wednesday conference on the Barron case began at 9.30 a.m., and that 'rumours were circulating in Raphoe that he'd been beaten to death'. Thirty Guards attended the conference, and afterwards questionnaires were distributed and the crime scene extended in a search for a possible weapon. Inspector Gallagher wrote that Paul 'Gazza' Gallagher was a suspect, as he had been ejected from the nightclub around 12.30 a.m. and 'had his uninsured car parked near the scene'. He also wrote that there were two other suspects, as Richie Barron 'had been in a row with one earlier in the night'.

Surprisingly, this contemporary note made no mention of any attempt by Superintendent Fitzgerald to contact Professor Harbison following Dr Barry's inconclusive findings. Gallagher also recorded in his diary that he was the acting district officer in Letterkenny on Wednesday 16 October. Other records suggest Superintendent John Fitzgerald, the district officer and superintendent in charge in Letterkenny district, had returned from his annual leave the previous day.

————

Sometime after midday on Wednesday, Sergeant Brendan Roache met Superintendent Fitzgerald. 'I'm setting up an incident room into the incident in Raphoe,' the superintendent told him. He asked Roache to find some people to run the room, which would coordinate and cross-check all the information collected by investigators. The superintendent also told him Professor Harbison would not be coming to Donegal, and Roache concluded it would be a hit and run inquiry.

Roache later met Sergeant Marty Moylan and Garda Tina Fowley. Moylan said he had some experience in the area, and they staffed the incident room. Roache divided his time between the incident room and the

Traffic Corps, where he worked. He also attended a traffic course at the time. 'I would have thought I was up to speed overall,' Roache said. 'There may be little snippets I would have missed, but overall I was up to speed.'

Tina Fowley was working the 'BSE desk', coordinating Garda efforts in controlling cattle movements across the border. When the Barron incident room was set up, her superior, Sergeant Marty Moylan, moved her desk into the incident room. 'There was no particular person appointed in charge of the incident room,' she said. 'Because Moylan was my superior, my approach was he was in charge of me. If I needed to check something I would check either of the sergeants.'

Tina Fowley divided her time between BSE duties and the Barron investigation. 'Along with my BSE duties, I was charged with maintaining the original statements file,' she recalled. She summarised statements for the investigation team, and filed the summaries for any investigator to examine. Another Garda, John O'Toole, came on board later.

Fowley said that those most familiar with the case 'in order of knowledge' were Sergeant Moylan, Garda John O'Toole, Sergeant Roache, and then herself.

Incident rooms keep a correspondence log to record all information on a case. The first record in the Barron correspondence book is not until Friday 18 October 1996, two days after Roache was told to put a team together, and five days after Richie Barron died. The first twenty pages of the book are missing. Entries between 12 November 1996 and 15 February 1997 are also missing. The last dated entry in the book is on 8 August 1997, with one undated entry after that. John O'Toole suggested the first pages in the book might have been used for another case, but no one could explain the later missing pages.

A Garda incident room also keeps a register of all tasks to be completed by the investigation team, known as the jobs book. Jobs are recorded on the left-hand side of the book, and the officers assigned to the tasks, the results, and any comments are recorded on the facing right-hand page. As each job is completed, it may in turn lead to new jobs, for example if a completed statement required further corroborating statements to be taken.

On that Wednesday, 16 October 1996, scenes of crime officer Garda Niall Coady collected another blanket which had been used to cover Richie Barron from Mattie McBride. More statements were collected that day, as the incident room tried to build up a picture of what had happened.

Among those interviewed that day was Mark Quinn, owner of the Town & Country bar. He told Garda Phil Collins he saw Richie arrive at 10 p.m. He made a comment about Richie's haircut, and Richie joked, 'They cut the black bits and left the grey bits.' Some time later Quinn intervened in the row between Richie and Mark McConnell. Around

11.20 p.m. he noticed Richie was gone. Mark Quinn also worried about the licensing laws. He told the detectives the bar was almost cleared by 12.45 a.m., with only Gerard and Kay Quinn, Irene and Frank Dolan, Laura Dolan and her boyfriend Jimmy remaining. He said he closed up just after 1 a.m.

Alison McBride, who made the 999 phone call, told Sergeant Paul Heffernan and Garda John O'Dowd that she remembered checking the time as she made the call; it was 1 a.m.

On Monday, Gardaí had collected four statements, all concentrating on Richie Barron's movements. They interviewed two publicans, Old Frank McBrearty and Rodney Gibson; Sidney Vance, the last person to see Richie alive; and Manny Hegarty, who was in Frank McBrearty's bar when Sergeant Joe Hannigan called there.

On Tuesday, the Gardaí took five statements. One came from another barman, Eugene Gamble at the Suile Tavern. One came from Jacqueline Hunter, who saw Richie going into town; one from David Parke, who saw him leaving as he went up Irish Row; and one from Sean Duffy, one of the first people to find Richie on the road. Finally, they spoke to Martin Quigley, who described the row between Richie and Mark McConnell in the Town & Country bar.

By Tuesday evening, they had built up a rough idea of Richie's movements through the pubs of Raphoe, including the two rows he had in the pubs. There were nine statements on file. Only one mentioned Mark McConnell, and none mentioned Young Frank McBrearty.

By Wednesday evening, Gardaí had taken an additional seventeen statements. Six of these were concerned with Richie's movements, and the cars seen on the road around the time he went up Irish Row. Two were from concerned people who saw him lying on the road after he was found. Nine of them concentrated on the fight in the Town & Country. The focus was shifting.

Late that Wednesday night, Inspector John McGinley called to see Mark and Roisin McConnell along with Detective Garda Michael O'Malley and Raphoe Garda Phil Collins. O'Malley interviewed Roisin McConnell. She told the detective that Mark dropped her and their son Dean off at his granny's house, Anna Quinn in St Eunan's Terrace at around 7 p.m., and headed to the Town & Country. About an hour later Roisin walked to the pub, joining her sister Katrina Brolly, Eunan Brolly and Mark. A while later, Roisin's brother Paul Quinn arrived with his wife Sue. Mark and Mary Bogle, and Roisin's cousin Charlotte also joined the group. Mark and Paul played pool. She saw Derek Ayton and Richard McBrearty at the bar.

At some point, one of her sisters told her that Mark and Richie Barron were 'having words'. She stood in front of her husband, and bar owner

Mark Quinn got in front of Richie. Mark went to the pool room. The Brollys left the pub around 12.15 a.m., and Roisin was refused a drink at 1.10 a.m. Roisin left with Mark shortly afterwards. On their way to Frankie's nightclub, they spoke to Stephen McCullagh, and they stopped at Sarah's Café to order curry. Old Frank McBrearty let them in for free, and they stayed in the nightclub for about fifteen minutes. Roisin's sister Edel Quinn told her Richie had been knocked down, but he wasn't dead. They left the nightclub, went to collect some baby things for Dean from Tullyvinney, came back and collected their curry order, and went to the Brollys' home on Railway Road.

Mark McConnell gave his statement to Garda Phil Collins. Inspector John McGinley was present when he made his statement, and Roisin was giving a statement to Detective Garda Michael O'Malley at the same time in another room. Roisin said her statement was made about 10.45 p.m. that night. Although the heading of the statement recorded that it was taken at Raphoe Garda station, McGinley confirmed at the tribunal that the statements of both Mark and Roisin McConnell were taken in their home.

Mark said that when he went to the pub he met the Brollys. Another family, the Bogles had joined them some time earlier. He placed the time of the row with Richie at around 10 p.m. It began when Richie said to him: 'You're some excuse for a McBrearty.'

Mark answered with something like 'Sit down to fuck, I'm not a McBrearty.' Richie went to take his coat off. 'His pose wasn't a friendly pose. He became aggressive and angry,' Mark said.

'Go on up home out of the road, you're an ould man,' Mark told Richie. Pub owner Mark Quinn got between them, saying, 'I don't want this bother about my pub.' Mark said that after about twenty minutes, he was told Richie was gone. 'It was around 11 p.m. at this stage.' They left the pub around 1.20 a.m.

Mark told the Guards he chatted to Stephen McCullagh and his wife on the way to the nightclub. Mark and Roisin then stopped in at Sarah's Café to order a takeaway, which they would pick up after the nightclub. They got to Frankie's at 1.30 a.m. In the nightclub, they heard Richie was dead. Mark and Roisin left at 1.45 a.m. Edel Quinn and her boyfriend Edmund 'Ebby' Walsh came with them. They dropped over to their house in Tullyvinney to get baby things, picked up their takeaway at Sarah's Café and went to the Brollys.

Mark believed the Gardaí helped fuel the rumours that Richie Barron was murdered, by asking everyone who made a statement if they saw Mark McConnell, and what he was wearing. 'People were coming back to me telling me this. This is the reason rumours were spreading like wildfire,' he told Inspector McGinley at the tribunal.

The investigation was looking into the movements of a man who spent a Sunday night on a pub crawl. Most of the witnesses were drunk at the time. Their times varied wildly. If the murder theory was to work, Mark McConnell had to leave the bar around 12.30 a.m. at the latest, in order to have time to reach Richie Barron and assault him before he was discovered. Unfortunately for the theory, half the witnesses the Guards spoke to said Mark McConnell was still in the Town & Country after 1 a.m., by which time Richie Barron had been found lying on the roadside. This time of 12.30 a.m., when some of the witnesses believed they saw Mark after he left the Town & Country bar, would become a crucial part of the 'Garda template' for Mark's involvement in the 'murder' of Richie Barron.

Eventually, a total of seven witnesses would say Mark McConnell left the Town & Country around 12.30 a.m. Another seven would say the time was 1.30 a.m. Inspector McGinley said he chose to believe the sober witnesses, bar owner Mark Quinn and barman Martin Quigley. He didn't believe witnesses would worry about late drinking hours in a pub when a murder investigation was in place. Yet Martin Quigley made his statement on Tuesday, at a time before O'Dowd passed on the murder rumour to Chief Fitzpatrick, and McGinley himself told the tribunal the investigation was still regarded as solely a hit and run inquiry at that point. Mark Quinn was questioned on Wednesday 16 October, when both possibilities were still being looked into, but at a time when McGinley said the murder theory had only the status of a rumour and the burial had gone ahead without a full forensic post-mortem examination.

Anybody who had made a statement to support Mark McConnell's alibi became a suspect, Sergeant Joe Hannigan later told the Morris tribunal. 'It was believed that they were covering his movements for the relevant time,' he explained. This was particularly true if the potential suspects were related to the McBrearty family, however remotely.

'If the statements were unclear or if the times covered Mr McBrearty or Mark McConnell, that's how they came into the frame,' is how Hannigan summed up the Garda viewpoint.

No one approached Martin Quigley to take a second statement as the timing became a critical issue. He told the tribunal he had given an early time to avoid getting his boss in trouble for late opening. If he had known it would lead to a murder investigation, he would have given the correct time.

In his statement to Garda Phil Collins, Mark McConnell explained that he didn't get on with Richie Barron. This dated back to 'an incident at the Baker's Corner' several years earlier, although the incident had involved Richie Barron's son Stephen, not Richie Barron himself.

Baker's Corner (also known as the Beehive) was a nightclub in the nearby town of Killygordon. Garda Padraig Mulligan prepared a report on the incident during the Barron investigation, describing how it had led to bad blood between the McBrearty and Barron families, which he later delivered to Inspector McGinley. Even by the most serious account, the argument in the Town & Country between Mark McConnell and Richie Barron was hardly serious enough to provoke a deadly assault. But the Baker's Corner incident now provided a stronger motive for assault and murder. The row was no longer a few heated words exchanged in isolation. It became part of a pattern. The families had been at each other's throats for years. The older generation stayed out of it for the most part, but for the younger McBreartys, McConnells, Barrons and others, there was long standing ill will.

The report which Padraig Mulligan sent in to Inspector McGinley was titled 'History of events/incidents involving the Barron family, the McConnells and the McBreartys'. It began with an account of the incident at the Baker's Corner, which involved Stephen Barron, Derrick 'Darcy' Connolly and others, with some of the McBreartys and Mark McConnell on the other side. Stephen Barron's version was that Mark McConnell and a McBrearty assaulted their friend, Derrick 'Darcy' Connolly. Stephen then attacked one of the McBreartys. Stephen Barron was ejected from the nightclub along with the McBreartys.

'On the following evening,' Mulligan wrote, while Stephen Barron and his friends were chatting in the Diamond in Raphoe, 'Frank McBrearty Junior assaulted Stephen Barron. He struck him with a stick he was carrying.' When a friend tried to help Stephen, 'Frank McBrearty Junior went back to his father's pub and returned with his brothers Andy and John. He was also carrying a length of angle iron on his return. He used this to assault the lads on the corner. This matter was reported to the Gardaí by the Barron family. The McBreartys then reported the incident the previous night in Killygordon and both matters were investigated.'

According to Mulligan's account, Martin Ayton, Derek 'Darcy' Connolly and Stephen Barron were convicted and sentenced to community service, while Young Frank McBrearty received a one-month suspended sentence on account of using an iron bar. 'During the course of the row at Raphoe, Richie Barron arrived and Frank McBrearty Junior is alleged to have said that on the next occasion he would use a shooter,' Mulligan wrote.

At the tribunal, Young Frank gave a slightly different account. The District Court judge had listened to the claims and counter-claims as the youths tried to justify themselves, he said, finally throwing his hands in the air and declaring: 'Enough, the Probation Act to the lot of you!', and warning them he didn't want to see any of them again.

Old Frank recalled at the tribunal: 'The whole lot were all brought to court. They all got community service. But that didn't stop me and Richie. Me and Richie never had a word about it. I used to meet him at Mass on Sundays and I used to see him at a lot of funerals. He was a great man for funerals. When this thing happened [at Baker's Corner], me and Richie got together to see if we could get the families to make it up, and [Richie's wife] Nora objected to it. She went on ahead to court with it.'

Mulligan's report outlined a list of less serious events in the years after the row at the Baker's Corner. In 1994, Stephen Barron allegedly broke a headlight in a car parked outside the Parting Glass. Andy McBrearty and two others went looking for Stephen, he wrote, but Richie Barron 'beat them out of the street'.

In 1995, Stephen Barron 'had words' with Mark McConnell's brother Michael in the Suile Tavern. A week later Stephen and Richie Barron met Michael McConnell in the Suile Tavern. Richie said something to Michael, and the barman had to separate them. While the barman was between Richie and Michael, Stephen Barron got past him and hit Michael, who left the pub. Garda Mulligan went on to report that as the Barrons left the pub, they in turn were met by Michael McConnell, Eddie McBrearty and 'a group Stephen describes as boys from the town'. The ensuing fight was not reported to the Gardaí.

In his report to Sergeant Joe Hannigan and Inspector John McGinley, Mulligan wrote that according to Stephen Barron there had been no further trouble between the groups since 1995, except for 'the odd bit of verbal abuse'.

Chapter 5
Two Suspects Have Emerged

On Thursday 17 October scenes of crime officer Garda Niall Coady left Donegal at 7.30 a.m. He was on his way to the National Forensic Science Laboratory in Dublin with the exhibits and forensic samples he had gathered where Richie Barron was found, and from Letterkenny General Hospital.

'Conference re suspicious death at 9.30 a.m. to 11.30 a.m.,' Inspector Jim Gallagher recorded in his journal. 'Inspector McGinley doing the book. Went through the evidence and handed out jobs. Two suspects have emerged but there is no evidence that they were at the scene. House to house inquiries to continue and all pubs to be visited, and each patron to be visited.'

The 'book' is the investigation jobs book, the log of all tasks to be carried out by the investigation team. It records all statements to be taken or cross-checked, and evidence to be searched for. The investigation was in its fourth day, and there were now two suspects in a possible assault, 'Mark McConnell and one of the McBreartys.'

In works of fiction, detectives are often brilliant and eccentric individuals, making intuitive leaps of logic to solve crimes. In reality, police work is slow and methodical, much of it taken up with cross-referencing files. The byword is thoroughness. Richie Barron spent the last night of his life in the pubs of Raphoe, so one of the first jobs in the investigation was to take statements from the bar owners and staff in the town. In turn, each person mentioned in the statements would then be approached for a statement. In turn, the people they mentioned would lead to new jobs, and to more again.

Further jobs were generated by speaking to the McBride family, who made the 999 call, to Lee Parker, Sean Duffy and Edward Johnston, who were the first to arrive at the scene. Everyone they saw then had to be interviewed.

The investigation began to gather momentum. A total of twenty-five statements were taken by Gardaí working the case on Thursday 17

October, as they spoke to the people who were in Raphoe on Sunday night.

Derek Ayton told Sergeant Paul Heffernan he spent Sunday 13 October in the Town & Country. He met Richie around 11 p.m. Richie was drinking whiskey and water and bought Derek a vodka. Derek was in the pool room when the row took place, but afterwards he heard Richie apologising to Mark Quinn. Quinn told him to forget about it. Ayton left shortly afterwards, and next saw Richie as he was leaving the Suile Tavern. Ayton went for chips, then went to his family home. Between 12.40 a.m. and 12.45 a.m. there was a knock on the window. It was Paul 'Gazza' Gallagher. Ayton went out to see what he wanted.

'I'm looking for a push,' Gazza told him. 'My car has broken down.' Derek helped Gazza get his car started, and went back inside. It was close to 1 a.m. He snoozed on the couch, and fell asleep until his sister Glenda woke him to tell him Richie Barron was dead.

Gazza was a prime suspect in the early hit and run investigation. Two anonymous telephone calls to Letterkenny named him in the early hours of Monday morning. He was in the right place, at the right time, and eye-witnesses reported he was driving erratically.

Gazza was busy on Sunday 13 October. The 22-year-old habitual thief from Letterkenny lived across the border in Castlederg, and at the time was driving a battered, cream-coloured Renault. The car was in bad shape, the brakes were dodgy, and the ignition key was missing. Gazza had rigged the ignition so he could start it using an old spoon. Still, it had only cost him fifty quid, so it was a bargain.

Gazza broke into a farmhouse early on Sunday evening. He picked up some cash, a billhook and a chainsaw. Maybe he could flog them later, he figured. Getting rid of the chainsaw was easy enough, Gazza soon found a buyer. The newly acquired riches in his pocket, Gazza decided the billhook was worthless. On his way from the sale, he threw it over a hedge.

Years later, Garda George Healy told the Morris tribunal that a local farmer, Hugh Stewart, had reported the theft of a chainsaw and £120, and a few days later told him he was also missing a slash hook or billhook. That was the last he heard about it until he was questioned by the Carty team.

Gazza headed to his mother's home in Letterkenny, and parked the battered Renault outside on a hill. While he was inside, the brakes slipped, and the car rolled down the hill until it hit a neighbour's wall and fence, damaging the fence and the car. Garda Dan Curran visited the scene and took note of the damage to the fence and to Gazza's car.

It wasn't the first encounter Gazza had had with the Guards. At the Morris tribunal, Gazza testified that in May 1996 he had been abducted, tied up like a chicken and brought across the border from Northern

Ireland to Donegal to be delivered to Garda detectives. A team of Garda detectives were waiting for Gazza at the border. There were several outstanding warrants for his arrest. The Guards told him he was under arrest, and brought him to Letterkenny.

Gazza said he heard his kidnappers on mobile phones arranging with the Guards where he would be picked up. 'I asked to see a solicitor and a doctor. I didn't get none,' he said. He was 'black and blue' and had blood on his face. He was asked about drug dealers in Castlederg.

The next day, when Superintendent John Fitzgerald found out what had happened, he ordered Gazza released. The affair offended Fitzgerald's sense of justice; the Gardaí hadn't caught Gazza fair and square. He let Gazza go, so he could return to the North and report the alleged kidnapping to the RUC. As Gazza remembered it, the outstanding warrants against him were not executed until six months later, after Richie Barron's death.

On 6 September 1996 Chief Superintendent Denis Fitzpatrick sent a report about Gazza's alleged kidnap to the Assistant Commissioner. Gardaí had been told Gazza would be travelling across the border to Donegal, but did not know he would be tied and brought against his will, the report stated. 'There was obviously a criminal act carried out on both sides of the border,' Fitzpatrick reported. Gazza had been unlawfully imprisoned and brought to the border.

On the night of 13 October 1996, Gazza decided to head to Raphoe with his brother Packie. He parked above the town, off Irish Row. He walked down to the Diamond and met a friend outside Frankie's. The two went inside.

Glenda Muldoon, Gazza's ex-girlfriend, arrived at Frankie's with her friend Paula McLaughlin at 12.30 a.m. Five or ten minutes later Gazza spotted her across the dance floor. Gazza had gone out with Glenda for two years, but it was not the happiest of relationships. The Muldoons were a highly successful business family from Castlederg in Northern Ireland, and they disapproved of her relationship with the ne'er-do-well Gallagher.

When he spotted her, Gazza knew he had to talk to her. She'd broken up with him three weeks before. He pleaded with her to take him back, but Glenda didn't want anything to do with him any more. She walked off the dance floor, but Gazza persisted, following her. A friend of hers called a bouncer, 'a small fat man', and he moved in quickly. 'I believe that Paul Gallagher was put out of the disco at about a quarter to one,' Glenda told the Gardaí later.

Young Frank and the bouncer marched Gazza to the door. Old Frank noticed them, and asked what was going on. 'He's barred,' Young Frank explained. 'He hit some boy with a bottle last weekend.' Gazza had spotted one of his abductors at the previous week's disco, and had taken impulsive revenge for the indignity of being trussed up like a chicken in the back of a van the previous spring.

Gazza later recalled that Young Frank told him not to worry, Old Frank would forget about his barring in a couple of weeks. Old Frank sent one of his doormen, Sean Crossan, outside a couple of minutes later, telling him to check in case Gazza was hanging around, planning revenge by breaking a window. Crossan didn't see Gazza when he checked outside. Crossan then went to deal with two young women who were sick in the car park.

Gazza headed back to the Diamond, and walked up Irish Row to get his car. There was no starting the battered Renault, so Gazza called in to a nearby house, looking for help to get the banger going. It was at this point that Derek Ayton helped Gazza push-start the car. From his bedroom window, Paul Ayton watched his brother helping Gazza.

Several independent witnesses saw Gazza expelled from the disco at around 12.40 or 12.45 a.m., or shortly afterwards when he asked Derek Ayton for help starting his car and then drove back down to the Diamond in Raphoe. An objective look at this evidence should have told Gardaí how unlikely it was that Young Frank McBrearty would have had time to then leave the nightclub, travel the several hundred yards from there to assault Richie Barron, and return within the timeframe allowed. But no one ever drew the obvious conclusion from the information the incident room collected.

When Gazza got back down to the Diamond, he drove past Frankie's, hoping to spot Glenda outside, but there was no sign of her. He turned round at the Tech, and headed for Lifford. He wasn't speeding when he drove down to the Diamond and past Frankie's, he said later.

Jackie Craig was sitting in a car in the town. She saw Gazza arrive back in the Diamond, shortly after Lee Parker drove up Irish Row. Irish Row forks in two; Lee took the left turn to Townparks and Mongorry, where he found Richie Barron lying on the road. Gazza had been parked in the Close, on a road which forks off to the right from Irish Row. Lee didn't pass anyone on the way up the hill, so it seems Gazza was still with Derek Ayton looking for help starting his car when Lee drove out of Raphoe.

Outside Lifford, Gazza spotted a Garda checkpoint. The banger was uninsured, so Gazza turned and headed to the border by another route. From there, he headed to Derry city, took the upper deck of the Craigavon bridge and made his way to Desmond's garage on the Strand Road, where he bought petrol and cigarettes. The security camera at the filling station recorded him getting petrol at 1.56 a.m.

It was late, but Gazza still couldn't get Glenda out of his mind. She'd broken up with him, and had him thrown out of Frankie's. He headed to her home in Castlederg. He tried throwing stones at her window to get her attention, but there was no answer. Gazza wasn't to know she was still in Raphoe. After a few minutes he gave up and left.

On the way back to Donegal, Gazza broke into the Border Inn in Castlefin, and stole the cash in the tills. He headed back to his mother's home in Letterkenny, arriving at around 4 a.m. His sister was home, but there was no sign of his brother Packie. After a few minutes, Gazza decided to head back to Raphoe to look for Packie.

Packie was nowhere to be found in Raphoe. Gazza decided to head back to Castlederg. On the way he gave a lift to a young man with a bloodied face. Gazza didn't know it, but the man had got the cut in a fight with Packie earlier that night. Gazza had exhausted his petrol supply, and the Renault gave up the ghost outside Castlederg. When the car died, he walked to Castlederg, to spend the night in a caravan he and Packie kept there. He was in bed at 6 a.m.

Glenda thought it was odd Gazza wasn't outside the disco when she left at about 3.20 a.m. He was usually parked outside, waiting for her. At a disco in Strabane a few weeks before, he'd even come up to her as she got into a jeep, banging on the window trying to get her to talk to him. Glenda saw Gazza's brother Packie. 'It's a wonder Gazza is not driving about,' she said. Packie agreed.

Gazza slept through most of the day on Monday 14 October. Eventually, he stirred himself, got some fuel for the Renault, and headed to his mother's house in Letterkenny. When he got there, his mother asked him if he had anything to do with Richie Barron. Packie had spoken to the Gardaí and said his brother was 'wild drunk and driving around'.

That night, Gazza broke into Dunnion's Café in Ballybofey, and stole £1,000 in 50p coins from the slot machines. On Tuesday 15 October, Gazza tried to sell the battered Renault. He brought the McGinley brothers out to it, but they weren't interested. It was scrap. Still, they agreed the wheels were worth salvaging, and Gazza agreed to sell them the tyres. He dumped the car at the edge of a forest, and put a match to it. 'It was scrap, nobody wanted it. I didn't want it lying about the house,' he recalled.

Gazza needed a new car. He picked up a Ford Escort for £350. He paid in 50p coins.

Gazza thought it was Tuesday night that he headed to Raphoe to see if he was still barred from Frankie's. Young Frank laughed when he saw Gazza walk in the door. 'Half the Guards in the country are looking for you,' he told him.

Gazza ordered a Budweiser, and paid in 50p coins. Young Frank kept up the slagging. Gazza wasn't bothered by it. Afterwards, what stuck in Young Frank's mind was that Gazza paid for everything with 50p coins.

Several of the Garda statements collected on Thursday 17 October focused on Gazza Gallagher. As well as the information from Derek Ayton, Damien Martin Callan told Detective Garda PJ Keating he was in Raphoe with his girlfriend, Jackie Craig. They spent the evening in her car talking to friends, and among others, he saw Paul Gazza Gallagher.

Declan McCullagh, the barman at the Suile Tavern, spoke to Detective Garda Pat Flynn. He heard Richie knocking on the door at about 11.45 p.m. 'He was drunk but not legless,' Declan remembered. 'I've seen him worse.' Richie and Manny Hegarty got into a row over money Manny said he was owed, and Manny got a cut on his head. When everyone calmed down, Declan let Richie out, and asked him did he want a taxi. 'No, I'll walk it,' Richie said. Declan watched Richie walk past Duffy's butchers. Declan said he left the pub at 1 a.m. and went to his girlfriend in Convoy, but she was in bed so he came back to Raphoe and went to DJ's chip shop around 1.15 a.m. There were four or five people there. As he left DJ's he saw Mark and Roisin McConnell coming from the Diamond and heading to Frankie's. He went down the street to his brother Stephen McCullagh and Liam Sweeney, who told him Richie had been knocked down. They went up to the scene, and left after the ambulance came. Declan McCullagh's statement punched another hole in the Garda murder theory, placing Mark in the Diamond on his way from the pub at about 1.15 a.m., by which time Richie Barron's body had already been discovered by Lee Parker and the ambulance was on its way.

————

Old Frank McBrearty was born in August 1944 in Donegal. 'In Raphoe, Co. Donegal, three miles out in the country,' he told the Morris tribunal. 'I have four brothers. Three brothers, a twin brother and myself, and a sister, six of us.'

Frank attended a small school in Drummucklagh, outside Raphoe, ending his education when he was eleven or twelve. 'I went to work with a farmer,' he remembered, 'and then I went to work in a bakery for two months. My father worked with the Donegal County Council, and my mother was a housemaid, housewife.'

Frank 'didn't like the inside work' so he didn't last long in the bakery. 'I went to the Irish Army, 1960. I was based in Athlone, Mullingar, Cork and Dublin. I was in the infantry first, then transport. I was in the Congo in 1961, in Africa.' Frank took great pride in his military service, in particular his six months on peacekeeping service with the UN in the Congo, and brought his UN peacekeeping service medals with him when he went to the Morris tribunal. He remembered it as a challenging time. 'There was people killed and there was people wounded. We were guarding an 84,000 refugee camp where there were people had diseases of all descriptions. We were staying in camps. We were against the Belgian rebels and the Congolese. I was stationed in Zulu Camp, and I was on an 84mm recoilless, protecting the Irish soldiers up front at the tunnels. And I was also along with the Gurkhas and the Malayans.

'There was attacks where the Mass was said on a Sunday. There was attacks along the road. There was bombing and there was shooting . . . There was attacks from the Belgian Congolese. They were trying to take over the Belgian Congo. They were mercenaries . . . I felt sorry for the young people there in the camps, where there was no food, starvation. A lot of people dying every day there.'

At the time, Frank was only seventeen. 'I finished and then I went home, and then I went to Scotland,' he recalled. He also worked in London, in 'the civil engineering business' and 'in tunnel work'.

One night in 1973, as Frank McBrearty was coming out of a pub in the Gorbles area of Glasgow, one of his friends told him to look out, there was a man coming towards him from behind. Frank turned around and thought the man had a knife. Frank hit him, the man fell on the footpath, hit his head and died. Frank was charged with culpable homicide. He pleaded self-defence, and the jury returned a verdict of not guilty.

Rumours about the death would haunt Frank McBrearty for the rest of his life. The slur that he had murdered a man followed him when he moved home to Ireland, and some said it was the root cause of the hostility between the younger generation of McBreartys and Barrons that led to the Baker's Corner incident.

Frank McBrearty came home to Raphoe in 1976, bringing with him a wife and four boys, and settled in Tullyrap, three miles outside Raphoe. With his savings of around £100,000, he bought a public house, and over time expanded the business to include a successful nightclub.

'It was a very small pub, turning about £100 a week. I built it up over the years,' he recalled. 'I extended the premises. I turned it into a Country and Western/disco entertainment centre. I had to demolish old sheds, cattle sheds. I built all the stuff myself. For two years I had a public bar, and then I went into the entertainment business. Country & Western music, and running some discos. Very little discos, mostly Country & Western music. At the very beginning we were running four nights.'

Frank McBrearty involved himself in the local boxing club, and charity work. 'The charity thing, I ran twice for Lord Mayor. When they say Lord Mayor, the title is only for collecting money, and the tickets were all £1 a ticket. So you go out around and you sell the tickets, and I sold the most tickets, for the boxing club I sold six thousand, which was £6,000. And I done the very same for the football club, the two football clubs. And that's how I became Lord Mayor, and I haven't been replaced, I'm still Lord Mayor for twenty years. Nobody took it up, they weren't able to beat me at collecting the pound a ticket.

'You couldn't accept donations of £100 or anything like that. You had to sell the ticket. I done it in my car, I went round all the places. I went around the doors, around the doors of my neighbours. I had no involvement in the football, but I had an involvement in the boxing. I trained the young people. I showed them how to defend themselves. I knew a bit about karate and judo as well. There used to be a boxing club in Raphoe years and years ago. My uncle was an amateur boxer. My mother's brother. And then I opened it up again in the Seventies, and I trained them. And we appointed them trainers, and I became president of the club, forever, for life now. I'm the president of that club now, there can be other presidents, but I'll always be the president.'

For Frank, proud of his humble start in life and how far he'd come, the honorary title of Lord Mayor of Raphoe was a shining achievement, one he took great pride in. It gave him a certain status in the community, and he took his role as a leading citizen seriously.

Even so, Frank's years as a publican hadn't been without the occasional clash with authority. At the Morris tribunal, Young Frank told how his father had been approached by a sergeant in the town and asked for 'loans' over the years, in return for which Frank—like all other publicans in the area—would be allowed to stay open after hours serving alcohol on Saturday, his most profitable night. The 'loans' began shortly after the sergeant arrived in the town, when the sergeant asked Frank for a 'sub' to tide him over until pay-day. These 'loans', varying from £20 up to £250 to £300, were never repaid. Old Frank told tribunal investigators 'the final straw' came when the sergeant asked for a £30,000 bridging loan to buy some property. Frank went to Gardaí in Letterkenny and made a formal complaint about the sergeant, who he said 'wasn't fit to wear the uniform'. Eventually files were sent to the DPP. However, the sergeant took early retirement, the DPP recommended no prosecutions in the case, and the matter was dropped. The McBreartys believed that other Gardaí held a grudge against the publican for costing this sergeant his job.

Frank told the tribunal he hadn't known Richie Barron in Scotland, they didn't work together, but he got to know him when he returned to Raphoe. 'My mother and my father were personal friends of their family,' he remembered. 'We got on very, very well.' Richie was barred from Frank's pub after he fought with a customer, 'but I didn't fall out with him. I just told him not to come back. We had no fight or no argument or anything like that. I was the boss of my premises, I wouldn't allow any carry-on.'

———

Gazza Gallagher was mentioned in at least three civilian statements on Thursday 17 October. His name had already come up in two anonymous telephone calls recorded by Alpha communications centre early on Monday morning. One of these anonymous calls had been passed to Detective Sergeant Sylvie Henry to investigate. Gazza's brother Packie had also told McDwyer and Birney that Gazza was driving wildly and drunk when they got back to Raphoe from the hospital early on Monday morning.

Detective Sergeant Sylvie Henry was putting some of the pieces together. The RUC had spotted Gazza at the border at a time that fitted the break-in at the Border Inn. The break-in at Dunnion's Café the following night also fitted Gazza's style. They'd spent Tuesday searching for his cream-coloured Renault 9, before finding the burnt-out shell in the woods near Letterkenny. Henry had discovered that Gazza had paid £350 for his new Escort car in 50p coins, matching the money stolen at the break-in at Dunnion's.

That evening, Detective Sergeant Sylvie Henry swore out an 'information' to a local peace commissioner, PJ Blake. He laid out his case against Gazza for the Dunnion's break-in. The key piece of evidence was the knowledge that Gazza was making large value purchases and paying with 50p coins.

At the back of Henry's mind also must have been the question mark over Gazza's movements the night Richie Barron died. He'd been expelled from the nightclub around the right time, he'd been seen driving at speed that night, there were calls to Alpha naming him as a possible suspect, and he'd burnt his car, making any forensic examination next to impossible.

Armed with his search warrant from the peace commissioner, Henry made plans to arrest Gazza on Friday morning.

Chapter 6

Captain Hook

A t 8 a.m. on Friday 18 October, armed with his search warrant to look for a large quantity of stolen 50p coins, Detective Sergeant Sylvie Henry and a party of Guards entered the Letterkenny family home of 21-year-old Paul Martin 'Gazza' Gallagher.

Earlier in the week, Henry and Inspector Jim Gallagher had called to the Parting Glass and spoken to Old Frank McBrearty. They asked him if anyone had left the nightclub before the disco finished the night Richie Barron died. Frank told them his son had ejected someone, but didn't know his name. The three travelled out to Tullyvinney, where Young Frank was working on his new house. Old Frank asked Young Frank to have a word with the Gardaí. Young Frank told Henry and Gallagher that he ejected Gazza at around 12.30 a.m. 'He was his usual arrogant self but at the time I felt he was being co-operative and remained in the car,' Sylvie wrote later.

Inspector Jim Gallagher's journal entry for Monday 14 October made no mention of Gazza Gallagher. On Wednesday 16 October, however, he noted 'Paul Gallagher Dr McGinley Road a suspect as he was put out of the Parting Glass nightclub at 12.30 a.m. and had his uninsured car parked near the scene.'

Henry's Friday morning search of Gazza's family home for 50p coins proved fruitless, but the detectives found Gazza hiding behind a wardrobe in his parents' bedroom. At 8.50 a.m., Henry arrested Gazza on suspicion of the Monday night burglary at Dunnion's Café, Main Street, Ballybofey. He was taken to Letterkenny Garda station and detained under Section 4 of the Criminal Justice Act, 1984.

Gazza's mother's house was near the station, the drive there took a mere five minutes. After he was processed by member in charge Garda PJ Lynch, Gazza was placed in a cell at 9.06 a.m. Four minutes later, Lynch was relieved by Garda Jackson, who was custody officer until Lynch returned at midday. The 1984 Criminal Justice Act allowed the Gardaí to hold a prisoner for up to six hours in the investigation of a crime. The detention can be extended for a further six hours if necessary, on the approval of an officer of superintendent rank or higher. Custody regulations signed in 1987 set out the mechanics of the detention, including meals for the prisoner, access to legal advice, and how many Guards can question him at any one time. The Judges' Rules, a set of principles dating from a keynote legal decision in 1918, require among other things that prisoners are cautioned that they have a right to silence before questioning. The 'Rules' (there are nine in total) were formulated by Lord Chief Justice Alverstone, and along with the Treatment of Persons in Custody regulations signed by Minister for Justice Gerard Collins in 1987, govern the treatment of prisoners in Garda custody. After Gazza was informed of his rights, he had a visit from his solicitor and was given breakfast, before his interrogation began.

Gazza was interviewed by several teams during his time in custody, but for only ten minutes by Sylvie Henry, his arresting officer, between 4.10 p.m. and 4.20 p.m. At the Morris tribunal, Gazza claimed that Sylvie Henry told him he was being blamed by Young Frank McBrearty for Richie Barron's death. He claimed Sylvie Henry put a statement in front of him, telling him that Young Frank had made it. Gazza said that it was as a result of this that he decided, if Young Frank was fingering him, he would blame Young Frank for Richie Barron's death. Henry flatly denied the accusation.

When lawyers at the tribunal pointed out that Young Frank's statement said nothing about Gazza hitting Richie Barron in a traffic accident, Gazza said he had not read the statement at the time. 'It was said to me anyway,' he insisted. 'I didn't look at it, it was thrown on the table.' Henry told the tribunal that Gazza's claim was nonsense. Young Frank did in fact make a statement about the 50p coins on Friday 18 October, but according to Detective Garda Michael Carroll, who took the statement, this didn't happen until after Gazza was released from his Section 4 arrest on Friday evening.

Gazza's credibility presented a problem for the tribunal. Not for the first time, they would have to deal with a witness who had lied several times, and changed his story when it suited him. Other witnesses contradicted parts of his story.

The Morris tribunal decided that Gazza 'could not possibly be relied on as a witness of truth'. Over the years, he had changed his story too many times. Mr Justice Morris wrote that 'in respect of any conflict of fact concerning meetings and interviews between Detective Sergeant Henry and Paul Gallagher, the Tribunal accepts the evidence of Detective Sergeant Henry.'

Gazza admitted to the tribunal that he made a series of false accusations against Young Frank, implicating him in the death of Richie Barron, the first of which was that he was told by Young Frank to burn his old Renault 9 banger. In an effort to shift the blame at the tribunal, he tried to blame Sylvie Henry, claiming the sergeant had threatened him with jail for the death of Richie Barron during his arrest. However, there is no record of any allegation from Gazza until two weeks after the arrest, when Gazza spoke to Henry at a bail hearing. The story grew with time. Gazza claimed he was given £500 in cash by Young Frank (much of it in 50p coins!) and that the billhook he'd stolen from a farmer's home was either given to him by Young Frank, or left in his car by Young Frank, who told him to get rid of it. Henry said it wasn't until a court hearing some time after the arrest that Gazza began making the false allegations against Young Frank in a bid to make bail. The paper trail discovered by the tribunal supported Henry's account.

As teams of detectives interviewed Gazza throughout the day, he eventually gave a fairly complete account of his movements during the week, but left out the break-ins he had committed. After he was released from custody, he was immediately arrested on foot of outstanding bench warrants dating back several months as he left Letterkenny Garda station. According to Gazza, these were the same warrants on which he'd been arrested when he was allegedly kidnapped and dumped at the border in May 1996, and later released because Superintendent John Fitzgerald felt the Gardaí hadn't caught him fair and square.

Fingerprints lifted at Dunnion's by scenes of crime examiner Niall Coady were sent to Detective Sergeant Henry Benton at Garda HQ the following Tuesday, 22 October. On 6 November, these prints were matched to the set taken from Gazza when he was arrested.

By the time the tribunal began, Gazza had already admitted that most of the accusations he made against Young Frank McBrearty were lies. He still insisted that Sylvie Henry threatened him with jail for the death of Richie Barron during his arrest, but the record didn't back this up. The jobs book maintained by the Garda investigation contained several jobs relating to Gazza. The first, Job 23, covered the anonymous telephone call naming Gazza as someone who was driving erratically the night Barron died. Job 26, dated Wednesday 16 October, noted that Gazza's burnt-out car had been found, and made plans for a forensic examination. Job 86, dated Friday 18 October, matched the information Gazza gave the detectives while in custody. Jobs were assigned to verify that Gazza refuelled in Derry, and to identify the young man he gave a lift to on the way from Raphoe to Castlederg. The notes at Job 86 made no mention of any allegations about Young Frank McBrearty giving Gazza money, or telling him to burn the car or dispose of a billhook. There is no mention of these allegations until Job 237, the report from Sergeant Henry that Gazza found a billhook in his car, which he threw away. This tallies with Henry's account that Gazza began to make false accusations in a bid to make bail.

Job 86 generated quite a bit of activity, as details of what Gazza said were checked out. On Thursday 24 October, Detective Sergeant Sylvie

Henry and Detective Garda PJ Keating travelled to Shanganagh Castle, an open prison for young offenders in Dublin, where Packie Gallagher was being held. Packie told the detectives he'd been on weekend release the weekend Richie Barron died, and travelled to Raphoe with Gazza around 11 p.m. that night.

Packie saw Gazza's ex-girlfriend Glenda Muldoon around 12.30 a.m. He met up with Glenda again after the disco, and then chatted to another girl until 'some boy with a moustache and tattoos' took offence and asked Packie if he was chatting up his girl. Packie said they were just friends, but the exchange of words led to a fight anyway. Packie explained how 'five Strabane boys' intervened on his side of the fight, and he ended up walking home from Raphoe to Letterkenny. Henry and Keating must have smiled at the irony. Gazza had later given a lift to Packie's assailant, the 'boy with a moustache and tattoos'.

———

In Letterkenny Garda station, while Henry and his team of detectives were questioning Gazza Gallagher, the Barron conference room was moving from a hit and run inquiry to a murder investigation. There was a case conference that Friday, 18 October, headed by Superintendent John Fitzgerald, Inspector John McGinley and Inspector Jim Gallagher. They traced the movements of Andy McBrearty. As a result, Andy was eliminated as a suspect. He could not have been 'one of the McBreartys' referred to in O'Dowd's tip-off who assaulted Richie Barron along with Mark McConnell, because he was not in Raphoe at the time. His girlfriend Patricia McGrath drove him home, and she was sober and certain of the time. They'd left Raphoe around midnight.

Two other McBrearty brothers, Eddie and John, were also ruled out. By a process of elimination, 'one of the McBreartys' had to be Young Frank. No one stopped to wonder if the tip-off was simply wrong and none of the McBreartys had anything to do with Richie's death.

Niall Coady, the scenes of crime officer, attended the Letterkenny conference on the case, and spent the rest of that Friday carrying out forensic examinations on several cars. By then, he remembered later at the tribunal, the emphasis had changed to a possible murder investigation. There were rumours about Young Frank McBrearty and Mark McConnell, 'that they had carried out an assault and killed him'. He said he might have heard such rumours from other Gardaí as early as the Tuesday or Wednesday of the first week.

Garda John O'Toole also attended the conference and said the hit and run theory was not abandoned by everyone, but was being pursued by

Sylvie Henry through Gazza Gallagher 'and in fairness to him he never gave it up'.

Gazza was a prime suspect in the hit and run investigation in the early days. Two anonymous telephone calls to Letterkenny named him in the early hours of Monday morning. He was in the right place, at the right time, and eyewitnesses reported he was driving erratically. However, in the light of all the facts, he seems an unlikely culprit.

Although several witnesses saw him come flying down Irish Row at speed minutes after Lee Parker went up Irish Row, Parker himself passed no car on his way up to Mongorry. At the top of Irish Row, the road forks, with Mongorry to the left and the Close to the right. Gazza had parked in the Close.

Earlier, in the disco, Gazza made a beeline for Glenda Muldoon as soon as he saw her, and was ejected from the disco shortly after. Old Frank McBrearty had just arrived back from escorting his son Andy to his car when Gazza was ejected. On the way, he'd met Richie Barron, who was still outside the Suile Tavern. Minutes after Gazza was ejected, Old Frank sent Sean Crossan to make sure he wasn't hanging around. Crossan saw no one. It seems likely Gazza walked across the Diamond, up Irish Row, over to the Close and his car, and was getting help from Derek Ayton to give his car a push start when Lee Parker drove up the road. Minutes later, Gazza arrived in the Diamond.

Gazza's behaviour could be considered odd if he had just struck a man with his car. He arrived back at the Diamond at speed, attracting attention. He drove past Frankie's, so that several people saw him. He then drove to Strabane, Clady, Derry, Castlederg and Letterkenny, a journey which could have brought him into contact with any of several random RUC or Garda border checkpoints, even if he knew from experience where the major stops were likely to be.

Gazza drew more attention to himself by throwing stones at Glenda Muldoon's window, and risked being caught in the act when he broke in to the Border Inn on the way back from Castlederg to Letterkenny.

Most bizarre of all, having made it safely to his mother's house in Letterkenny, he then drove back to Raphoe along the road where Richie Barron died, and once more risked crossing the border to Castlederg looking for his brother Packie. Gazza had no way of knowing the Guards would have left the scene unattended.

In custody, Gazza proved himself a skilful liar, sticking to the truth for the most part. The fewer false details are added to a story, the fewer lies had to be remembered. He told the truth about getting thrown out of Frankie's, getting a push from Ayton, driving to Derry, visiting Glenda's house, and returning to Letterkenny, leaving out only the break-in at the Border Inn. Every trip Gazza made had a reason. He went to Derry for petrol, Castlederg to see Glenda, Letterkenny because it was his family home, and back to Raphoe and Castlederg looking for his brother Packie.

His account of his movements on Monday was similar. Understandably, he made no mention of the break-in at Dunnion's, where the poker machines yielded a lucrative harvest of 50p pieces, but there was no reason for him to lie about anything else. He went to Letterkenny because it was his family home, and to Raphoe to find out if he was barred. He went to Ballybofey to do a break-in, so he told the Guards he'd gone to a disco there.

Detective Sergeant Henry might still have harboured suspicions about Gazza before and during his arrest on Friday, but he was also well aware that Gazza would say anything that would pass the blame. Gazza did just that a week later, throwing around wild claims about Young Frank in an attempt to move suspicion away from himself, and muddy the waters for everyone.

Henry acknowledged at the tribunal that he was sceptical of Gazza's later claims about the billhook and payoffs from Young Frank McBrearty, but still they had to be followed up. He organised a search for the bill-hook. Henry's tenaciousness in chasing down what Gazza told him would earn him the nickname of 'Captain Hook' among the investigators on the Barron case.

Chapter 7

We Had a Mindset

Between three days and a week after Richie Barron died, Noel McBride got a call from William Doherty. 'Did you hear Richie Barron got killed?' Doherty asked him.

'I did,' said Noel.

'If the Guards come questioning you about being in Raphoe that night, say you were,' Doherty told him. 'Say you were in McBrearty's car park to do a job in the Tech in Raphoe, and say you saw McBrearty, Young Frank McBrearty and Mark McConnell coming down through the car park. Say he stopped with a bouncer, Marty McCallion, and then he went into the Tudor Lounge to get in.'

Doherty told McBride to specify times in his statements, to say he heard the clock ringing the hour. The story was simple enough. McBride was to say he was outside DJ's Chip Shop, then decided to rob the vocational school, and that was when he saw the two cousins. In the weeks that followed, Doherty would phone McBride again, urging him to make a statement to the Guards. 'I'll give you another hiding if you don't,' he threatened. Doherty had beaten up McBride about a month before.

Over the years, McBride would vary his account of why he did as Doherty asked him, variously claiming that he did as he was asked by Doherty out of fear or because he was promised money. However, he consistently blamed Doherty for the statements.

Noel McBride and William Doherty had been childhood friends, although they'd lost contact as the years passed. The week before Richie Barron died, Noel spent the day at a christening party thrown by his sister Stephanie for her daughter Meghan. Afterwards, at a party in Roper's Lantern Inn in Killygordon, Noel met Sharon Alexander. The two hit it off, and the following Sunday, Sharon invited Noel as her guest to the christening for her sister Mary Gallen's daughter Emma.

For the second Sunday in a row, Noel spent the day in Roper's Lantern Inn in Killygordon. At the end of the night, he went with Sharon and her family to a nightclub in Ballybofey, and spent the night in her brother's caravan in Killygordon.

As far as Doherty was concerned, he had found the perfect foil to frame Young Frank McBrearty and Mark McConnell, in his own words 'the only man stupid enough to do it'. The weekend after Richie Barron died, Doherty told Garda John O'Dowd that there was a witness. By the end of October, the Raphoe Garda would know the name of the witness— Noel McBride.

––––

Garda Tina Fowley recalled a case conference on the Saturday following Barron's death, 19 October 1996, which was not recorded in minutes. Present at the conference were the incident room staff, Sergeants Marty Moylan and Brendan Roache, Garda John O'Toole and herself, Superintendent John Fitzgerald, Sergeant Joe Hannigan and Garda John O'Dowd from Raphoe, and two or three members of the detective unit.

The same day, Sergeant Joe Hannigan spoke to Philomena Laird, one of the workers in Sarah's Café. She told him that Mark and Roisin McConnell came into the café to order a chicken curry for collection after Frankie's disco 'between 12.30 a.m. and 12.35 a.m.' She remembered that Manny Hegarty and Annie Caulfield were in the café at the same time.

Even taken at face value, before the inconsistencies with other statements emerged regarding the times she gave, Philomena Laird's statement should have pointed to Mark McConnell's innocence. Instead, it was used against him.

Declan McCullagh, the Suile Tavern barman, had already told the Guards in his statement on Thursday 17 October that Manny and Annie left the bar 'between 12.45 a.m. and 1 a.m.,' and he himself left at 1 a.m. He went to see his girlfriend in Convoy, but she was in bed, so he returned to Raphoe, where he bought some chips at about 1.15 a.m. While he was in the chip shop, he saw Mark and Roisin McConnell going across the Diamond. McCullagh's statement was bad news for anyone following the murder theory. If Mark McConnell had met up with Young Frank McBrearty in time to intercept and assault Richie Barron before 1 a.m., it was hardly likely that he'd still be in the Diamond at 1.15 a.m.

Like Philomena Laird, Declan McCullagh was a sober witness. He wasn't drinking that night, he was working. If the sequence of events he relayed was true, then Philomena must have been mistaken about the times. Leaving aside the times, the sequence of events must be that Declan McCullagh left the bar at the same time as Manny Hegarty and Annie Caulfield. While they went to Sarah's Café, McCullagh drove to Convoy and back, a round trip of at least ten minutes. Allowing another five minutes for a brief conversation in Convoy, it was at least fifteen minutes later when he returned to Raphoe and saw Mark McConnell crossing the square.

Declan's brother Stephen McCullagh spoke to Detective Garda Pat Tague on the same day that Philomena Laird made her statement to

Sergeant Joe Hannigan. Stephen held the lease on the Suile Tavern, but he had Sunday nights off and Declan took care of the pub instead. He told Tague he spent the night in Friels'pub with his wife Ann, and left 'sometime around 1 a.m.' They bought chips, and waited outside the Suile Tavern for a taxi to pass.

While he waited, Mark McConnell spoke to him for a few minutes as he crossed the Diamond. Just after he left, Sean Duffy then arrived and told him the news about Richie Barron. Stephen's brother Declan arrived, and they travelled up to the scene together. Clearly, the accounts of Declan and Stephen McCullagh confirmed each other. Ann McCullagh told Detective Garda Pat Tague that as she went for chips, she saw Manny Hegarty and Annie Caulfield 'sitting in Manny's car outside the Suile Tavern'. If they sat in the car before going to the café, this would account for the fifteen minutes or so between the time Declan McCullagh saw them leave the Suile Tavern, and when he saw Mark McConnell crossing the Diamond on his way to the café. The interlocking stories from Manny Hegarty and from Stephen, Ann and Declan McCullagh provided strong evidence that Philomena Laird had to be wrong about the time. Nobody ever went back to her to check.

It is the job of an incident room to tease out such discrepancies. The witnesses should be re-interviewed, to see if the inconsistencies can be resolved. Stephen McCullagh was not re-interviewed by Gardaí until 25 November 1997. Declan McCullagh was not reinterviewed until 18 January 1998. Ann McCullagh was only interviewed once. Philomena Laird was not re-interviewed until 22 September 1997. When she was questioned by Gardaí again, almost a year later, she would tell the detectives she was mistaken, and she saw Mark McConnell at 1.20 a.m., not 12.30 a.m. Other statements that day, from Edel Quinn (who saw her sister Roisin and Mark McConnell arrive at the disco around 1.30 a.m.) and from Paul and Sue Quinn (who said Mark McConnell was still in the Town & Country after 1 a.m. when they left by taxi) also coincided with Mark's account of his movements.

'Within a fortnight, John O'Dowd came in with the information that Frank McBrearty Junior and Mark McConnell were seen coming down the car park,' Sergeant Roache said. Other statements and information also came in about Young Frank McBrearty's movements. Profiles of Frank, Mark McConnell and Roisin McConnell were prepared, intended to give an accurate time-line of each individual's movements. Plans were made to search for a murder weapon.

That Sunday, a cryptic entry was made in the Barron investigation correspondence book. It noted that a young woman 'was in Frankie's car park with boyfriend'. The supposed witness 'saw Frankie McBrearty (Junior) coming down McBrearty's car park—on Sunday night, Monday

morning—he was covered in dirt and he was wet'. Official jobs were created to interview the young girl and her boyfriend. Investigation Job
number 131 dealt with the task of interviewing this potential witness.

The entry in the correspondence book is the first written record of
what Justice Morris called the 'Garda template' for the investigation, the
notion that Young Frank intercepted Richie Barron on his way home,
assaulted him, and made his getaway back down the field to the car park
and from there to the nightclub. It was not until a year later, in November
1997, that the young woman was interviewed. She was amazed to be asked
for a statement. She'd gone into Raphoe to get chips from DJ's takeaway
that night, but had never been anywhere near the nightclub car park. She
didn't even have a boyfriend at the time. The supposed report was a 'ghost
sighting', the first of many. It set up the template, but was not pursued.

The second week began with a Monday morning conference in
Letterkenny. The conference marked the first day on duty in his new
posting in Donegal for Detective Superintendent Joe Shelly. The 25-year
veteran was appointed Border Superintendent in the division on 17
October 1996, and took up duty on 21 October 1996. In the role of Border
Superintendent, his job was to co-ordinate information on subversive
activity in the county, and act as a liaison point with RUC officers on the
other side of the border.

However, Shelly soon found that in Donegal, Kevin Lennon was the
de facto border superintendent, even though his official job description
was District Superintendent in Buncrana. Lennon had so impressed
Chief Superintendent Denis Fitzpatrick with the McGlinchey charade
back when he was a detective inspector and Fitzpatrick was border superintendent, that he effectively had free rein in counter-intelligence and
anti-subversive operations.

At the tribunal, Shelly recalled that all intelligence in Donegal was to
be 'vetted by Kevin Lennon', and that Lennon's role in intelligence
gathering 'was much wider than his own district'. Shelly claimed he had
to use 'back door' methods to keep up with what was going on. He kept
tabs on local subversive activity by talking to the sergeants in the division,
and to Inspector John McGinley, and said he didn't get to see what was
recorded on c77 forms, the secret reports sent in on local paramilitary
activity.

Chief Superintendent Denis Fitzpatrick disagreed with Shelly's self-
portrait of an officer cut out of the loop. Copies of the c77s were kept in
the Divisional Office where the border superintendent could view them
at any time, he said.

Shelly painted a picture to the tribunal of an officer somewhat at a
loose end in Donegal, left without most of his official job description. If
Kevin Lennon had unofficially taken over most of his job, he needed to

find some other way to make himself useful. The Barron investigation gave him an outlet for his energies.

'Superintendent Shelly and I are two totally different people in our make up. Superintendent Shelly has a big presence, and when he walks in to a room, he's there,' John Fitzgerald memorably recalled at the tribunal. 'He has a loud voice. This is absolutely no reflection on Superintendent Shelly, he has a loud voice, and he has a different temperament or make-up to me.

'But having said that, I know the man, and I would have known the man for years on his investigations, and he would always consult with me. He wasn't the sort who would come in and take over the show or anything like that.'

The Monday morning meeting, Shelly's first in Donegal, covered what was known to date on the case. There was some work 'to be finished' on Gazza Gallagher's car, but he had been effectively—if not formally—eliminated as a suspect in most minds at the conference at that stage. A statement from Glenda Muldoon two days later would effectively fix the time Gazza was thrown out of the nightclub at around 12.40 to 12.45 a.m., ten to fifteen minutes after Glenda arrived at the Parting Glass.

However, eliminating Gazza as a suspect would also create problems for anyone who favoured Young Frank and the assault theory. Gazza himself told the Gardaí that he was thrown out of the Parting Glass by Young Frank, and this was confirmed by other witnesses, although not by all of them. Frank was also involved in a second incident at the nightclub around 1 a.m., when a group of men from Northern Ireland were expelled. Several witnesses saw Young Frank at the nightclub at 1 a.m. If the assault theory was to work, this left young Frank with a bare ten to fifteen minute window—from 12.45 to 12.54 a.m. (when Lee Parker found Richie Barron) in which to meet Mark McConnell, plot revenge, assault Richie Barron and run several hundred yards across open scrub on a cloudy, rainy night guided only by the light of a two-day-old new moon, all without being seen. And even if this was possible, there were several witnesses who said Mark McConnell was still in the Town & Country pub at the other side of the town until after 1 a.m.

Mark McConnell's name came up several times in the conference notes on 21 October. Then there were the two telephone calls to Letterkenny hospital the night Richie Barron died.

'We applied to track the two calls that were made to the hospital on the night, purporting to come from the Barron family,' Superintendent John Fitzgerald remembered. Detective Sergeant Sylvie Henry was appointed to follow up on the calls. Henry prepared a request which he forwarded to Crime & Security Branch, the Garda intelligence section in Garda Headquarters which coordinated all requests for telephone records in criminal investigations.

Henry's letter to Crime & Security laid out the essential facts of the case. Barron was found lying by a roadside just outside Raphoe on 14 October, and pronounced dead at Letterkenny hospital. 'The cause of death is unknown, but foul means is now a serious possibility,' Henry wrote.

Henry went on to give an account of a telephone call taken by the hospital receptionist, in the early hours of that morning. The first came from a man claiming to be Barron's son-in-law, 'John McCarron'. When the receptionist checked with Mrs Barron and found that Richie didn't have a son-in-law of that name, the caller hung up.

'It is possible that this was the culprit, checking to see how Richie Barron was,' Henry wrote. 'It is also possible that it was a nosey person. In any event, it is essential that the caller be identified by the investigation team.' Henry requested a trace on incoming calls to Letterkenny hospital between 2 a.m. and 2.45 a.m. 'as a matter of extreme urgency'.

The following day, Tuesday 22 October, Chief Superintendent Denis Fitzpatrick signed off on Henry's phone trace request, and forwarded it to Crime & Security. It would be months before the investigation team received an official reply, despite its 'extreme urgency'.

'That official reply from Crime & Security only came in January 1997,' Fitzpatrick recalled. Telecom Eireann was experiencing delays in handling Garda requests for phone records at the time, in part because of the increased volume of requests from Gardaí every year, in part because of delays caused by a planned changeover to newer technology to track telephone calls.

———

Superintendent John Fitzgerald chaired the second conference of the week, on Tuesday 22 October. The conference record contains some notes that filled in some more of the gaps in the Garda theory that Richie Barron was murdered, for instance '1 a.m. Frank McBrearty plus one other came through car park—Trousers wet', and later 'Culprit may have come down by the dirt track to the Technical school. Search'. Superintendent Joe Shelly confirmed at the tribunal that more searches were conducted that day.

The information that Young Frank was seen at 1 a.m. came from John Patton, a farmer who lived in Drumkeen, near the town of Ballybofey.

Patton recalled that he was first asked if he had seen anything in Raphoe at a vehicle checkpoint one week after the night Richie Barron died. 'I just said I saw Frank McBrearty,' Patton recalled. The Garda who spoke to Patton recorded that he saw nothing unusual.

At the Tuesday conference, Detective Garda Pat Tague was ordered to follow up on the possible lead with John Patton. Tague was stationed in Lifford in 1996, and knew the Patton family. He was fifteen years in An Garda Síochána, all but six of them as a detective. 'He was asked to develop that information and he went out to Mr Patton on that evening,' John McGinley recalled. Tague was accompanied by Detective Garda Pat Flynn.

John Patton was a 38-year-old single farmer who lived with his parents on their family farm. On the night Richie Barron died, he was in Letterkenny visiting his brother, and left to return home around 12.30 a.m. Patton had broken up with his fiancée the previous Thursday, and normally they would have gone to Frankie's nightclub in Raphoe on Sunday nights. At a crossroads halfway between Letterkenny and Ballybofey, Patton changed his mind about going home, and turned for Raphoe instead.

Patton parked outside Sarah's Café when he got to Raphoe. As he got out of the car, he checked his watch. It was 12.55 a.m. He crossed the road to the disco.

'When I was walking into the Parting Glass, I seen Frank McBrearty Junior and another man just walking five or six yards from the entrance to the doors of the disco,' Patton explained at the Morris tribunal. Patton didn't recognise the second man along with Young Frank. The two men were 'just five or six yards from the door of the disco when I was walking in' and 'seemed to be walking normal'.

Patton was reluctant to talk to the two detectives, and wouldn't make a statement. Tague believed that Patton didn't want to make a statement because he lived in a 'fairly republican area'.

'It's a traditional reluctance in that area. People would be reluctant to have dealings with Guards,' the detective explained at the tribunal. 'I thought my familiarity with the Pattons might breach that and he would be prepared to talk.' Patton, however, was reticent.

John Patton's cousin Seamus Patton had joined An Garda Síochána in 1990, and was stationed in Lifford. He recalled that Detective Garda Patrick Tague had asked him if he was related to John Patton. The Garda confirmed they were first cousins.

Detective Garda Tague told Garda Patton the Barron investigation was 'now turning into a murder investigation'. He asked the young Garda to visit his cousin and get a description of the man or men seen with Young Frank. Garda Patton was reluctant to interview his own cousin, but a man was dead, possibly murdered, so he accepted the task. The 'bottom line' was to identify the men seen with Young Frank. Unfortunately, John Patton could give no more help to Seamus Patton than he had to Patrick Tague.

Garda Patton reported back to Detective Garda Tague, but made no written record of the conversation until three years later when he was asked for a report by the Carty inquiry.

Because John Patton would not make a statement, Tague wrote down what he and Garda Seamus Patton had gleaned from the interview afterwards in a memo for Inspector John McGinley. '12.55 a.m. to 1 a.m. on 14/10/1996, as this witness was going into the Parting Glass from the Main Street direction, he saw two or three men running down the car park towards the Parting Glass entrance,' Tague wrote. 'The first man was young Frank McBrearty, no idea of who the others were. No idea if witness went into the disco but these men did not come in. He is absolutely sure of his times and of his identification of Frank McBrearty Junior. He describes young Frank McBrearty as being "rise" looking and he thought he was like someone who had given someone a beating.

'When he heard of Richie Barron's death, he came to the conclusion that McBrearty may have been involved. He is absolutely terrified of McBrearty and is already under the impression that McBrearty was watching him in the Parting Glass last Sunday night. He wants no more contact with the Gardaí. This is an honest, decent hard-working young man.'

John Patton was mystified when this memo was shown to him at the Morris tribunal. He said he had not told Detective Garda Tague that Young Frank looked like he'd given someone a beating. He said he had not told the detective he was 'absolutely terrified of McBrearty and was convinced McBrearty was watching him'. He said he had seen one other person with McBrearty, not two, and they were walking, not running.

Patton said he told Detective Garda Tague he wanted his information kept confidential because he 'just wanted to keep himself to himself'. Tague gave the memo to Inspector McGinley in a sealed envelope to protect his source. The conference was not told John Patton's identity.

Tague's note said that Patton saw 'two or three men running down the car park'. The first man was identified as Young Frank McBrearty, the identity of the other two unknown. Young Frank was 'rise' looking, a local dialect word meaning excited or agitated, and 'like someone who had given someone a beating'. The detective told the tribunal he 'honestly didn't put a lot of weight on the description of Young Frank McBrearty outside his premises, looking 'rise'. As far as he was concerned, there was nothing unusual in a nightclub bouncer looking worked up.

Tague said his report to McGinley was 'an interpretation' of what Patton told him and Garda Seamus Patton. He felt Patton was 'jumping to conclusions', and imagining that Young Frank was staring at him. 'What I believe is that John Patton had himself terrified by whatever conclusions he came to. This fear was his own doing.'

The garbled account of what Patton was saying meshed with the 'template' recorded a few days earlier, that Young Frank was seen coming down the car park with another man, and that he was wet and covered in dirt. The information from John Patton 'was misrepresented to the incident room team,' Mr Justice Morris found. 'Its relevance to the overall picture is that it appears to have conjured up a picture for what might have happened to the members of the incident room and it appears that they adopted it as being the facts of the case.'

The same day that Tague was assigned to interview John Patton, Garda Padraig Mulligan submitted his own statement on the events the night Richie Barron died. Mulligan glossed over his illicit visit to a pub while on duty, describing how he and Garda John O'Dowd went 'for a spin in the town and outside areas of the town'. Mulligan then described how at about 1.15 a.m. he saw 'two fellows fighting in the street outside of Frank McBrearty's disco. They went up towards St Eunan's Terrace direction as one was chasing the other.' Mulligan told the two men to behave themselves, and asked the two where they were from. He recalled they told him they were from Artnagarven.

Mulligan then told how he'd found out about Richie Barron from Stephen McCullagh, gone to the scene, and from there to the hospital, before returning to Raphoe and from there travelled to Lifford Garda station where he prepared a report on Barron. Mulligan took time in his report to mention twice that he did 'not recall seeing the McBreartys or any other person outside the Parting Glass disco during the row'.

Mulligan's information was slightly off, as the incident room would have seen from another statement that came in the same day. Liam O'Donnell, a doorman at the nightclub, described the expulsion from the nightclub of the men who ran towards St Eunan's Terrace around 1 a.m. He described them as 'boys from Aghyaran' near Castlederg, not Artnagarven. Another staff member from the nightclub, Marty McCallion, described the same incident in a statement the following day, 23 October, placing it between 1 a.m. and 1.15 a.m. Two days later another staff member, Gerard Coyle, also described the incident. He didn't remember when it happened, but he also remembered the four men involved were from Aghyaran, and Young Frank was there at the time.

According to the McBreartys, these four Northern Ireland men were IRA members on weekend parole from HM Prison The Maze, where they were serving sentences for terrorist offences. They had gone to Frankie's for a night out, and although they would return to the prison the following morning, crossing the border to Donegal was technically a violation of their parole.

Michelle Scott also described the incident in her statement to Gardaí on 23 October. She described how she'd gone to Sarah's Café where she heard about Richie Barron, and as she arrived back at the nightclub, there was 'a scuffle taking place'. Geoffrey Dolan also saw the fight, and then saw John O'Dowd and a Garda in uniform talking to the men involved.

From these statements, the sequence of events could be reconstructed. Shortly after 1 a.m., a row in the nightclub led to the expulsion of four men from Northern Ireland. The row continued outside, where Geoffrey Dolan saw it. As two men ran up St Eunan's Terrace, he followed to see what would happen. Mulligan and O'Dowd, just back in Raphoe shortly after 1 a.m., also saw the incident, and Geoffrey Dolan saw the Guards talk to the men in St Eunan's Terrace. Meanwhile, back at the nightclub, the rest of the men were still arguing, and Michelle Scott caught the tail end of the scuffle as she arrived with the news she had just heard from Sean Duffy about Richie Barron. Shortly afterwards, Geoffrey Dolan saw Michael and Charlotte Peoples leaving the nightclub, and the McConnells arrived minutes later. The whereabouts of Frank McBrearty and Mark McConnell that night should have been clear to the incident room staff examining the statements. Because they didn't see it, an ill-conceived murder investigation gathered momentum.

––––

Another layer would soon be added to the investigation, this time bringing Old Frank McBrearty under suspicion. The first formal report of any behaviour that might be called intimidation happened on the two-week anniversary of Richie Barron's death, 28 October. Garda John O'Dowd reported that Old Frank McBrearty approached him around 3 a.m. that morning and asked him 'Do you sleep well at night?', called him a 'black-guard', and said money meant nothing to him. O'Dowd also reported that Old Frank's nephew Michael McConnell verbally abused him. Garda Dan Curran also filed a report on the encounter.

As a result of O'Dowd's report, Frank was eventually charged under Section 6 of the Criminal Justice (Public Order) Act, 1994, for using threatening, abusive or insulting words or behaviour in a public place. It would be the first of over 100 District Court summonses served against Frank, his family and employees. Frank's annoyance at O'Dowd may have been inspired by what Frank had heard from a member of his staff, Michael McGahern. The Army corporal worked part-time in the nightclub, and had gone to make a statement to Gardaí at Frank's urging. Frank had told him the Guards wanted to interview him, and McGahern called to Raphoe Garda station on Thursday 24 October.

At first, McGahern recalled, Sergeant Joe Hannigan refused to interview him, saying he was under the influence of drink. McGahern told him he was completely sober, but tired and red-eyed because he'd just driven that day from Cork to Donegal. O'Dowd and Collins agreed to interview McGahern. 'The two of them were there, Garda Collins was doing most of the writing, Garda O'Dowd was firing the questions,' McGahern recalled.

McGahern said O'Dowd asked him how much Frank was paying him, and he retorted that it was none of the Guard's business. O'Dowd told him 'this is a can of worms, I hope you don't get caught up in it'. Old Frank told the tribunal that when he heard of this, he brought McGahern to see Superintendent John Fitzgerald and make a complaint. In a statement to the tribunal, Frank said he was 'afraid the Gardaí were trying to frame myself and my family for something we did not do'. Frank had already complained about the frequent visits and searches around his car park by Gardaí.

Frank also said that before meeting Fitzgerald, he'd come across John O'Dowd at the entrance to his pub in the early hours of Monday 28 October. 'I asked him why did he say those things to Mickey McGahern. I asked him was he trying to frame us for something we did not do,' he wrote later. 'I said to him how do you think we are going to be able to sleep in our beds at night. I'm sure you'll be able to sleep all right, trying to frame myself and my family. I told him I would never forgive him until the day they took my coffin up the street in Raphoe and into the graveyard. I was speaking to Garda Curran and told him, you know Fr Harkin is our friend and your friend and you know we are not like that. He did not reply to me.

'It was this sort of treatment from Garda O'Dowd and Garda Curran that made me feel I had to speak to Superintendent Fitzgerald to find out what was happening in Raphoe and to my family,' Frank wrote.

———

Mark McConnell's next door neighbour, Martin Laird, remembered that Raphoe was 'buzzing with rumours' in the week after Richie Barron died. He'd heard on the grapevine that Barron was murdered, and Mark McConnell was involved.

On Sunday 27 October, two weeks after Barron died, Garda John O'Dowd and Garda Dan Curran went to meet Laird. Laird told them that on 14 October, around 8.20 a.m., he saw Mark McConnell leaving the Town & Country pub as Laird stood admiring the sign he had painted above the pub doorway. Laird's report would give the Garda investigators another doubt to hang over Mark McConnell.

Laird worked as a supervisor on a FÁS social employment scheme run by the local Tidy Towns committee to keep the streets clean in the town.

He left his home a little after 7 a.m. on 14 October and walked from Tullyvinney to Raphoe. Laird would later tell his parents that as he went about his work clearing up litter in the town, he thought he saw Mark McConnell leaving the Town & Country pub early that morning. He also told Tommy Doherty, a local taxi driver.

The taxi driver in turn told Garda John O'Dowd about the reported sighting. It seems he also told others, because Darcy Connolly, a friend of Richie Barron's, gave the same information to Detective Garda Pat Flynn. In his notebook, Flynn recorded that 'Martin Laird . . . saw Mark McConnell leaving Mark Quinn's 7.30 a.m.—8 a.m. Monday morning'.

In a second statement to Detective Garda Joe Foley on 2 December 1997, Laird said he 'did not mention the sighting of Mark McConnell to anyone I can remember'. Laird initially told the Morris tribunal in 2003 he had told no one what he saw except his parents. Recalled to the stand on 12 April 2005, he added that he told Tommy Doherty, the taxi driver.

Taxi drivers are commonly befriended by Gardaí. Working late hours and travelling as they do, they are often in a position to notice something that might prove helpful to an investigation. Interviewed by the Carty team, O'Dowd told them that Tommy Doherty supplied him with information.

Through O'Dowd and Flynn, the information made its way to the Garda conference. Job number 232 was straightforward: 'Martin Laird to be interviewed—statement required in relation to Mark McConnell leaving or not 8.20 a.m.'

Martin Laird also said that Patrick Quinn, a brother-in-law of Mark McConnell's, was missing from work on the morning he saw Mark McConnell. The only person there when he arrived at work that morning was Billy Strain.

Laird told the Morris tribunal that Garda John O'Dowd and Garda Dan Curran 'just wanted to know my movements because I am out early every morning'.

The tribunal noted 'serious difficulties with Mr Laird's evidence'. Mark McConnell felt that Laird was at best mistaken about the time, as he had not visited the Town & Country until much later that day. Laird said that shortly before he saw McConnell, he met Sheila McBride, who told him about Richie Barron's death. The tribunal noted that 'there was also a statement from a Ms Sheila McBride to the effect that she did not think she could have been in Raphoe at the time suggested by Mr Laird and she had no clear recollection of the 14th of October'.

In summary, the tribunal concluded that 'though Mr Laird is an honest man, he may be mistaken in his evidence'.

At the time, however, Laird's statement 'caused considerable scepticism on the part of the Garda Síochána in relation to the account furnished by the McConnells', in the words of the tribunal. Combined with the garbled report of what John Patton saw, and the mistaken times given by the café workers, it added to the picture of the McBreartys and McConnells lying about their movements. The investigators grew more and more convinced that they knew who was guilty.

––––

Liam Fleury is a forensic chemist employed in the national Forensic Science Laboratory attached to Garda HQ. On 17 October, he received from Garda Niall Coady the exhibits in the Barron case, including Barron's clothing, dentures, hair and blood samples, glass, paint flakes and a 'strand of hair' found at the scene. Coady also handed over the yard brush used to sweep the scene clean the following morning.

A week after he got the samples from Coady, Fleury received from Detective Garda Michael Jennings samples from Gazza Gallagher's burnt-out Renault 9, including the 880IH number plates, glass, wheels, a floor mat, and a sellotape lift from the exhaust. Jennings also forwarded the fencing posts the car had rolled into in Letterkenny early on Sunday evening and Richie Barron's wrist watch.

In the weeks that followed, the Forensic Science Laboratory would receive further samples from Coady, mainly hair and dirt samples from other cars. None of these provided any evidence of forensic value.

Fleury's conclusion after examining the exhibits from Richie Barron was that 'nothing was found to support the suggestion that Richard Barron was knocked down by a motor vehicle'. In a letter to the Morris tribunal in August 2002, the Forensic Science Laboratory said that Fleury 'was asked by the Garda scenes of crime officer to examine the exhibits with a view to determine if a car accident death was involved'. From this it appears Fleury was never asked to look for evidence of an assault, but in any case the forensic science laboratory noted that there was 'nothing to suggest a definite assault or a definite hit and run'.

At the tribunal, Fleury was critical of the failure to preserve the scene in Raphoe. 'Even if a scene had initially been "contaminated" by people helping the injured, it should still be preserved as soon as Gardaí arrived.'

Minuscule traces of red paint on the face of Barron's watch were similar to the paint on Barron's own red Bedford van, Fleury concluded, but it was 'on the low side of a match', and there was insufficient paint for a definitive test. He found no smears of oil or paint on Barron's clothing, something which usually—but not always—indicates a traffic accident.

'However, I would have to qualify that by saying myself and my colleagues have come across a small number of cases in the laboratory, cases where we've known that cars have gone over people and nothing was found,' Fleury later told the Morris tribunal. 'The absence of paint or trace elements doesn't exclude the possibility [a car collision] is what happened.'

On Tuesday 29 October 1996, two weeks after Barron's death, Inspector John McGinley and Detective Superintendent Joe Shelly called to see the scientist in Dublin. 'I suppose a turning point in the case was probably when Superintendent Joe Shelly and John McGinley spoke with the people in Forensic and there was nothing at that stage,' Fitzgerald recalled. 'We would have focused I suppose more on the suspicion of murder aspect.' From that point on, whatever lingering suspicions there were that Barron died in a hit and run were quelled. It was now a clear murder hunt.

The Guards would continue to collect statements from patrons in the pubs, building a full picture of Richie Barron's movements. They would collect statements from the youngsters in the town who watched the comings and goings up and down Irish Row. Evidence from some of the cars at the scene would be processed. But the focus was on Mark McConnell and Frank McBrearty. When and where were they seen? How did they appear? And crucially, the search was on for witnesses who could place the two men near the spot where Richie Barron died.

By the end of October, Gardaí regarded anyone who made statements which contradicted their view that Frank McBrearty and Mark McConnell were murder suspects as a potential suspect themselves.

The lack of forensic evidence of a hit and run (which was equally a lack of evidence of assault) was interpreted as positive evidence of assault. The row in the pub between Barron and Mark McConnell provided a motive. The confused report of what John Patton said seemed to place Frank McBrearty in the right area. The clincher was the report from Garda John O'Dowd that he was 'working on something', and would be able to find a reluctant witness who would place McBrearty and McConnell at the scene.

Sergeant Joe Hannigan recalled that Gardaí believed Michael Peoples was the 'third man' John Patton might have seen. Peoples, a Letterkenny native, was married to Charlotte Eaton, a cousin of Roisin McConnell.

'Anybody . . . making a statement that tend[ed] to support the fact that Mark McConnell couldn't have been at Townparks in Raphoe at 1 a.m. on the night of 14 October became a suspect,' Sergeant Hannigan told the tribunal. 'It was believed that they were covering his movements for the relevant time.' This was particularly true if the potential suspects were related to the McBrearty family, he added.

'We had a mindset at that stage, based on information that they were seen coming down through the car park. There was the thing that Mr

McBrearty was supposed to be agitated. If statements were brought to the conference that were at variance with what we thought was right, these people became suspects.'

The investigators thought they were on the right track, and never stopped to ask obvious questions. Instead of doing their job and cross-checking statements thoroughly as they came in, an inexperienced incident room team and lackadaisical management let them slip. No one thought to wonder why none of the witnesses who saw Richie Barron turn up Irish Row at 12.30 a.m. saw Mark McConnell, since the Garda theory said he should have been crossing the Diamond on his way to Sarah's Café around the same time.

Looking back on the experience at the Morris tribunal, Marty Moylan put his finger on the nub of the issue. 'Because of drink, people's memory of times are clouded,' he explained. His perception was that the witness accounts of people's movements were trustworthy, but any estimate of times they gave were unreliable. What mattered was to concentrate on the sequences of events and how they meshed together.

However, there were some fixed times in the official record. Instead of accepting a witness's estimate, everything should have been related to those times. Michael Peoples' ATM withdrawal was recorded by the bank at 12.19 a.m. for example. The 999 calls were logged just before 1 a.m. The ambulance arrived at the scene thirty minutes later. Witnesses remembered seeing the ambulance any time between 12.30 a.m. and 1.30 a.m., showing how unreliable time guesses were. Instead of accepting times from these witnesses, the investigation room should have concentrated on the times they knew, and from there built an accurate picture of what happened. If they had done this, the investigation room would also have picked up the inconsistencies in the accounts of later witnesses damaging to McBrearty and McConnell. The conspiracies and the cock-ups could have been uncovered.

———

Just after midnight in the early hours of Sunday 27 October 1996, detectives from the Buncrana district arrested five men in an IRA training camp near a remote farm in Malin, at the northern tip of County Donegal.

At the scene, detectives found two AKM assault rifles, 100 rounds of ammunition, a rocket launcher and an improvised rocket grenade packed with Semtex. The five men, all with addresses in Derry, were arrested under Section 30 of the Offences Against the State Act.

The men were brought to the Special Criminal Court in Dublin on 28 October, where they were charged with several offences, including possession with intent to endanger life.

Judge Dominic Lynch, one of the three judges sitting in the Special Criminal Court that day, had written to the government to resign from the non-jury court in early July. His delisting from the court was approved by the government on 1 August, and published in *Iris Oifigiúil*, the official State gazette, but a 'chapter of accidents' in the Justice Department meant he was not told of this for three months, when a copy of *Iris Oifigiúil* was faxed to him.

Lawyers for the five men would argue that the Special Criminal Court was not properly constituted on the days Judge Lynch had sat since August. The case dragged on for several months before a resolution was reached, and the five men were eventually convicted in July 1997.

Inspector Jim Gallagher lost contact with the Barron investigation as a result of the Malin case, dealing with the paperwork it generated. To a lesser extent, Joe Shelly, as border superintendent, was also involved in the Malin case, although he remained involved in the Barron investigation. The Malin affair served as another distraction from the Barron investigation.

———

On 29 October, the day after the Malin five were brought before the Special Criminal Court in Dublin, Gazza Gallagher had a bail hearing in the District Court in Letterkenny. He asked to talk to Detective Sergeant Sylvie Henry.

Gazza told Henry he wanted bail. He was desperate to get free, to try and patch things up with his girlfriend. He told Henry that on the night Richie Barron died, Young Frank McBrearty asked him where he'd parked his car. Gazza told Henry that later, Frank told him there was something in his car, and to get rid of it and burn the car. He described how he'd later found a billhook in his car—the billhook he'd stolen—and thrown it into a field. He described the location of the field. Henry met Gazza later in November, while he was held in Mountjoy prison. Gazza continued to spin his lies. He told the sergeant he was given £500 by Young Frank, mostly in 50p coins. He said his car had been turned around since he'd parked it, and that the spare wheel and the spoon he used to turn the ignition were missing.

The Morris tribunal concluded that Gazza 'made up this story either because he believed Frank McBrearty Junior had said something to his detriment to the Garda Síochána or because he felt under suspicion himself and wished to deflect that suspicion onto Frank McBrearty Junior. He probably heard something of the rumours implicating Frank McBrearty Junior in the death of the late Mr Barron and concocted a suitable story on that basis.'

Garda Niall Coady found the billhook during a search on 31 October, labelled and removed it for forensic analysis, and also bagged and removed the sod of turf on which it lay. Both were sent to Dublin. Naturally, the forensic tests would find nothing of value.

Henry wasn't sure quite what to make of Gazza's story. If Barron's death was a hit and run, Gazza was still his prime suspect. 'I was getting more suspicious of his involvement in the matter and I went to the prison to speak to him because I felt that he wasn't telling the truth,' he told the tribunal. 'It was then I think that he said about Frankie McBrearty having given him the £500 in the toilet the night before, and when I asked him then what the denominations were in he said—I forget now exactly the words he used—but that some of them were 50p pieces. I told him straight up, I said you're lying to me because I said nobody had the 50p pieces only yourself from the burglary.'

Henry also told the tribunal that Gazza claimed he was given the money around 11.30 p.m. at the disco, over two hours before Richie Barron died. Henry didn't put much weight on what Gazza told him, but he did follow up, checking the forensics on the hook and re-interviewing Gazza. After his visit to Mountjoy, he was convinced Gazza was spinning tall tales to get bail.

Henry reported back to the Barron case conferences on his progress with Gazza. 'It wasn't ranked as important, at that stage. From an early stage, the two main suspects and the thrust of the inquiry was focused on Frank McBrearty Junior and Mark McConnell,' Sergeant Joe Hannigan recalled.

'We never believed the billhook was a runner,' John McGinley said later. 'We didn't believe it existed until it was found, and when it was found it added more fuel to the fire.'

McGinley said that he gave Henry the nickname 'Captain Hook' as a joke during a meeting on the case. At another conference, he asked Sergeant Henry 'what progress have we made with Dr Hook?', and later again, had at one point turned to Henry and said 'perhaps Dr Hook would answer that question'.

'It wasn't in any way a slight or a derogatory thing,' McGinley told the tribunal. 'It just came up in a lighter moment at the conference.' He told the tribunal the nickname was not intended to turn Sergeant Henry away from the avenue he was investigating.

Chapter 8

A Psycho on the Other End of the Phone

Charlotte Peoples is the daughter of Catherine 'Dolly' Eaton, and wife of Michael Peoples. On the night Richie Barron died, Charlotte and Michael were in Quinn's Town & Country pub and the Parting Glass disco in Raphoe. Charlotte's mother babysat for the couple, and after they arrived home and told her the bad news about her friend Richie, a distant relative, she decided to phone the hospital.

Dolly Eaton knew the hospital would only give out information to close family members, so although she was a second cousin of Richie's, she told them she was his aunt. The call was one of two asking about Richie that night—the other came from the home of Eunan and Katrina Brolly—where the callers identified themselves incorrectly, something the hospital staff discovered when they checked with the Barron family.

Rodney Bogle, a friend of Charlotte and Michael, also phoned their home that night playing a prank. 'He was joking that he was looking for a taxi to New York,' Charlotte remembered. 'I knew it was Rodney straight away when he phoned. I had rang Rodney back then and Rodney came over to the house.' Rodney sat up talking with Charlotte and Dolly for a while before they retired for the night.

The Guards knew about the two calls to the hospital, but the official reply to Detective Sergeant Henry's request for a phone trace was not completed until 14 January 1997.

Legally, any officer of chief superintendent or higher rank may request telephone records as part of a criminal investigation. For administrative convenience, Telecom Eireann had requested that all such requests come from a single source within An Garda Síochána. A chief superintendent in Crime & Security, Michael Diffley, was the designated contact point with the phone company in 1996. Chief superintendents throughout the country forwarded requests to him, and he passed them on to the phone company. Diffley told the Morris tribunal that Gardaí were constantly calling and pestering him at the time because of delays in processing requests.

By 9 November 1996, it is not possible to say what the Guards knew about the phone calls to the hospital. But suspicion was pointing at the Brollys and Peoples for other reasons. Mark and Roisin McConnell said they had spent the night with the Brollys, and called up to the Peoples the next morning for breakfast. Both families confirmed this story. However, Martin Laird's statement that he saw McConnell leaving the Town & Country pub around 8 a.m. that morning, and statements from other witnesses who thought they saw Roisin McConnell walking from her home to Raphoe that morning, both cast doubt on the McConnells' account. If the Brollys and Peoples were supporting that account, it could be because they were part of a false alibi, the investigation concluded.

————

John O'Dowd kept pressing William Doherty for more information. Doherty in turn used his influence over the Garda to deepen his suspicions. But O'Dowd kept insisting the leads he was getting weren't strong enough. They needed proof. By early November, Doherty and O'Dowd hatched the hoax blackmail plan. They would make one of the suspects think someone had seen something, and Doherty would demand payment. Then, if the suspect offered to buy off Doherty, that would be the proof they needed. An innocent man would react in outrage to a blackmail threat, but a guilty man would pay for silence.

On 5 November 1996, in the early hours of the morning, Doherty telephoned Old Frank McBrearty. Frank made a note of what the caller said in the two calls, at midnight and 2.30 a.m. 'You fucking done it Frank, didn't yous? You, Young Frank and Mark McConnell, I seen yous with my own eyes. I seen yous killing him, and you went down the field down into the car park. . . Sure didn't you kill a man in Scotland, you murderer? . . . You have seventy-two hours to get £10,000. I got your phone number, and I'll get you Frank, Mark McConnell as well.'

Old Frank ignored the crank caller. He contacted Superintendent John Fitzgerald, and told him what had happened. Doherty's first blackmail entrapment scheme had failed.

On 9 November Doherty tried again. This time, he chose Michael Peoples. Whether it was Doherty who added Peoples to the mix, or whether he got the name from O'Dowd, is not clear. It seems Doherty was the first to mention his name. The Patton information was ambiguous: Young Frank was seen in the car park with one or two men. The note Old Frank took of the call on 5 November, referring to 'You, Young Frank and Mark McConnell', suggests he too was a possible candidate, at least in Doherty's mind.

Doherty told O'Dowd his witness saw McBrearty and McConnell. It appears that in one theory, Michael Peoples was added as the third man. According to this scenario, Michael had not come all the way down the car park with the others, instead making his getaway through the grounds of the vocational school, 'jumping over the Tech wall'.

Michael Peoples didn't recall any nasty calls before 9 November 1996. Charlotte remembered harassing phone calls before 9 November, but that day was different. The first call asked simply 'Is that the Peoples?' and then hung up.

The second call, within sixty seconds of the first, involved lengthy abuse. Michael Peoples didn't recognise the caller's voice, though it was a Donegal accent. The caller told him he'd killed Richie Barron and demanded £5,000 to keep quiet. The money was to be taken to a pub outside Raphoe called the White Cross Inn. Michael asked for a number to call the blackmailer back, but the caller made up a fake number.

There was 'a psycho on the other end of the phone so we called the Guards,' Charlotte told the tribunal. While the Peoples waited for a Garda to arrive, there was a third call. Michael tried to keep the caller on the line. In a statement he made the next day, he was able to give details of the call.

'Is this Michael Peoples?' the caller asked. Michael said it was.

'Remember the carry on that you were at on Sunday night?'

'What carry on?'

'You know what carry on.'

'I don't know what you're talking about.'

'You killed Richie Barron. I seen ya. I seen you and your wife outside the Parting Glass at twenty past one... I seen ya running down the field. I seen you hitting Richie Barron with the baton and running down the field.'

'You're only talking shite.'

'You're going to Mountjoy. You better have your hole ready. I want money, I'm going to the Guards.'

'Fuck off,' said Michael. Charlotte at one stage took the phone, he remembered. 'Why are you doing this to us?' she asked.

The Peoples had called the Guards in Raphoe to complain about the chilling calls, and Michael spoke to Detective Garda Pat Flynn when he arrived at their home. Flynn told him several people had received nuisance calls. 'Cases like this bring the cranks out of the woodwork,' he told the worried couple.

Flynn said another Garda would call the next day and set up equipment to monitor and trace back any future calls, Michael Peoples said.

The Peoples asked Detective Garda Flynn to go to the White Cross Inn, but he said it would be a waste of time. The detective felt the calls were the work of a crank, and there was no point going on a wild goose chase to a pub looking for a blackmailer who didn't exist. He said that phone calls couldn't be monitored, it would take too long. Charlotte remembered Flynn saying, 'You wouldn't believe the many crank calls being made.' He told them he was going off duty, but he would leave a note at Raphoe station for Garda Phil Collins.

Flynn said he advised the Peoples to 'monitor the phone calls and find out who was making the calls and where they were coming from'.

Charlotte Peoples was completely dissatisfied when the detective left. 'Anything he was asked to do, he had no interest in doing it,' she said. She would have welcomed it if he offered to tape calls, but he had not asked.

After Flynn left, the telephone rang again. 'Are you going to take me serious?' the caller asked.

'Why don't you go to the Guards?' Michael responded.

'I was in a robbery that night and I left my fingerprints all over the place, that's why I can't go to the Guards,' the caller said.

This time, the caller demanded £2,000. Playing along in the hope of finding out who the blackmailer was, Michael protested there was no way he could find that kind of money, and they began to haggle. They eventually settled on £1,000. The caller told Michael he would meet him at a pub at the White Cross Inn in Drumbeg, outside Raphoe. The caller told him to be at the pub at 11 p.m. He was to look out for someone in a black leather jacket, a white T-shirt and brown corduroys.

There were four calls in total early in the evening, at 8.08 p.m., 8.09 p.m., 8.14 p.m. and 8.23 p.m. Michael tried to string the caller along, pleading poverty, saying there was no way he could raise the huge sums being demanded. After four calls, he had 'negotiated' the blackmailer down to £1,000. He was furious. Charlotte was in a state, and some idiot was calling him a murderer. He was determined to find out the crank's identity.

The fifth call came at 10.06 p.m. Flynn had been no help getting the Gardaí to trace the calls, but Michael Peoples had managed to get his hands on a dictaphone machine. He recorded the call.

'Have you got the money? Are we going to meet?' the caller demanded.

'Aye. No problem.'

'Have you got the money?'

'I'll give you five hundred pound. I cannot raise any more than that.'

'I'm not a hard man to bargain with you know.'

'Five hundred cash is all I have.'

Michael Peoples agreed to meet as arranged earlier at the White Cross Inn. 'There'll be no trouble,' he added.

'Be on your own,' the caller warned.

'I'm coming on my own.'

Michael Peoples went to the White Cross Inn to investigate, along with his father-in-law, Charlie Eaton. When they left, Charlotte rang the

Raphoe Garda station to tell them what was going on. It was after 10 p.m., the station was closed. The call forwarded automatically to Letterkenny. Charlotte told the Guards in Letterkenny what was happening. She asked them to send someone to the White Cross Inn to help Michael, in case the blackmailer showed up. Michael took no cash to the White Cross Inn, but he brought the dictaphone recorder. He'd also arranged for a friend to go ahead alone. He would sit in the bar before Michael arrived, to see if anyone reacted when Michael came in.

Everything was in place. Charlie Eaton stayed in the car, while Michael Peoples went into the pub, but he didn't see anyone fitting the blackmailer's description at the White Cross Inn. The arrangement was to meet in the toilets of the pub at 11 p.m., so he went there and waited. He then went outside and stood around in case someone would approach him. 'Nothing happened,' he told the tribunal.

They returned home. The next day, Michael made a statement to Garda Phil Collins, and handed over the tape recording of the final call. He told the Garda the caller had a local accent, perhaps forensic analysts would be able to identify the blackmailer's voice. Michael also told Collins he had no objection to his phone line being monitored in future if it helped track down the hoaxer. Garda Collins told Peoples the tape would be sent for analysis to Dublin. 'I was happy with that,' Peoples said.

Collins passed the micro-cassette tape to the Barron incident room in Letterkenny. From there, Sergeant Brendan Roache gave it to scenes of crime examiner Garda Niall Coady. The tape, labelled BR1, was forwarded to the forensic scientists at Garda HQ for analysis.

When Michael Peoples was arrested for murder on 4 December 1996, one of the grounds used was that he was prepared to 'bribe someone to keep quiet' about the alleged murder of Richie Barron.

The Peoples were not asked to sign any formal authorisation by Gardaí to see their phone records, but when Charlotte was arrested in December 1996, she was stunned to discover Detective Michael O'Carroll knew about the phone calls made to Letterkenny hospital by her mother Dolly the night Richie Barron died. 'I had an idea then they must have had my phone records,' she told the tribunal.

In 1997, a private investigator hired by Old Frank McBrearty to investigate Barron's death, Billy Flynn, advised Michael Peoples to get the tape recording back from the Gardaí. Michael asked Sergeant John White for it. White told him Garda Collins was off sick, and he knew nothing about it. Michael tried on several occasions to get the tape, before it was eventually returned to him. The tape is now in the hands of the Gardaí again, handed over to the Carty team when they came to Donegal to investigate the repeated complaints about what was happening in Raphoe.

The tape quality was too poor for Forensics to make any voice print identification. Several years later at the Morris tribunal Carty investigator Detective Garda Richard Caplice identified the voice on the tape as William Doherty's, but this unscientific identification was challenged by Doherty, who represented himself. The retired detective was adamant his identification was correct.

On the day Doherty made the calls to the Peoples, John O'Dowd and Phil Collins were working the 2 p.m. to 10 p.m. shift in Raphoe Garda station. O'Dowd had arranged to meet William Doherty that night, and picked him up about half a mile from his home around 9.30 p.m. Phil Collins was covering things back at the station, and would sign out both Guards at 10 p.m. Doherty was excited. 'I think I've solved the murder,' he told O'Dowd.

Doherty explained how he'd phoned Michael Peoples, and bluffed him, telling him he'd been on a robbery and seen him assault Richie Barron. Peoples took the bait, Doherty said, and was offering to pay him to keep quiet. They were going to meet at 11 p.m.

At the Garda's home, O'Dowd went upstairs to change into his 'civvies', and he heard Doherty on the phone as he came back downstairs. 'I'm not a hard man to deal with,' Doherty was saying. The meeting was on, Doherty reported. Peoples would be at the White Cross Inn at 11 p.m. with £500.

As O'Dowd explained it, it was not until this point that the enormity of what was happening hit home to him. He'd allowed himself get caught up in a blackmail plot. Demanding money with menaces was a criminal offence. Worse, a phone call from his home could be traced. He dropped Doherty home, and drove to Raphoe Garda station. The occurrence book contained an entry from the Peoples, complaining about the phone calls. O'Dowd claimed he then went to the White Cross Inn. He said he didn't see Peoples, but saw Charlie Eaton 'getting out of a car'.

'I was in a panic at that stage and I went home,' O'Dowd confessed in his statement on 18 October 2004, when he finally admitted to knowing about the hoax extortion phone calls. But even this belated admission seems to contain less than the full truth. The tribunal was doubtful if O'Dowd had ever gone to the White Cross Inn. Michael Peoples had told the tribunal that Charlie Eaton stayed in the car while he went inside the pub, so O'Dowd couldn't have seen him 'getting out of a car'. Tribunal investigators had visited the White Cross Inn, and came away convinced that if O'Dowd had been there, Michael Peoples would have seen him. Michael Peoples did not see anyone he recognised. O'Dowd never went

to the White Cross Inn, because he had no need to. He was already supplying information to the incident room in October 1996 that Michael
Peoples had been seen 'jumping over the Tech wall', and might have been
involved in or witnessed the supposed murder of Richie Barron. Once
Michael agreed to go there, that was all the 'proof' he needed of his guilt.

To this day, William Doherty denies knowing anything about the
phone calls. He told the tribunal that his friend Noel McBride made the
calls, first from his own home, then from O'Dowd's home. Doherty said
he didn't even realise what the calls were about at the time. McBride for
his part denied any knowledge of the phone calls. He said he hadn't even
met O'Dowd at that stage, and wasn't in his house until the following
spring.

After listening to his version of events, the chairman decided
Doherty's account was 'self-contradictory and utterly implausible', and
accepted McBride knew nothing about the hoax.

————

O'Dowd didn't know what to do about the mess he'd got himself into. On
Monday 11 November he travelled to Dublin with a team of Guards investigating the Barron case. RTÉ's *Crimeline* programme was covering the
case, and Superintendent John Fitzgerald would make an appeal for
information on the national broadcasting service. O'Dowd was part of
the line-up sent to advise the production team and handle any calls from
members of the public. In a bizarre twist, O'Dowd could be seen in the
background answering phone calls in the *Crimeline* studio less than
forty-eight hours after he had been involved in the hoax extortion call
plot against Michael Peoples.

On Wednesday 12 November, O'Dowd was back in Donegal. He decided
to go to his confidant Kevin Lennon, the Buncrana district superintendent. Lennon had been appointed by Chief Superintendent Denis
Fitzpatrick to supervise the handling of William Doherty. Lennon would
know what to do.

O'Dowd told Lennon what had happened. He explained about the
phone calls, how Doherty was winding Peoples up, how a payment had
apparently been agreed, and how the last call was made from his own
home. Lennon told him not to worry, he would sort things out. 'Leave it
to me,' he told the worried Garda. 'Basically both of us were of the belief
that it was a silly thing at the time,' O'Dowd told the tribunal.

In the days that followed, O'Dowd asked Lennon what was happening
again and again. In his own words, he 'pestered' his agent supervisor,
demanding to know if his problem had been sorted out. Eventually,
Lennon told him he'd spoken to Detective Superintendent Joe Shelly, the

border superintendent, and everything was fine. In fact, Lennon never spoke to Shelly about the calls. His reaction to the news was to do little or nothing, except to advise O'Dowd to change his finishing time in the station records and on his A85 worksheet to 10.30 p.m. on 9 November 1996. This would provide him with an alibi if the phone calls ever came to light. He could say he was still working at the time. O'Dowd changed his record and also the records of Garda Phil Collins, who was working the same night. O'Dowd hoped that would be the end of it. 'I know it was a silly thing to do now, but I did that,' O'Dowd admitted ruefully at the tribunal, after coming clean in part about the telephone call. 'It was a big elephant on my back, but there's no elephants on my back now believe me.'

Kevin Lennon denied knowing anything about the phone calls. When O'Dowd finally admitted in October 2004 that he not only knew about them, but had told Lennon about them within days, Lennon was furious.

'I am saying Sir that not until June of 1997 did I get to know about the phone call,' Lennon told the tribunal chairman. 'When I did get to know about it I wrote about it to the various authorities and to the sergeant in Raphoe.'

'In July 1997 Garda O'Dowd came in with a document from [private investigator] Mr William Flynn, saying he didn't make the call,' Lennon recalled. Flynn had obtained phone records showing the call to the Peoples at 10.06 p.m. had come from O'Dowd's home telephone. Lennon said he then told O'Dowd to go to Garda investigators looking into the calls and tell them what Flynn had said, and asked him specifically who had access to his house, and who had a key to his house. O'Dowd told him no one had access.

Lennon said he then told O'Dowd to get a record of his phone calls and bring it in to the detectives investigating the calls. 'For eight years long Sir, Garda O'Dowd has lied and lied to me about this affair. It's as simple as that Sir,' Lennon protested.

But it was Lennon who lied, the tribunal decided. He knew about the calls, and played an integral part in the initial cover-up. When O'Dowd came clean about the calls, Lennon had no option but to deny everything.

Within five years, Lennon had gone from the rank of sergeant to superintendent, thanks in large part to the credit he received for his work thwarting the efforts of the IRA in Donegal, and the interception of several large IRA bombs. These bombs were in fact a series of elaborate hoaxes planned by Lennon and his friend Detective Garda Noel McMahon through their manipulation of Adrienne McGlinchey, the daughter of Letterkenny-based businessman and former Senator Bernard McGlinchey, who they controlled and presented as a Garda informer infiltrating the IRA. But Lennon's ambition didn't stop with the superintendent's job in Buncrana. He wanted to be a chief superintendent, perhaps eventually commissioner. Doherty was the ideal candidate to help him carry out another deception, with the help of Garda O'Dowd.

The vehicle for the deception would be the c77 intelligence gathering system, deeply flawed in its design and poorly controlled in Donegal. Garda intelligence was recorded on the forms and submitted to Crime & Security Branch in Dublin, but there was no requirement to identify the source of the information, either by name or by a code name or code number. Crime & Security had no way to check the credibility of the sources behind c77 intelligence, and had to rely on the assessment of the Garda supplying the information. By an adept handling of the information that went up the line to the chief superintendent's office in Letterkenny, and to Crime & Security in Dublin, a local petty criminal like Doherty could easily be re-packaged as an IRA infiltrator.

O'Dowd had sent the first two Doherty c77s to Dublin on 8 November 1996, the day before the Peoples extortion hoax. There would be forty-three in total, all of them elaborate works of fiction. O'Dowd's phone calls show he was in regular contact with Lennon in October and November 1996, even before the hoax. Lennon was not going to jeopardise the plan just because Doherty was making harassing telephone calls, and willingly helped O'Dowd cover his tracks. He had his sights on bigger things.

Preparations for the *Crimeline* programme had begun as early as October, when Superintendent John Fitzgerald wrote to Nuala Finn, the sergeant in charge of liaison with the programme, outlining the details of the case. The superintendent said the Guards were following four lines of inquiry: accidental death; hit and run accident; assault; and robbery. He referred to 'local innuendo that [Richie Barron] was waited upon or followed at the scene'.

Forensic tests showed no evidence of a hit and run accident, Fitzgerald wrote, and it could not be determined whether the blunt instrument that struck Richie Barron was 'a car or other instrument'. The reference to the lack of forensic evidence suggests the letter was written at the end of the month, after Inspector John McGinley visited Dr Liam Fleury at the national Forensic Science Laboratory.

'There are a number of routes of escape available to the attackers by both foot and car,' Fitzgerald wrote, 'and we would be most anxious that the scene and the surrounding area would be professionally recorded by your section for TV presentation.'

'Full coverage of this Investigation is requested on the Crime Line programme. It may help to solve our case,' he continued. 'Please find attached, a location map of Raphoe with index.'

The map used on *Crimeline* caused its own share of controversy. By the time the ordnance survey map was translated into television-friendly graphics, arrows were added to the map pointing from where Richie Barron died, one pointing southeast towards the Parting Glass nightclub, the other curving southwest towards the 'Tech'.

The arrow pointing to the nightclub 'carried with it an innuendo', the tribunal would hear years later. 'What business has the arrow doing there?' tribunal chairman Mr Justice Frederick Morris demanded of Superintendent John Fitzgerald, who appeared on the programme.

'Well I don't know,' a hapless Fitzgerald replied. 'The whole intention of this was to give people a general idea of the area and to get help.'

'Who put the arrow there?' the judge asked again.

'Well I didn't put it there and it wasn't put there for any devious reason,' was all Fitzgerald could say.

Old Frank McBrearty also complained that the scale used in the graphics was distorted, exaggerating the size of the nightclub and car park and giving them prominence. The maps made it look like he owned half of the town of Raphoe.

Brian Murphy, a barrister hired by the Garda Representative Association to put John O'Dowd's case at the tribunal, returned to the question in his own cross-examination of Fitzgerald. Murphy first pointed out that his client, a mere Garda, had no input into the creation of the graphics. His function was simply to answer the telephones if any member of the public rang in with information.

'In any event you don't know which members of An Garda Síochána dealt with RTÉ in respect of the diagram?' Murphy asked Fitzgerald.

'I have no idea about that arrow, and I wouldn't have been conscious of it on the programme,' Fitzgerald answered, adding that he wanted to keep both assault and hit and run options open during the broadcast.

The map also showed a road or pathway between the spot where Richie Barron was found and the nightclub. Justice Morris described this as 'what appears to be an ordinary road which the assailants may have taken, down this rather back road'. Tribunal barrister Peter Charleton later stated that 'the road shown on the *Crimeline* map simply doesn't exist, and never existed'.

———

On Wednesday 13 November 1996, the investigators held a case conference in the incident room in Letterkenny Garda station. Telephone calls were one of the items on the agenda. The investigators wanted phone traces. However, they wanted more than a trace on the blackmailer who called Michael Peoples. Also on the list were the hoax extortion calls to Old Frank a few nights earlier, and checks on the two public telephone boxes in Raphoe, one in the Diamond, the other in St Eunan's Terrace. The detectives also wanted traces on calls made to McBrearty's pub the night Richie Barron died, and calls made from the Town & Country pub.

The Guards had a theory: Mark McConnell and Young Frank McBrearty got together and decided to teach Richie Barron a lesson. But how did Mark and Frank hatch the plan, if they were on opposite sides of the Diamond? There must have been a phone call, and the detectives wanted proof.

The conference discussed Michael Peoples' complaint that someone attempted to extort money by saying he assaulted Richie Barron. Some thought the fact that Peoples went to the White Cross Inn to meet the blackmailer was a sign of a guilty conscience. Michael's straightforward actions, reporting the blackmail attempt immediately, taping one of the calls, making a full statement the next day to Garda Phil Collins and handing over the tape, all of which strongly suggested his outraged innocence at a false accusation of murder, simply didn't register with the investigators.

The conference decided to send in a request to see where the calls to the Peoples came from, to see if it was 'anyone connected to the Peoples as opposed to a genuine crank caller'. The investigation team also sent in a request for the records of the phone calls the night Richie Barron died, calls to and from Old Frank, and from the public call boxes.

The hit and run was no longer treated as a realistic option. The same conference notes also mention 'Searches—to be left till near arrests.' The plans to arrest were first mentioned in conference notes as early as 24 October, ten days after Richie Barron died, and were now well under way.

Detective Sergeant Sylvie Henry had already requested the records of the phone calls to Letterkenny hospital the night Richie Barron died. But the response to his request to Crime & Security was taking forever. Telecom Eireann were legally required to hand over phone records if they were requested to by a chief superintendent, but the task was a nuisance, it required computer time, time the company felt was better spent getting the bills out to customers to get their money in.

At the time, the State-owned phone company was busy gearing up for privatisation as Eircom. Billing was a priority, Garda inquiries had to wait until after office hours. But the company was also cutting back on overtime as part of its cost-cutting programme. In its favour, the company was installing new computer systems to streamline Garda requests, but perversely this also led to delays in processing the requests as the bugs were sorted out in the new software.

The delays at Telecom Eireann were well known within the force. A new arrangement to allow the police access to phone records, put into legislation in the early 1990s, had become a victim of its own success. In 1993 the company received 234 Garda requests for phone records. By 1997 the number of requests annually had grown to 1,300. Michael Diffley, the Crime & Security chief superintendent assigned to deal with phone traces at the time, wrote to the company on 30 January 1997 to complain that 503 non-Dublin phone requests were still outstanding from the previous year. 'I had meetings with the carrier, with the people in Portlaoise, I discussed it with the Department of Justice. It was an ongoing battle,' Diffley remembered.

An internal phone company memorandum on 10 February 1997 showed only 45 of 358 Garda requests were processed between June and September 1996. Things looked better between September and December 1996, with only 9 of 224 requests outstanding. However, from December to February 1997, 62 of 117 requests were not completed. The system was erratic at best.

Diffley told the Morris tribunal he or his staff would 'take it up verbally or in writing' with the Investigation Branch of An Post, based in the GPO, who dealt with requests from An Garda Síochána to telephone companies, if they received complaints about delays.

His successor Dermot Jennings, now an Assistant Commissioner, also agreed the delays were unacceptable. 'Umpteen phone calls I have got from investigations all around the country trying to put pressure on Eircom and this was done on a regular occasion even by myself contacting the people in the GPO to see if they could speed things up,' he recalled.

However, while official requests took some time to deal with, over 1,000 of the 14,000 staff at the phone company could look up customer records at their terminals. As the tribunal would discover, it appeared some staff members at the phone company were happy to help Guards and private investigators who needed an 'informal' phone search.

At the 13 November conference, Inspector John McGinley mentioned the delays in getting phone records, and said that if anyone at the conference had contacts they would be as well to use them or they could be waiting months for results.

Despite the importance placed on obtaining telephone records for the investigation by the first conference after the calls to Michael Peoples, an official request for the phone records was not prepared by Inspector John McGinley for Crime & Security until a week later on 21 November.

Detective Sergeant Henry had already sent in a request looking for the incoming calls to Letterkenny hospital the night Richie Barron died 'as a matter of extreme urgency'. On 22 October Crime & Security duly forwarded his request, assigned the reference number 58/10/96, to the Investigation Branch of the post office based at the GPO. From there it went to the phone company, where it was assigned the internal reference code 1019/96. By early November, Henry still had not received any answer.

A second request for all calls from the two public telephone boxes in Raphoe, one in the Diamond and the other in St Eunan's Terrace, was processed at Crime & Security on 22 November 1996. Crime & Security assigned this request the reference number 54/11/96. The reply to this request was received at Crime & Security on 3 December 1996. The request seems to be an attempt to discover if the extortion hoax to Michael Peoples, and a similar attempted hoax call a few days earlier to Old Frank McBrearty, were made from a public call box in the town.

Inspector John McGinley prepared another request for telephone calls, date-stamped 21 November 1996 in the Letterkenny superintendent's office. The request involved a total of eight telephone numbers. These included the two Raphoe public telephone boxes, this time covering the entire period between 11 p.m. on 13 October and 11 p.m. on 9 November, that is from Richie Barron's last night in Raphoe until the date of the hoax blackmail calls to Michael Peoples. McGinley also requested details of all incoming and outgoing calls to the home number of Old Frank McBrearty, the McBrearty nightclub, Geoffrey Dolan, Eunan and Katrina Brolly, the Town & Country pub, and Michael and Charlotte Peoples on 14 October. Calls involving the Peoples' number on 9 November were also sought. This request would not be forwarded from the chief superintendent's office in Letterkenny to Crime & Security until the middle of December. On 12 December, Crime & Security Chief Superintendent Michael Diffley forwarded the request to the GPO Investigation Branch. Crime & Security assigned this request the reference number 19/12/96; Telecom Eireann filed it as 1126/96.

After McGinley made his appeal to the Guards at the 13 November conference to 'use their contacts' to speed up phone requests, Garda John O'Toole approached the inspector. He told him about his brother-in-law, a detective inspector called Patrick Nyhan in Crime & Security. Perhaps Nyhan could help.

'I think it was after a conference, or perhaps during one, but I know that Inspector McGinley made the comment that if anybody had any contacts to contact them and see could they speed up the getting of the phone calls, or the incoming and outgoing phone calls from various numbers that had been applied for officially,' O'Toole testified at the Morris tribunal.

'As a result of that I contacted my brother-in-law, Detective Inspector Patrick Nyhan, who is based in Crime & Security. I explained the situation to him, that we had applied for these through the normal channels, and that we had experienced delays, and that there was frustration, and asked him if he could help us get the phone calls, about the information that we had sought.

'As I said the calls had been applied for officially, and I used the application form that had been sent away through normal channels,' O'Toole said. (O'Toole was mistaken in this—the official request prepared by McGinley did not go to Dublin until December). O'Toole read the numbers and times to Nyhan. To the best of his memory, the numbers he gave to Nyhan came from the request prepared by McGinley and date-stamped 21 November. 'I must say that my recollection is that I thought I did this earlier than 21 November,' O'Toole said in evidence. 'But it was certainly a list very like that, and those would appear to be the numbers and the times that I had, that I had checked with him.'

'And what did you request your brother-in-law who was working at Crime & Security to do?' O'Toole was asked.

O'Toole said he explained to his brother-in-law the delays being experienced in getting phone records, and 'asked him if he could speed it up or if he could get the calls. And he said he would get back to me. And I think about a week later or a number of days, a week later, he contacted me by phone at the Garda station, and he asked me for the fax number, and he faxed me down information in relation to some of the phone calls. He did say that he was unable to get incoming calls, and was only able to get outgoing calls from some of the numbers. And I went to the communications room, to the fax in the communications room, and collected the data when it came through, and brought it to the incident room.' O'Toole then went through the printout with Sergeant Marty Moylan.

The fax from Nyhan to O'Toole no longer exists. 'It wasn't our intention to use it as evidence, and to be honest I wasn't that happy about the manner in which I obtained it and I didn't want to hold on to it. We had taken whatever relevant information from it, created jobs, and then some time afterwards I discussed it with Sergeant Moylan again and we decided, it was decided it be destroyed, and I destroyed that information.'

O'Toole said he thought he contacted Nyhan in 'late October, early November' but having seen the 21 November application at the tribunal, felt 'it could have been late November either'. He said this was the only occasion on which he had contacted his brother-in-law to fast-track bureaucratic delays in getting records, but added that 'it wouldn't be unusual for say the officers in an investigation to ring up people that they knew informally to try and speed it up in headquarters'.

Detective Inspector Patrick Nyhan was not called to give evidence at the tribunal, but he was interviewed by tribunal investigator Michael Finn on 5 October 2004, four days after O'Toole gave his evidence.

Nyhan said he asked O'Toole if an official application had been made, and was assured it had. He took down the details, and went to see his chief superintendent Michael Diffley to 'give it a push', but Diffley was not in his office when he called in. Nyhan called the GPO Investigation

Branch. He spoke to 'a fellow who was very helpful', though he could not recall his name. A week or so later, he received an envelope with a compliment slip through the internal mail system 'and inside it was a number of sheets with telephone, I think it was outgoing calls'.

Nyhan phoned O'Toole in Letterkenny, and asked him for the Garda station fax number. He faxed the sheets to his brother-in-law. Nyhan said this was the only time he had ever contacted the Investigation Unit looking for telephone records.

John O'Toole and Patrick Nyhan both agreed that the 'informal' request for telephone records only resulted in information on outgoing calls from the specified numbers.

After he eventually learned that telephone records were obtained 'informally' by the Letterkenny investigators, Inspector John McGinley said that knowing the phone calls to the hospital came from the homes of the Peoples and Brollys pointed the investigation in their direction, making suspects of the Peoples and the Brollys. This in turn led them to seek outgoing call records from the Brolly and Peoples' phones. However, pressed by the tribunal lawyers, McGinley said he did not know how the records of the call to Letterkenny hospital were obtained.

When he was recalled in 2006 during the inquiry into the arrest and detention of Katrina Brolly, McGinley expanded on his recollection. 'The first aspect of the telephone records that arose was in relation to the telephone calls to the hospital. There was two telephone calls received in the hospital by persons purporting to be the Barron family, enquiring about the health of Richie Barron on the night he died.'

'Obviously the Barron family didn't make the calls and Sergeant Henry applied for those and the result of those calls were that one was made from the Brolly household and the other was made from the Peoples household.'

'Subsequent to that in the early part of November there was extortion telephone calls made to Michael Peoples. On 20 or 21 November I made application to Crime & Security to have telephone calls made from those three numbers that we were aware as a result of the hospital trace that the calls were made from Brollys and Peoples and the other, the extortion telephone call to Michael Peoples, I applied for those on 21 November and there was also, I think, a couple of telephone boxes or some other calls in it as well.'

In other words, McGinley said the request for outgoing telephone calls from the Brolly and Peoples homes on the night Barron died came as a result of the answer to the trace on incoming calls to the hospital, and he had that information on or before 21 November 1996.

McGinley went on to say that to the best of his knowledge, the results of this inquiry were not available by early December, when the Gardaí moved to make arrests. Joe Hannigan, Tina Fowley and John O'Toole all felt the results were known before 4 December 1996. John White remembered being given details of the hospital phone call by John O'Toole before he interviewed Katrina Brolly on 4 December. McGinley said the results of the hospital query were what led the investigation to look for the Brolly and Peoples records in November 1996. The hospital query did not come through officially until January 1997. This suggests there may have been more than one 'informal' record search. O'Toole and Nyhan said they only made one 'informal' search. Apparently, other Gardaí also had access to 'informal' channels.

The word 'illegal' is never used in the Morris report to refer to the O'Toole/Nyhan search for phone records. Neither is 'unofficial' or 'irregular', both words used at tribunal hearings by barristers as they danced around what O'Toole and Nyhan had done. O'Toole's own barrister, Ms Sean Quinn, merely referred to 'procuring telephone records . . . through a fast track channel'. The strongest criticism of the operation came from solicitor Paudge Dorrian, who while questioning O'Toole on behalf of Sergeant John White said the records were 'illegally and improperly obtained'. In his report Justice Morris described this invasion of privacy as an 'informal enquiry'. O'Toole and Nyhan destroyed the records of their 'informal' search. For this and for by-passing proper channels laid out in the statutes they are criticised. But they are never called law-breakers, even if their actions were unwitting and they believed they had a chief superintendent's authority. The 'fellow who was very helpful' in the GPO was never identified.

In 1996, the power of the Gardaí to get telephone records was governed by the Data Protection Act (1988) and the Interception of Postal Packets and Telecommunications Messages Act (1993). The 1988 Act makes it a criminal offence to obtain access to personal data, or disclose personal data, without the prior authority of the data controller or data processor. The 1993 Act creates an offence if 'information concerning the use made of telecommunications services' is disclosed without authorisation. While Michael Peoples told the police to go ahead and monitor his phone if it would help in tracking down the crank blackmailer, no permission was obtained from the Brollys. Without the authorisation of a chief superintendent, something that didn't exist until mid-December 1996, the 'informal enquiry' was illegal.

Chapter 9

Who is Mister X?

Inspector John McGinley was looking for a tape recorder. Reports were coming in that Old Frank McBrearty had intimidated witnesses. Inspector McGinley and Detective Superintendent Joe Shelly decided to go to see Frank and speak to him about the allegations. McGinley wanted a record of the meeting, in case there was any trouble afterwards about what was said.

Garda Tina Fowley thought Inspector McGinley asked her for a tape recorder before he and Shelly went to meet Frank McBrearty. McGinley's recollection was that he had used his own recorder to tape the meeting. Both agreed that he had given her the tape afterwards to type a transcript of the conversation. Fowley would later hand in the transcripts to the authorities.

McGinley felt Frank was making life difficult by 'pursuing witnesses and following the Guards around'. Frank, on the other hand, felt the Guards were trying to frame his family, and said he only spoke to members of his staff about what was going on.

'We were investigating a crime,' McGinley remembered. 'But Frank McBrearty was investigating it too, and his investigation in tandem with ours was causing huge conflict, and making it difficult. I would go so far as to say had he stood back and let us investigate, we would have established different facts. I'm not saying they weren't justified, I'm just saying where we were at that time. It had an influence.'

On Wednesday 20 November 1996, McGinley and Shelly approached Frank McBrearty at his pub, the Tudor Lounge. Unknown to Shelly, McGinley secretly recorded the conversation. McGinley later wrote a report for the Carty team setting out the reasons for the meeting. There were reports that Frank was 'hindering' the Garda investigation into Richie Barron's death by 'following the investigating Gardaí around Raphoe; parking and remaining in the vicinity of houses where Gardaí were carrying out enquiries; questioning witnesses who were interviewed by Gardaí and telephoning other witnesses seeking to find out what the Gardaí were asking. This conduct was making it difficult for people to come forward and assist Gardaí and in general was unhelpful and was hindering the investigation.'

'We had a discussion with him,' McGinley explained. 'We made him aware of our concerns and asked him to desist from these activities and allow the Gardaí to carry out their investigations and conduct their inquiries.' McGinley also gave the Carty team a copy of the transcript Garda Tina Fowley had typed up.

———

When the two senior officers arrived at Frank McBrearty's pub, they introduced themselves and explained that they 'just wanted a wee word' with the publican. McGinley secretly turned on the tape recorder.

'What's wrong now?' was Frank's first question.

After a few moments of small talk, the Guards explained the reason for their visit. 'We are investigating a matter out here at the minute and it would seem that you are investigating it too.'

'No I'm not,' said Frank. The publican said he had asked his staff what the detectives were saying about him, and asked why everyone was being asked about Young Frank and himself, when they were both at their work the night Richie Barron died. He pointed out that he was the one who told his staff to make statements to Gardaí in the first place.

He denied he had followed Gardaí in the town or watched them, and asked which Garda had said he was doing so, and what houses they were visiting at the time.

The officers explained they were 'concerned that people would be afraid to talk to us'.

'I'll tell you now how all this happened. I sent people to the Barracks to make statements, and they were fucking interrogated. They were not asked to make proper statements, they were asked about me and mine, I have the notes down at the house that they asked them,' Frank complained.

He told the officers that rumours his family had something to do with Richie Barron's death had started because he had reported a Garda sergeant for alleged misbehaviour years before. 'Some of the Guards mortally still hate me. They never forgave me for reporting his carry on.'

The old complaint had nothing to do with why they were there, the officers told Frank. They'd come to see him because of reports that he was seen outside people's houses while Gardaí spoke to them, and had approached people and telephoned people after they were interviewed. The meeting ended at that.

———

The encounter was reported to the next Richie Barron case conference on Thursday 21 November. Under the heading of 'Intimidation of witnesses', the notes recorded 'Frank Snr spoken to by Insp McGinley and D/Supt Shelly. Direction to log visits/followings by McBrearty snr, Keep file live—report on further breaks.' The notes made no mention of the secret recording.

The investigation was in trouble. The bare suspicion of murder was all they had to show for a month's work. The scene hadn't been preserved, and Gardaí had failed to preserve Barron's clothes at the hospital. It was hardly surprising therefore that Dr Liam Fleury's forensic tests found no evidence, either of a hit and run, or of an assault. There was no murder weapon, and there were no witnesses to the presumed assault. There were discrepancies in Mark McConnell's movements that night, but for every witness who contradicted his account, there was another who verified it. Dr Barry's autopsy was inconclusive, and there had been no definitive post-mortem forensic examination by the State pathologist, Professor John Harbison. The information from John Patton was ambiguous at best, and anyway he wouldn't make a statement. Reports that other witnesses might help place Mark McConnell or Young Frank McBrearty near the scene had come to nothing. The *Crimeline* appeal for information had produced nothing concrete. (In fact the message register for the initial investigation notes only one response to the *Crimeline* programme. The Guards dutifully recorded how a caller in Waterford, on the other side of the country, 'suggested Belgian or French mafia may be involved! They are involved in the movement of illegal growth promoters in this country.' Incredibly, Gardaí in Waterford were contacted to take a statement from the caller.)

Remarkably, John McGinley cited the *Crimeline* response at the Morris tribunal as evidence that the investigation had been thorough, not simply targeting the McBreartys. In evidence to the tribunal he said there were lots of rumours during the investigation, including rumours about Richie Barron's own family, members of the Travelling community, and 'Russian and French Mafia'. All of these had to be investigated and eliminated, and 'they were put out of the frame,' he maintained. McGinley argued that the only suspects who could not be eliminated were the McBreartys.

Short of launching an inquiry into the French connection, the investigation had run out of places to go by mid-November. There were still jobs to be completed (the notes record 'Approx 80' statements to be taken), but they were loose ends. None of them promised anything that would allow the team to make an arrest. Only one inquiry seemed to hold any promise. The notes recorded 'John O'Dowd working on something'. There was a proposal that the Lifford and Raphoe station crews and the desk crew should tidy up 'loose ends', and 'everyone else to revert back'.

The conference called for ideas from the floor, 'Suggestions of what could be done'.

O'Dowd was indeed 'working on something'. William Doherty hadn't just tried to solve the case by making hoax blackmail calls in a bid to bluff the supposed perpetrators. Doherty and O'Dowd knew they needed 'the final part of the jigsaw', someone to place McConnell and McBrearty at the scene. Doherty later told the Morris tribunal that O'Dowd asked him if he would make a statement doing just that, but he responded: 'The only person stupid enough to do that would be Noel McBride.'

O'Dowd claimed that Doherty 'drip fed' him information, first telling him Richie Barron had been murdered, then that there was a witness who had seen Young Frank McBrearty and Mark McConnell coming down the car park from the spot where Richie was found to the nightclub. The witness was afraid of the McBreartys, and didn't want to come forward. O'Dowd insisted he took any information he received into the conferences on the case, 'delivering this to conference as it came in'.

Robert Noel McBride was a childhood friend of Doherty's, they went to school together. His father was also Robert McBride, so Robert Noel was known by his middle name to avoid confusion. In their closing submission to the tribunal, his legal team presented Noel as 'a simple, nervous, fearful man with very limited reasoning, articulation or judgement and poor retention of detail and even poorer memory'.

By mid-November, O'Dowd had the name of the witness from Doherty. Noel McBride was in the car park, and saw the suspects as they made their getaway back to the nightclub. Doherty and O'Dowd's telephone records show they telephoned McBride several times both at his home and at his girlfriend's home, but McBride didn't want to make a statement.

Noel McBride's girlfriend, Sharon Alexander, was fifteen years old in 1996. On Sunday 6 October, a week before Richie Barron died, Sharon went to the christening of Stephanie McBride's daughter Meghan. After the christening, the party went to Roper's pub. There, Sharon met Stephanie's brother Noel McBride for the first time, and they finished the night at the Parting Glass disco. 'We went out together that night and he is my boyfriend since,' Sharon remembered when interviewed by Guards a year later.

The following Sunday, there was another christening. This time it was for Sharon's sister Mary. Once again, the reception party was in Roper's pub in Killygordon, and Sharon invited her new boyfriend. Noel and Sharon spent the evening together, and at about 10 p.m. left to go to a disco in Ballybofey. They stayed at the disco there until 2 a.m., and Noel spent the night in a mobile home belonging to Sharon's brother. Noel didn't go to work on Monday, he spent the day with Sharon. That night he got a lift from Sharon's uncle back to his home in Figart, just outside Raphoe.

'About two or three weeks after I started going out with Noel we were in Killygordon one night walking about and Noel told me that he got a call from a friend that he had not heard from in a long time,' Sharon remembered. 'He said it was William Doherty. That was the first I heard of William Doherty.'

'After that Doherty started ringing my home on a regular basis looking for Noel. Sometimes he would ring twice in one night. After a couple of months of this Noel would tell me run and answer the phone and if it was Doherty to tell he was not in.'

Doherty wasn't the only caller. 'Garda O'Dowd rang our house a good few times looking for Noel,' Sharon remembered. 'I answered the phone a few times that John O'Dowd rang and I gave the phone to Noel. Noel would tell me afterwards it was John O'Dowd.'

Doherty told O'Dowd that McBride would say he had seen Mark McConnell and Young Frank McBrearty coming down the car park at 1 a.m. But although O'Dowd and Doherty pressed McBride, he wasn't willing to make a statement.

While Doherty said he was put under pressure by O'Dowd to get a statement from McBride, and did so only to stay on the Garda's good side because he feared him, he did admit he gave one piece of information to O'Dowd. Back in June, a television aerial was stolen from 'the Tech', the vocational school in Raphoe. Doherty told O'Dowd that Noel McBride stole the aerial.

At the 22 November case conference, there was a discussion of what to do next. The talk turned to the Veronica Guerin murder in Dublin six months earlier, and the tactics used in that investigation. Detectives working on the high-profile Guerin case broke the criminal gang behind the assassination by working in from the outside. Low level criminals on the edge of the gang were arrested and questioned, and that in turn led the detectives to bigger fish until they reached the Godfathers at the top. Because so many were arrested, the gang could never be sure who was giving the Guards information.

The plan hatched and put to the conference was simple. Detectives would make a series of arrests in Raphoe under the cover of investigating local petty crime, the kind of stuff that had been 'let slip' because resources were concentrated on the Barron investigation. There had been a break-in at DJ's chip shop, another at Sarah's Café. There was a broken window to be investigated. And of course, there was an aerial, stolen from the local Tech six months earlier.

'Five or six people were to be arrested. This was in the expectation they would have the shield of being arrested for crime ordinary and made divulge information about the death of Mr Richie Barron,' Garda Tina Fowley recalled. Nominations for arrests were called for. In all, there were five cover arrests, intended to disguise the sixth arrest, Noel McBride.

Different Guards gave varying accounts of what happened. Tina Fowley was the first to name the operation 'the Guerin strategy' at the tribunal. 'The approach adopted was the investigators start at outer edges of criminal activity, bring those people in, and eat in to the criminal world,' she testified.

Superintendent John Fitzgerald said that before the arrest he asked John O'Dowd 'Who is Mister X?' several times, but was not told. He testified that those were the exact words used. Yet Sergeant Marty Moylan said the name 'Mister X' was not applied to McBride until after his arrest, when it was decided on in order to protect his identity. The name 'Mister X' does not appear in any conference note until 3 January 1997.

Chief Superintendent Denis Fitzpatrick recalled being told 'a month or so in, near a month' that there was a key witness who would be known only as Mister X. 'I was told there was information leaking from the system and this was to counteract this,' he recalled. 'I thought it was Doherty at first, and I was told no, it was a witness.' But he could not remember if he was told who Mister X was.

John O'Toole, who worked in the incident room with Moylan, knew nothing of a 'Guerin plan'. He did not recall suspects being named. Superintendent Fitzgerald told Justice Morris 'there was no concerted effort in that way, but obviously the people that are named there were the people who would have had information about the Richie Barron case'. He said there was no decision to question the youths about Richie Barron, there was no sweep in order to hide Noel McBride's arrest.

Inspector McGinley said the Raphoe sergeant Joe Hannigan 'indicated to conference that other crimes were happening in Raphoe that required attention and that local Gardaí would require time to attend to these crimes'. He said the superintendent gave approval to investigate these crimes.

Joe Hannigan rejected any suggestion that he had requested help from the conference in clearing up petty crime in the town because ordinary policing was slipping behind.

O'Dowd rejected as 'pure nonsense' the assertion that the arrests were merely to clear up outstanding local crimes on the books in Raphoe. They were to give cover to McBride, with the chance of a 'Guerin strategy' bonus, as the Guards could also question the others arrested and 'see what they knew' about Richie Barron.

'I don't think it was ever discussed openly, but it was to bring those fellows in to give cover to Noel McBride,' was Phil Collins's recollection. This order came from higher up the chain of command, he added, 'at least Inspector McGinley, maybe higher'.

O'Dowd thought the plan was fully in place by 26 November. At 8.56 p.m. that evening, his phone records show a 3 minute 17 second telephone call to Inspector John McGinley's home. O'Dowd said this was to let the Inspector know everything was in place for the arrests. McGinley had no memory of the call, and thought he might not even have been home that evening. O'Dowd's telephone records also show a 3 minute 33 second call to Buncrana District Superintendent Kevin Lennon, just before he rang McGinley. The following day, Thursday 28 November, William Doherty rang John O'Dowd, and they spoke for fourteen minutes.

———

Noel McBride was arrested at 6.15 p.m. on Friday 29 November 1996 by Garda John O'Dowd at his girlfriend Sharon Alexander's home, and taken to Letterkenny Garda station, where the member in charge, Garda Dan Curran, took his details. Curran was acting member in charge for Garda Martin Leonard, who was on his meal break. Curran explained to Noel McBride his rights, and took custody of his property, £103.79 in cash, a key, and a social services card. At 7.10 p.m., Garda Phil Collins took Noel McBride to an interview room. Five minutes later, Garda John O'Dowd joined them. At the same time Garda Martin Leonard returned to duty, taking over as member in charge and custody officer from Garda Dan Curran. At 8 p.m., a meal was ordered for Noel McBride. At 8.20 p.m., O'Dowd left the room. Fifteen minutes later, Sergeant Martin Moylan went in. At 8.40 p.m. McBride was given his meal. At 9.40 p.m. he was 'placed in his cell for a short period of rest'. At 9.55 p.m. Collins and O'Dowd again brought him to the interview room. At 10.20 p.m., Martin Leonard wrote in the custody record that Noel McBride was 'notified that he was free to leave and was released from Garda custody'. His property was returned. Those are the bare facts of Noel McBride's detention on 29 November, as recorded in the custody record at Letterkenny Garda station.

When Noel McBride was asked about the night Richie Barron died, he told the Guards he was at a reception after a christening in Roper's pub. Phil Collins went to check the story. Mrs Kathleen Roper checked the bookings, and told Garda Collins the McBride christening was on 6 October, the Sunday before Richie Barron died. Apparently Noel McBride did not recall that he was at a second christening in Roper's on Sunday 13 October, that of his girlfriend's niece, Emma Marie.

According to Collins, McBride initially denied stealing the aerial from the Tech. However, he said he did have an aerial in his shed, which he had taken from an old house. Collins contacted Garda Eamon Earley at Raphoe Garda station to get this aerial.

Collins then told McBride a Garda was going to get the aerial, at which point McBride admitted the theft. Collins said the Guards decided to wait until Earley arrived with the evidence before taking a statement.

While they waited, O'Dowd asked McBride if he was in Raphoe and had any information about the night Richie Barron died, but McBride told them he was at a christening for his sister Stephanie.

O'Dowd left the interview room at 8.20 p.m. Despite the crucial point the McBride interview had reached, O'Dowd went home for his dinner, although fast-food snack boxes were brought in for McBride. 'I went down to my own house for something proper to eat. I don't like that stuff,' was his explanation.

Shortly afterwards Sergeant Marty Moylan entered the room, and McBride was given a meal. Collins said he and Moylan continued to talk with McBride as he ate his meal. It was at this point that Noel McBride began to tell them what he saw in Raphoe. Collins then decided to contact Inspector McGinley and tell him they had a witness in the Barron case. However, according to his phone records, O'Dowd also called McGinley, from his home during his meal break.

O'Dowd said that when he got back from his meal break, Phil Collins said to him: 'Your man said he was in Raphoe.' He thought Inspector McGinley arrived within a few minutes. With O'Dowd back at the station, and Garda Earley arrived with the aerial, the Guards decided to 'clear up the other matter first'. They told the tribunal that Garda Phil Collins took McBride's statement admitting the theft of the aerial. They then explained to McBride that he was released from custody, and he voluntarily agreed to stay in the cell and talk about the night Richie Barron died.

'You take this one, I took the last one, I'm a bad old writer,' O'Dowd later said Collins told him.

At the time the tribunal heard evidence about the arrest of Noel McBride (he gave his evidence in the summer of 2004), it did not have available the expert evidence of Professor Gisli Gudjonsson. The Icelandic psychologist, who lectures in King's College London, specialises in the psychology of interrogation, and has given evidence in several high-profile miscarriage of justice cases, including the Birmingham Six and the Guildford Four.

In his evidence, Gudjonsson explained how a combination of pressure from interrogators and a suggestible and psychologically vulnerable prisoner could easily lead to false confessions. In Noel McBride's case, it would lead to a false witness statement.

Duly broken on the aerial, and with his alibi in Killygordon the night Richie Barron died also in tatters, McBride eventually completed a statement saying what the Guards wanted to hear: he saw Mark McConnell and Young Frank McBrearty coming down the car park at 1 a.m., and being let into the nightclub. Thanks to the information fed into the incident room by O'Dowd and Doherty since the investigation began, the Guards already knew—or thought they knew—what McBride had seen: McBrearty and McConnell in the car park at 1 a.m. McBride named five other individuals in his statement, people he said he saw at various times and places in Raphoe that night. A cursory check would confirm all of these people were indeed in Raphoe that night. Statements had been taken from them.

Even so, a thorough cross-reference with the other statements would have revealed serious discrepancies in McBride's account. McBride said he saw Martin Neilis going into Frankie's nightclub at 10.30 p.m. However, Neilis said he was in McCarron's pub, the Tir Chonnaill, until 12.30 a.m. McBride said he spoke with Derek and Sean Crawford before 11 p.m., and they went into the nightclub. However, the Crawfords in their statements say they were barred from the nightclub, and stayed in the Suile Tavern until after 11.30 p.m. McBride said he saw Andy McBrearty twice going into the nightclub, and spoke to him. But Andy was with his girlfriend the entire night, and didn't speak to anyone on the one occasion he went to the nightclub. McBride said he saw Damian Murphy going into the disco at 11 p.m., and fixed the time because he heard the town clock chime. Damien Murphy was in the Tir Chonnaill bar from 8 p.m. until 12.30 a.m., where he was playing music. Finally, McBride said Sean Crossan, one of the McBrearty employees, was not in the car park when he was there at 1 a.m. Crossan in his statement said he was there from about 12.40 a.m. taking care of two girls who were sick.

Sergeant Marty Moylan said the Guards were worried McBride's name would get back to Old Frank McBrearty and he would be intimidated, and as a result his statement was not followed up to verify its details. 'In hindsight I suppose it should have been done, but that was the way it was.'

Marty Moylan said that McBride initially denied being in Raphoe, and that at some stage Garda O'Dowd said, 'I was in Raphoe myself, I saw you.' Moylan said that at the time he believed Garda O'Dowd. However, after he discovered the following year that in none of the 500 or so statements in the Barron file system did anyone mention Noel McBride, Moylan did not approach O'Dowd for a statement to confirm McBride's account. In fact, Moylan never said anything to O'Dowd—or anyone else—about O'Dowd claiming to have seen McBride until 28 January 1998 when he made a statement outlining his dealings with Noel McBride.

'All I remember saying to him was that we had information that he was in Raphoe that night,' was O'Dowd's version. 'The information I had was from William Doherty.'

If Moylan heard O'Dowd say he saw McBride in Raphoe while taking the Barron statement, then this would have been at 9.55 p.m. at the earliest, as it was not until then that O'Dowd entered the interview room after returning from his meal break. Moylan could not have heard O'Dowd say anything before his meal break, as he did not enter the room for the first time until O'Dowd had left. O'Dowd telephoned Inspector McGinley from his home at 9.33 p.m. If Moylan's recollection is correct, this meant McBride was still protesting he knew nothing about Raphoe twenty-two minutes after O'Dowd had phoned McGinley, apparently to tell him the witness was talking. Clearly McBride's acceptance of the proposition put by his interrogators, that he was in Raphoe the night Barron died and saw something important, was not as clear cut as the Guards maintained. He was still reluctant to make a statement.

At the Morris tribunal, O'Dowd denied saying he saw McBride in Raphoe. He said he simply told the witness he had information to the effect that he was in Raphoe. McBride was technically a free man, able to walk out the front door of the Garda station at any time. However, after he was released from custody, he found himself in a room with three uniformed Guards. To leave the station, he would have had to walk through four closed doors. At his trial on charges of making false statements that night, the Judge decided it was never clear to Noel McBride that he was no longer in custody. The distinction between 'I saw you in Raphoe' and 'you were seen in Raphoe' might well have been lost on McBride—and Moylan.

McBride said he just wanted to get out of the station. He would have told the Guards whatever they wanted. Moylan had gone upstairs, brought a copy of the aerial photograph of the Parting Glass nightclub, and pointed out different areas on it. You were here, you saw them there, they went here, he said Moylan told him. Moylan drew a rough sketch of the car park, showing the same locations. McBride said one of the Guards banged his fist on the table, shouting at him, telling him he had been in Raphoe.

By the time Inspector John McGinley arrived at the station, Noel McBride had already technically been released from custody. The Inspector 'popped his head in the door', and saw Moylan, O'Dowd and Collins with Noel McBride. Moylan told him that McBride was making a statement about what happened in Raphoe. 'That's fine, continue on, see you later,' was the inspector's response.

McGinley checked the custody record and satisfied himself that it showed Noel McBride had been formally released from custody and was in the station voluntarily, not under any duress to make a statement.

Martin Leonard, the member in charge, said he was told at 9.50 p.m. by Garda Collins and O'Dowd that Noel McBride was staying on, and that he was released from custody. Standard procedure is to bring a prisoner to the front desk to release him, return his possessions to him, have him sign for them and indicate whether he has any complaints, after which the prisoner is free to go. Leonard agreed that when he went to the interview room to hand McBride his belongings and tell him he was free to go, it was 'not normal'. Moylan said he explained to the prisoner 'in plain language' that he was free to go, and that Leonard did the same. McBride said no one ever told him he was released from custody.

Weighing all the evidence, the tribunal chairman found that O'Dowd and Collins conspired to coerce a false statement out of McBride 'in oppressive circumstances'. O'Dowd was the 'driving force', and Collins his 'willing and able accomplice'. Moylan was 'swept along by the other two'. Garda Martin Leonard, the custody officer, failed completely in his duty to protect the prisoner, and was happy that Noel McBride should be oppressed. John McGinley knew that McBride was arrested under the pretext of theft of an aerial in order to question him about Raphoe, but wasn't aware of the conspiracy to force a statement out of McBride.

It was not until 2 a.m. that Noel McBride finally walked out of Letterkenny Garda station. His signed statement was a breakthrough for the Barron investigation. It was the catalyst that would allow the investigation to move to the next phase. The arrests could begin.

Because of the rumours that Old Frank McBrearty was intimidating witnesses, the Guards felt it was crucial to protect McBride's identity. To avoid leaks, the decision was made to keep his name from the majority of officers working the Richie Barron case. He was to be referred to only as 'Mister X'.

'The system in the incident room would have picked up on the Mister X statement if it was given the opportunity,' Garda Tina Fowley complained. But because they did not know who Mister X was, they could not verify from cross-checking other statements if he was in Raphoe. Of course, one member of the incident room staff did know who Mister X was. Marty Moylan was there when the statement was taken. However, it was not until 1997 that he cross-checked the other statements in the files against Mister X.

Moylan said that in hindsight he felt he was drawn into taking the statement by Collins and O'Dowd, and didn't realise at the time the pressure McBride would have felt in a Garda station interview room with three uniformed policemen. 'At the time I didn't cop it, to be honest,' he told the tribunal. 'It didn't occur to me. It should have.'

'My view would be that William Doherty started it off, and John

O'Dowd got involved and went along with it. Now I can't answer for Garda O'Dowd but that's my opinion,' he theorised.

In the journal he handed to the Morris tribunal, Superintendent John Fitzgerald wrote for Friday 29 November: 'Statement in Raphoe case putting Frank McBrearty and Mark McConnell in car park at vital time. This matter would need full checking out and try to corroborate if possible.' This is precisely what did not happen.

Inspector McGinley said the statement was taken at face value. 'In our view it seemed to amount to a measure of corroboration at the time,' he testified. 'We didn't think that the man had any agenda. And we had no reason to think that there was any underlying thing going on there.

'Looking back on it now, what we did clearly wasn't adequate. However, where we were at the time we genuinely believed that there was sufficient there, and it was supported by other factors there.

'We genuinely thought that we were on the right road, and we thought that for a considerable time. When one looks back on it now, one can have a different view. There's no way that we would have gone down that road if we believed there was anything wrong. This was what we believed was a very positive sighting, at the vital time, coming from the right direction.'

The chairman was more scathing. He concluded that Inspector McGinley, like other senior officers, had become emotionally caught up in the investigation.

———

The pre-arrest conferences were told the Mister X statement existed. Inspector McGinley told the conference that a witness said Young Frank McBrearty and Mark McConnell were seen walking down the car park at 1 a.m. This placed them less than 400 yards from where Richie Barron was found, at around the time he died.

Despite attempts to keep the identity of Mr X secret, his name appeared in the statement. Near the end, the following passage appears:

'The phone rang and I answered it. The caller said "can I speak to Noel McBride" and I replied "speaking here". The caller then said "I seen you up in the car park in Frankie's one Sunday night, don't go to the Guards or else." I immediately hung up.'

On the morning before the arrests, Sergeant Brendan Roache recalled how he arrived for a conference on the case, and saw John McGinley reading through the statement and laughing to himself. He'd just spotted the giveaway passage. 'So much for Mister X', he said to Roache.

McGinley did not remember any objections to the statement at the conference, or to the decision to begin arrests.

'This was a young man who presented himself without any agenda, we believed,' he said in evidence. 'Put together with all the factors before it, it was decided there was enough there to arrest Frank McBrearty and Mark McConnell.' It was also decided to arrest other people 'who were giving them alibis and so on'.

———

When Noel McBride got home, William Doherty phoned him and asked him if he wanted to make some money by making another statement against the McBreartys. Doherty already knew one statement had been made when Noel McBride was arrested. Doherty had pursued him to make the statement against the McBreartys, told him what he should say, told him what time he should say he saw the McBreartys. Now Doherty had demonstrated he had the power to get him arrested. Noel felt there was no telling what Doherty could do if he didn't go along with him.

Doherty for his part protested that while he pressurised McBride into making statements, he in turn was coming under pressure from John O'Dowd, the Garda he identified as the architect of the entire conspiracy.

Wherever the pressure was coming from, McBride was terrified of Doherty. Doherty had influence over the Guards. He could get people arrested. Doherty sweetened the threats with offers of money, but also threatened him. Doherty had power. 'He's much smarter than I am,' was McBride's comment at the tribunal.

Junior barrister Ms Sean Quinn best illustrated the power Doherty held over McBride. Quinn represented the Association of Garda Sergeants and Inspectors (and several individuals at those ranks) at the Morris tribunal.

Tom Creed, a senior counsel representing John O'Dowd, first questioned McBride. The witness agreed that it was William Doherty who put him under pressure. Doherty represented himself, and during his questioning, revealed that he knew Old Frank McBrearty had visited McBride while he was held in Loughlin House open prison to talk about what had happened to his family. McBride at the time was on remand, pending a trial for making false statements and wasting Garda time. He was later acquitted. Cross-examined further by Doherty, McBride reversed himself, and said it was O'Dowd, not Doherty, who put him under pressure. Creed rose again to re-examine, and again McBride tried to reverse himself, this time saying he didn't know who had put him under pressure. When Doherty again got to his feet, the chairman had had enough. The 'ping pong' questioning would have to stop, he would make up his own mind based on what he had heard.

Sean Quinn began her cross-examination by asking Noel McBride if it was scary hearing all the things Doherty knew about what happened while he was in Loughlin House. 'Doherty knew who your cellmate was when you were in prison and what you said to him,' she said. 'He knew what you said to the Guards the day after you made your statement.'

'That's scary isn't it? That's a bit frightening. You can't even be in prison but he knows what you're saying to people. He knows that Frank McBrearty came down to see you in prison, that's kind of scary as well, isn't it?'

'That's right,' McBride answered.

'He knows almost everything about you, and what goes on in your life, whether you're in prison or whether you're out, isn't that true?'

'That's true.'

'And that's kind of scary, isn't it?'

'Yes.'

'This is a guy who can beat you up. Even though you're a big strong guy, he beat you up. And you think he's going to be back out in about a week's time, isn't he, when his trial is over?'

'That's right.'

'Why are you covering up for him?' Quinn asked. 'Why won't you admit he was the one?' Quinn said the only version of events that made any sense was that Doherty told McBride what to say.

Doherty told the chairman he had met McBride's cellmate, and this was how he knew McBrearty had visited him in prison. 'I don't think at any time in my life I have scared Mr McBride,' he told the judge. Turning to McBride, he told him there would be no reprisals from him after their court cases were completed.

'I hope so,' McBride answered.

Perhaps William Doherty provided the first inspiration for McBride's statement of 29 November 1996. Perhaps John O'Dowd was its source. Perhaps they worked together. Whichever it was, the cross-examination of McBride showed Justice Morris how easily McBride could be coerced into saying what his questioners wanted to hear. Morris was unwilling to accept without question that McBride was, in the words of one lawyer, 'a gormless auld divil', but did accept he was a man of limited intelligence, while Doherty 'showed considerable intelligence'. Fed the script by Doherty, and questioned in oppressive circumstances in a Garda station, it was inevitable that McBride would eventually crack and make a statement telling the Guards whatever they wanted to hear.

Chapter 10

The Power of Arrest

To the McBrearty family, they're the Four Dublin Boys. Detective Sergeants John Melody, Gerry McGrath and Eamon O'Grady, and Detective Garda John Fitzpatrick were members of the Special Detective Unit, an elite serious crimes squad based in Harcourt Square in Dublin. Officers in the squad are experienced in handling high-profile cases, conducting interrogations and getting confessions from suspects. In December 1996, the officers were assigned to Operation Cobra (also known as the Cobra Unit), set up to tackle a spate of armed robberies in the Dublin area.

It was a busy year, and Garda resources were stretched to the limit. Cobra Unit members were also seconded to work on the Veronica Guerin murder, the murder of Detective Garda Jerry McCabe during an armed robbery in County Limerick, and several other high-profile cases. In 1997, following an internal re-organisation by An Garda Síochána, the National Bureau of Criminal Investigation (NBCI) was created, incorporating detectives from several existing units.

A couple of days before the planned arrests in the Barron case, on 2 December 1996, Detective Superintendent Joe Shelly contacted his counterpart in the Special Detective Unit, and the 'Four Dublin Boys' were ordered to Donegal. There they were briefed about the Barron investigation by the senior officers, District Superintendent John Fitzgerald, Detective Superintendent Joe Shelly and Inspector John McGinley, and by Sergeant Marty Moylan from the incident room.

For the next couple of days they immersed themselves in the case, studying the statements and evidence collected by the Letterkenny incident room since 14 October. On 3 December, the Four Dublin Boys visited the crime scene along with Sergeant Marty Moylan, walking around Raphoe and getting a feel of the local geography, before attending the final pre-arrest conference in Letterkenny where they were given briefing files and maps of Raphoe. The briefing was chaired jointly by Detective Superintendent Joe Shelly, Superintendent John Fitzgerald and Inspector John McGinley.

Along with the Four Dublin Boys and the senior officers, Fitzgerald, Shelly and McGinley, the incident room staff and all those involved in the next day's arrests took part in the conference. Given the number of planned arrests, it was quite a crowd.

———

Although the McBreartys did not learn about him until much later, there was a fifth Garda from Dublin in Donegal. Detective Sergeant Joe Costello was attached to the Garda Television and Technical Support Section based in the Technical Bureau at An Garda Síochána HQ.

'It was also agreed by management in charge of the investigation that the services of the Garda Technical Support at Garda Headquarters should be requisitioned as the services of this section might be of assistance to the investigation,' Shelly recalled. 'I made contact with Detective Sergeant Joe Costello who was the member in charge of this unit and he agreed to travel to Donegal to assist in the investigation if required. The type of assistance that might be required that I had in mind would be technical covert surveillance of suspects which might come to light arising out of the interviews.'

Later, Justice Morris would note that it was symptomatic of the disorganisation in Donegal that Shelly contacted Costello directly, rather than going through the formal chain of command. Not only that, but no one seemed to have a clear idea what exactly it was that Costello was supposed to do once he got to Donegal.

'My duties involved me in assisting Garda investigation on a nationwide basis in supplying and maintaining video and still photography, night vision equipment, lecturing to training courses within the Garda Síochána,' Costello said in a statement on his visit to Donegal. 'We were very much involved in big public events in installing and monitoring CCTV at such as Pop Concerts, International Matches of all codes.

'On 3 December 1996 I was contacted by phone by Detective Superintendent Joe Shelly who was then stationed at Letterkenny Garda Station. He informed me that he was making arrests on the following day, 4 December 1996, in relation to the death of Richard Barron at Raphoe, Co. Donegal. He informed me that he may need some form of technical assistance in the event of any disclosures from the subsequent interviews. We did not discuss the matter any further on the phone.

'I went to Donegal that evening, 3 December 1996. On my arrival at Letterkenny I sat in at the end of a conference which was being held there, in relation to the impending arrests. I spoke to Joe Shelly and other members of the Detective Branch after the conference. I got no specific instructions or requests from anyone at that time. I was told that a number of people were to be arrested the following morning and that I was to be available in Letterkenny Garda station the following morning and made myself available.'

Costello's statement was made following an allegation by Detective Sergeant John White that conversations between those arrested on 4 December and their solicitors and visitors were secretly recorded by Gardaí at Letterkenny Garda station.

'I was not requested to perform any duty at Letterkenny Garda station on 4 December 1996,' Costello said. 'I spent my time mainly in the Sergeant I/c's office. I remained on standby duty in Letterkenny until 7 December 1996. I was not asked for and I did not render any technical assistance to the investigation while I was in Letterkenny Garda station from 3 to 7 December 1996.'

The pre-arrest conference argued over whether Gardaí had the power to carry out one of the arrests. 'I recall Sergeant Brendan Roache express the view that a woman could not be arrested for being an accessory after the fact as she was deemed to be acting under the influence of her husband,' John McGinley recalled. 'This arose in the context of Roisin McConnell, and Sergeant Roache was of the view that she could not be arrested for the crime of aiding and abetting her husband.'

'I recall that I sought advice on the matter from the office of the Director of Public Prosecutions, in that I discussed this with a legal assistant of that office at that time,' Joe Shelly remembered.

Schedules were drawn up and distributed to those attending the conference, including the officers assigned to each arrest and the interview teams for each suspect.

There was another briefing in Letterkenny station early on the morning of Wednesday 4 December 1996. Afterwards, the Four Boys from Dublin travelled with Sergeant Joe Hannigan and others to Young Frank McBreaty's house at 67 Elmwood Downs. The Four Dublin Boys had a specific job that day—they were to interrogate Young Frank McBrearty after his arrest. The final preparations were in place.

A total of nine arrests were planned: Old Frank McBrearty, Young Frank McBrearty, Mark McConnell, Roisin McConnell, Michael Peoples, Charlotte Peoples, Edel Quinn, Katrina Brolly and Mark Quinn. Garda Martin Leonard was assigned as station orderly, member in charge and

custody officer for the day, as specified under the provisions of the
Criminal Justice Act 1984. It would be his responsibility to ensure that the
prisoners' rights were respected in custody.

Leonard was a member of the Traffic Corps in Letterkenny. He joined
the force in 1978, and spent four years in Burnfoot, then four in Killybegs,
before his transfer to Letterkenny in 1986. He was the local representative
in the Garda Representative Association, in effect a shop stewart.
Although assigned to the Traffic Corps, he frequently worked as station
orderly, and was chosen for his experience in that role during the mass
arrests. Because of the number of arrests, some of the suspects would go
to Lifford Garda station.

After the early morning meeting, Detective Superintendent Joe Shelly
and Chief Superintendent Denis Fitzpatrick left Letterkenny to travel to
Finner Army Camp near Bundoran. They would not return until late in
the afternoon.

————

At 8 a.m. on 4 December 1996, Detective Sergeant Mick Keane arrested
Michael Peoples for murder. It was the first arrest in the Barron investigation. In an undated statement (most likely prepared in early 1998 as a
response to Michael Peoples' civil action for wrongful arrest) Keane wrote
that he arrested Michael Peoples 'under Common Law for the murder of
Richard Barron'.

The first hint Michael Peoples had of the oncoming storm came the
previous evening, around 8 p.m. He had heard rumours before then, but
only that Young Frank was involved in Richie Barron's death, nothing
more than that, no hint that his own name was being mentioned, save the
unpleasant blackmail calls to his home on 9 November.

'On 3 December, around 8 p.m., I received a phone call,' Michael
remembered. 'The caller said he was from the Garda forensics department in Letterkenny and he wanted to talk to me about the telephone
calls to my house on 9 November. I says okay. He says, do you want to
meet up with me.

'I thought that's good, there's somebody looking into this, it's being
looked after, and they wanted to discuss times to meet me. I went through
the times, he asked me what time did I finish work and I told them I
started at 5.30 a.m. and I finished around 12 p.m. or 1 p.m. that day.

'I thought it strange myself that there was a forensic department in
Letterkenny Garda station, but I just took the caller's word.'

As a result of the call, Michael arranged for his brother to do his bread
run the following morning. He planned to go to the station to see what

help he could offer to the forensics department. The detectives in Letterkenny didn't know this, and sat outside his home early the next morning, waiting to arrest him on his way to work. One of the detectives later complained to Michael that he'd been outside his home freezing since 5 a.m.

'I got a knock on the door at 7.45 a.m. There was a bang on the door at 7.45 a.m. and there was a Guard standing—he didn't identify himself, he just says Hello, Michael.

'I was kind of shocked, I wasn't expecting anybody at that time of the morning. He knocked at the door and he says look, I need to talk to you for a few minutes. I says, what's wrong? . . . He says there's a few discrepancies in your statement.'

At first, Michael thought the Garda meant his statement about the telephone calls, but the Garda told him he meant his 'other statement', the one he made following the death of Richie Barron.

'I asked him to come in to the living room. He says no, no, come on out to the car. I says, I'm not dressed, come into the living room. He more or less insisted I go out into the car. I says look, I have to get dressed. He says okay, do that.'

As Michael went upstairs, Charlotte asked him what was happening. 'There's a Guard downstairs, he wants me to go out to the patrol car to talk about my statement.'

'Is there anything wrong?' Charlotte asked. 'What's wrong?'

'I don't know,' Michael answered.

Michael went outside and got into the patrol car. He recognised Detective Garda Pat Flynn, the detective who'd visited his home the night he called to complain about the extortion phone calls. 'How are you doing, Pat?' he asked. Flynn didn't answer. 'I was kind of taken aback by the fact that he did ignore me,' Michael recalled.

The first person to speak was Detective Sergeant Mick Keane, who asked him 'Tell us what happened to Richie Barron.' Michael told him he didn't know.

'He says aye, you know something,' Michael remembered. 'Like ordinary conversation. He shouted at me and he says, you lying bastard, you. He shouted at me. I was taken aback. I was shocked, like, somebody shouting at me like that. I said, I don't know what you're talking about, and he put his left hand on my shoulder and he says, I'm arresting you for the murder of Richie Barron. I was just in complete shock. I says, I need to tell my wife. I opened the door. He shouted at me, close that door, I'll tell your wife. I was in the back of the car, I wasn't handcuffed, I wasn't nothing. If I had wanted to get away, I could have got away, all I had to do was open the door and run. It was just shock, I couldn't believe what was happening at the time.

'He went down to the house, told Charlotte whatever story he told her, I think he told her I would be back in a few minutes, and proceeded then to Lifford in the car.

'On the way to Lifford station, I think he asked me who owned the house I was living in. I told him it was my house. He asked me how did I afford that. I looked at him as much as to say, it's none of your business, I think I answered then I have a mortgage the same as everybody else. He made a remark then, he says Jesus, I thought you were going to hit me there. Just being intimidating. I don't know what kind of angle he was going at.

'I didn't know what he meant by it. Whether he wanted the boys in front to think I was going to hit him or whatever it was, he made a remark like that.'

In his statement, Keane said he cautioned Michael Peoples and explained the arrest 'in ordinary language'. The detective sergeant then took Peoples to Lifford Garda station, where he explained the reasons for the arrest to the member in charge, Garda Bosco Gallagher.

Gallagher authorised the detention of Michael Peoples under Section 4 of the Criminal Justice Act at 8.20 a.m. This allowed the Gardaí to hold Michael Peoples and question him for up to six hours. The detention could then be extended for another six hours, provided it was approved by a superintendent or officer of higher rank.

Michael was asked if he needed a solicitor. He told the detectives he didn't need one. 'I thought, they've made a mistake, we'll straighten it out here now at the station and I'll be released. I was under the impression I was going to be released in half an hour.

'But then the interview proceeded, I just got the feeling it was going to be a long day, so I asked then for a solicitor.' Michael said that during the first interview, Detective Garda Pat Flynn and Detective Garda Thomas Burke asked him about his movements the night Richie Barron died, 'no problem, just civilised questioning. There was no abuse, there was no shouting, roaring, physical or anything,' Michael recalled. Detective Garda Pat Flynn told him he didn't believe he should be there, which relaxed him. Looking back, Michael was uncertain if the detective was unsure or if it was a tactic to put him at ease. He remembered a relaxed atmosphere. He had no cigarettes, and Burke let him smoke his.

At one point, Flynn asked Michael Peoples about the phone call from his home to Letterkenny hospital the night Richie Barron died. Michael said he didn't know who made the call. Then a thought struck him. 'If you can get that call,' he told the detective, 'you can find out who phoned me on 9 November.'

'No,' said Flynn. 'These were got a different way.'

About halfway through the interview, Flynn mentioned that Michael wasn't the only person arrested. Michael realised that relaxed or not, he wasn't going to be released after half an hour. He asked for his solicitor, Ciaran Dillon. The Gardaí tried to contact the solicitor, but his phone line was engaged. After several unsuccessful attempts, they sent a patrol car to Letterkenny to find Dillon. The interview lasted just under two hours, from 8.27 a.m. to 10.22 a.m. At the end the notes were read over to Michael. He refused to sign them, and was brought to a telephone, where he spoke to his solicitor. Dillon told him not to sign anything. When they finished speaking, Michael was given breakfast.

———

By the time Michael Peoples arrived in Lifford, the second arrest had been made. Roisin McConnell was stopped at a checkpoint in Raphoe and arrested by Detective Sergeant John White at 8.18 a.m. as an accessory after the fact to murder.

'They were letting other cars in front go on ahead and they stopped our car,' Roisin remembered. 'I thought there was an accident or something and then John White, he came around to the back of the side door where I was. I thought it was somebody belonging to my family was in an accident or something. He asked me was I Roisin McConnell and I says that's right. He told me to step out of the car and all I could hear that morning was, you're arrested for the murder of Richie Barron. I never heard accessory, nothing. He could have said it, but all I heard was murder.'

White, then newly promoted to sergeant rank and stationed in the small town of Carrick in the west of the county, was an experienced detective who had worked for several years in Dublin. At the pre-arrest conference he was nominated to arrest Roisin McConnell.

John Dooley, a Detective Garda stationed in Glenties, assisted White in the arrest, along with Detective Garda Padraic Scanlon from Letterkenny and Garda John Harkin from Newtowncunningham. Roisin was travelling to work at Fruit of the Loom along with her friend Lorna O'Donnell and Lorna's sister Mary Pearson when the car was stopped. As the Gardaí led Roisin across the road to the patrol car, she turned to her companion in the car and yelled 'Lorna, go and get Mark'.

'Don't be making a show of yourself,' White told Roisin as she shouted to Lorna. Roisin was placed in the back of the car with White and Dooley, and the Gardaí drove her to Letterkenny Garda station.

'John White turned around and started on about it was a vicious attack and a vicious murder and it was animals that done it, and he was raising his voice to me at this stage,' Roisin recalled. 'I can't remember what else he was saying.' None of the other Gardaí said anything. Roisin asked White if Richie Barron was murdered. White repeated what he had said before. A vicious attack, a vicious murder, Mark and Young Frank were animals.

'Do you have a lot of evidence?' Roisin asked. 'What evidence do you have on him, if you have evidence on him why are you not lifting him?'

In fact, Mark was 'lifted'. Four minutes after Roisin was arrested, Garda John O'Dowd placed his hand on Mark McConnell's shoulder and told him he was under arrest for murder. O'Dowd was accompanied by Detective Garda Patrick Tague, Detective Garda Mick O'Malley and Detective Sergeant Jim Leheny. The time was 8.22 a.m. O'Dowd reported afterwards that Mark replied, 'I'm ready to go, lads.'

'Roisin had headed off to work at around about 8 a.m. I was at the house watching the child,' Mark recalled later in an interview. 'Dean was just one and a half years old at the time. We were still in bed. The knock came to the front door of the house first, and I didn't bother answering it. Then the knock came to the back window of the bedroom, and I shouted "Who is it?" They said it was the Guards, and they told me to come to the front door. I suppose the first thing I thought was something had happened with Roisin on the way in to work.

'I went to the front door and I was met by Garda John O'Dowd. He put his hand on my shoulder, and told me that he was arresting me for the murder of Richie Barron. At that stage I went weak at the knees, as you can imagine. I was standing just in my night clothes, just a shirt and my underwear, and the child was standing behind me as this was all happening. There were maybe five, maybe six Guards in the driveway at the same time, with two patrol cars.

'O'Dowd then told me to compose myself, and to go in and get dressed, so I went back in, the Guards followed me in the door, I got my clothes on, and dressed the child. As we were coming out the door, there was a Bangharda present, and she went to reach for the child. Where she was going to take him I have no idea, but I refused to give the child to the Bangharda. I kept the child in my arms. Meantime, Roisin's sister Edel had came out to our house, to inform me that Roisin had been arrested in Raphoe.'

In the weeks before the arrests, Edel had heard the rumours about Mark McConnell and Young Frank McBrearty. 'We were more worried for Roisin, about Mark, if he was arrested,' she remembered.

Edel rose at about 7.45 a.m. on 4 December 1996. 'It was dark so I had the light on and I pulled the curtains and I seen a car, a Dublin registered car parked over the roadway a bit and I just thought, right, strange the way it was sitting but I just thought, okay,' she remembered. 'I had my breakfast and I got ready for work and I left. When I came out of the house, as I was walking along, the car started to go by my side, drive by my side . . . I remember thinking, this is strange.'

From the Terrace, Edel walked up Guest House End towards the Diamond. The strange car drove up the Terrace. Halfway up Guest House End, Edel met Lorna O'Donnell, who stopped and waved her into the car. Lorna told Edel that Roisin had just been arrested, and that she was on her way to get Mark. Edel got into the car, and they drove up to Mark and Roisin's home in Tullyvinney, just outside the town. 'When we got there, the house was surrounded with cars and people.'

Meanwhile the strange car had arrived in the Diamond. The Gardaí waited for Edel to arrive, not knowing she'd met Lorna while walking down Guest House End. Eventually, they got a call on the car radio. Edel was up at Mark's house.

At the house, Edel was first told to wait in the car, and then that she should go to work. But as Lorna pulled the car out of the drive, Detective Garda Pat Tague stopped the car, opened the door, and asked her to get out.

'He put his hand on my shoulder and told me he was arresting me for accessory after the fact for the murder of Richie Barron and asked me if I understood what it meant and I said, no,' Edel remembered.

'You know who murdered Richie Barron,' Tague told her.

'All the pins and needles I had for Roisin, the shakes, everything left me,' Edel remembered. 'I went numb. I couldn't believe it. I just went totally numb . . . I just thought, this is crazy like, sure how would I know who murdered Richie Barron.

'He took me and put me in a patrol car outside the house, he put me in the back and he was in the front, then he turned around to me and he says to me to tell him who murdered Richie Barron and he wouldn't tell anybody, it'd just be between me and him. He said it's not a thing they go out and do every day, arrest people for murder, that they had a lot of information and statements concerning me, that was why I was arrested. I just told him I didn't know, I didn't know nothing.'

Edel Quinn was arrested by Detective Garda Patrick Tague at 8.35 a.m. She was taken to Lifford Garda station, while Mark went to Letterkenny.

Mark's main concern was to take care of Dean. He dressed quickly, grabbing a pair of tracksuit pants and top, and picked up a baby bag with some nappies and creams. 'I went to the front door,' he remembered. As he stepped outside, Garda Gina Lohan 'put her hands out to reach for the child as I came out the door and I told her, I swore, no fucking way are you taking my child,' he recalled.

'You'll have to take me to his Granny's house,' Mark told the Gardaí.

When Mark said in a statement on 18 February 1998 to Chief Superintendent John Carey, assigned to deal with his case by the Garda Complaints Board, that Garda Lohan tried to take Dean from him at his house, Detective Sergeant Jim Leheny responded with a statement that the only Gardaí at Mark's home were himself, John O'Dowd, Pat Tague and Michael O'Malley. However, in a statement to the Morris tribunal on 17 January 2003, Lohan said she 'was present at Raphoe Garda station on duty when Roisin McConnell, Tullyvinney, Raphoe was arrested. I then travelled to the home of Mark McConnell accompanied by a number of other Gardaí where Mark McConnell was arrested. I recall entering Mark McConnell's home. I recall my duty was to be present as it was known that his child would be there.'

The Gardaí agreed with Mark that they would drop Dean off with his grandmother, and Detective Garda Mick O'Malley told him to lock the house. As he did so, O'Malley put his hand out and Mark gave him the keys. 'I was never arrested before, I suppose I was in shock and I was a bit afraid too into the bargain. He put his hand over towards my hand and I gave him the key. The keys to the car were also on the bunch of keys.'

In a statement dated two days later, on 6 December 1996, Leheny wrote that he asked Mark if he had any objection to his car being taken to Letterkenny for forensic examination. Mark said he didn't and handed over his car keys. Mark told the tribunal that this was 'complete and utter lies', and he didn't even realise the Gardaí had taken his car until they saw it in Letterkenny Garda station later that day.

Detective Sergeant Jim Leheny's first involvement in the case was on 2 December 1996, when he attended a pre-arrest conference in Letterkenny. The following day he read up on the case, visited the scene in Raphoe, and spoke to Garda John O'Dowd.

Leheny joined An Garda Síochána on 24 March 1965. In 1975, he was appointed to the Detective Branch in Buncrana, and in 1986 he was promoted to sergeant and transferred to the Traffic Corps in Letterkenny. In 1987, he returned to Detective Branch as a sergeant, and was transferred to Donegal town, where he stayed until his return to Buncrana in charge of the Detective Branch in 1995. Leheny had a fractured relationship with his superintendent in Buncrana, Kevin Lennon. The sergeant disapproved of Detective Noel McMahon, whom he regarded as unpredictable. McMahon, however, was Lennon's protegé. Together, Lennon and McMahon had skilfully executed a series of bogus arms finds which enhanced Lennon's reputation and kick-started his career, painting a false picture of Adrienne McGlinchey as an IRA informer.

Leheny, Garda John O'Dowd and Garda Gina Lohan drove Mark and Dean to Mark's mother's house. 'I went in towards the house with the child in my arms, followed by Leheny and O'Dowd, both of them, they entered the house along with me,' Mark remembered. 'Gina Lohan stayed in the car . . . My mother was quite shocked. I went down to the room with the child and she was fairly shocked to see me . . . She says, what are you doing down? I says, I've been arrested for the murder of Richie Barron. She got up in a very bad state, both her and my father. They came up into the kitchen. My mother was crying and my father was in a bad state. I remember my mother saying to John O'Dowd, Mark didn't kill anybody, and John O'Dowd agreed with her. He says, don't worry, I know he didn't. Don't worry about it.

'I had to sit her down and try to calm her down first, she was pure white, white as a ghost. I got her a glass of water and she felt a bit faint and we got her settled down and then I just—whatever I had in the bag, I just left it and then the Guards took me out of the kitchen.' As they drove to Letterkenny, Mark heard on the police radio that Michael Peoples had been arrested.

––––

'You have one argument with a man and you're blamed for murdering him,' Garda John Harkin recorded Roisin as saying while the Gardaí drove her to Letterkenny. 'How many people did murder him?' she asked.

White asked her if she knew Richie Barron. 'I just knew him to see,' she replied. Roisin asked if she could make some phone calls. She was worried about Dean, she would need to arrange a babysitter if Mark was arrested. 'I can have a solicitor as well?' she asked. White told her she had that right.

'I will not get any this time of morning,' Roisin said. She thought for a moment. 'I don't need a solicitor. I done nothing wrong,' she decided.

Roisin arrived at Letterkenny Garda station at 8.40 a.m. As she got out of the car, White said to her, 'Roisin, tell me this here, do you believe in God?'

Roisin looked at him and said 'I do.'

'That's good, because so do I,' White said as he led her into the station.

Custody officer Garda Martin Leonard took the details from White and Dooley, and explained to Roisin her rights. She wanted to find out if Dean was okay, but told him not to phone her mother. 'I don't want my mother contacted because she doesn't keep well at times,' she explained to Dooley. Leonard noted her request for a solicitor in the custody record, but refused her request to contact her family because, as he said later, it 'might hinder the investigation'.

After processing, Roisin was taken to the interview room opposite the duty sergeant's office on the ground floor, according to a statement made by custody officer Garda Martin Leonard on 12 February 2002, while Mark McConnell was taken to one of the detective branch offices on the first floor.

––––

Charlotte Peoples was still in bed along with her three-year-old daughter when Michael came upstairs to tell her the Guards wanted to talk to him about a few discrepancies in his statement. He had to get dressed because the Gardaí wouldn't speak to him in the house.

'Why don't they come in to the house?' Charlotte asked.

'No, they want to talk to me in the car outside,' Michael told her.

A few minutes later, there was a knock on the door. Charlotte went downstairs. 'We're just taking Michael away,' the detective told her. 'He should be back in a wee while.'

At first, Charlotte didn't realise Michael was under arrest. When she figured out what was happening, she phoned her mother, Dolly Eaton, who agreed to come down. While she was on the phone, she saw a car go past with Mark McConnell inside holding Dean on his knee, followed by another car. 'It looks as if Mark McConnell is being lifted as well,' she told her mother.

Charlotte called Michael's parents in Letterkenny. They drove to her house. Charlotte didn't realise Michael was in Lifford, she thought he'd been taken to Raphoe Garda station. She decided to go there along with Michael's father, to find out what was going on.

'I was given the job to arrest Charlotte Peoples from the previous conference the night before,' Detective Sergeant Sylvie Henry told the Morris tribunal. 'We went out to the house and I think it was her mother that told us that she was gone down to the Garda station because Michael had been arrested earlier. We went down as far as the Garda station and Charlotte was there.'

Raphoe Garda station looked deserted when Charlotte got there. She rang the 'Green Man' door buzzer, gave her name and said her husband was taken away this morning and she wanted to know where he was. 'Hold on a minute,' said the voice at the other end.

While Charlotte waited, Sylvie Henry pulled up in his car. He got out, along with another plain clothes detective and a female Garda in uniform. 'These boys are bound to know something,' Charlotte said to Michael's father.

Charlotte barely had time to ask Sylvie Henry what was going on.

'Hello, I'm Charlotte Peoples, I'm looking for my husband Michael, he was taken away from the house this morning,' she said.

'You are Charlotte Peoples?' Henry asked.

'I am.'

Henry flipped open his wallet, showing her his Garda ID, placed his hand on her shoulder and told her he was arresting her as an accessory after the fact to the murder of Richie Barron. Charlotte barely heard the words.

Henry arrested Charlotte Peoples at 9 a.m. It was one hour since Michael had been arrested. There were now five people in custody.

Charlotte was taken to Letterkenny Garda station for processing. There she met Garda Martin Leonard, who took the details of the arrest, and asked her if she wanted a solicitor. She told him she didn't need one, she hadn't done anything. After processing, Charlotte was taken to a ground floor interview room near the cells.

At 9.15 a.m., Garda John O'Dowd and Detective Sergeant Jim Leheny arrived at Letterkenny Garda station with Mark McConnell. Because of the volume of prisoners, Garda Martin Leonard authorised Garda Willie Cannon to assist him as a custody officer. Cannon was an experienced officer with thirty-three years in the force, twenty-six of them spent in Letterkenny.

In an undated statement, Garda John O'Dowd said he told Martin Leonard that Mark was under arrest for murder, and gave the reason for the arrest—the 'Mister X' witness statement from Noel McBride. In a later statement, also undated, O'Dowd added to the reasons for the arrest the row between Mark and Richie Barron in the Town & Country pub, and a 'false alibi' given by Roisin. Leonard in a 1998 statement recorded the row, Roisin's 'false alibi' and McBride's statement as reasons for the arrest.

Leonard was satisfied with the explanation of the arrest given by O'Dowd, and at 9.17 a.m. he detained Mark under Section 4 of the Criminal Justice Act. Mark was taken to Room 234 on the first floor, opposite the Detective Branch office, by Detective Sergeant Jim Leheny and Detective Garda Mick O'Malley. Mark told the detectives he would answer questions but would not make any statement until he had a chance to speak to his solicitor.

'Detective O'Malley was very aggressive,' Mark later told Chief Superintendent John Carey. 'He was roaring and shouting and kept calling me a murdering bastard and that I'd never see my wife and wain again. They asked me to stand up now and again. Detective O'Malley then would ask me to stand up. They both pushed me from side to side from one to the other. They were with me for a couple of hours at first.'

———

While Mark McConnell was taken to his interview room, and as Charlotte Peoples arrived at Letterkenny Garda station, Young Frank McBrearty was stopped at a checkpoint on Thorn Road in Letterkenny.

While Frank worked to get his new home built in Raphoe, he lived in a rented house in Elmwood Downs outside Letterkenny, along with his wife Patricia, their newborn daughter Leanne, one-year-old daughter Shannon, six-year-old Chantelle, and Wee Frankie, at seven the oldest of the children.

'My wife had severe abdominal pains and she had been admitted to the hospital on a couple of occasions during the period we were living at Elmwood Downs,' Frank recalled later. 'One of the times then she took a severe attack of abdominal pain and she was subsequently rushed in to Letterkenny hospital and they discovered that she needed her gallbladder removed. She had her gallbladder removed roughly three weeks, four weeks before I was arrested.

'She went through a rough time because they did laser surgery at the start and one of the cameras failed during the operation and they had to rush her from one theatre into another theatre and then cut her open. She was left then with thirty-six staples in her stomach.'

Frank's sister-in-law Jackie Gallagher, who lived in Falcarragh, was also staying in the home to look after Patricia McBrearty and help with the two youngest children. Frank's target was to get his new home finished and his family settled in Raphoe before Christmas Day. He worked days at the site, and nights in the pub.

'I got up to take the children to school,' he recalled. 'The wife was in bed because she had a very severe operation. My sister-in-law helped get them ready to put them into the car. I reckon it was between 9.10 and 9.20 a.m. that we headed up off for Raphoe school.

'We were up at the top of Elmwood Downs and the road was slippy that morning, and as I was driving down the hill I actually nearly lost control of the car, only I was going easy. I pulled out into the main part of the road, which leads to where the sewer works were and there was a bus with parents putting children on the school buses.'

About fifty yards from the school bus, Frank saw a checkpoint. He recognised Sergeant Joe Hannigan, who was standing on the road with his hand up. At first, Frank thought it was an early morning drink driving checkpoint. As he stopped, a Garda patrol car pulled up in front of him. Frank wound down the window to speak to Hannigan. The sergeant asked him to get out of the car.

Frank thought there were up to twenty or twenty-five Gardaí at the scene. He recognised several of them—PJ Keating with his distinctive strawberry-blond hair, Patrick Cafferkey, who had purchased a farm outside Raphoe, Martin Anderson, who had taken a statement from him about Gazza Gallagher a few weeks earlier, along with Mick Carroll who occasionally had a drink in the Tudor Lounge, Tina Fowley and John O'Toole, who had worked in the Parting Glass nightclub on drug squad operations, and of course Joe Hannigan, his local sergeant in Raphoe. Others were strangers to him.

Hannigan put his hand on Frank's shoulder, and told him he was under arrest for the murder of Richie Barron. He was handcuffed and taken to a patrol car, and put in the back seat.

The Gardaí said it was a smooth arrest, apart from Frank's loud protests of innocence. The children were upset because of his shouting, but three Guards took them home to their mother, while Frank was taken to the Garda station.

Frank's version is different. He claimed that as he was arrested, he was called a murderer, his children were shouted at, he was punched or pushed in the back and poked in his ribs. Justice Morris was unimpressed by his claims. It was an efficient and dignified arrest in the circumstances, he decided.

———

Sergeant Joe Hannigan was assigned the duty of arresting Young Frank for murder. 'Thorn Road was convenient to Frank McBrearty's home at Elmwood Downs, Letterkenny, and I knew that he would be travelling to Raphoe that morning,' Hannigan later wrote.

'From my experience and knowledge of Frank McBrearty Junior I believed there was a possibility that he would react in an aggressive and violent manner to his arrest and I had sufficient manpower available should such an event occur,' Hannigan wrote.

In addition to Hannigan, the arrest team was made up of Detective Garda Patrick Cafferkey, Detective Garda Martin Anderson, Sergeant Michael Brennan and Garda Tina Fowley, who was assigned to take care of Frank's children once he was arrested. The Four Dublin Boys, Detective Sergeant Gerry McGrath, Detective Sergeant Eamon O'Grady, Detective Sergeant John Melody and Detective Garda John Fitzpatrick were also present, but played no part in the arrest. According to the Garda version, John Melody travelled back to Letterkenny in the patrol car with Frank. In an undated statement Melody recalled that Frank 'became abusive in the back of the patrol car and was complaining about being arrested'.

Tina Fowley, Martin Anderson and Mick Brennan took Chantelle and Wee Frankie home. Fowley and Anderson were both based in Letterkenny, Fowley worked in the Barron incident room, and Anderson was attached to the detective unit. Brennan was a sergeant based in Burnfoot, one of the Gardaí drafted in to help deal with the volume of planned arrests. Brennan remembered that when they got to the house, Frankie and Chantelle ran inside, and they were met by Patricia McBrearty, who 'was very abusive towards myself and Garda Fowley and continued to shout and roar at us. Garda Fowley asked her if we could come into the house but she was more abusive. At that stage we decided that it was better to leave matters alone and left.'

'She was quite upset and I could understand why she would be upset,' Brennan told the Morris tribunal. 'We were after informing her that her husband was after being arrested and we had the unenviable task of bringing back her two kids to her.'

Patricia McBrearty saw her husband's car pull up from her upstairs bedroom window. She was expecting Frank—after he dropped the kids off at school he was due to drop Jackie off at the hospital. When a stranger got out of the passenger side door, Patricia wondered if Frank had given a lift to a friend from Raphoe. Moments later, Chantelle and Frankie got out of the car, upset and crying, and ran towards the door. With thirty-six stitches in her abdomen, Patricia could not move fast. She was still walking towards the stairs when she heard her sister Jackie open the door to the Gardaí.

'I could hear the kids crying and I could hear them saying downstairs, your husband has been arrested for murder,' she recalled at the tribunal. The Gardaí had assumed that Jackie was Frank's wife.

'I made my way downstairs and my sister was saying to them, "What do you mean? What are you saying?" They just kept shouting, your husband has been arrested for murder. The kids just kept on screaming. I came down the stairs and I was like, what's happening, what's going on? I just can't describe what it was like. They must have realised then that it wasn't his wife that they were talking to because then they said it to me, your husband has been arrested for murder. Frankie was shouting Mummy, tell them Daddy's not a murderer, Mummy, they said Daddy's a murderer. Chantelle was screaming and shouting saying, Daddy didn't kill anybody Mum, Mummy tell them. I suppose my voice was raised, their voices were raised, but the only reason I was raising my voice is because I was trying to be heard over the kids' voices.'

The Gardaí left the home, and drove back to the station.

Arresting Young Frank in front of his children 'was the most awful stupid decision altogether, one of the most stupidest decisions I ever saw,' Detective Garda Patrick Cafferkey told the Morris tribunal. 'Any Guards that were working with me would be of the same opinion.' But the order came from the senior officers at the pre-arrest conference, Superintendent John Fitzgerald, Detective Superintendent Joe Shelly and Inspector John McGinley. The decision was made, and a Garda doesn't have the luxury of debating orders from high ranking officers. Justice Morris concluded that the Gardaí made the best of a bad situation. They had no power to enter Frank's home, and couldn't wait until after the children were at school because they didn't know where Frank would go afterwards. Arresting him near his home allowed them to return the children quickly to their mother.

When the arrest party arrived at Letterkenny Garda station at 9.30 a.m.

with Frank McBrearty, Garda Martin Leonard was still processing Charlotte Peoples. They waited in the dayroom until Leonard was finished.

To protect against wrongful arrest, the Criminal Justice Act (1984) requires that the custody officer is satisfied that any arrest is valid. When Garda Martin Leonard was free, Hannigan explained to him the reasons for arresting Frank. The arrest was based on a witness statement placing Frank and Mark McConnell 'coming from the murder scene', 'a history of disagreements and rows' between the families, and 'the fact that bouncers at McBrearty's nightclub had given false alibis'.

Leonard was apparently satisfied at this, and authorised the detention under Section 4 of the Act, handing Frank a 'Form C72' and explaining his rights. Leonard later wrote that Frank demanded to see a solicitor, and 'banged the table' in front of him. 'He was standing over me, I felt threatened and one of my colleagues pulled him back from my table,' he wrote. 'McBrearty was using very abusive language and I told him that I was merely letting him know his rights and that I was the member in charge to see to it that he was getting his rights and to be treated properly while in Garda custody.' Frank signed the custody sheet to acknowledge he had been given notice of his legal rights. This was the first of several documents he would sign in Garda custody.

The paperwork completed, Frank was taken to Room 225 on the first floor at 9.40 a.m. Leonard got back to his work, he had to telephone Frank's solicitors. There were now six people in Garda custody, four of them in Letterkenny. Leonard was in for a busy day.

In his second report, Mr Justice Frederick Morris concluded that in Mark McConnell's case, 'notwithstanding the tribunal's determination that the ultimate responsibility for the arrests lies with the senior officers directing the investigation, whose suspicions in respect of Mr McConnell were unreasonable', the arresting officer, Garda John O'Dowd, 'was directly responsible for manufacturing the evidence on which his reasons for arresting Mr McConnell were based. He was centrally involved in the forced statement of Robert Noel McBride on 29 November 1996. His actions in this regard were also mala fide. No lawful arrest can occur where the agency effecting the arrest is responsible for manufacturing the evidence on which the grounding suspicion was allegedly based. This basic proposition applies to all of the arrests that occurred as a result of the McBride statement. There is therefore no need to traverse all of the arrests in detail.'

In short, the tribunal concluded that all the arrests on the morning of 4 December 1996, and those that followed later, were unlawful.

The chairman went on to note that the arrest of Michael Peoples illustrated 'the chaotic nature of the management of the investigation. The fact that both the arresting officer and the senior officer who ultimately extended the period of detention of the prisoner, ultimately claim to have arrested him for a separate offence to the one for which he was, in fact, arrested amounts to a complete disregard for the most basic principles of law.'

'The Tribunal has come to the conclusion that nobody is sure why and for what offence Mr. Peoples was arrested,' the chairman decided. 'His arrest can be seen as a crude attempt on the part of the investigation team to put pressure on the chief suspects. This is a clear abuse of the power of arrest.' The chairman went on to describe the fact that Michael's attempt to identify a blackmailer who accused him of a murder he did not commit was used as a reason to arrest him as 'absurd'.

'What is apparent, however, is that there were a series of theories floating about the incident room as to the supposed involvement of Mr Peoples in the death of the Late Mr. Barron,' the chairman wrote. 'The Tribunal cannot but feel that some individual, or group of individuals in the incident room were manipulating this situation.'

Chapter 11

I Was Left With Nothing

On the way to the station, Mark McConnell learned over the car radio that Michael and Charlotte Peoples had also been arrested, but not much else. His memories of being processed by Garda Martin Leonard at the station were vague. He remembered being brought in to the station, and little more. Beginning at 9.20 a.m., Mark was interviewed by Detective Sergeant Jim Leheny and Detective Garda Mick O'Malley. 'I was very nervous and afraid and very apprehensive about the whole thing but apart from that there was nothing really said until such time as I got into the interview,' he recalled. The Garda notes record a straightforward interview in which Mark gave an account of his movements the night Richie Barron died. Mark's memory was somewhat different.

'I remember it being very abusive,' he told the Morris tribunal. 'I thought with O'Malley coming into the room at least it was a face that I knew and it would have helped a bit maybe during this interrogation. But he came into the room and went completely ballistic, O'Malley. Shouting and roaring, calling me a fat murdering bastard. It was just abuse from the start of the interview until the end. From the get go they were very abusive. Especially O'Malley.

'As far as I can remember I was brought upstairs, somewhere on a long corridor into a room. I can't remember was I took in by O'Malley and Leheny or was I took in by somebody else or who came in when. But as soon as the interview started he was a Jekyll and Hyde kind of a character, just went completely berserk.

'They were pushing me from one to the other and telling me to come clean, that an innocent man had been murdered and kept going over the same thing, same thing, how they had all these witnesses that could place us at the scene and people had seen us coming down through the car park, very reliable witnesses and just in general just abusive during the whole period.'

Mark described a see-saw interview, with periods of abuse followed by calmer interludes where the detectives would sit down and ask questions. Each time he recounted his story, he was called a liar. 'Anything I told them they accused me of lying. They went over my movements going up the town, into the café, up into the Parting Glass. Telling me that I had met Young Frank by arrangement, they seemed to think. They seemed to think that there was some kind of phone contact between myself and Frank Junior. They just didn't believe anything I said.

'They kept going on about this great witness they had that had seen me and Frank Junior coming down the car park. I says, that's complete and utter lies. They said this person is sure because they heard the town clock chime one o'clock while yous were coming down through the car park. I says, whoever he is, he's a complete Walter Mitty character, it definitely didn't happen because I wasn't up in the car park that night. They said no he's a very credible witness and we stand by him.'

Just over an hour into the interview the word came that Mark's solicitor James O'Donnell was in the station. The detectives left the room. The interrogation was 'hard going', Mark told O'Donnell . 'Stick to your story,' the solicitor advised him.

In a memorandum he recorded that day, James O'Donnell wrote that Mark told him 'he was being questioned by Garda Mick O'Malley. The client told me that the questioning Guard had said that his statement was a pack of lies. He said that he had been seen by the Guards going with Frank McBrearty up a road to murder Richard Barron. They said that they had witnesses who had made a statement on Wednesday or Thursday after the murder.'

Mark told the solicitor he'd told the Guards he had made a phone call to the hospital from Eunan and Katrina Brolly's home asking about Richie Barron. He said the Guards had taken his house and car keys, and told him that Old Frank McBrearty was harassing witnesses and putting people under pressure to change their statements. They'd told him he 'went up the road with young Frank McBrearty Junior and bludgeoned Richard Barron with an iron bar'.

The solicitor told Mark not to say anything other than what he had already said in his statement, and to contact him again if the Gardaí told him he had to make a statement, or asked for blood samples.

The meeting lasted forty minutes until 11.10 a.m., when Leheny and O'Malley resumed. The interview continued until 11.35 a.m., when the Gardaí say they read over the notes they had taken to Mark, who refused to sign them on his solicitor's advice.

Meanwhile, James O'Donnell asked the member in charge, Garda Martin Leonard, for copies of Mark's interview notes, a copy of the statement he made the week Richie Barron died, and a copy of the custody record. The requests were refused.

Mark McConnell took issue with the interview notes the Gardaí said they took. 'It's far more aggressive than that portrays,' he told the tribunal. 'I can't even remember anybody writing on a sheet of paper.'

———

After processing, Young Frank McBrearty was taken to Letterkenny Garda Station Room 225, the 'Bunker', at 9.40 a.m. According to the interview notes handed in afterwards by Detective Sergeant Eamonn O'Grady and Detective Sergeant Gerry McGrath, when he was asked if he understood the formal caution that anything he said could be taken down and used in evidence against him, Frank said 'Yes, this is a load of shite lads, I am an innocent man.' The mixture of vulgarity and protestation of innocence set the tone for much of the rest of the day. At the Morris tribunal, Frank said he would not use the word 'lads', as it was 'Dublin slang'. Differences of opinion between Frank and the Gardaí over what was said would also become a recurrent theme.

'They first of all introduced themselves,' Young Frank recalled. '[They] told me about Veronica Guerin, that they were the people who was investigating the Veronica Guerin murder, that they weren't cowboys, like the Donegal Gardaí were.'

Frank said he got into 'heated confrontations' with O'Grady. The detective told him he too had been a boxer, and Frank said to him 'you couldn't have been much good with the shape of your face'.

The interview was interrupted at 10.20 a.m., when Frank's solicitor James Sweeney arrived. Frank complained to him about being arrested in front of his children, and asked the solicitor to make sure his wife was okay.

In his case notes, Sweeney wrote that Frank was 'upset and emotional at the time. He said that he was arrested in front of his children while taking them to school. The police car pulled in front of him as he was leaving the housing estate in which he lives. He was adamant he was innocent and [they were] trying to pin the murder of Richie Barron on him.' Frank was extremely concerned about his children, and Sweeney told him he'd check they were okay. After the solicitor left, Frank was given tea and toast.

Frank was asked if his father was interfering with witnesses, and the Guards again put their theory to him, that he and Mark were upset when Richie insulted the McBreartys, and they had a witness who saw him in the car park. 'I am an innocent man,' Frank protested.

The Gardaí read over their notes to Frank at the end of the interview, and he refused to sign them. Frank told the tribunal no notes were read to him, and he didn't remember anyone writing, although it could have happened and he didn't notice. He agreed the topics covered in the first series of notes were discussed, but said the notes presented were sanitised, free of the abuse and vulgar language used in the room. The tribunal's conclusion was that he was 'in a particularly volatile and aggressive humour', and the two detectives would have spent a considerable amount of time trying to calm him down, with much of the abuse and vulgar language coming from Frank himself.

Just after midday, at 12.04 p.m., Detective Inspector Gerard McGrath and Detective Inspector Eamonn O'Grady left the room, and were replaced by Detective Sergeant John Melody and Detective Garda John Fitzpatrick.

The first interviewers to question Charlotte Peoples were Detective Sergeant Sylvie Henry and Garda Debra (Debbie) Kyne. The questioning began at 9.30 a.m. as soon as Charlotte was processed by Garda Martin Leonard.

'I found it okay,' Charlotte told the Morris tribunal. Sergeant Henry knew she had been unwell with pleurisy, and told her he would make arrangements so that she wouldn't be put in the cells, she would be allowed to rest in the interview room. Charlotte's mother, Catherine 'Dolly' Eaton, knew she was unwell, and went to the Garda station to see her daughter. When she got there, she was refused access by the custody officer, Garda Martin Leonard, but she handed in the medication her daughter needed. Garda Willie Cannon delivered the medication to Charlotte at 11.20 a.m. Leonard's entry in the custody record says Charlotte told him about her medicine, and he despatched Sergeant Joe Hannigan to Raphoe to collect it. Dolly remembered that when she arrived at the station with the antibiotics, Martin Leonard told her that Hannigan had been sent to get the medicines.

Around the same time, according to the custody record, Garda Leonard told Charlotte there was a solicitor in the station, and asked if she wanted to see him. She declined. Charlotte had no memory of the conversation. She explained to the tribunal that later in the afternoon, she was told there was a solicitor in the station if she wanted to see him, but by then she had been told that Ciaran Dillon would call to see her. She asked if the solicitor was Dillon, and when she was told it was someone else, she said she didn't need to see him. Charlotte said she didn't know Dillon was coming to see her until after she saw her mother in the mid-afternoon, and therefore couldn't have refused a solicitor in the morning. Possibly when James Sweeney and James O'Donnell arrived in the station to see Young Frank McBrearty and the McConnells, Garda Leonard asked Charlotte if she wanted to see them too, and she refused for the same reason she had earlier forty-five minutes earlier at 9.30 a.m. She figured since she hadn't done anything, she didn't need a lawyer.

Charlotte accepted that the interview notes recorded by Henry and Kyne were an accurate account of the questions and answers during the first interview. Henry began by cautioning Charlotte, then asked her if she knew Richie Barron.

'I always knew him to see but I got to know him better since my cousin Mark Quinn opened the pub from drinking there,' she replied.

'Did you see him often?'

'I could have seen him in there other nights.'

'Did you ever have any run in with him?'

'No, he gave me and Paula Eaton my sister and Rodney Boyle a lift to Strabane in his van one day.'

The questioning continued in the same vein. Charlotte told the detective she didn't really know the Barron family except to say hello to, and Henry moved on to the night Richie died. Charlotte explained how she left the Town & Country around 12.30 a.m. along with her husband Michael and Geoffrey Dolan, and went to the Parting Glass. There she met her sister Paula and Rodney Bogle. Her cousin Edel was there with her boyfriend too, and later Roisin arrived. When they asked about the row with Richie Barron, she told Henry she saw 'a bit of a scuffle but it was over very quickly'.

'Do you know about the tapes?' Charlotte asked Henry. 'About two weeks ago a man called on the phone and said he had seen my husband kill Richie Barron and seen me come out of the Parting Glass with my husband and I was crying, which I wasn't.'

'Did you recognise the voice?' Henry asked.

'No I didn't, he looked for money, I think £6,000.'

'How did you feel hearing this?'

'How do you think, I was devastated. I answered the phone, he asked to speak to my husband Michael, I didn't recognise his voice.'

'How did you know what was said?'

'I could hear my husband on the phone and the caller mentioned that he had seen my husband Michael kill Richie Barron.'

'What did your husband say?'

'Michael said to him to call the Guards and tell them all he knows. The caller said he couldn't because he was in a robbery that night and his prints were all over ... He said to Michael to meet him at the White Cross at 11 o'clock that night, it was a Saturday night. Michael said, sure that will do and hung up.'

'Do you know who it was?'

'I don't know who it was.'

'What happened then?'

'I went on the phone and asked him why are you doing this to us, and he said "call in all the Guards if you want".'

'Did ye go to the White Cross?'

'We rang the Guards and Pat Flynn came out and said four others got calls as well.'

'Was that the last you heard?'

'He rang back again before 11 p.m., Michael answered the phone this time.'

'What time was it?'

'Phil Collins has the times.'

'Was he still on for the meeting?'

'He said he wanted £2,000 now. Michael said would he take £500, and he said I'm not a hard man to bargain with.'

'Did your husband go to the White Cross?'

'Michael went to the White Cross but nobody came.'

As she explained the story of the blackmail calls to Henry, Charlotte did not know that the calls were cited as part of the reason to arrest her husband. Henry moved the topic back to the night Barron died, asking how she heard the news about Richie Barron. She told him she heard about it as she was leaving the nightclub. She went outside and told Geoffrey Dolan, and they drove after Michael, who was walking down the street. Charlotte told Michael the news about Richie, and they decided to go up the road to the scene, unsure if it were true or just a rumour. There were a few people at the scene, but the Gardaí hadn't arrived yet. They turned and went home.

'Did anybody make a phone call from your house?' Henry asked.

Charlotte knew her mother had phoned Letterkenny hospital to ask about Richie. But she was under arrest, and she knew her husband had been picked up too. She didn't want anyone else arrested, least of all her mother.

'Nobody made calls from our house,' she told the sergeant.

'I was afraid they were going to arrest Mammy and bring her in, that's the only reason,' she explained at the Morris tribunal. 'Because I knew it was Mammy who had made the phone calls, so I was afraid, that's the only reason I lied about it.'

At 11.07 a.m., Detective Sergeant Henry and Garda Kyne left the interview room, and Detective Garda Mick Carroll and Detective Garda Michael Jennings took over. Before the changeover, Detective Sergeant Henry forgot to read over the interview notes to Charlotte or ask her to sign them.

Carroll and Jennings began their questioning of Charlotte Peoples by repeating the standard caution. Again they went over Charlotte's movements the night Richie Barron died. Again, she told the detectives she made no phone call, the only phone call that night came from Rodney Bogle, who phoned their house pretending to be a drunk looking for a taxi to America, a drunken prank. A few minutes later, Charlotte rang Rodney back, keeping the joke going, and told him his taxi was waiting outside. Rodney laughed, and came over to the Peoples' house for a chat with Charlotte and Dolly.

'Were there subsequent phone calls made to your house about this matter?' the detectives asked.

'There was,' Charlotte answered.

'Who made them?' they asked.

'I don't know, but I would love to,' she replied. Once again, she told the story of the anonymous phone caller who accused her husband of murder and demanded money, how Michael contacted the Guards immediately and tried to find out who the caller was by going to the White Cross Inn.

'Do you know of any reason why anybody would ring your house looking for money from you in relation to Richie Barron's death?' the detectives asked.

'No. We want to know why he picked on us,' Charlotte told them. 'That is why we called the Guards in. We want to keep on the right side of the law. Whoever done this to us even if he is a next door neighbour, I want to see him taken up for this.'

At one stage during the morning, Charlotte heard someone shouting 'Is there any toilets in here?' She recognised the voice—Young Frank McBrearty.

'Where's the toilets in here? And I'm an innocent effing man and there is no justice in this,' she recalled. 'I remember hearing that at one time.' Young Frank's voice was the only one Charlotte heard, she didn't hear any detectives shouting.

At 12.50 p.m., Michael Jennings read over the interview notes to Charlotte. She agreed they were correct and signed them. Because of her recent illness, Charlotte wasn't taken to the cells during the lunchtime break. Leonard had ordered a dinner for her, but she wasn't hungry, so he gave her a cup of tea in the interview room.

In Lifford Garda station, after he was served breakfast, Michael Peoples was visited by his mother, Bridget, and brother, Liam. Michael wrote out an order for supplies from the bakery for the following morning's bread run. Custody officer Garda Bosco Gallagher read over the note before giving it to Liam. Bridget and Liam left at 10.51 a.m. 'I didn't feel under any pressure at that time,' Michael said. 'I didn't eat my breakfast, just the shock of the thing. I didn't realise what was involved, didn't know what was ahead of me that day, put it that way.'

Michael was sure it was all just a horrible mistake. Somewhere the Guards had got their wires crossed, his report of the anonymous black-mail attempt had been taken up wrong. All he had to do was explain what happened, and everything would be cleared up. It helped that Detective

Garda Pat Flynn was one of his first interviewers. Flynn had called out to his home the night of the extortion calls. He knew the score. Flynn had said to him as they went to the interview room, 'Look Michael, I don't even know why you're here. I don't believe you had anything to do with this.' He'd get this mess sorted out soon enough. The first interview, with Flynn and Garda Thomas Burke, was relaxed, and Michael had been confident the confusion would be sorted out until Flynn told him about the other arrests. Michael realised he might not be free quite so soon after all, and asked for a solicitor. After Flynn and Burke, he was served breakfast, and then got a phone call from his solicitor Ciaran Dillon and shortly afterwards, a visit from his mother and brother. He found out that Charlotte was among those arrested. He told his mother to make sure she got to see Ciaran Dillon too.

The second interview began at 11.23 a.m. Michael Peoples was questioned by Detective Sergeant Mick Keane and Garda Phil Collins. 'That interview, that was a horse of a different colour,' Michael remembered. 'That's when it changed.'

'They started the interview and the first thing I remember, they asked me a question, I don't know what the question was, I just remember "You're a lying murdering bastard". [Keane] shouted that at me.

'He asked me several questions and every time I answered the question, I don't remember the questions, I don't remember the answers, but I remember being called a lying murdering bastard. That was his volume for the day, more or less anything I said he didn't like it, you're a lying murdering bastard. To be quite honest I was sitting terrified, I'm just being truthful about it. It was a hateful, hateful situation to be in.

'I didn't know what was coming next . . . There was no threat at this stage of physical violence but I was waiting on it to happen. That was the atmosphere that was created. I was waiting that day to get it. By a pack of thugs. That's my opinion of them. Thugs.'

Michael was never struck during his arrest, but the fear was there, the awareness that it could happen at any time. And if it did, who could he complain to? In theory, he had the right to complain to the custody officer, Garda Bosco Gallagher, who was charged with protecting his rights, but as he explained afterwards: 'Garda Gallagher, he's not independent, he's not an observer to watch it, he's a Guard. I'm in a Garda station. Being intimidated by Guards. So the complaint is going to go as far as the front door, it's going to stop.'

During the second interview, Michael was not allowed to smoke. Garda Collins blew smoke in his face. His own cigarettes were in front of him but when he reached for them, Mick Keane said 'don't you touch them'. When Michael pointed out that Collins was smoking, Keane said 'I'm in charge here, you're not polluting my air.'

The later interviews blend together in Michael's memory. He remembers being told he didn't murder Richie Barron, but he 'helped a few boys do it', and that he'd 'brought them down to the house where I washed their clothes in my washing machine'. He was asked if he'd been given a £500 bribe by Old Frank McBrearty.

Michael told the tribunal the Guards knew he was innocent when they arrested him. They had used the extortion phone calls as a reason to arrest him. Why, he asked, would he go to the bother of reporting the calls, making a tape of the caller to give to the Guards, and making a statement about the affair the next day, if he had anything to hide.

'It's a joke, they knew before they arrested me,' he told the tribunal chairman. 'They knew I should never have been arrested. They didn't arrest Geoffrey Dolan who was with me the whole night. Wasn't arrested. It wasn't accidental or nothing else. It was pre-planned, premeditated. They knew I shouldn't have been arrested. It was just abuse. If I did to that man down there now, if I did what he did to me, if I tricked him into getting into a car and held him for twelve hours and terrorised him I would still be in jail. He can do it to me. He's still getting paid. He's only a thug.'

The second interview finished at 2 p.m. Michael was taken to the cells and given lunch. He then got to see his solicitor, Ciaran Dillon. The solicitor told Michael that Charlotte was under arrest too, that he'd tried to see her in Letterkenny but she declined to see him.

The solicitor told Michael 'they'll probably get abusive and they'll probably get rough. Just don't let them get to you, don't let them intimidate you.' Dillon's words were no comfort to Michael.

Michael Peoples' third interview, again with Detective Garda Pat Flynn and Detective Garda Thomas Burke, began at 3.23 p.m. 'That was more or less a continuation of the same, from the first one. There was nothing out of the ordinary or no abuse. They'd ask the question and I would answer it,' he recalled. Michael told the detectives that the call from his home to Letterkenny hospital the night Richie Barron died was probably made by his mother-in-law. The interview ended at 6 p.m.

Scenes of crime officer Garda Niall Coady had travelled from Letterkenny to Lifford, where he took fingerprints and palmprints from Michael Peoples at 6 p.m. Garda Michael Murphy took Michael's photograph. At 6.15 p.m., Detective Sergeant Michael Keane and Garda Phil Collins entered the room again.

'[T]here was a lot of shouting and roaring going on and it was really hyped up and at one stage I says I don't know nothing and thumped the table, or banged the table,' Michael recalled.

'And he says don't you thump the table or I'll thump you, and the conversation came around then to this poor man Richie Barron, look what happened to him, and with this he was going to show me the autopsy photographs, he says to Phil Collins, get the autopsy photographs. I says I don't care, it doesn't bother me. I wouldn't be squeamish or nothing like that. And he says, you're a heartless bastard. Phil Collins left the room to get the photographs. There was only me and him was in the room. He walked away from the table. He walked over to the left-hand corner of the room. There was a broken leg of a chair, a steel leg of a chair, it was about I suppose two foot long. He was kind of bent over and he had this in his hand and he was looking back at me like this and he was hitting it into his hand.'

'He didn't speak, he didn't do nothing. I was just sitting there, at this stage I thought he is going to hit me with that, and I am going to make a run for the door, and Collins is outside the door. They created that atmosphere for that to happen. Collins came back into the room and sat down and he didn't bring no photographs with him then. I thought now, he went [into] the corridor and I thought I'm going to get it here now, I was wondering what to do. At that stage I thought I was going to be assaulted and I would have defended myself, I would have had to. It's just a natural reaction. It was fear. I was terrified.'

In fact, Collins did have the autopsy photographs in his pocket, he later admitted to a tribunal investigator, but had a qualm of conscience about showing them to Michael. However, the judge wasn't convinced that Keane had intended to threaten Michael if he picked up a chair leg, believing that there were 'many circumstances in which this incident could have occurred which could be innocently explained and accounted for'.

Michael was told he would be charged with murder at a special court sitting in Donegal, that he wouldn't see the light of day for fifteen years, and his wife Charlotte would get seven years, leaving his child without parents. He was told Charlotte had confessed.

Finally, the clock ran out. Keane looked at his watch. Michael remembered the detective sergeant looked up at him and said 'Out of here to fuck.' Michael was taken downstairs, his property and money were returned. He was released at 7.53 p.m. 'Mick Keane followed me out the door,' he remembered. 'I'm not sure if I signed the release or not. But he walked me out to the door and I thought I was going to be arrested again. He put his hand on my shoulder as I was opening the door and he just says Michael, and I was just waiting for the whole thing to start again. He leaned over to me and he says to me if there is anything I can ever do for you just give me a shout.'

'I felt like turning around and busting his mouth and that's the truth. He left me shaking.'

Michael Peoples was free to go, but the effects of the arrest would be long-lasting. His business suffered. No one wanted to buy bread from a murder suspect. 'I gave up my bread run,' he said later. 'Business did go down, because people thought I was involved, sales did go down. I was living on £118 a week, my mortgage was £80 a week, I had no arse in my trousers and that's the God's honest truth. Only for my mother and father, and Charlotte's mother and father, I would have been out on my ear. I had nothing. I was left with nothing. It was lethal.'

––––

Roisin's first interview in Letterkenny Garda station went smoothly. 'They just more or less asked me about my whereabouts that night and I told them everything,' she recalled.

Roisin made one mistake going over the events the night Richie Barron died. She thought Mark was delayed going into the nightclub because he stopped to speak to Daniel Lynch. In fact he spoke to Geoffrey Dolan. She also told the detectives that while she was in Sarah's Café, she spoke to Wilma Barnett. The two detectives exchanged a look at the information. Roisin told them that Wilma was married and lived in Castlederg, and her mother had built a new home outside Raphoe.

During the interview, Roisin's solicitor arrived at the station, and the interview was suspended. After speaking with Roisin, the solicitor asked for copies of Roisin's original statement, her custody record, and interview notes taken by the Gardaí. 'Sergeant White said he had no problem giving him the two statements,' Roisin remembered.

While Roisin spoke with her solicitor, White left the room to get authority to hand over the statements. At 11.50 a.m., White returned and told the solicitor he couldn't have the copies. Detective Garda John Dooley and White asked a few more questions, and at the end of the interview, Roisin agreed the notes were correct, but declined to sign on her solicitor's advice.

Nobody could tell Roisin what happened to Dean. She asked the detectives who was minding the toddler, and asked her solicitor to find out if everything was all right.

According to the custody record, Detective Garda Padraig Scanlon and Garda John Harkin took over from White and Dooley around midday, and were joined about thirty minutes later by Garda Gina Lohan. Roisin could only remember interviews with White and Dooley until lunchtime 'because whenever they came in after dinner time, I thought I was glad to see three different people coming in rather than White and Dooley being in with me, and I thought it strange all morning that a bangharda wasn't with me.'

Harkin told the tribunal he took notes of the questions asked by Scanlon, and read them over to Roisin, but she again declined to sign them on her solicitor's advice. The interview finished at 12.45 p.m., and she was brought lunch.

———

While Michael Peoples was upstairs in Lifford, Edel Quinn was downstairs in what the Gardaí called 'the medical room'. Edel had refused a solicitor, because like Michael, she didn't think it would be long before the Gardaí realised their mistake and released her, a couple of hours at best. Edel had arrived at the station just before 9 a.m. Custody officer Bosco Gallagher took down her details and told her what her rights were, but she didn't really take in what he was saying. At 9 a.m. she was taken to an interview room by Detective Sergeant Des Sheridan and Garda Pauline Golden.

'They were insisting that I said that Mark was crying, that he was crying in the disco. And I told them that I hadn't said it,' Edel recalled. 'They told me that I had said it to him, the two of them were insisting that I said it in the interview. I said well if I did I didn't mean to say it. I think it was that interview that [Garda] Pauline Golden had told me I was going to Mountjoy for fourteen years.

'They wanted to know the truth and I didn't know nothing. So she obviously felt that I was hiding something and that, more or less, that if I told them that I probably wouldn't do the fourteen years.'

The questions revolved around Mark McConnell. What time had he arrived at the nightclub? Edel told the detectives he arrived around 1.30 a.m. The answer didn't fit with the Garda theory, and they pressed her on it. 'They wanted him in before one o'clock but it was just constantly more or less the time.'

Edel thought the first interview with Detective Garda Des Sheridan and Garda Pauline Golden 'was grand. Sheridan asked the questions and he wrote them down . . . And then when he finished he asked me to sign them and I signed them . . . That was calm enough.' The interview ran from 9 a.m. until just after 11 a.m., when Sheridan and Golden were replaced by Detective Garda Michael O'Grady and Detective Garda Brendan Regan. One or more combinations of these four Gardaí would interview Edel throughout the day. The interviews blurred into one another. A decade later at the Morris tribunal, she could remember the things that were said to her, but not always who said what.

After a time, Edel began to believe the Gardaí knew that she knew nothing. They couldn't look her in the eye. 'Every time I stared at one of them, they would have to look away and then eventually one of them said to me at the end of it that I seemed to do this kind of thing before, that it wasn't the first time I seemed to be in a station and was interrogated. But I don't know which one of them said it,' she recalled. 'Maybe they thought I was cheeky, I don't know.

'They asked me about my father, what age he was when he died and about me being in confessions, when was the last time I was at confessions, and did I go to the funeral, and did I go to the wake, which I hadn't and I hadn't been in confessions. I took it that they must have thought I went and confessed, got it all off my chest to the priest in confessions, but I hadn't been in confessions either.

'The way I took it was that they must have thought that whatever guilt that I had I passed it on to the priest, that I felt grand then leaving the confessional box.'

At the tribunal, Edel also remembered being told by Gardaí that Roisin had confessed in Letterkenny. 'She must be lying, because I didn't know,' she told the detectives. When she got to speak to her solicitor after lunch, his note was that the Guards told her Charlotte had confessed.

Edel remembered being told that the Gardaí had been following her for weeks before the arrest, 'and that there was a room full of photographs of me in Lifford station'. The detectives were able to tell her which bedroom in her mother's home she slept in, and that she had a television in the bedroom. One of the detectives decided to explain to Edel what accessory to murder meant. He told her she was the same as the man who drove the motorbike when Veronica Guerin was shot.

At midday, Edel got a visit from her sister, Katrina Brolly. 'Katrina got in to see me and she was very nervous. She just asked me what was going on and I had said to her, oh they think that I know who murdered Richie Barron . . . She got in for about ten minutes and it was then that I found out that my cousin Charlotte and her husband and Frank McBrearty was arrested. I thought it was just me and Roisin and Mark at that stage. Then she told me about the other three and I just thought, this is crazy. She got in for about ten minutes and she left again then.'

Edel had not asked for a solicitor when she was first arrested. It is likely that it was the news that there were six arrests that made her worried enough to ask for one. After Edel left, Regan and O'Grady questioned her again until 1 p.m., when she was brought to the cells. Meanwhile, Ciaran Dillon contacted the station, and told custody officer Bosco Gallagher he would call down to see Edel.

At 2 p.m., Edel was brought back to the 'medical room'. Shortly afterwards, she was told her arrest had been extended for another six hours. 'When they just said about the extension of six hours, I didn't know then that when they got to there they could get another extension or what was going to happen. I didn't know if I was ever going to get out of there.'

Shortly afterwards, Edel was told her solicitor had arrived, and she got to see Ciaran Dillon. The lawyer asked Edel if she had eaten, and advised her to eat at every opportunity she got. It would be a long day, and meals would give her a break from the questioning. He told her he believed she was innocent, and advised her not to sign anything. His notes recorded that the Gardaí told Edel she was 'as good as a murder[er] because what I know of the murder' and kept calling her a liar, and that she was told Mark McConnell had changed his clothes in Quinn's Town & Country pub afterwards, and that 'Charlotte Peoples has let go and told them. Charlotte is a mental case. She has let go.' (At the tribunal, Edel thought it was Roisin she was told had 'let go'). Edel told Dillon her arrest was 'like a nightmare'.

At 2.50 p.m. Dillon left, and Edel was questioned again by Sheridan and Golden. She got another break at 5.30 p.m., when she was brought to the cells and given a meal of chicken and chips and orange juice to drink. After she had eaten, Edel was photographed and fingerprinted. At 6.30 p.m., O'Grady and Regan questioned her again.

Shortly after 7 p.m., Edel's mother, Mrs Anna Quinn, arrived and was allowed to see her. 'She had come back from Letterkenny,' Edel recalled. 'She was down seeing Roisin and she got in to see me and was just asking how I was and all and I just said I was grand and that I was just cold, my feet had been cold all day and I just said to her have you a fire on . . . I just wanted to stay calm for her sake.'

Anna Quinn's visit was brief, a little over ten minutes. After she left, O'Grady entered the 'medical room' again. 'Your mother seems to believe you,' he said. Edel said nothing. 'But then again my mother would too,' O'Grady added.

Probably the most bizarre incident of Edel's arrest came during her final interview with O'Grady and Regan before her release. As Edel insisted yet again that she knew nothing, Regan asked her if she was willing to swear on a bible that she was telling the truth. When Edel said she was, Regan produced a book. Edel put her right hand on it and swore she knew nothing about what happened to Richie Barron.

'Then he turned it around and it was a Garda Síochána book . . . I just kind of shook my head, I put my eyes to the ceiling and he told me that I looked relieved to find out it was a Garda Síochána book, that it wasn't a Bible.' Edel remembered the 'dictionary size' book had a yellow cover and a Garda Síochána badge on the front.

Edel was released at 8.22 p.m. Anna Quinn was not long home when her daughter arrived. 'She came home and she came in and she started to—she just went to bits,' Mrs Quinn remembered. 'She started to cry and she just went—she just went completely to bits, you know . . . She was innocent and how could it happen, that the Guards could do that, you know . . . She wouldn't lie in the room that she usually lay in . . . I lay in a back room and I had to swap the room with her, give her the room that I had and let me lie in the back room . . . She wouldn't lie in it any more, she thought they were watching her. She stayed up the stairs then most of the time. She had to go then to see a psychiatrist. Then with Roisin and everything, she just took over worrying more about Roisin than she worried about herself.'

Edel later told the tribunal: 'Just the way it is, with all this happening and Roisin having the nervous breakdown, an awful lot of what happened to me was put aside because she was so badly affected that what happened to me was really nothing compared to the way she was. So as time went on then, it was just my life just revolved around this . . . I want to get on with my life . . . I put an awful lot behind me because I wasn't getting on with my life. Every time I met a Guard I was in fear. So it was either get on, forget about it, get on with your life or stay with it and be bitter. So that's why there's an awful lot that I can't remember, who and what.'

Edel was released from Garda custody in Lifford around the same time Roisin was released in Letterkenny. Katrina had gone to collect her sister in Letterkenny, and shortly after, Edel and her mother got word that Katrina had been arrested. Edel and Mrs Quinn went to Katrina's home to look after her children and allow Eunan Brolly go to Letterkenny to see his wife.

'The whole night I never slept and all I kept thinking about was they said to me about going to my work, about going back to my work would I not be ashamed. So the main thing in my mind was I was going to work that morning,' Edel told the tribunal.

'I had done nothing wrong and I was innocent. Where I worked there was about 700 people worked there. I walked in and some people spoke, some people couldn't look. Like I say I don't know if half of it was through embarrassment, that they didn't know what to say to me or half of them believed it. I was in for half a day. I took a pain in my chest and had to leave, it was just exhaustion. So then afterwards I was out one night and I was in a bar, I kind of tried to stay away from Raphoe and I went to Ballybofey and I was walking from the toilets and there was a group of people and I got a punch in the stomach as I was walking past and I stopped to look and there was a gang of them so I walked on. And then there was another night I went to the toilet and I was followed into the toilet by a group of women and they were saying about Raphoe, if you went into Raphoe you wouldn't get out of it alive, if you went to Raphoe for a drink . . . and I had to come out of the toilet. I couldn't wash my hands because they were waiting on me to hit me. So that was kind of what was happening to us.'

In May 1997, Edel went to see Ciaran Dillon again, to ask advice about what had happened to her. 'The only thing I remember about going to

Ciaran Dillon is saying to him about a civil action and he told me not to do it, because I wouldn't have the living of a dog if I did because the Guards would harass me. And I left then with that there, with him giving me that advice I left. I says okay, I wasn't taking a case against them.'

Shortly before she gave her evidence to the Morris tribunal in 2006, Edel moved to Dublin. 'Just with Raphoe being the way it was, there was a lot of hatred in Raphoe,' she explained. 'The Barrons had been told their father was murdered, they had a lot of rage, then you had our side that were being blamed for it. So if you went into a bar, you always met somebody from the Barrons or their friends or whatever, so there was always staring. I used to try and always drink outside Raphoe and then at the end, I just wanted to get away from Raphoe. I was made redundant in my job, so it was my best opportunity to get out of Raphoe and come to Dublin.

'As for the Guards, the way we were brought up, they were there to protect us and, at the end of the day, they done the harm to us. But we ended up having to spend a Christmas with Roisin in a psychiatric unit over what they done. Her baby was a year and nine months and we had to sit and play with him in a psychiatric ward.'

Chapter 12

Rambo and the Pussy Cat

Charlotte Peoples knew her husband had been arrested. She was still at home that morning when the detectives came and told her they were taking Michael away. She knew Mark McConnell was in custody too, she'd seen him in the back of a Garda car as she was on the phone to her mother, and she'd heard that Frank McBrearty had been picked up. She learned that Roisin McConnell was under arrest almost by accident. The door to her interview room was opened, and down the hallway she heard a bangharda's voice ask 'Do you want a cup of tea, Roisin?' Garda Debbie Kyne was standing by Charlotte's door at the time. Charlotte asked if Roisin McConnell was in the room next door. 'I can't tell you that,' Kyne told her, but she nodded her head anyway, confirming that Roisin was next door.

After lunch, Charlotte Peoples was told that Superintendent John Fitzgerald had given his approval to have her fingerprinted and photographed. At 2.05 p.m., the interviews began again, first with Detective Sergeant Sylvie Henry and Garda Debbie Kyne. The interviews went as before. Henry left the room at the half hour mark, and was replaced by Detective Garda Michael Jennings. He was in the room less than fifteen minutes when he left again, to allow fingerprinting and photography. Garda Niall Coady took Charlotte's prints, while Garda Michael Murphy photographed her. As they worked, Garda Martin Leonard told her that Superintendent John Fitzgerald had extended her detention for six more hours.

At 3 p.m., Coady and Murphy left, and Jennings returned. He was there barely ten minutes when Charlotte was told her mother was in the station. At 3.15 p.m., Dolly got to see her daughter, supervised by Debbie Kyne.

'Sylvie Henry came in and he was actually chatting with Mammy in the interview room,' Charlotte remembered. Dolly told Charlotte that the solicitor Ciaran Dillon had been to see Michael in Lifford Garda station, and would call to see her later. At 3.45 p.m., Dolly left the station, and

Sylvie Henry and Debbie Kyne returned. They were in the room with
Charlotte until 5 p.m.

———

Mark remembered the second interview with Detective Garda Pat Tague
and Sergeant Pat Hennigan as 'fairly aggressive questioning, but no physi-
cial, nothing like the first interview'. After lunch, he was photographed
and fingerprinted, and told he would be held for another six hours. At
2.16 p.m., Detective Sergeant Jim Leheny and Detective Garda Mick
O'Malley returned, and his third interview of the day began. No Garda
notes survive from this interview.

One incident stood out for Mark. At one point, Detective Garda
O'Malley left the room, and he had a 'fairly cordial' conversation with
Detective Sergeant Jim Leheny. 'But as soon as O'Malley re-entered the
room Leheny started verbally abusing me, as if he had been since
O'Malley had left the room.

'We talked about a number of things. I think he talked in general—at
the time I was severely overweight and the conversation got up over that
and how he'd lost weight and stuff like this, it was just an ordinary
conversation. I can remember then when O'Malley re-entered the room
Leheny started to get—it was as if somebody had turned a switch on him,
and he started being abusive. The way I took it was he was trying to make
it look as if he had been involved in some hard questioning of me while
O'Malley had been out of the room.'

Mark remembered O'Malley as much more aggressive than Leheny. 'It
was nearly as if he had a personal friendship with Richie Barron the way
he was taking the whole thing,' he explained. 'I don't know if he had a
personal relationship with Richie Barron or even knew him but he
seemed to take it even more personal than most of the other Gardaí.'

At 2.45 p.m., Inspector John McGinley entered the room. At the same
time, Mark's solicitor James O'Donnell telephoned the station, having
been given a message that Mark wanted to speak to him. Mark spoke
briefly on the telephone to O'Donnell. The Guards wanted a blood
sample from him, and he wanted the solicitor's advice. O'Donnell told
Mark to give blood, but to ask for a split sample, and keep one sample
himself. While on the phone, Mark complained that he'd been pushed
around during his first interview, but that no one would tell him the
name of one of the Gardaí involved. O'Donnell, worried about what was
happening to his client, decided he would call down to the station.
Meanwhile, the doctor arrived and took a blood sample from Mark, who
was then questioned by Inspector John McGinley.

'He started to question me and as the questioning went on and as he didn't like the answers he also started to raise his voice,' Mark recalled.

'He was questioning me very aggressively and shouting and roaring, he was totally fixated also with Frank Senior . . . He had this theory in his head that Frank McBrearty had convened some kind of a meeting in the Parting Glass of all the people involved in the supposed murder of Richie Barron and that he had coached everybody on what to say and everybody was to keep their stories right and he more or less thought that Frank McBrearty was coordinating some kind of cover-up, which I told him was a load of lies.

'Things calmed down again for a minute and he sat down in his seat and started asking general questions about my movements. He told me that I was lying about leaving the Town and Country pub at 1.20 a.m. He says it was more like midnight, 12.20 a.m. He said he had witnesses that could prove it. He said that we have statements from two people who seen you in the café at 12.20 a.m.

'I said, they're either mistaken or they're lying. I says I don't believe that, because I took it that it was probably the people that worked in the café that he was on about, I says I don't believe you. I don't believe that these people could have made that mistake because I know what time I was in the café at.

'He said these are genuine, hundred percent statements. These people have no reason to lie. They're only ordinary working class people. He also went on about the Noel McBride statement. He didn't name Noel McBride and also the feature of all interviews was the ringing of the town clock at 1 a.m. as Noel McBride was in the car park. He then left the interview room for a period of time and came back in with two statements.

'He wouldn't tell me who they were, but I knew who they were. I knew the two statements that he was reading from was the people that worked in the café. He put the two statements down on the table and read them out.' Mark wasn't sure what to make of the statements at the time. He even thought McGinley might have made them up.

At 3.20 p.m., solicitor James O'Donnell arrived at the station and asked to see Mark. During their telephone conversation, Mark had mentioned that 'he was being abused by one particular member of the Gardaí', the solicitor recorded at the time, but when Mark asked Garda Willie Cannon for the name of the Garda, Cannon refused to tell him.

When O'Donnell arrived at the station, he spoke to the custody officer, Garda Martin Leonard, who in turn consulted Inspector McGinley. The inspector checked the custody record. Mark had seen the solicitor that morning and spoken to him several times on the phone, and McGinley decided he'd had more than reasonable access. He refused the visit. When Leonard told O'Donnell, the solicitor said he'd received a complaint,

wanted a doctor to see his client, and asked Leonard to record in the custody record that his client was abused. Leonard refused, and recorded
baldly in the custody record only that the solicitor 'made allegations'.

After the solicitor left, Leonard went to the interview room and asked
Mark if he was okay, and did he need a doctor. According to the custody
record, Mark 'made no complaint'. No one in the interview room bothered to ask the custody officer why he was asking such an extraordinary
question. 'I didn't even know the solicitor was looking to see me,' Mark
told the Morris tribunal.

According to the custody record, Inspector McGinley, Detective
Sergeant Leheny and Detective Garda O'Malley left the interview room at
3.55 p.m., when the doctor arrived to take Mark McConnell's split blood
sample. After he'd finished, McGinley, Leheny and O'Malley continued to
question Mark McConnell until 4.31 p.m. The notes McGinley took are
the only notes of the afternoon interview. No notes from Leheny and
O'Malley survive.

McGinley claimed that he handed in the notes he took to the incident
room within days at most, but an analysis of the numbering system used
by the investigation team showed that, as late as March 1998, the notes
were not in the system. There was 'a body of evidence that tends to suggest that the originals of the notes came into existence after the interview,'
Justice Morris wrote, though he went no further than that, save to find it
regrettable that it was 'a repeated feature of these detentions that when
notes became unavailable or lost there was no explanation required of the
person whose responsibility it was to make and preserve the notes'.

The chairman did not accept that Inspector McGinley handed the
notes in to the incident room in December 1996, and felt that the lack of
a satisfactory explanation for what happened 'cast suspicion on the
behavior of the interviewing Gardaí'. It would not be the last time that
McGinley faced controversy over interview notes at the tribunal.

McGinley's interview ended when Garda Niall Coady arrived. The
scenes of crime officer wanted the clothes Mark was wearing the night
Richie Barron died, as they might contain forensic evidence. As it happened, Mark was wearing the same clothes the day he was arrested. Mark
agreed to give Coady his clothes, and Coady arranged for replacement
clothing from the local Dunnes Stores. Leheny told the Morris tribunal
that because of the abrupt end to the interview, he didn't get a chance to
read over Mark McConnell's interview notes to him, and decided he
would leave it until later.

Roisin McConnell was given her lunch in the same room where she was interviewed. While she ate, her detention also was extended by Superintendent John Fitzgerald. She was half expecting the news, as her solicitor had told her it was likely to happen. Shortly after she was told, she was fingerprinted and photographed. The custody record shows Detective Sergeant John White and Detective Garda John Dooley re-entered the room at 2.25 p.m.

'That was the time that John White told me that my child would be taken off me and put into care,' Roisin recalled. 'I was going to jail for seven years and I probably would never see my son again and he said that Frank McBrearty Senior was sitting back laughing at us all. And he made me swear on my wain's life that Mark McConnell had nothing to do with the death of Richie Barron.

'I swore on my wain's life that Mark McConnell had nothing to do with it. And then he started then, he started to roar and shout, I was nothing but a dirty lying murdering bastard, that I would use my child in that way . . . It was the worst thing that he said to me.'

White also accused Roisin of having an affair with either Young Frank or Old Frank, and called her a slut and a whore. Although the notes taken by White and Dooley show Roisin was asked if anyone made a phone call after she arrived in the Brollys', Roisin said she was asked only about a telephone call from Mark Quinn's Town & Country pub to the Parting Glass nightclub (one Garda theory held that this call explained how Mark McConnell and Young Frank McBrearty decided to beat up Richie Barron), but no one asked her about the telephone calls she asked Mark to make from the Brollys' home to Letterkenny hospital, or any other calls.

'If they had asked me questions about the telephone calls I would have said Mark phoned the hospital and I would have told them I phoned Dolan's,' Roisin told the tribunal. 'They never mentioned any phone calls from Brollys' house at all . . . They just kept on about the phone call from Mark Quinn's pub to Frank McBrearty's, that it was Mark phoning young Frank Junior.' In fact, the phone call was between two women, making arrangements for babysitting that night, and took place before the encounter between Mark McConnell and Richie Barron.

Roisin said that the detectives told her she hadn't stayed with the Brollys at all that night, and neither had Mark. She had no memory of either detective taking notes during the interview. Dooley sat at the desk, while White strode about, animated. At 4.10 p.m., Garda Gina Lohan accompanied Roisin on a toilet break. The interview ended shortly after the pair returned, at 4.20 p.m. The custody record shows Garda Lohan sat with Roisin from 4.20 p.m. until 4.40 p.m. Roisin had no memory of the interlude, which ended when Garda John Harkin arrived to begin the next interview. She thought that Dooley and White left the interview room, and a few moments later the next interview started. Roisin did, however, remember a conversation with Lohan later on, after a visit from her mother.

In her statement, Garda Lohan said that 'Initially the prisoner's demeanour was calm but then altered in that she became tearful and suddenly emotional. While tearful she spoke of embarrassment of her being arrested and the difficulty she found in the situation of sitting in the Garda station as a prisoner. I did not caution Roisin McConnell while I supervised her nor did I interview her in any way concerning the matters for which she was arrested as this was not my function. I made attempts to pacify the prisoner by listening to her and asking if she required anything. At 4.40 p.m. Garda Harkin entered the interview room and began interviewing Roisin McConnell.'

In his note of the interview that followed, Harkin also wrote that Roisin was 'tearful' when he entered the room. Shortly after the interview began, Inspector John McGinley entered. According to the custody record, the officers in the room at that point were McGinley, Harkin and Lohan.

Harkin had asked a few questions, writing as he went, before McGinley arrived. Once the inspector came in, Harkin took a back seat, writing down the conversation between Roisin and McGinley. Roisin remembered that as McGinley described to her what the Gardaí thought happened, he called her husband 'a big fat pussy cat' and referred to Young Frank as 'Rambo'. Harkin's version is less colourful. The following is an excerpt from his interview notes:

'Roisin, what is the position here?' the inspector asked.

'They are saying that I left Quinn's pub with Mark earlier than I did,' Roisin replied.

'What time are you saying you left the pub at?'

'Not earlier than 1.15 a.m.'

'What about these people who saw you and your husband long before this?'

'They are mistaken. If they saw me, they saw me in Quinn's.'

'What sort of woman are you, are you a good woman?' McGinley asked.

'There are worse than me,' Roisin answered.

'Are you a religious woman?'

Roisin shrugged her shoulders and laughed.

'I would say you are a good person and I am going to tell you what happened that night and you tell me if I am telling a lie,' McGinley said. 'Your husband Mark McConnell had a row with Richie Barron in the pub. There were no blows struck but he insults the McBreartys and he insulted your husband. He did not like it. He left the pub with you and you ordered your food after walking over and meeting the McCullaghs. You went into Frankie's on your own. Mark met Frankie McBrearty and told him what happened. They decided to teach Richie Barron a lesson. They walked up through the car park and met Richie Barron staggering home as he always did. He got one wallop and that was it. As far as they were concerned, Richie was down—he got a wallop, he often did before—it was no big deal. They were not to know the man would die. They left him and went back down. Walked down in fact and went into the Parting Glass. Now tell me, did I tell you a lie?'

'Yes,' said Roisin. 'It's all lies.'

'Why?'

'Because I know it's a lie.'

'What do you mean, you know it's a lie?'

'Because he wouldn't have it in him.'

'What does that mean? What do you mean he wouldn't have it in him?'

'He could not do that, murder a man like that.'

Nine months later, Harkin's notes led to one of the more bizarre incidents in Donegal, apparently sparked after McGinley decided that he was 'embarrassed' at having asked Roisin about her religious beliefs at the beginning of the session. McGinley would ask Harkin to amend the notes, removing the embarrassing questions, and amending the beginning to the long question he asked, replacing 'I would say you are a good person and I am going to tell you what happened that night and you tell me if I am telling a lie' with 'I am going to put this scenario to you and you tell me if I am telling you a lie.'

McGinley planned to remove earlier versions of the questions from the Garda incident room, but the operation was botched, and conflicting versions of the notes, both handwritten and typed, remained in the system. Eventually, McGinley had to forge a set of notes himself, and claim they were contemporaneous, in order to explain the discrepancies in the Garda files. Strangely, despite all the subterfuge, McGinley left in place the substance of the long question, which Young Frank McBrearty and tribunal barristers later pointed out bore a striking resemblance to the confession the Dublin detectives interviewing Young Frank would produce later that night. McGinley's antics with the different versions of his notes meant he had to return to the tribunal after giving his evidence and apologise for perjuring himself, once Garda Harkin came forward and told the full story.

Justice Morris was unimpressed at the conspiracy to amend the notes in Garda files, altering the official record. To this end McGinley had sought the aid of Detective Garda Brian McEntee (later promoted to sergeant) who worked as a clerk in the border superintendent's office. Sergeant McEntee's evidence at the tribunal was 'deliberately evasive' and he 'knew more at that time than he is prepared to admit now,' Justice Morris concluded. McGinley was 'the prime mover behind a conspiracy that not only denied fair play to Roisin McConnell, but implicated two other Gardaí in wrongdoing. McGinley, the judge concluded, had abused his rank and deliberately perjured himself.

Disturbingly, the tribunal did not find it unlikely that original notes would be removed from the investigation files by Gardaí, and noted 'the frequency with which the tribunal's business has been hampered by the disappearance of original documentation and exhibits from Letterkenny station over the last number of years'. The entire conspiracy involving McGinley, Harkin and McEntee would have remained a mystery had Garda John Harkin not eventually come forward at the tribunal and told the truth.

Roisin remembered that at one point, she told McGinley she wasn't going to answer any more questions. 'Roisin, you're like an IRA woman, that's the way the IRA goes on here,' he told her. McGinley left the interview room at 6 p.m. Harkin wrapped up the interview fifteen minutes later. Roisin's mother, Anna Quinn, wanted to see her.

———

Between 4.35 p.m. and 6 p.m., Detective Sergeant Pat Hennigan and Detective Garda Pat Tague questioned Mark McConnell. 'It probably turned out to be one of the most severe interviews of the lot,' Mark told the tribunal.

'I remember Tague coming into the room, holding the same book that I had seen numerous times during the day and smiling, and he said to me, what do you think is in this? I says, I haven't got a clue. He then slapped the photos, well the book on the table and he then sat down and done a bit of an interview with me. He never mentioned the booklet for a time, just went over general issues and started to get a bit aggressive. I remember at one stage him digging at my shins underneath the table with his own foot.

'More or less he was calling me a murderer, said that I told nothing but lies during the whole day and that he was going to sort me out. And with that he got up and he reached for the book and again asked me what did I think was in the book, and I says I haven't a clue. He came towards me and opened the book and I could see the photographs of Richie Barron inside the book. I didn't want to look at them because I wouldn't be a great person looking at something like that, even at a wake or a funeral.

'I wouldn't particularly like looking at a corpse, but especially on this occasion because it was so graphic. I looked away from the pictures. He then reached for me by the ear and made me look at the photos. I still didn't look at them. He also grabbed for my hair. I eventually got sight of the photographs and he started saying, look what you done to Richie Barron, this is your work, this is you and Frank Junior's work, what's happened to this man. And as I say, the photographs were very graphic in detail.

'I can remember one of Richie Barron lying on a slab. As far as I can remember he might have been bare from the waist up, I'm trying to remember. I'm trying to put it out of my mind but I remember a blood-soaked pillow. I can remember a picture of his hand. I can remember a picture but the only way I can describe it that it was the inside of his brain. I can remember a date superimposed on one of the corners of the picture.

'I can also remember there was a picture of a car . . . They showed a car. I think there was two cars but I can remember one car in particular. It was a kind of sky blue or dark blue—I can't remember, it was blue in colour anyway, a Cavalier.

'I think, I'm not sure but there was some damage done to the car and I remember passing a comment, is that the car that knocked Richie Barron down, that knocked him down, and Tague took this as me taking the piss and started to get angry at me even passing the comment.'

In fact, the car had nothing to do with the Barron investigation. It had been found several miles away, and eliminated by Gardaí in the early days of the investigation, but the same roll of film was used to record it and the Barron post-mortem examination. That Mark was able to describe it—and the other photographs on the roll of film—so accurately convinced Justice Morris that he was telling the truth.

'There was very little questions or answers in that interview,' Mark recalled. 'It was more abuse more than anything. [Tague] was doing childish things like poking me in the eye and he was digging me in the sides on my ribs and stuff like this, tried to provoke me anyway. But as for interviewing during that interview, I can't recall any interviewing of any sort. There was a wee bit at the beginning but apart from that there was very little.'

At one point, Garda Martin Leonard, the custody officer, looked in and asked if everything was okay. Mark complained that he was being abused and shown pictures. Leonard asked the Guards if they saw the prisoner being abused. Both men answered no. Leonard turned back to Mark. 'What the fuck are you complaining about?' he asked.

'That was the end of it, there was not much point,' Mark explained. 'If the custody Guard who is there supposed to protect you, what is the point in making any more complaints as far as I was concerned. I was in a desperate situation at that time and I didn't know what way this interview was going to go. They had given me the impression the whole day that it was only a matter of time before I was going to be charged with the murder.'

_____

There was another 'changing of the Guard' with Charlotte Peoples at 5 p.m., when Detective Sergeant Sylvie Henry and Garda Debbie Kyne were replaced by Detective Garda Mick Carroll and Detective Garda Michael Jennings.

Carroll wanted to get to the bottom of the phone call from the Peoples to Letterkenny hospital, but Charlotte was denying there was any phone call. He had an idea. 'I pretended that I had made a phone call on my mobile phone,' he told the tribunal, 'and asked the person I pretended to call if they knew exactly what time, or what time they said exactly the phone calls were made to Letterkenny General Hospital.

'At that point Charlotte Peoples gave in that there was phone calls made to Letterkenny General Hospital from the house. Then later on in the evening I stepped outside the door of the interview room and stepped back in again, and I said to Charlotte Peoples that her husband Michael had admitted to having knowledge of the murder of Richard Barron, and her answer to that was that if he did, that she knew nothing about it. And I asked her did she think that her husband would set her up like this and her answer to that was in the negative. I can't remember what it was. But that's all it was about it. We moved on and we continued on with her memo of interview after that.'

The successful subterfuge, which led to Charlotte explaining how her mother phoned the hospital, is covered in the interview notes in a brief few lines.

'Q. Have you thought over the questions we asked you earlier, if there were any more phone calls made from your house?'

'A. I have. There was another phone call. That's the only lie I told.'

Charlotte went on to explain that she'd said nothing about the telephone call earlier in order to protect her mother. Enough people had been arrested already, she didn't want her mother to have to go through the same thing. 'She was just enquiring about Richie Barron. There was no harm in it,' she told the detectives.

Charlotte wasn't sure when the topic came up, but she also remembered being accused by Jennings and Carroll of having an affair. 'Jennings actually turned around and he says oh come on, he says, we all have skeletons in the cupboard', Charlotte recalled. At 6 p.m., the interview ended. She was allowed a rest, and brought a meal.

_____

Young Frank McBrearty began his evidence to the Morris tribunal covering his treatment in Garda custody on 9 October 2006, five days before the tenth anniversary of Richie Barron's death. The first day of evidence was fractious, with Frank accusing the tribunal of 'corruption' and 'cover-ups'. At the end of a long day, the tribunal adjourned his evidence until 23 October, when it planned to spend a week in Donegal to facilitate Old Frank, who was busy trying to get the nightclub back in shape after suffering flood damage. Young Frank's second session lasted three days, as he grew more and more heated, until he walked out rather than face cross-examination 'until the Minister for Justice gives me the same rights that he affords himself and the Garda Commissioner before this tribunal and the AGSI and the GRA'.

It was a risky strategy. Frank risked jail time and hefty fines if he was found in contempt, and unless he completed his evidence to the tribunal by accepting questions in cross-examination, no findings could be made against any of the Gardaí he alleged mistreated him. Without a case to answer, the Gardaí didn't even have to attend the tribunal. They were entitled to their good names, and if they were denied the right to confront their accuser, they didn't have a case to answer.

Young Frank relented and returned on 15 January 2007 to face cross-examination. The following day, he walked out again after a particularly heated exchange with Tom Murphy, the solicitor for the Garda Representative Association. Lawyers for most of the Gardaí involved had cross-examined him by then, but some did not get the opportunity, notably those representing John White, John O'Dowd and the Garda Commissioner.

Young Frank's evidence to the tribunal was at times confused and disjointed. He claimed he had difficulty pinning down times and events, but was adamant that he was mistreated physically and verbally from the moment of his arrest. He disputed many of the details in the custody record, and even questioned whether it was written on the day of his arrest. Among his more florid allegations was the theory that statements were rewritten by forgers so that signatures would match those on documents he denied signing while in custody.

Frank frequently boasted to the tribunal about his self-control in the face of the hostility he claimed he endured from his interrogators. 'God definitely was on my side that day,' he told the tribunal. 'It's a miracle to this day that I didn't hit Melody and Fitzpatrick. I don't know how I was able to keep my hands off them. I am being honest about it, it's a miracle. God definitely was inside me that day, because I'll tell you, what I felt like doing to them.'

Several times, Frank tried to leave the interview room. He claimed he was poked and kicked throughout the day, as the detectives tried to provoke him so they could charge him with an assault on a police officer, although he also claimed he pushed Detective Garda John Fitzpatrick 'over onto the table', but was not charged as a result.

Some time after 6 p.m. on 4 December 1996, Frank McBrearty was shown photographs of Richie Barron. The images had a lasting effect on him. His friend Marty McCallion later described how he had 'a bad colour' when he spoke about them. What else was said to Frank during that session, no one is certain. The tribunal felt that neither Frank nor the detectives involved had told the full story. What Justice Morris was able to conclude was that most of the allegations Frank made against various Gardaí he encountered during his arrest and throughout his period in detention were unfounded, and that he had made a number of wild allegations. Possibly, the aggression Frank claimed he endured from Gardaí was designed to bolster his claim that he never made a false confession, reinforcing the image of a man standing up in the face of intimidation in such a way that he could never have admitted to something he didn't do.

At one point, Frank told the tribunal, a Garda said 'Rambo went up the field and the big fat pussy cat followed him,' the same comment that Roisin McConnell attributed to Inspector John McGinley. When he was asked if he was certain of this, and it wasn't something he overheard from somebody else or read in the paperwork supplied by the tribunal, he said he was 'absolutely sure about it'.

Detective Garda John Fitzpatrick remembered that as he went in to begin his first interview, Sergeants McGrath and O'Grady told him that 'Frankie was an aggressive man, he was a volatile man. They said that he'd answer questions and he said that when they made the notes and they read them over to him, he said they were correct. But he said he refused to sign the notes.'

Fitzpatrick recounted how early in the first interview, Frank stood up out of his chair. 'I said, Frank, if you want to stand up we'll stand up as well, and John Melody stood up and I stood up and then we sat down.' Fitzpatrick said his focus during the interviews was 'keeping him nice and calm and keeping him on track, not clashing with him, not in any way aggravating the situation, just keeping him talking and agreeing with him'.

Detective Sergeant John Melody also said he was told Frank McBrearty was 'a very volatile person'. For most of the day, Frank protested his innocence, but between 5 p.m. and 6.10 p.m., 'a change came over him towards the end of the interview. He started to answer the questions differently. Then he said to us he would think about making a statement,' Melody explained. 'I can't say what made him change his mind. I've no idea what made him change his mind.'

Chapter 13

Confessions

Charlotte's interview ended at 6 p.m. and she was allowed a rest in the interview room. Mark McConnell's interview also ended at 6 p.m., and he was placed in the cells. He was given a meal at 6.10 p.m., at the same time that Young Frank McBrearty's interview ended. He too was taken to the cells. Roisin's interview ended shortly afterwards, and she got a visit from her mother, Mrs Anna Quinn.

Shortly after 6 p.m. then, all four Letterkenny prisoners were left alone. This was no coincidence, the Dublin Four told the Morris tribunal. The break had been planned in advance, so that all the interview teams could get together and compare notes on their progress to date. The meeting was not a full-blown 'top table' conference led by the senior officers, like those that preceded the arrests, they explained, but a 'round table' conference where information was exchanged. The Dublin Four said that while no one else was getting anywhere, they told the conference about Frank's closing comment that he would 'think about it', and said they thought he might be ready to make a statement. Few Gardaí from Donegal could remember the 'round table gathering'. John McGinley and John Fitzgerald said they knew nothing about such a meeting. Joe Shelly said he wasn't even in the station at the time, he'd spent most of the day in Finner Army Camp with Chief Superintendent Denis Fitzpatrick, and after they got back to Letterkenny he met with a local banker about a fraud investigation, then went for a bite to eat. Jim Gallagher wasn't involved in the Barron investigation after the first week or so, and spent most of the day writing up files from the previous day's District Court, and 'running the ordinary business of the station' while Fitzgerald concentrated on the arrests.

Garda Tina Fowley knew nothing about the conference; at the time she was in Raphoe, with Detective Garda Noel Jones and Garda Padraig Mulligan, taking a statement from Roisin McConnell's sister Katrina Brolly. Sergeant Brendan Roache said he heard nothing about a planned conference, and left the station around 6 p.m. to get a meal.

Garda John Harkin remembered two 'mini-conferences', although he wasn't sure of the times, but he thought the first took place after 6 p.m., 'about tea time'. Harkin remembered very little of what was said, apart from an exchange between Detective Garda Pat Tague from Lifford and Detective Sergeant Gerard McGrath from the 'Cobra' unit. McGrath asked if anybody had heard mention of a dog barking the night Richie Barron died, which he figured was something Frank McBrearty might have mentioned during an interview. Nobody knew anything about a dog barking in the night. Harkin also remembered Tague saying he wasn't making much progress with Mark McConnell, and asked if any of the Dublin Four wanted to question him. 'I believe that it was an offer that was posed by Detective Garda Tague and I think it was rejected by Detective Sergeant McGrath', Harkin told the tribunal. Harkin couldn't remember if anyone mentioned making progress with Frank.

At the second 'mini-conference' about an hour later, Harkin remembered a decision was made to arrest Roisin McConnell's sister Katrina Brolly. He said he was told to go with Detective Garda Mick O'Malley and take a statement from her husband Eunan Brolly in Raphoe to 'clarify an inconsistency', but couldn't recall what the 'inconsistency' was.

Meanwhile, the clock was running down. The Criminal Justice Act allowed the Gardaí to hold suspects for a maximum of twelve hours. At that point, they had to be either charged with a crime, or released.

––––

While the detectives were intimately aware of the time, the prisoners were kept in plain rooms, without watches or a clock to refer to, and had difficulty measuring time. Charlotte Peoples thought it was sometime in the afternoon that she first realised something terrible was happening to Roisin in the interview room next door. 'I was actually sitting in the interview room and my door was open and Roisin had actually passed down by and there was a bangharda with her and her mother was with her,' she remembered. Roisin's mother, Anna Quinn, was logged in at 6.16 p.m., and left the station at 6.45, according to the custody record, which seems to fix the time.

'I remember she [Roisin] was carrying this silver tray but her mother then had passed up just shortly afterwards again,' Charlotte recalled. 'But I mean they didn't see me. But I remember just sitting looking out of the door and these two boys coming walking down past and it was actually the man with the beard, it was the beard that actually threw me . . . I didn't know that they could have beards in the force, was he a Guard, you know, for I never seen a Guard with a beard.' (John Dooley, the detective who interviewed Roisin McConnell, wore a distinctive beard.)

Detective Garda Mick Carroll and Detective Garda Michael Jennings then arrived to question Charlotte, and a shouting and roaring started up again next door. 'I heard somebody saying you lying bitch you, I heard them saying you lying bitch you, murdering B- and that,' Charlotte remembered. 'But I heard a clash and to me it was this silver tray that I had seen Roisin carrying.' Charlotte asked the detectives to go next door and intervene. 'I had pleaded with them, I was crying and I had said to them please go in and stop what's going on next door,' she told the tribunal.

As Charlotte grew more upset at what she was hearing, Carroll rose from his chair to calm her. 'Please go in and stop what is going on,' Charlotte pleaded.

'Don't worry, this isn't going to happen to you,' Carroll told her.

'Please, go in and tell them to stop,' Charlotte begged. 'She didn't do anything, tell them to stop, she doesn't deserve this.'

Carroll went to place a comforting hand on Charlotte's shoulder to calm her. Charlotte misinterpreted his intentions. 'I actually thought this is it, I thought this is where he's just going to pull me and this is where I'm going to get it now,' she remembered. 'I said to him you can go on ahead now, I don't care any more, I says you can batter me, you can throw me up against walls, you can do whatever you want to do to me now, I can't tell you any more than what I am telling and that's the truth.

'It went quiet for a wee while, it did go quiet. Because when it went quiet I was sitting there and I was sort of waiting to hear the run of feet in the corridor or to hear sirens pulling into the barracks for I thought they had done something to her and it started back then again, the noise. The noise started back again.'

Charlotte had harsh words for Carroll and Jennings, and their failure to react to what happened next door. 'To start off with, I thought it was their duty when they knew what was going on next door, they shouldn't have stood by and let it happen anyway. They shouldn't have. They should have went in and stopped it. They shouldn't have been allowed to get away with what was going on next door, they should have went in and stopped it. So I believe that I was just being used. I was on medication and that, and to me I was just being used, that that was a form of mental torture with me. That maybe they thought they would have broken me.'

In May 2006, Carroll and Jennings admitted for the first time that Charlotte was upset by what she heard happening in the room next door. They said they reassured her that the same thing would not happen to her, but denied that she asked them to intervene next door. The tribunal was satisfied that she asked them to do just that, and her request was ignored. The tribunal criticised Carroll and Jennings for their failure to say what happened until after Dooley and White admitted Roisin McConnell was abused.

A few days after Carroll and Jennings came forward, Detective Sergeant Sylvie Henry admitted that he too had found Charlotte upset when he and Garda Debbie Kyne took over the interview at 8.30 p.m. He said he had taken the step of asking the member in charge, Martin Leonard, if everything was all right next door. Martin Leonard said he couldn't remember such an exchange, which Henry first mentioned a decade after the event. Debbie Kyne, who at the time was only a student Garda, gave her testimony 'in a freeflowing and direct manner', and told the truth, and her failure to act was excusable as she would have followed the lead of Sergeant Henry, the more experienced officer in the room. Henry, who was regarded overall as 'an honest and careful Garda', could have done more to find out what was happening next door. 'It is only when experienced and honourable Gardaí stand back and do nothing of an effective nature that abuse of the kind which has been admitted in respect of Roisin McConnell can take place,' Justice Morris concluded.

Charlotte remembered how at one point Carroll left the room, and returned shortly after. 'Charlotte, the murderer has now confessed and has said that you did know something about the death of Richie Barron,' he said. 'He said that you did know.'

'Well if someone has confessed to a murder in here today, they've framed me,' Charlotte replied.

'Do you think would your husband frame you?' Carroll asked.

'Well if Michael has admitted to a murder or anything like that, he has framed me but he didn't do anything, because I know he didn't do anything.'

For ten years, Carroll denied telling Charlotte her husband had confessed. It was not until two days before Charlotte gave evidence, on 16 May 2006, that he made a statement explaining what he had done. 'I believe that it was in my last interview with Charlotte Peoples that I put it to Charlotte Peoples that her husband Michael had admitted to having knowledge of Richard Barron's murder,' he wrote. 'I recall that she replied that if he did, she didn't know anything about it. I then asked her did she think her husband would set her up like this. I can't exactly recall what her reply was to this but I do recall it was in the negative. I did not labour this point, nor did I go on about it. I only ran it by her the once.'

At the tribunal, Carroll explained that he had earlier got Charlotte to admit her mother phoned the hospital the night Richie Barron died by pretending to check up on telephone records, and thought a similar trick might work again if he pretended Michael Peoples had confessed.

Detective Sergeant Sylvie Henry's first interview had ended at 11.07 a.m., but before leaving, Henry hadn't read over his notes to Charlotte. Shortly before the deadline for her release, Henry sat with Charlotte and read over to her the notes from his first interview. After he read over the notes, Henry asked Charlotte if there was anything she wanted to add. Charlotte told Henry why she'd said earlier to him that she knew nothing about a phone call from her home to the hospital. 'I didn't mean any harm, just protecting my mother,' she explained. Charlotte signed the amended notes, witnessed by Kyne and Henry, who wrote the time beside the signatures, 8.53 p.m. There is a slight discrepancy in times, as Charlotte was released from Garda custody at 8.50 p.m. according to the custody record.

Charlotte didn't make any complaints when she signed the custody record. 'I didn't think about anything, I just wanted to get out,' she explained. Michael's father collected her at the Garda station and brought her home.

'Afterwards I was sort of trying to deal with what had happened and actually then I fell into depression and I had been attending a psychiatric unit in Letterkenny. I had been put on medication,' she told the tribunal.

'My health deteriorated . . . I didn't want to leave the house and I actually didn't go out of the house. Mammy actually had my daughter, she was three . . . She had had her living with her for a month, for I had no interest in her. I had no interest in anything.'

Charlotte's ordeal and its after-effects also affected her husband deeply. Justice Morris noted in his report that the only time Michael Peoples lost his composure while in the witness box was when he spoke about his wife.

———

At 6.15 p.m., Roisin McConnell was told her mother was in the station to see her. As she was taken to the visitor's room, John White passed.

'Somebody says where are yous taking her or something, and somebody said that her mother was there and that they were taking me to the visiting room, and John White, he turned around and he said "all that murdering bitch deserves is a cell",' Roisin remembered.

Anna Quinn was able to tell Roisin all that had happened that day. When her solicitor James Sweeney saw her earlier, he had only been able to tell her that another woman was arrested—Roisin guessed it was either her sister Katrina Brolly or her cousin Charlotte Peoples. Now she learned Charlotte was under arrest in Letterkenny, and that her sister Edel was in Lifford. Nine hours after her arrest, Roisin finally found out what no Garda would tell her all day. Dean wasn't in Garda custody, he was safe and sound at home with Mark's parents. Anna Quinn gave her daughter a pack of twenty cigarettes. The two women chatted for half an hour before Anna had to go. According to the custody record, Roisin was given a meal after Anna left. She didn't remember a meal, only a cup of tea.

At 7.25 p.m., White and Dooley arrived again. White didn't waste any time. 'You've had a good enough day all day, put out that cigarette now and get off the chair,' he barked as he threw an envelope of photographs on the table. As Roisin rose from the chair, he grabbed the chair and sent it flying across the floor. In the next room, Charlotte Peoples heard the noise, and thought it was the silver tray she'd seen Roisin carrying earlier.

Roisin moved back until her back was against a filing cabinet by the wall. White began roaring and shouting, and told her to stop leaning against the filing cabinet. Roisin moved away obediently, towards the middle of the floor. White shouldered Roisin, so that she was thrown towards Dooley. He shouldered her in turn back to White, so that she bounced between the two men like a shuttlecock.

White reached for the photographs. They showed Richie Barron's post-mortem. Dooley was looking at White, who lifted the photographs and held them in front of Roisin's face. 'I started to close my eyes tight and every time that I opened my eyes, I could get a glance of blood so I had to close them tight again,' Roisin said. 'They kept doing this here and I had no other choice but to look at the photograph then. White kept roaring and shouting that this was the work of my husband and that I was nothing but a dirty lying murdering bastard.'

'This is the work of your husband,' White told her. He said Roisin had told nothing but lies all day. She was Satan. She was the devil. 'He was roaring and shouting that much that the spits was coming out of his mouth and hitting me in the face and I had to keep wiping my face and at one time in that interview he was frothing at the mouth . . . I thought it was never going to end. I was scared.

'I eventually had to look at photographs, like I would keep closing my eyes tight and the photographs was up at my face and I kept closing my eyes again and then eventually then whenever I did look at the photographs, the lights was being turned on and off.'

Roisin moved away from White, away from the horrific images. White told Roisin that someone in Raphoe would stab her, and when it happened he would spit on her grave. He told her Richie Barron would come back and haunt her. Roisin could only protest that she was innocent. White asked her to swear on her father's grave. Roisin refused the blasphemous order. 'There's some good in you then,' White said.

White asked Roisin if she would pray to her father to tell the truth. 'I'll say a wee prayer for Richie,' he told Roisin. 'Bless yourself.'

Roisin made the sign of the cross. They both stood in silence for about five minutes. White broke the silence. 'Well, were you speaking to your father?' he asked.

'Aye, I was,' Roisin answered.

'What did he say?'

'He said that I was telling the truth the whole day.'

The answer infuriated White. He began to shout again, calling Roisin a dirty murdering bastard, a lying murdering bitch as he punched the table and punched the wall. Roisin was terrified, certain that White was going to hit her. Desperate to get out of the room, she told the detectives she had to go to the toilet. Dooley and White summoned Garda Lohan, and she accompanied Roisin to the toilets. It was 8 p.m. Roisin had been in the room with White and Dooley for thirty-five minutes. Ten minutes later, after Lohan brought her back from the toilets, Garda Martin Leonard told her she was released from custody. 'You don't have to go back into that room,' he told her.

'But my coat is in there,' Roisin answered.

'Somebody will get it for you,' Leonard told her.

Leonard produced the custody record. 'Have you any complaints?' he asked.

'I do have a complaint,' Roisin told him. 'Them two boys was pushing me in to one another in that room.'

Leonard smiled. 'Do you need a doctor?' he asked.

Roisin looked at Leonard. 'You're just as bad as the two boys in the room,' she thought to herself. 'No,' she told him, 'I don't need a doctor.'

'I suppose you're not going to sign this either?' Leonard said, indicating the custody record.

Roisin nodded.

Officially released from custody, Roisin asked for a telephone. She rang her mother's house, looking for someone to come and collect her.

———

Mark McConnell couldn't remember if he was given a meal when he was taken back to the cells at 6.10 p.m. At 7.05 p.m., according to the custody record, he was taken back from the cells by Detective Garda Mick O'Malley and Detective Sergeant Jim Leheny. The record shows that O'Malley left the room forty minutes later to be replaced by Sergeant Pat Hennigan. Mark disagreed with the record. There were several Guards in the room during his final interview, he told the Morris tribunal.

Mark knew Roisin had been arrested, Edel had told him when she arrived at the house that morning during his own arrest. He knew Michael and Charlotte Peoples had been arrested too, because he'd heard it over the car radio as the Guards brought him to the station. Early in the day, he'd guessed Young Frank had been picked up too—the Guards were accusing Frank of the murder along with Mark. As the day went on, he could hear

Young Frank shouting from about mid-afternoon, and 'it was really get-ting hot and heavy by the time my last interview was coming about'.

Mark McConnell wasn't entirely sure who told him Young Frank had made a statement. 'Frank is blaming you for the murder,' he was told. 'It's about time now Mark that you got your side of the story across. He's going to sink ye and we're willing now to take a statement off you. You can outline how the murder happened. We've a fair idea that you weren't to blame for the murder but we need details of what happened.'

'I don't care what Frank McBrearty has signed or what you say about Frank McBrearty Junior, I'm not admitting to no murder because I've nothing to do with it,' Mark told the Guards.

As Mark continued his protest, Inspector John McGinley arrived. He told Mark he had Frank's admission. In his hand, he held several hand-written pages.

'There was a big build-up to this, the production of the statement, that was the only thing I could hear. Young Frank shouting and roaring and they created a massive build-up that Frank had confessed. They said that Frank Junior was crying for his father in the interview room, that's what the roaring was, that he wanted his father,' Mark recalled.

At the end of the last page, Mark saw a signature. Frank McBrearty Junior. 'I knew by looking at it that it wasn't his signature,' Mark explained. The document just looked wrong. McGinley sat down and began to read the 'confession'.

'I'll never forget the opening line of it,' Mark explained. 'I knew, the minute that he said the opening line I knew definitely that young Frank wouldn't use that kind of phraseology. Something to the lines of I, Frank McBrearty, am showing remorse for what I have done. And the minute that line was said to me I knew right away that there was something fishy about the document and I let him read on and read on and like I remember before he had finished the reading of the statement—because it was fairly lengthy, as I say it was four pages plus—I remember the custody Guard coming in to the room, that my time was up and he was nearly at the end of the statement, and I said, even though I was desperate to get out of the Garda station, I wanted him to finish the statement and it was only maybe—he was five, six lines from the end of the statement and he finished it. And when he had fin-ished it he told me, well what do you think of that. I told him in no uncer-tain terms what I thought about it. I told him the best way I can put it, but I put it a lot cruder than this, that he would be far better going and relieving himself in the toilet and wiping his behind with it. That's the exact words I said to him about the statement, I said to him it was a load of rubbish. Because I know for a fact I had nothing to do with Richie Barron's death.'

Mark McConnell was released from Garda custody at 8.20 p.m., ten minutes before a confession emerged from the interview room where Young Frank was being questioned. Mark described a confession written on four or five pages, while the confession in Young Frank's case is written on two sides of a single page. The wording of the opening line is also significantly different. The confession Mark was shown was bogus, an attempt to bluff him into making an admission.

———

As Mark McConnell was led down the halls to the custody desk, he was convinced he was going to jail for something he didn't do. He wondered if he would ever see Roisin and Dean again. 'Martin Leonard was sitting at the table and whoever brought me down they were more or less saying, we're bringing you Mark now to charge you. When we got as far as the table I can remember a book sitting open, some kind of a book, and I thought this is the point that they were going to charge me with the murder. But it turned out that they were releasing me, but I didn't know that at the time.' Mark signed the custody record to say he had no complaints. He was free to go.

'I walked in to the foyer of the police station, we had no lift home, and I remember Roisin sitting there and she was overly calm, to tell you the truth. I thought she would be in terrible state once I'd see her, but she was sitting there just kind of in a trance outside in the foyer.'

Roisin McConnell was still waiting for her brother Paul to collect her when Mark was released. When she saw him for the first time, wearing a strange grey sweatshirt and pants, she thought he was wearing prison clothes and was going to be charged. Mark quickly reassured her, explaining that the Guards had taken his clothes for forensics.

———

Roisin McConnell's sister Katrina Brolly is married to Eunan Brolly. At the time of the arrests they had three children, Peter (twelve), Debbie (ten) and Christine (eight). Eunan, a musician, knew Mark McConnell through bands they'd played in together, and the families were close. December 4 would be one of the longest days of Katrina's life.

'A friend of my sister's, Lorna O'Donnell, came to my house before 8.30 a.m.,' Katrina remembered, 'and she could hardly get out what was wrong because she was crying.'

Lorna had given Roisin a lift to work, then gone to Roisin's home when she was arrested and after Roisin called to her 'Lorna, go and get Mark.' On the way, she met Edel Quinn and told her what had happened, and

saw both Edel and Mark McConnell arrested at his home. She then went
to tell Katrina what had happeened to her sisters.

Eunan wasn't working that day, so he took care of getting the children
ready for school, while Katrina went to get her brother Gerard. Together
they went to see Katrina's mother, Mrs Anna Quinn, while Eunan held
the fort at home. They then got in touch with Mark's mother, Hannah
McConnell, and brought over baby things for young Dean. While they
were there, they got word that Young Frank had been arrested too.

'Then my mother phoned to say that another cousin of mine,
Charlotte Peoples, and her husband were lifted.'

'So we went back up home again and my aunt Dolly Eaton, Charlotte's
mother, was in her house. So I went up to see her and we phoned
Letterkenny and I asked—I think it was Martin Leonard I was chatting to
about going down to visit them, and he told me to come ahead.

'We still didn't know what was going on. There was my brother
Gerard, my brother Patrick and Charlotte's mother Dolly and myself
went to Letterkenny, and when we got to Letterkenny Martin Leonard
came out and he was laughing as if it was—I don't know what he
thought, and I said could I visit Roisin and he said, no. My aunt asked
could she visit Charlotte and she was told no.

'I asked about Edel then and he laughed and says, oh Edel's not here,
Edel's in Lifford. I thought why didn't he tell me that when I had phoned.

'They wouldn't let us visit anybody in Letterkenny. So we went to
Lifford then and I got in to see my sister Edel in Lifford. That would have
been early, maybe it could have been between 11 a.m. and midday or just
after it.'

'They were—well they were a lot nicer than they were in Letterkenny,
put it like that.

'I went in and I know there was Guards sitting in the room with Edel
and I said to Edel, what's going on, what's wrong. She was just looking,
she was in pure shock, she says that they told her that she had something
to do with the death of Richie Barron. So that was the first time that we
actually knew what it was all about.

'She just was pure shocked and dazed . . . at this stage she hadn't got a
solicitor or anything and I think I said to the Guard about a solicitor and
I says, does she need one and he said, oh well, that's up to you whether
you want to get her one or not.

'I went home to tell my mother, you know, all that had happened, that
I had seen Edel but they wouldn't let me visit Roisin and you know, to
check on her and check on the children again and I was just up and down
all day.

'And then I went home again, you know, to get the children something
to eat and it was more or less just up and down all day.

'I had a little part-time job just cleaning offices, just up at the top of my road and Christine, my youngest daughter, used to come up with me, I'd only be away maybe about half an hour. I used to go up about five o'clock. I did notice a car coming down whenever I was going up and braking. But I went on to work and whenever I came back to the house, they were in the house. There was Padraig Mulligan, Tina Fowley and Noel Jones.

'They must have been there from about 5 p.m. if it was the car that I had seen, you know, whenever I was going up. I came back around about 5.30 p.m.

'Well Noel Jones wanted to question me. I think actually now from what my daughter [Debbie] has said that one of them actually questioned her, she was only ten at the time, that one of them questioned her . . . I just don't think that they should have been questioning her, you know.

'To be quite honest, with all that was going on that day, I actually don't know what he was on about, it just wasn't registering with me. I didn't know why they were there, especially whenever I had two sisters lifted and like my mind just wasn't registering anything for to come, you know, at that time of the evening to take a statement.'

Katrina's first statement, given to Garda Phil Collins on 16 October, two days after Richie Barron died, gave an account of her movements up until the time she and her husband arrived home from the Town & Country, shortly after midnight on 14 October. The new statement continued her account of the night from that time, covering how she got the children to bed, and how Mark and Roisin McConnell arrived some time later. Mark, Roisin and Eunan were still asleep when she left for work the following morning.

After the Guards left, Katrina made dinner for the kids, then went back up to her mother. She had barely gone when the Guards called again to the Brolly home. Two Guards arrived looking for Katrina, and Eunan told Noel Jones she'd gone to her mother, and gave them directions. As they were leaving, Detective Garda Mick O'Malley and Garda John Harkin arrived. O'Malley and Harkin took another statement from Eunan, again focusing on the morning after Richie Barron died, and what time he and Mark McConnell left the house to collect Mark's car. Harkin and O'Malley stayed chatting with Eunan until close to 10 p.m.

When Katrina got to her mother's home, her brother Paul was there, along with his wife Sue, and Roisin rang from Letterkenny to say that she was being released. Paul said he would go down and collect her. Katrina went along with Paul.

'I sat in the car. Paul went in,' she recalled. 'I was sitting in the car and the next thing, I saw Tina Fowley coming down, but then she went away out around the car. Then she came over to the passenger door and asked

me to open it and I opened it and she asked me to step out. That's when
Garda Tague, he had come along then, and he arrested me.

'I was told not to speak to anybody on the way in. But while we were
standing there another Guard came and said that they were to bring me
in the back doors.

'We went in, Martin Leonard was still there, and he says to me, oh
you're back again. I said I was. Then somebody had came in and says
about that they had told my brother Paul to go on ahead without me, that
I was being kept.

'I think I was read my rights and all and they said about a solicitor,
phoning a solicitor and I says, I don't need a solicitor. I says, as far as I'm
concerned I'm innocent and I don't need a solicitor. I was taken to a room
then.'

Katrina Brolly was arrested at 8.25 p.m. After she was processed, she
was brought to Room 113 in Letterkenny Garda station. As she entered the
room, she could hear Frank McBrearty 'roaring'. It would be a long night.

Once he met Roisin in the front foyer, Mark wanted out of the Garda
station as quickly as possible. Roisin told him that her brother Paul was
on his way to collect her, so they went outside to wait. When Paul found
them, he told them that Katrina Brolly had just been arrested.

———

The Morris tribunal called it the Garda Template. The theory, explained
at the pre-arrest conferences and put to Roisin McConnell by Inspector
John McGinley, was simple. Mark had a fight with Richie Barron in the
Town & Country. Afterwards, he got in touch with his cousin Frank. They
decided to 'teach Richie a lesson'. They waylaid him on the way home,
assaulted him, and made their getaway down the car park to the nightclub. Throughout the day, the Four Dublin Boys put the Garda Template
to Frank McBrearty, recording the questions in their own notes. Beside
each question, they recorded Frank's vehement denials.

Between 2.48 p.m. and 4.05 p.m., for example, Detective Sergeant
Eamonn O'Grady and Detective Sergeant Gerry McGrath told Frank they
had 'a statement from a person who saw you up on the embankment at
the back of the car park of Frankie's Nite Club'. They told him they had 'a
statement from a person who saw you knocking on the window of the
Tudor Lounge with Mark McConnell at about 1.15 a.m. and that both of
you were let in'. This witness told them that Frank and Mark 'both came
down the embankment at the back of Frankie's Night Club at 1 a.m. and
that you went to the entrance to the disco and spoke to a bouncer. Then

you and Mark McConnell went around to the Tudor Lounge and were let in at 1.15 a.m.' This witness saw Frank and Mark 'up at the back of the car park of Frankie's Nite Club at 1 a.m.'

'Why is your father questioning people about this investigation, about what questions the Guards are asking and who the individual Guards are?' they asked.

'Because my father is very nervous, he's worried about his business,' Frank answered.

'What do you mean, he's worried about his business?'

'My father is a fucking eejit. He shouldn't be interfering.'

'So you know that your father has been interfering with this investigation?'

'Yeah, I told him to stop and leave the Guards to do their job but he wouldn't listen. He's that sort. He never fucking listens and he never tells me anything anyway.'

'Do you realise that your father has been intimidating people who were questioned by the Gardaí in relation to this investigation?'

'My father wouldn't intimidate or threaten anybody, that's just the way he goes on, he doesn't mean anything by it, he's just worried, that's all.'

Between 5 p.m. and 6.10 p.m., Detective Sergeant John Melody and Detective Garda John Fitzpatrick put it to Frank that he 'met Mark McConnell and he told you what happened in Quinn's pub, and the two of you decided to do something about it after Richie Barron was seen heading for his home drunk.

'A number of people saw you and Mark McConnell coming over the hill at the car park of the club just after Richie Barron was killed,' they told him. 'We have written statements that they saw the two of you.'

'Isn't it a fact that your father asked all of the employees in the bar and the club what the police had asked them and demanded that they make statements to him about what they said to the police?'

'Frank, we know it did happen. Didn't one of your employees leave an account of this intimidation, and hasn't your father offered a bribe to a witness not to give evidence against you?'

'The two of you were seen that night coming across the car park of the Club at about 1.03 a.m. We know this for a fact. Tell us the truth about what occurred that night.'

Frank made an angry denial to every question. He was an innocent man, he told the detectives. The witnesses were liars. He'd never been up the car park, never met Mark McConnell, never murdered Richie Barron. The detectives tried a change of tack.

'Could it have been that the two of you only meant to give Richie Barron a hiding to teach him a lesson?' they asked.

Frank didn't answer.

'Richie Barron from what we know had severe head injuries. We know that he received a blow from some sort of blunt instrument on the top of his head near his forehead. Did you or Mark McConnell hit him on top of his head?'

'I'm saying nothing.'

'Frank, we need to know the truth. Did you deliberately plan to murder Richie Barron?'

'I murdered nobody. I wouldn't do that.'

'Tell us the truth then. What happened that night with Richie Barron?'

'I'm saying nothing.'

'We know that the McBreartys were having a lot of hassle from Richie Barron, but he didn't deserve to be killed. Would you agree with that?'

'Of course I agree with that, but he wasn't causing a lot of hassle.'

'Didn't he have a row in Quinn's pub earlier that night with Mark McConnell and embarrassed him in front of his wife and friends? Wasn't Mark McConnell very angry over what had occurred and when he told you about it the two of you decided to do something about it when you saw Richie Barron drunk and making his way home?'

'That was Mark's business, it had nothing to do with me.'

'You went along with sorting Richie Barron out when Mark McConnell told you what the row was about, isn't that true?'

'I'm saying fucking nothing.'

'All we want is the truth. What occurred that night? Tell us the truth.'

'I didn't murder nobody. I'm saying nothing more.'

'You should think about telling us the truth about what happened that night. The facts are that Richie Barron died as a result of one or more blows to the head. Either you or Mark McConnell hit him on top of the head with something, we don't know what it was, only you or Mark can tell us that.'

Again, Frank made no reply.

'You should consider telling us the truth and make a written statement about what happened that night. Do you understand?'

'I'll think about it,' Frank said.

The interview ended at 6.10 p.m. Frank was allowed a toilet break, given two painkilling tablets, and shortly afterwards a meal. At 7 p.m., Melody and Fitzpatrick took Frank back to the interview room. By 8.30 p.m., they had a confession.

At the tribunal, John Melody said that something changed in Frank just before the 6 p.m. break. 'A change in answering the questions alerted us to the possibility that maybe we were asking the wrong questions here,' he told the chairman. Melody said that he didn't say so in as many words, but in asking Frank if he 'only meant to give Richie Barron a hiding', he and Fitzpatrick were 'asking him to consider the proposition' that this wasn't a murder, only an assault gone horribly wrong.

By 6.10 p.m. then, Young Frank had all the information he needed in order to tell the Dublin detectives what they wanted to hear. And by asking him to 'consider the proposition' that this was only an assault gone wrong, they offered him a carrot: admit to a lesser crime, and the interrogation will end. However, the detectives professed puzzlement at what might have induced Frank to admit to something he hadn't done in order to stop the questioning, when he had only another couple of hours to go until his release. The detectives denied there was any stick to go with the carrot. Frank had been a difficult man to interview, but he had not been abused or assaulted in custody, they maintained.

'Looking back at it,' Melody told the tribunal, 'certainly I don't know what came into the man's head, whether he's reiterating what he has been told or whether there's some truth in it or not. We know now that it's a false statement.'

'My job was keeping the man calm,' Fitzpatrick told the chairman. 'Frank McBrearty Junior stated he was making a statement. In that statement you'd have got nowhere with the man unless he was calm. Now, that was my job, I was keeping the man calm.' Despite this, Frank went off on several 'tangents', and the confession was compiled slowly, virtually one sentence at a time, punctuated by rants from Frank as Fitzpatrick worked to keep him calm and Melody wrote down what he said.

This account, with its images of Frank going off on sustained rants then pausing to add another line or two to his confession before launching again on another tangent, simply wasn't credible, Justice Morris felt. What exactly happened in Room 225, he could not say for sure, save that Frank was 'subjected to inappropriate behaviour', including being shown post-mortem photographs which he was later able to describe in detail. However, Frank had also exaggerated the level and scale of the abuse he endured, and made numerous false allegations. Beyond that, the tribunal could not say for sure what happened, save that—for whatever reason— Frank 'completely disintegrated during his period of detention, such that his will crumbled and he made a false confession due to the pressures that were on him at that time'. The chairman found that 'this could have happened due to inappropriate behaviour by the Gardaí, or without any such behaviour, simply because the prisoner found the pressures of his detention too great to bear'.

The first page of the controversial statement reads in full: 'Listen I'll tell you what happened on the 14.10.96. I heard that Richie Barron was up to his old tricks again, mouthing about the McBrearty's, Mark McConnell, he's my first cousin told me this. He had a row with him in Quinn's pub that evening. His wife, Róisín was also there. Mark was very annoyed over the row and what Richie Barron said to him. When he came over to the club, that is Mark McConnell he told me that he had seen

Richie Barron heading towards home and that he was drunk. We decided that we would head him off at the top of the road. We went up the back way across the car park and got onto the main road. We waited for Richie Barron there. We intended having a word with him. We saw Richie coming. He was on his own. I picked up a bit of timber. When we stopped him he lashed out at us but he missed. I hit him a slap on the head and he fell back. We then ran. I dropped the timber I had on the way back. We got into the club and it wasn't until later that I heard that Richie had been knocked down by a hit-and-run. Michelle Scott told me. My father found out about what happened and he said he would look after it for us.'

On the second page the statement reads: 'My father never intimidated anyone. He never offered to my knowledge money to anyone to not give evidence against me. This statement has been read over to me and it is correct.'

The second page is signed 'Frank McBrearty Junior' and witnessed 'John Melody, Detective Sergeant 8.25 p.m.'. Underneath is a second signature, 'John Fitzpatrick, D/Garda' and the date, '4/12/1996'.

——

For years, Young Frank would deny vehemently that he made a confession, or would ever break under questioning. The statement was a forgery, or the Guards got his signature with a trick, he claimed. Most of his outbursts and walkouts at the tribunal were sparked when barristers got to the subject of the confession.

Frank's case was bolstered in June 1999 when Garda Tina Fowley told the Carty team that sometime on 4 December 1996, Inspector John McGinley showed her a copy of Frank McBrearty's signature and a photocopy of a document containing the signature, and asked her, 'Is it a good likeness?' Fowley laughed, but she wasn't sure what to make of the incident. When she told Sergeant Brendan Roache about it afterwards, he said it was probably another of McGinley's practical jokes. Fowley told the Carty team that the confession from Frank McBrearty was not the document McGinley had shown her.

McGinley denied anything like the incident had happened, declaring that he was mystified why Fowley would make such an allegation. Giving evidence in November 2006, the only explanation he could offer was the possibility that a joking remark could have been horribly misinterpreted by Fowley. Comparing his own handwriting with Frank McBrearty's, he might have shown the two to Fowley saying: 'Léann an púca an rud a scríobhann sé féin' [the pooka can read what he himself writes], meaning his own handwriting was as bad as Frank McBrearty's. 'I could have said something that he was as good a scribe as myself,' he told the chiarman. At another point, McGinley said that for a prank he had walked into the incident room 'and said that I had interviewed Frank McBrearty for the last three hours or something and he admitted the whole thing to me,' but did not believe Fowley—or anyone else—could have taken the joke seriously. McGinley said he had been afraid to admit to something even remotely similar to what Fowley described when the Carty team approached him, because he knew Frank was denying he made a confession and claiming his signature was a forgery. Too much was happening as the Carty team dissected the Barron investigation, and he didn't want to give any credibility to the allegation.

After listening to both sides, the tribunal concluded that McGinley had not forged the false confession from Frank McBrearty. But he did find that McGinley had written a bogus confession, which he then showed to Mark McConnell in a bid to get him to make an admission.

In the early 1970s, a young detective with the Reykjavik Criminal Investigation Department in Iceland was building a reputation as a stickler for verifying confessions. In one case, a man confessed to murder, but the weapon could not be found. Gisli Gudjonsson and his fellow detectives sifted through refuse at the Reykjavik Corporation Rubbish dump for two days before they found the murder weapon, verifying the confession.

Gudjonsson had good reason to be suspicious of confession evidence. Early in his police career, he made an arrest following a complaint from a member of the public. Gudjonsson took a statement in which a witness named the man who had stolen her purse. The witness was reliable, Gudjonsson had no reason to doubt the statement, and he made an arrest.

'I presented that witness testimony to that individual, who had a history of alcoholism and [he] said, well, I must have done it,' Gudjonsson told the Morris tribunal. 'I can't remember doing it but I must have done it.' The suspect signed a confession to the crime. Later, the woman telephoned Gudjonsson full of apologies. 'I'm terribly sorry, I found my purse, it was never stolen in the first place,' she told him.

The lesson stuck with Gudjonsson. He'd done nothing wrong, and yet he'd obtained a false confession. If his witness hadn't found the missing purse, an innocent man could have gone to jail. His interest in the psychology of false confessions and their causes led to a new career, and eventually he left the police force to pursue his studies, and became the Professor of Forensic Psychology at King's College, London.

Gudjonsson believes there are three basic types of false confession. Voluntary false confessions, such as the one the supposed purse-thief made; coerced-compliant confessions, where suspects try to reduce pressure by telling interrogators what they want to hear, and coerced-internalized confessions, where suspects actually come to believe they really did commit the crime.

The professor has become a familiar face in courtrooms around the world, as he gives expert evidence in criminal trials and appeals. Among others, he gave evidence on behalf of the Birmingham Six and Guildford Four.

Among the concepts Gudjonsson uses in his analysis is Interrogator Bias, which 'may result in police officers being particularly vigilant and receptive to information that is consistent with their prior assumptions and beliefs, whilst ignoring, minimizing or distorting information that contradicts their assumptions. Information that does not support the interviewer's hypotheses may be erroneously interpreted as lies, misunderstanding, evasiveness or defensiveness.'

Just as important was the suggestibility of the suspect, his willingness to accept what interrogators tell him. A similar but different measure was the compliance of the suspect. Suggestibility measured the willingness of a suspect to accept what his interrogators told him. Compliance measured his willingness to go along with something in return for a reward, for example to plea to a lesser charge in return for a reduced sentence.

Gudjonsson is also critical of police tricks, such as 'Mutt and Jeff' routines (also known as 'Good Cop, Bad Cop'), bluffs, and 'prisoner's dilemma', where one suspect is told his accomplices have confessed, and he faces a stiff punishment unless he too makes a confession. Mostly though, Gudjonsson argues for objectivity. Police interrogators have to remain impartial, and avoid getting caught in the emotion of a crime, learning to listen to what suspects (and indeed witnesses) are telling them, not to what others may believe. Or as the fictional Sergeant Joe Friday might have put it, 'just the facts Ma'am'.

Gudjonsson gave evidence at the Morris tribunal on Day 442, 27 April 2006. His research provided a way for Justice Frederick Morris to understand what happened a decade earlier in Room 225 of Letterkenny Garda station on 4 December 1996. The forensic analysis demonstrated that the signature on the confession belonged to Frank McBrearty, and showed no evidence of forgery. Unless Young Frank had somehow been tricked into signing, something happened in that room which deeply traumatised Frank. Gudjonsson provided the framework to explain at least part of the mystery.

At 8.30 p.m., the interview teams changed. Melody and Fitzpatrick left the room, and McGrath and O'Grady took over. During the changeover, Melody brought his colleagues up to date, reading over the confession. The statement was sparse in its details. 'I believed that we had work to do,' McGrath told the Morris tribunal. 'There were a number of issues that could be developed in relation to this particular statement. It was just an admission to an altercation . . . Sergeant Melody said to us, go in there and see how you can progress this further.'

As soon as he went into the room and cautioned Frank, Gerard McGrath 'received this volley of abuse from him saying that he had already made a statement, that he cooperated with the other two and that he wasn't going to answer any more questions about Richie Barron'.

'He continued with this type of abuse towards us,' McGrath recalled. '"I am not going to talk about the Richie Barron case any more." He was absolutely resolute in relation to that. He would not engage with us in relation to that and we went from there to why won't you talk to us, Frankie? Why can't we talk about this? He was absolutely resolute, would not engage with us at all concerning this investigation.'

Between 8.30 p.m. and 9.16 p.m. the detectives tried to get Frank to expand on his earlier statement, but to no avail. Sometime before 9 p.m., McGrath drafted a statement based on what Frank had said to him as he entered. Eamonn O'Grady spoke to Frank, about his father, about his boxing career, about anything he could think of to engage him.

McGrath realised the clock was ticking. He showed Frank the basic statement he'd drafted, and asked him if he was willing to sign it. He began to read it over, and Frank grabbed it out of his hand. Frank read it over, and signed it.

The second statement reads in full: 'I have already made a statement to the other two Gardaí. I have cooperated with them. I told them the truth about what happened.'

At 9.16 p.m., Frank was taken to the custody desk for release. Two minutes later, he signed the record to say he had no complaints. He was free to go.

Chapter 14

Long Day's Journey into Night

'Frank was in a terrible state when he came out,' Mark McConnell recalled. 'The only thing he said to me was, don't believe anything them lying bastards said to you in there.'

With that ambiguous remark, Frank walked past Mark, not stopping to talk any further, his eyes fixed straight ahead.

Mark and Roisin met James Sweeney, the solicitor, and told him that Frank had been released and had set off on foot from the Garda station. 'Knowing the state of mind he was in earlier that day, I was concerned about him, where he would go,' James Sweeney recalled. 'So I hopped in the car and went in search of him and I found him about halfway between the Garda station and his own house.'

Frank was 'extremely distressed, very distressed', Sweeney said. 'He was marching along the road. I persuaded him to get into the car. He was very upset at the manner in which he was treated in the station, that he was being accused of what he was accused of and the manner of his interrogation.'

———

Superintendent Fitzgerald took the confession the two Dublin detectives gave him, and brought it to the incident room. The statement was discussed, and Fitzgerald then left the room with the document. He told the Morris tribunal he went to brief the DPP's office and get directions, but was unable to get through to anyone from the office, despite trying several numbers. Young Frank was released, and Fitzgerald told the tribunal that because he 'wasn't going anywhere', he didn't bother trying the DPP's office the next day during office hours. The tribunal was unimpressed with Fitzgerald's evidence. No effort was ever made to contact the DPP, Judge Morris decided, because Fitzgerald was 'apprehensive in relation to the validity of this statement'. When he left Letterkenny in early February 1997, instead of leaving the document behind, Fitzgerald took it with him. He kept it locked in his safe for several years, and would only hand it over to the Carty team 'in exchange for a receipt'. Rightly or wrongly, the tribunal concluded, Fitzgerald was convinced that if he let the statement out of his sight, it would disappear. If that happened, Fitzgerald was determined he would not be blamed.

_____

After she was processed by Garda Martin Leonard, Katrina Brolly was taken to one of the interview rooms by Detective Garda PJ Keating and Garda Gina Lohan, just before 9 p.m. Katrina didn't remember much that happened during this first interview. She recounted her movements, going over what she had already said in her statements to Phil Collins and Noel Jones.

At 9.20 p.m. Detective Sergeant Paul Heffernan entered the room, and five minutes later Keating left. Detective Garda Noel Jones arrived a couple of minutes later. Five minutes later again, Garda Martin Leonard arrived and told her James O'Donnell was in the building.

'I was told there was a solicitor in the building and it was up to me, they couldn't let him see me unless I agreed to it. I says, well if he's in the building, I'll see him.'

The solicitor told her that at midnight, the detectives would ask her if she wanted to rest for the night. 'They'll let you sleep and then in the morning they'll get you up at eight o'clock again and you'll not be out of here till two o'clock,' he told her, and advised her to stay up and get the interrogation over with if she could.

_____

In December 1996, Mark Quinn had been running the Town & Country bar for about six years. He lived above the business along with his wife Donna and their children. Oliver, the youngest, was born just a few days before Richie Barron died. Two days after Barron died, on 16 October, Mark Quinn made a statement to Garda Phil Collins. He heard nothing more from the Gardaí until 4 December.

Mark Quinn is a cousin of Charlotte Peoples, and of the three Quinn sisters, Edel, Roisin (McConnell) and Katrina (Brolly). He'd heard about the arrests, and gone to see Charlotte. When he got there, he discovered she'd been picked up, along with Michael Peoples. After speaking to Charlotte's mother, he left to get back to work at his pub.

'I was just leaving my cousin's house, driving up St Eunan's Terrace, and a patrol car stopped me,' he recalled.

'The blue light went on in the patrol car and I pulled over and I was just sitting in the car.' Mark Quinn was arrested at 5.05 p.m. on 4 December 1996. The arresting officer was Detective Garda PJ Keating.

Keating tried to handcuff Mark Quinn, and Sergeant Joe Hannigan intervened to say, 'I know that man there, you've no call to handcuff him.' Mark Quinn was put into the back of the patrol car and taken to Letterkenny Garda station. He was in shock, and wasn't quite taking in everything that was happening.

'On the way down, Sergeant Hannigan said that the Murder Squad was waiting for me in Letterkenny,' Mark Quinn told the tribunal. 'Tell us now what you know before the Murder Squad gets here. They're waiting for you in Letterkenny,' he recalled Hannigan said to him.

'I was very frightened. I didn't really know what was going on. I was confused and didn't really know what was happening,' Mark said.

'I was taken into Letterkenny, into a Garda station and I just recall them telling me to take my shoes off and putting me into a cell.' Mark could only remember 'bits and pieces' of what happened to him. He had no memory of being processed by the custody officer, or informed of his rights. He thought he was left in the cell for about twenty minutes.

According to the official custody record, Mark Quinn was processed by Garda Martin Leonard when he arrived at Letterkenny. At 5.40 p.m., the booking completed, Mark Quinn was taken to the Traffic Sergeant's office for questioning by Sergeant Joe Hannigan and Detective Garda PJ Keating.

'There was a lot of, "Tell us what you know". They just kept going over and over and over it again. "You know something. Tell us what you know",' Mark Quinn recalled. He told the Gardaí that when he arrived in the bar during the confrontation between Mark McConnell and Richie Barron, all he saw was the two men staring at each other. 'They insisted that it was a vicious, violent row.'

According to the Garda interview notes, Mark Quinn told the Guards that Mark McConnell left the pub 'well after 12.30 a.m., 12.45 a.m. I reckon'. He was asked if Mark McConnell came back to the pub again later in the night to clean and wash up. He told the Gardaí they were quite welcome to go to the pub and carry out any forensic tests they wanted. They told him Mark McConnell was back in the pub the following morning; he said that wasn't so, Mark wasn't there until the following afternoon.

The first interview notes were witnessed by Detective Garda PJ Keating and Sergeant Joe Hannigan. Mark Quinn couldn't remember Hannigan being there. He agreed that the interview notes reflected the kinds of questions asked during the first interview and the kind of answers he gave, and identified the signature as his own. 'I can't recall signing those,' he told the tribunal. 'But any notes that was given to me, I just signed.'

The official custody record shows that when Hannigan and Keating left the room at 7.50 p.m., they were replaced by Garda John O'Dowd and Sergeant Marty Moylan. In an undated statement, Moylan said he 'talked generally first about the death of Richard Barron and the events that took place in Mark Quinn's pub that night between Richard Barron and Mark McConnell'.

'I told him that I had read a lot of statements from people who were in his pub that night and that there were sizeable differences in the times that people stated they left his pub that night,' Moylan wrote. The custody record shows the second interview continuing until 9.35 p.m., when he was brought to the cells for a rest. Twenty minutes later he was given a meal.

It is possible that Mark Quinn, who admits he 'couldn't really believe it was happening, you know. I kept having to pinch myself', compounded the first and second interviews into a single session. In his mind, his lawyers argued, he was in the interview room from 5.40 p.m. until 9.35 p.m., a single session. The official record shows two teams interviewed him during this period, Hannigan and Keating first, then Moylan and O'Dowd. During the same period, he was visited several times by the custody officer. Barrister Ken Fogarty argued that this could explain why Mark Quinn recalled 'comings and goings' during his first interview.

———

'I was shown photographs of the post-mortem done on Richie Barron, photographs of him on I think a slab or table. That seemed to be the worst. It was a big one for me,' Mark Quinn told the Morris tribunal. As with much that happened, he couldn't put a time on when this occurred, but he remembered that he was given a meal at the end of the incident, which placed it during his second interview with Sergeant Marty Moylan and Garda John O'Dowd.

'A Garda came in with photographs and put them on the table and they were photographs of the deceased Richie Barron, different photographs of different parts of his body,' he remembered.

'I was at the table and [the photographs] were laid out in front of me and the shouting and banging of the table started again and you know what happened to this man, just went on like that.

'Someone came in and said something about a meal break or something I think, and I said I didn't want nothing to eat, I just wanted a cup of tea. Some uniform Guard suggested I ordered chicken and chips or a chicken box or something like that. They questioned me then again about what happened ... went on for a while, then a chicken box came in and that was put on the table . . . The photographs was still on the table and they said to me to—think of white brains when you're eating your chicken.'

Mark Quinn had difficulty telling the story at the Morris tribunal. The grotesque linkage of a fast food meal and Richie Barron's brain matter still upset him deeply, even a decade later.

Seven years later, in March 2003, Garda John O'Dowd was interviewed by Chief Superintendent Brian Steele Garvie, a senior officer of the Royal Canadian Mounted Police on secondment to the Morris tribunal as an investigator. O'Dowd told the Mountie that while he was interviewing Mark Quinn, the prisoner was shown post-mortem photographs by Sergeant Marty Moylan. He and Moylan were the only Gardaí in the room when the photographs were produced. Several of the prisoners complained afterwards through their solicitors and to the Garda Complaints Board that they were shown post-mortem photographs. O'Dowd was the first Garda to admit the practice took place, and it took him seven years to do so. Moylan wouldn't admit his part until days before he took the stand at the Morris tribunal, ten years after the event. As with much else, Moylan claimed he had blanked out the episode as a result of post traumatic stress from his experiences on United Nations duty in Bosnia.

———

At 10 p.m., after Katrina Brolly spoke with her solicitor, Garda Martin Leonard told her he was going off duty. He introduced her to Garda Thomas Kilcoyne, who would take over as custody officer.

Around the same time, Paul Quinn arrived at Eunan Brolly's home. Eunan was still talking to Detective Garda Mick O'Malley and Garda John Harkin. Eunan asked him where Katrina was.

'Katrina's been arrested,' Paul told him.

'You're joking,' Eunan replied.

Paul told him it was true. Eunan phoned Letterkenny Garda station, and spoke to Paul Heffernan. The sergeant confirmed that Katrina was being held. Eunan asked if he could see her. 'He says yes, come on down,' Eunan recalled. Eunan arranged for Katrina's mother and sister to come down to his house to mind the kids, and Paul stayed with them. Eunan went to collect Katrina's brother Gerard and Mark Quinn's wife Donna, and they left for Letterkenny. It would be after midnight before he got there.

According to the official custody record, Detective Sergeant Paul Heffernan and Detective Garda Noel Jones went to interview Katrina

Kevin Carty, the assistant commissioner sent to Donegal to investigate allegations of Garda corruption by the McBrearty family and others. His wide-ranging report, delivered to the Garda commissioner in summer 2000, was never made public. (*faduda.ie*)

Tony Hickey: The assistant commissioner was falsely accused in a fax sent to Fine Gael TD Jim Higgins in 2001. The tribunal was satisfied that the fax was composed and typed by Frank McBrearty Snr and former Garda PJ Togher. (*faduda.ie*)

Jim Higgins MEP, the former Fine Gael TD and justice spokesman, was the first to raise the issue of what was happening in Donegal, in Dáil Éireann. (*faduda.ie*)

Brendan Howlin TD: The Labour justice spokesman was briefed on the content of the 'anonymous allegations' by Martin Giblin SC, barrister for Frank McBrearty Snr. Days later he met Justice Minister John O'Donoghue along with his Fine Gael counterpart. (*faduda.ie*)

Frank McBrearty Snr: The Donegal publican was held for 14 days in December 1996, and was admitted to hospital for tests twice during his arrest. He complained regularly that he had to deal with the tribunal without the assistance of lawyers, since he could not afford the risk that he would not be awarded his legal costs. (*faduda.ie*)

Frank McBrearty Jnr had a troubled relationship with the Morris tribunal, walking off the stand several times as he gave evidence over the years (as for instance in the illustration above) and risking contempt charges and heavy fines. (*faduda.ie*)

Roisin and Mark McConnell: Mark was arrested three times for crimes which he did not commit, and which never in fact occurred at all. He settled his civil claims against the state for a reported €1 million in late 2007. Roisin suffered a nervous breakdown in the wake of her arrest in December 1996, and reached an out of court settlement shortly after the tribunal was set up.

Katrina Brolly: The first of the twelve who were arrested to give evidence of her ordeal at the Morris tribunal. She was praised for her 'quiet dignity and courage' in the report by Mr Justice Frederick Morris. (*faduda.ie*)

John Nicholson: The only Garda successfully prosecuted as a result of the Carty inquiry. The retired Garda pleaded guilty to four counts of uttering forged documents in a County Sligo District Court in 2003. The judge applied the Probation Act. *(James Connolly / PicSell8)*

Bernard Conlon: A small-time criminal living in Sligo, described by the tribunal as 'a completely unreliable witness whose evidence should only be approached with the utmost caution'. Conlon was recruited by Sergeant John White to go undercover in Frank McBrearty's nightclub, in a bid to prove the publican was serving drink after hours. Later, he falsely accused Mark McConnell and Michael Peoples of threatening him with a 'silver bullet'. *(faduda.ie)*

John Dooley *right*, with solicitor Damien Tansey): Detective Garda John Dooley was paired with Sergeant John White on 4 December 1996, and took part in the interrogation and mistreatment of Roisin McConnell and Katrina Brolly. His decision to come forward in 2005 and tell the truth to the tribunal 'courageously and honestly', allowed the tribunal to uncover the truth. (*faduda.ie*)

Joan Gallagher: The tribunal found the evidence that Garda Joan Gallagher pulled Katrina Brolly's hair during an interview in Garda custody 'overwhelming', and also that she lied about the incident to the Garda Complaints Board, as did her colleagues, and 'persisted with these lies in her evidence to the tribunal'. (*PA Photos*)

Phil Collins: During the arrest of Robert Noel McBride, the former Garda Phil Collins 'was brought in on the incident, and brought from his sick bed at that, in order to enhance the threat against McBride so that he could be persuaded to make the statement demanded of him', incriminating Frank McBrearty Jnr and Mark McConnell. (*faduda.ie*)

Derrick 'Darcy' Connolly: The tribunal found he 'coached' Roderick Donnelly on what to say in a false statement made in January 1997. (*Declan Doherty*)

Tina Fowley made several high-profile allegations in statements to the Carty inquiry, including that she saw Inspector John McGinley practising the signature of Frank McBrearty Jnr. She claimed that she faced intimidation from colleagues after speaking to the inquiry. (*faduda.ie*)

William Doherty: A phone call from William Doherty passing on a wake house rumour changed the Barron investigation from a hit and run inquiry to a 'murder hunt'. The petty criminal was a leading player in the events that followed.

John O'Dowd (*right*), the Garda handler for the notorious informant William Doherty, denied for years knowing anything about a hoax blackmail call made by Doherty using his telephone. **Martin Leonard** (*left*) was the custody officer in Letterkenny Garda station on 4 December 1996. 'Had he performed his duties as member in charge conscientiously and honestly, and had he given truthful evidence, then the entire nature of this scandal would have been uncovered earlier. Instead he has chosen to be part of a cover up.' Both men were later dismissed from the force by the Garda commissioner. (*faduda.ie*)

Padraig Mulligan: The Garda on duty in Raphoe the night Richie Barron died, he failed to respond to the initial 999 call, as he was several miles away in a pub at the time with his colleague, off-duty Garda John O'Dowd. (*faduda.ie*)

John White (*right*) the controversial former detective sergeant who was the focus of several modules at the Morris tribunal, pictured with **Paudge Dorrian** the solicitor who's interview with reporter Connie Duffy first led to the publication of allegations that Garda interview rooms were 'bugged' during the Barron investigation. The allegation was an attempt by Sergeant John White 'to distance himself from the central issues that he was being asked to explain at the time'. (*faduda.ie*)

Sgt Niall Coady: The scenes of crime officer was the first officer to examine the site of Richie Barron's death. Unfortunately, by the time he was notified and arrived at the scene, it had already been cleaned, and vital evidence was lost. (*faduda.ie*)

Michael Peoples had the misfortune to be wrongly arrested twice for crimes that never happened. So great was the confusion in Donegal, Justice Morris noted, that no one seemed quite sure on what charge he was arrested the first time. With him is **Charlotte Peoples**, who complained to the tribunal that during her arrest her pleas to detectives to help Roisin McConnell, who was being mistreated, were ignored. *(James Connolly / PicSell8)*

Tom Coffey: A detective employed by Billy Flynn, the private investigator hired by Frank McBrearty Snr to clear his family's name. Coffey re-interviewed many witnesses who were in Raphoe the night Richie Barron died, retracing the steps of the botched Garda inquiry. *(faduda.ie)*

'The next thing he came back and he says, your husband says you're a lying bastard, he was at his work that day. And I said to him, I says, I didn't say he wasn't at his work, I said he wasn't away to his work when I left the house.'

Solicitor Paudge Dorrian told the Morris tribunal that John White refused Eunan Brolly permission to visit his wife 'for fear that information may have been relayed to her husband by Roisin McConnell in relation to her questioning and other people who were questioned and that he could come in and relay that information and obstruct or impede the investigation.' The solicitor offered no explanation for White's apparent rage.

The decision, 'in flagrant disregard' of statutory regulations, was criticised by the Morris tribunal. White should have consulted with the member in charge, and noted the decision in the custody record. It was 'a pity' that Sergeant Heffernan, a 'compassionate and conscientious Garda', did not act as he should have done in respect of the visit, and did not object to White's decision.

Outside, Eunan asked Paul Heffernan when he could see his wife. The sergeant told him to call in an hour or so. When he got home, he phoned the station again. 'There was still no joy at that stage,' he recalled. Eunan called several times during the night. Sometimes, the phone would ring out. Other times, someone would answer, but nobody could tell him when he would see Katrina. It was after 7 a.m. before Eunan got to speak to Detective Sergeant Heffernan again. The sergeant told him he could come down to the station, his wife would be released shortly.

Katrina had no idea when she would be released. 'They had me convinced all night that I was being kept, first I was doing fourteen years, then the other two came in and I was doing seven years, then John White and John Dooley came in and they asked me how would I feel whenever I was looking after my sister's baby,' she remembered.

'Well I thought to myself they couldn't even get it right.'

Katrina told the tribunal it was her signature on interview notes taken by White and Dooley but said she couldn't understand why, when she hadn't signed anything until then, she signed those particular notes. When White and Dooley left, Detective Sergeant Paul Heffernan and Garda Sean Herraghty took over.

White and Dooley returned at 2.45 a.m., along with Garda Joan Gallagher. It was then that Katrina remembered things got rough. The photographs were thrown on the desk. No one is quite sure when they were left there. Katrina remembered they lay loose on the table; John White and John Dooley thought they were in an album inside a folder for most of the night. Dooley had the photographs with him during all three interviews with Katrina, but it was only during the second interview that they were produced.

'I was sitting at a table and they threw them, loose photographs,' Katrina remembered. 'There was a facial view and there was hands,' she told the Morris tribunal, 'They were loose.'

Katrina remembered the photographs being shoved almost into her face. John White, John Dooley and Joan Gallagher were all in the room at the time. 'They would have taken the photographs in and they threw them, they didn't mention, they just threw them on the table beside me so that I could have a view of them.' The lights were turned down. Katrina remembered one of the detectives saying to her 'Richie Barron will come back to haunt you tonight.'

'I said I wish to God he would, he might tell yous what happened him. Then I remember Mr Dooley thought I was too comfortable and he made me stand out in the middle of the floor and they were pushing the photographs into my face. Joan Gallagher was in the room at this stage and the next thing, I can't remember what question they had asked me and she said you lying bastard you, and she reached for my hair. And I told her to let it go.

'A few minutes later she reached for me again and I said to John White and John Dooley, I said that's it. I says I thought I was brought in here for questioning, not to be abused. They kept asking questions and she was standing behind me, over at the side and I wouldn't answer them.'

The impasse ended when White nodded his head to Joan Gallagher. 'It would have been a sign to get out of the room. So then they kind of turned all nice and Dooley pulled the chair up again and said, oh, sit down. You know, to sit down again. They started questioning again and I remember Dooley pulled like a wee slip of paper out of his pocket.

'It had a named person, and he asked me did I know her and I said I did. He asked me details about her and he says did you know that Mark McConnell's riding her. I looked and I started to laugh. He says do you know what riding is, Katrina? And I said I find that hard to believe. And there was a mention of Mark making a statement too that he had done it and I laughed.'

The detectives asked her what was so funny. They asked her if she would believe it when he appeared in court in the morning. 'No,' said Katrina, 'I will believe it whenever it comes out of Mark's mouth.' Then they told her that Mark McConnell was an abusive husband, and Roisin was terrified of him.

'I started to laugh again and he says oh, do you not believe that either, and I says no I don't.' Katrina was also told that her two young daughters would be taken away and put into care. John White said she had made a late night telephone call to Letterkenny hospital the night Richie Barron died. When she told him she hadn't, he claimed to have a tape of the call, and told her 'The more I listen to it the more it sounds like your voice.'

The Guards kept insisting Katrina had phoned the hospital the night Richie Barron died, and Katrina insisted just as vehemently that she hadn't. At the time, she did not know Mark McConnell had phoned the hospital from her house. He had initially refused to do so when Roisin asked him to find out if Richie was alright. Later, he called and gave a false name, then hung up when the receptionist checked if he was a relative. When he told Roisin he'd phoned but hadn't been able to find out anything, no one was sure whether to believe him or not.

White pitched a theory to Katrina, trying to get an admission. 'He knew it wasn't Mark that done it, that it was Young Frank, that Mark was just there, Mark stood back, but it was Young Frank. They asked me was I being bribed, was Frank McBrearty bribing me, was that why I was afraid to open my mouth and say anything. I said, no, nobody was bribing me.'

White pressed the point. 'He maintained that it wasn't Mark that done it, that it was Young Frank. He said that my son would be got, how would I feel whenever my son would be got. They must have thought that I had information, that I knew it was Young Frank, you know, that had done it. That he was maintaining that Mark just stood back and watched, that he had nothing to do with it.'

Twice during the session, according to the official custody record, Garda Tom Kilcoyne checked in and found 'all in order'. Kilcoyne told the Morris tribunal he had no memory of those brief visits, nothing out of the ordinary stuck in his mind. Apart from the brief visits to the room, Kilcoyne, who was also station orderly, remained at his station, down a corridor, through a set of double doors, in the public reception area at the front of the station. Unlike Leonard, who was member in charge until 10 p.m., Kilcoyne could not see the interview rooms. The daytime arrests had been planned, Leonard had Garda Willie Cannon to help him, and another Garda to man the reception area. The evening arrests were almost an afterthought—Kilcoyne was on his own.

From his station, Kilcoyne could not see who entered or left the interview rooms. He was dependent on others to tell him their comings and goings. Kilcoyne couldn't remember Eunan Brolly visiting the station to see Katrina around midnight. He thought he might have been bringing Donna Quinn to see her husband at the time and missed him. Or Eunan might have asked to see 'a Guard named Paul', and he might have gone to fetch Paul Heffernan without ever realising who Eunan Brolly was. No one told him Eunan was looking for his wife, or that he was refused a visit. As custody officer, it was his job to make the final decision on who did or didn't get a visit, and to record the incident in the custody record. None of Eunan's phone calls that night to Letterkenny were transferred to him. If they had been, he would have recorded them in the custody record, and asked Katrina if she wanted to talk to her husband. Finally, nobody told him Katrina had asked to phone home and check on her children.

———

According to the official custody record, after Donna left, Mark Quinn was questioned by Detective Garda Padraic Scanlon and Sergeant Joe Hannigan between 12.08 a.m. and 1.50 a.m. Unusually, Scanlon's overtime form A85 records that he went off duty on 4 December at 9 p.m. Scanlon wasn't rostered to work on 4 December, but he was called in to help with the interviews. He questioned Roisin McConnell at one point, but couldn't remember what he did after 9 p.m. until he was called in to question Mark Quinn just after midnight. Scanlon told the tribunal he took no notes during any of his interviews with Mark Quinn. Mark himself didn't remember seeing Scanlon or Hannigan at all after midnight. It wasn't until the end of the night that he saw the two men, he told the tribunal.

The custody record shows Scanlon leaving the interview room at 1.50 a.m., replaced by Sergeant Joe Hannigan. At some point, Mark Quinn recalled, he was questioned by 'two Gardaí in front of me asking me what I knew, tell us what you know. The same again, how much did Frank McBrearty give you? Different times, what time—it was just constant, going on and on, questioning.'

Between 2.30 a.m. and 3.30 a.m., Mark Quinn was allowed a rest period. He remembered being taken to the cells. 'I was a bit uncomfortable walking around, cold like, you know,' he explained. He'd been barefoot since his first interview. 'It was cold in the cell, yeah I was very cold in the cell . . . Like air conditioner blower, very cold air, when I was in the cell it was blowing in. I can remember it very cold, like. I can remember look-ing at my hands and they were pure blue with cold.'

The custody record says that after his 'rest period', Mark Quinn was again questioned by Detective Garda PJ Keating and Sergeant Joe Hannigan. This was the first time he could remember seeing Hannigan since his arrest. Keating, on the other hand, he felt he saw 'more than any other Guard'.

Just after 4 a.m., Mark was taken downstairs. A Garda told him he was free to go, he could phone home and arrange for his wife to collect him. 'I'll take him home,' Hannigan said.

Mark's property was returned—including his shoes—and he was given the custody record to sign, saying he had no complaints. 'Anything that was put in front of me, as I said before, I just signed it because I just wanted to get it over and get out,' he told the Morris tribunal. 'I was too frightened, I just wanted to get out.'

Mark Quinn didn't see a solicitor when he was in custody. He didn't go to a solicitor after he was released. There was no point. Who was going to investigate the Guards?

'I was so frightened, so scared of losing the business, we had a heavy mortgage and two young kids,' he recalled.

Donna Quinn remembered how her husband looked upset and drawn when he got home. 'I just gave him a hug and a kiss when he came in and he was very withdrawn and I suggested that he had a cup of tea and a piece of toast and sat down. I started asking questions then about what had happened and he just got up, went to the bathroom, and he said he was going to bed. That was it. He had thrown up his tea and toast and he went to bed,' Donna remembered.

'I tried to talk about it but Mark just didn't want to talk about it,' Donna recalled. 'He never wanted to talk about it. He's bottled everything up, has never really dealt with it, only maybe through alcohol.'

Mark couldn't face anyone after his arrest. Raphoe was a small town, everyone was talking about the arrests. No smoke without fire. Mark withdrew. When the pub was busy, he'd stand out the back rather than face the customers. Donna got the story from Mark in 'bits and pieces' in the years that followed. Whatever he told her, she wrote down. Mark didn't want to go to a lawyer for advice, but Donna was determined to help him confront what was happening. She'd sit with him and take notes as he told his story.

In February 2002, Mark Quinn finally went to see Ken Smyth, a solicitor acting for the McBreartys, the McConnells, the Peoples and others at the time. His only earlier record of his treatment in custody are the undated notes his wife Donna took of the things he told her, which she handed over to the Morris tribunal, and an interview with two members of the Carty team where he 'just told them what was happening,' though to the Carty team he concentrated more on the harassment of his pub business.

'After my arrest the fear that I was living in was unbearable. I couldn't talk to anyone. I was scared of a lot of people, especially anyone in a uniform,' he told the tribunal.

'The business just seemed to go quiet after . . . It was common knowledge that I was arrested. Didn't go too well to tell you the truth, I seemed to hit the bottle a lot harder. I really didn't want to see people or talk to people.'

———

Around the time Mark Quinn was released from Garda custody, there was a changing of the Guard with Katrina Brolly. At 4 a.m., Sergeant John White and Detective Garda John Dooley left the interview room. Detective

Sergeant Paul Heffernan and Detective Garda Sean Herraghty returned.

'I didn't come in here to be abused, I came in to be questioned,' Katrina complained.

Heffernan put his hands up. 'Sure I didn't touch you,' he said.

Having misinterpreted her complaint as directed against himself, Heffernan didn't press the issue any further. The tribunal did not criticise Heffernan and Herraghty for failing to act on what Katrina said to them.

'And by the way,' Katrina added, pointing at Heffernan, 'I didn't get my phone call.' Sean Herraghty had a pen in his hand. The pen came down on her finger. 'Don't you dare point your finger at him,' he said.

The interviews continued deep into the night. At 5.30 a.m., Katrina was allowed a rest for forty-five minutes, before Herraghty and Heffernan saw her again. Herraghty and Heffernan were then replaced again by White and Dooley. No notes survive from this interview, or from the earlier interview involving White and Dooley. No notes were ever made.

At one point, 'Dooley looked at his watch and said, I have been on the go now for nearly twenty-five hours,' Katrina recalled. 'White was leaning back, kind of sitting, he said "Katrina do you feel sorry for him? He hasn't seen his wife and wains in twenty-five hours."'

'I do surely,' Katrina replied.

'Go on, you lying bastard you,' White said.

'Sure I've been on the go nearly as long myself,' Katrina told him. White looked at his watch. 'I suppose you have,' he laughed.

Finally, Katrina was taken from the interview room back to the cells. The custody record shows she was released at 8.15 a.m., twenty minutes short of the twelve-hour maximum the Gardaí could hold her.

Katrina didn't remember signing the custody record as she was released. She couldn't understand how she would have signed any document saying she had no complaints. The signature was hers, she told the tribunal, she just didn't remember making it.

At the tribunal, Katrina was asked if she had considered 'saying something to get out of there' while under arrest.

'No. I was always brought up to tell the truth,' she answered. 'There was no way I was going to sit and tell lies just to save myself. Yeah they were trying to pressurise me into it but I kept telling them all night what they were saying wasn't the truth. But I was just called the liar.

'My husband brought me home. My mother was in the house because she had stayed down with my husband with the children and all and they were ready to go to school so I just sent them on to school and my mother said to go to bed for a while but I couldn't sleep.

'I went to the solicitor then, I think it was about 3 p.m., to make my complaint. I kind of went through it in a daze . . . I know Mark and Roisin was along with me.'

The meeting at VP McMullin & Co. was chaotic. Mark McConnell described how everyone was talking at once, trying to get their stories across. In the confusion, the hair-pulling allegation was mistakenly recorded twice, in both the complaints from Katrina and from Roisin. It was not until the Morris tribunal that the confusion was finally sorted out.

———

Ten days after her release, Roisin McConnell was admitted as an in-patient to St Conal's, a local psychiatric hospital, where she spent the next eight weeks. She was heavily medicated, and underwent three sessions of electric shock treatment. She believed the hospital staff were detectives 'in there just to get me', and didn't even trust her family when they came to visit her.

'From the times that I had got out, then my mind started to work on what they had done and everything and then I was trying to think, you know, who did kill Richie Barron,' she remembered. 'My head was just going. John White had said that Richie Barron was going to come back and haunt me. So I used to sit up every night, like I just couldn't sleep anyway and I could hear noises in the house, well I would imagine hearing noises probably. I just started to slowly go downhill.'

Chapter 15
The Don

On 4 December, Noel McBride—Mister X—made a second statement to Garda John O'Dowd. He claimed that a few days earlier,
Old Frank McBrearty gave him £500 to keep quiet. The Gardaí
in Donegal had planned to arrest both Old Frank and Young Frank on
4 December 1996, but they missed Old Frank. Already frantic with concern at what he suspected was a Garda plot to frame him and his family,
Old Frank left Raphoe at 5 a.m. that morning to drive to Dublin, where
he tried to meet Joan Burton, a Labour Party TD and Junior Minister in
the Department of Justice, 'about the harassment we were getting at our
nightclub and different things'.

Frank arrived back in Donegal around 7 p.m. on 5 December, and
called to his sister Hannah McConnell's home. A local priest, Fr Ciaran
Harkin, was there, and they brought Frank up to date on all that had
happened while he was away. 'There was a lot of anger,' Frank recalled.
'We were very upset.'

After a while, Frank left Hannah's and walked the thirty or so yards to
his own home, to collect any post and catch up on messages that had
arrived while he was away. He was on the phone when he heard the
commotion outside. Frank said that the front door was locked, and
before he could put the phone down and answer it, the Gardaí had gone
round to the back door. Sergeant Paul Heffernan said that when he
arrived Frank got up, locked his front door, and wouldn't let him in.

There were several Garda cars outside. Frank thought there were
'anything up to sixty' Guards at the door. It would not be his last exag-
geration. He remembered Detective Sergeant Mick Keane, Detective
Sergeant Paul Heffernan, Garda John O'Dowd, Garda Phil Collins, Garda
John Harkin, Detective Garda James Frain, Sergeant Joe Hannigan, and
Sergeant PJ Hennigan. Others at the search were Detective Garda Michael
O'Malley, Detective Garda Pat Tague, Garda John Forkan and Garda Niall
Coady (both later promoted to sergeant rank).

Despite the key part Noel McBride's second statement played in the
decision to search Frank McBrearty's home, none of the Gardaí present
knew about it. Garda John O'Dowd, Sergeant Marty Moylan and
Detective Superintendent Joe Shelly were the only people aware of its

existence. None of the Gardaí in the search party knew the main reason for the search, or what exactly they were looking for.

Over in Hannah's house, Frank's wife Rosalind saw the cars arrive. She went to see what was happening, along with her nephews Eamonn and Michael McConnell. 'There were words with Sergeant Hannigan,' Frank told the tribunal diplomatically.

When she got inside her home, Rosalind remembered three Guards, Frain, Harkin and Heffernan, in the front room. Frank told her to watch one of the other rooms, where Guards were searching. She tried to take notes, and wrote down one name, 'Sergeant Faulkner', possibly mishearing Garda John Forkan's name. Bizarrely, Rosalind sprinkled holy water on the Guards.

Before the Guards entered his home, Frank tried to phone Superintendent Fitzgerald's number to find out what was happening, but had no luck. The superintendent wasn't at home. He then dialled his doctor's number. 'The whole thing collapsed around me then, because the whole lot was all in the sitting room, Frain was there, Harkin was in there, Heffernan was there and Keane was there. They were all in around me.'

Sergeant Heffernan had a search warrant, issued under Section 29 of the Offences Against the State Act, signed by Detective Superintendent Joe Shelly. Old Frank said he remembered 'a piece of something in his hand but I never read it'.

When Dr Martin Coyne arrived, he examined Frank in his bedroom, and gave him a tablet. 'Essentially we were looking for any evidence that would link Mr McBrearty to the alleged intimidation of witnesses in any shape or form,' Paul Heffernan said, explaining the reasons for the search. Heffernan said that after Dr Coyne arrived and examined Frank, he spoke to the doctor, asking him if Frank was okay, and 'got a positive response'.

Dr Coyne in evidence said he would not have told the Garda it was inappropriate to arrest Frank, but 'voiced my concerns about the fact he should not be stressed.' Heffernan said he could not recall the doctor telling him Frank 'should not be stressed.' After speaking to the doctor, Heffernan arrested Frank McBrearty. Heffernan said it was always intended to arrest Frank McBrearty, regardless of what was found in the search, those were his orders. He was directed at a conference to read the statements and then apply for warrants. He was not told before the arrest that 'Mister X' had made a second statement about the McBreartys, alleging he was offered a £500 bribe.

Detective Garda James Frain said that when he tried to talk to Frank about the notes and documentation that were being taken, he was 'dismissive', and Rosalind 'used very foul language. She was very angry.' The detective said that at the time, he believed what he was told about allegations that Frank McBrearty was intimidating witnesses, and that the death of Richie Barron was a murder case, but added that since then 'my mind has been changed', explaining that 'over the period of this tribunal there have been some amazing revelations that I never knew about, and my colleagues never knew about'.

'It certainly took a lot of chat to get him out of the house, but there was no physical force,' Frain explained. McBrearty protested during the car journey from his home to Letterkenny Garda station, and 'it was a tirade of abuse from the time we left Raphoe until we got to Letterkenny'.

Sergeant John Forkan said that because there were allegations of bribery, he seized bank statements. Frank was abusive to the Guards, 'calling us bastards, but it wasn't directed to me, he didn't know me,' and 'roaring like a bull around the place'.

'It was hostile,' he concluded simply. 'I thought the Guards behaved respectfully.'

Frank complained several times at the Morris tribunal about the 'Don Photo'. Taken during a family occasion, the photo showed Frank sitting in a vest on a chair. The photo went missing, and he later learned it was pinned to a notice board in Letterkenny Garda station, with the words 'The Don' written underneath.

Frank was arrested by Sergeant Heffernan just before 8 p.m., on suspicion of intimidating witnesses during a Garda investigation, and placed in the back seat of a patrol car alongside Detective Sergeant Mick Keane. Heffernan got into the front passenger seat, and Frain drove.

Heffernan told how on the way to the station, Frank 'constantly shouted abuse from the back seat of the car' and told him 'that I would never work in Donegal again, words to that effect'. Keane said the publican shouted abuse at Heffernan and Detective Garda Frain. 'He was at times a wee bit abusive to the two members in the front. He probably didn't know them. He was maintaining they were of somewhat small stature to be in the Guards.' Frank also mentioned his standing in the community as a respectable businessman, his involvement with Raphoe boxing club, and winning the Lord Mayor competition.

The evidence of intimidation to justify the arrest of Frank McBrearty was presented to the Morris tribunal over several days, and consisted of approaches Frank made to several people who had made statements to Gardaí.

One instance involved Aileen Campbell, a part-time bar worker in McBrearty's nightclub. On 8 December 2006 she told the tribunal she was asked by Frank to write out the questions Gardaí asked her. She said that after she was interviewed by Gardaí, Frank 'asked about himself and Young Frank and Mark and all'.

'I had said I didn't remember seeing them, because I worked at the bar and he was up the front at the door . . . He said of course you seen me . . . He made a comment to me, of course you remember, you stupid looking . . . and he stopped speaking.'

Aileen felt 'a little bit embarrassed because it was in front of all the staff', and Old Frank asked her to write down what the Gardaí had asked her. She agreed to do so, but the next day, her parents told her not to make a statement for him because she was only a teenager and could get caught up in court proceedings.

The following night, Frank McBrearty asked her for the list of questions, and when she said she didn't have them, he said 'You're fond enough of the work here, aren't you?'

'That's up to you,' she told him, got her coat and left. The following week, Aileen visited the nightclub as a customer, and when she spoke to Frank 'he told me my job was there if I wanted it. I was there working for a year afterwards.' Aileen said she felt 'more uncomfortable and embarrassed rather than scared' by the incident. She said she was not concerned that Frank McBrearty would ask her to change her statement.

John Rouse was the member in charge at Letterkenny Garda station when Frank McBrearty arrived under arrest at 8.10 p.m. It was the first time he had met the Raphoe publican. While Frank was processed, his solicitor, James O'Donnell, arrived at 8.25 p.m. They spoke together for a while. Shortly after arriving, Frank requested a doctor, and Rouse made the phone call at 9.20 p.m. Before Rouse could make any phone call to the doctor, he had to escort Frank to the interview room. He then phoned looking for Dr Coyne, but when Coyne said he couldn't come, he telephoned Dr Ciaran Kelly, Coyne's partner in the practice. Kelly couldn't come either, and when Rouse told Frank, the publican said he didn't need a doctor. Frank made no complaints to Rouse about the detectives interviewing him before Rouse went off duty at 10 p.m., replaced by Garda Liam Dowd.

After he was processed and spoke to his solicitor, Frank was taken to the interview rooms. Detective Sergeant Paul Heffernan said he 'wasn't very co-operative, it was tense, it was difficult to get any structure out of it', and at one point he 'went over to the window and started praying'. Frank was 'volatile' and 'intimidating', and 'very forthright, very up front. He is a strong character.'

Frank was not physically abused by the detectives in custody, he conceded at the tribunal, but the very fact of his arrest was an outrage to his dignity. Each of the allegations the detectives put to him, he took as a personal attack. 'They would have been as well hitting me, the things they said were so offensive,' he complained.

Detective Garda PJ Keating said that during questioning, Frank shouted and banged a table, 'banging with his fists, his two fists on the table . . . He would get up off the chair and bang on the table.' At one point McBrearty 'got on his knees and started to pray'.

At 10.05 p.m., Frank took a phone call from Peter Murphy, a solicitor, and returned to the interview room. Three Guards, Herraghty, Heffernan and Keating, joined him when he returned to the interview room. Meanwhile Liam Dowd, the member in charge, noted in the custody record that he had contacted a Dr McGeehan, who agreed to come in and examine Frank. Five minutes later though, Dr Kelly arrived. Dowd brought him down to see Frank, then phoned to cancel Dr McGeehan.

Dr Ciaran A. Kelly examined Old Frank between 10.35 p.m. and 11 p.m., and directed the member in charge to take the prisoner to hospital. McBrearty told the tribunal he 'had pains in my arms, and across my chest'. The custody record entry at 11 p.m. recorded Dr Kelly telling the member in charge that 'the prisoner was in danger of having a heart attack or stroke and that he be taken to casualty'. Ten years later to the day, on 5 December 2006, Doctor Ciaran Kelly gave evidence at the Morris tribunal. The doctor stated there was no delay in getting McBrearty to hospital. He had gone to the station because he received a phone call from a member of Frank's family concerned about his well-being, and knew his partner in the practice had earlier examined Frank at his home.

'When I arrived there he was complaining of numbness and loss of power on the left side of his face, his blood pressure was raised, he was very distressed about what had happened and I formed the opinion that he was at risk of having either a stroke or a transcient ischemic attack and I recommended he be admitted to hospital. He was subsequently admitted to Letterkenny where that diagnosis was confirmed, and then he was moved on to Dublin,' Dr Kelly explained. He was happy that the Gardaí had responded with appropriate speed in allowing access and getting Frank to hospital.

Mr Brian Callaghan, a consultant physician, examined Frank when he arrived at Letterkenny General Hospital. He later told the Morris tribunal his patient had abnormal heart readings, suffered from hypertension, and complained of numbness in his hand. These were the symptoms of a possible heart attack, he explained.

Chapter 16

I Heard the Photos
Were Bad

Old Frank McBrearty was admitted to Letterkenny General Hospital just after 11 p.m. on 5 December. He would not return to the Garda station for a week. While in hospital, he was still under arrest as far as the Gardaí were concerned. 'There was a twenty-four-hour guard on me in hospital,' he complained. For their part, the Gardaí did their best to keep their presence discreet.

Earlier that evening, when Frank arrived home from Dublin, he found that the arrests the previous day were front page news: 'Arrests in Murder Hunt' was splashed over the front page of that morning's *Donegal Democrat*. Superintendent John Fitzgerald was quoted at length in the article, outlining the thoroughness of the police operation, with over 500 statements taken by a team of twenty detectives whose work he described as 'both intense and painstaking'.

The following week, while Frank was still in hospital, the *Democrat* of 12 December reported that 'The patient at the centre of a 24 hour guard by Gardaí in connection with the death of Raphoe man Richie Barrons [sic!] was this week transferred from Letterkenny General Hospital to a hospital in Dublin. The man, who is believed to be from the Raphoe area, was arrested on Sunday night under Section 30 of the Offences Against the State Act and became the tenth person to be arrested in the investigations.' This time, Chief Superintendent Denis Fitzpatrick was quoted, saying Gardaí were 'now following a definite line of inquiry'.

Frank was in fact the ninth person to be arrested, and he was picked up on Thursday 5 December. The following Sunday, Gardaí arrested Marty McCallion, one of the bouncers who worked in Frankie's nightclub.

A decade later at the Morris tribunal, Frank told how 'In a small town of 1,400 people, we were shamed,' so that he was unable even to go to the local graveyard to visit his mother's grave. 'We were spat on, we were assaulted,' he told the chairman. 'I have lost nearly all my life's savings, the banks, to try to fight for the truth.'

Marty McCallion was arrested just after he crossed the bridge dividing the twin towns of Strabane, Co. Tyrone, and Lifford, Co. Donegal, on his way to work at Frankie's nightclub, shortly before 10 p.m. on the evening of Sunday 8 December. The 31-year-old Tyrone native held down two part-time jobs, as a bouncer and doorman for Frank McBrearty in Raphoe, and as a barman in Strabane. He'd worked for Frank for five years, and knew Young Frank well—they boxed together.

The arresting officer, Garda John O'Toole, explained why he was under arrest, and the section of the Criminal Law Act which placed him under arrest, but as far as Marty was concerned, 'it was like Double-Dutch'. He thought he was being arrested because there was a bit of confusion about what time Paul 'Gazza' Gallagher was bounced from the nightclub, and the Gardaí wanted to sort it out.

He was taken to Letterkenny Garda station, read his rights and booked, and taken to the interview rooms within half an hour of his arrest, where he was questioned by John O'Toole and Detective Garda Mick Carroll until close to midnight. Five minutes before midnight, the member in charge, Garda Martin McDonnell, gave him the option of resting for the night, or continuing the questioning. Marty said he'd keep going. McDonnell, a rookie who still hadn't completed his training at the time, told the tribunal he'd only been in the force six or seven months by that night. He said he had little memory of the night, and the contents of the custody record were not necessarily what he saw, but also what he was told by the interviewers. Garda Dan Curran took over from McDonnell at 1 a.m.

From the moment of their release until they gave evidence at the Morris tribunal, several of those who were arrested in December 1996 claimed they were shown explicit photographs taken during Richie Barron's post-mortem examination. With equal fervour, the Gardaí would deny anyone was shown the photographs for years. Some continued to deny even in the witness box, while others admitted it had happened before then, often at the eleventh hour. Despite evidence from several suspects that it happened, and similar evidence in another module from seven Travellers arrested near Burnfoot in May 1998, every Garda denied there was a policy of showing post-mortem photographs to murder suspects.

Incredibly, one of the earliest written complaints about the post-mortem photographs is recorded in the interview notes taken by O'Toole and Carroll during their first interview with Marty McCallion on 8 December 1996.

Describing the wounds, one of the detectives told Marty that Richie Barron 'was in a bad way'.

'I know, I heard the photos were bad,' Marty answered.

'How do you know that?'

'Young Frank said to me—I saw him last night and I said to him you are a bad colour. He said to me if you saw what I saw you would be a bad colour too. He said that he saw photographs and that they were horrific…'

Marty told the tribunal his interviewers didn't seem surprised when he told them this. He added that Young Frank told him 'he was getting abused and hit, verbally and physically'.

O'Toole and Carroll continued questioning Marty McCallion until 12.45 a.m. Marty said he 'was treated fair' by O'Toole and Carroll. He went through his movements, told them he was working with Young Frank the night Richie Barron died, and described the major incidents he remembered from the night.

O'Toole told the tribunal he believed Marty 'was being honest. However, I do believe also that he was withholding.' He then qualified this to say that 'whilst he was being very candid in his answers, we still felt that there was a bit more and he wasn't being entirely honest'.

Interview notes taken later that night by Mick Carroll and Detective Garda Pat Tague also contained mention of the photographs. Marty told the detectives that Young Frank was 'pale looking', and added that 'he was shown photos here and that they had a bad effect on him'.

'I was surprised but I don't know if I actually believed him at all in relation to it, we just moved on from it,' Tague explained. He added that people who were arrested often gave 'a bravado report of what happened' after their release.

At 12.45 a.m., Detective Garda Martin Anderson and Detective Garda Padraic Scanlon took over. At 2.30 a.m., Marty got a break, an hour in his cell to rest. The third interview started at 3.30 a.m., this time Detective Garda Carroll was joined by Detective Garda Pat Tague. Ten minutes into the interview, Superintendent John Fitzgerald authorised the Gardaí to hold Marty for a further six hours, and photograph and fingerprint him. The custody record shows a succession of interviews as the night wore on. Carroll and Tague were succeeded by Scanlon and Anderson for a second time, then back to Carroll and Tague again.

Marty McCallion's account of the interviews caused some confusion at the tribunal. Each time the interviewers in the room changed, the tribunal counted it as a separate session. As far as Marty was concerned, there was one session with several teams of Guards until he got his break in the cells, and then a second interview 'when I came back out of the cell'. With the two sides at cross-purposes, it wasn't always clear who Martin was talking about when describing particular events, or which Gardaí might have shown him photographs.

Marty told the tribunal that 'the tone changed' during the second interview. A detective told him 'this is not a laughing matter' and told him he was arrested 'for conspiracy to murder after the event'.

'You must be fucking joking,' Marty replied.

One of the detectives 'raised his voice', and showed him the post-mortem photographs.

'Does that not bother you?' he asked.

'It doesn't bother me,' Marty answered.

The detective told him he wasn't bothered by the graphic images because he 'didn't do it, but you might as well have done it'.

Marty described to the tribunal a photograph of an 'aqua blue' Cavalier car among the post-mortem images, 'What's that about?' he asked the detectives.

At that, the booklet of photographs was pulled away from him.

Lawyers for the Gardaí tried various theories to the tribunal to explain how Marty was able to describe in detail the photographs he had seen, including the detailed picture he drew of the car for Michael Finn, the tribunal investigator. Roisin McConnell and Katrina Brolly were shown photographs—John Dooley had admitted as much several months earlier. Therefore, they argued, Roisin had described the photographs to Marty, and to cover up for his friend, he told O'Toole and Carroll a tall tale about Young Frank.

Other barristers argued that no detective ever showed the photographs to Marty, and he got the descriptions from Young Frank. Yet another theory was that Marty had seen the photographs during the inquest into Richie Barron's death in 2003, and as a result was able to describe them. Unfortunately for this theory, the photograph of a blue Cavalier car from a separate crime scene, which the tribunal saw because it was developed from the same roll of film, was not included in the folders of photographs used at the inquest. Finally, the lawyers claimed Marty was after money, and was making the claim to boost the damages he could earn in the High Court.

Gardaí also took issue with Marty's description of the book in which the photographs were bound. Garda booklets had a yellow cover, with black spiral binding, they argued, while McCallion described a brown covered booklet. Eventually the tribunal chairman looked up from his notes to tell one Garda he'd seen 'loads' of albums during his legal career. 'Have you ever seen the red ones? I've a couple upstairs actually,' he asked. The Garda insisted that 'generally' Garda albums were yellow.

Marty didn't like the way the tone had changed during the second interview. There was an edgy feel to the room, more aggressive than before. Early in the night, with O'Toole and Carroll, he'd had a conversation. This time, detectives weren't listening to what he had to say. He was being accused of murder, shown photographs of grisly injuries. 'I'll cooperate, but if you give me a hard time, it'll be the longest twelve hours you ever spent in here,' he told the detectives. 'I told them I'd help them in any manner at all, I would answer their questions,' he explained to the tribunal. 'If they would treat me with respect, I would treat them with respect.' Things calmed down a bit after that.

He told the tribunal he didn't complain at the time that he was shown post-mortem photographs, because as far as he knew, it was part of standard policing practice, and had only found out when the tribunal began that it shouldn't have happened. Overall, he said he didn't have an issue with the way he was treated in custody.

All of the Gardaí denied showing any photographs to Marty McCallion. The tribunal could not identify which Garda showed him the photographs. 'The fact that nobody admits to the showing of these photographs to Mr McCallion suggests to the tribunal that the Gardaí involved knew that there was no good reason to do so,' the chairman noted.

Gina Lohan, who took over as custody officer from Dan Curran at 6 a.m., told the tribunal that exhibits, such as photographs, would be fetched by the interviewing detectives themselves, and the member in charge wouldn't know anything about it unless they told her or made a record of it in their interview notes. 'I never saw photographs in the interview, nor did I know if any Garda was showing them,' she told the tribunal. None of the other custody officers saw anything out of the ordinary.

Marty remembered that for the final interview, there were a lot of Guards present. 'It was more or less a chat before I was being released,' he explained. He was asked about how much he was paid to lie about the night Richie Barron died, and told the detectives 'It'll take more than thirty pieces of silver for me to sell out Frank McBrearty.' He had already made a statement to Sergeant Joe Hannigan back in October, but that morning he made another. It told pretty much the same story as what he'd already said to Hannigan, but went into much more detail about his movements the night Barron died. He was released from custody at 9.45 a.m. on Monday morning.

———

From 5 December to 12 December 1996 Old Frank was in Letterkenny hospital, except for 11 December when he was taken to James Connolly Memorial Hospital in Blanchardstown, Dublin, for tests. 'The hospital was absolutely brilliant to me, and the doctors and nurses. I have to thank them very much,' he recalled. He was less impressed with the fact that at all times there were two Guards 'watching the prisoner'.

Detective Garda Jim Frain said he had never seen a prisoner admitted to hospital and held for so long previously. 'I think there was the opinion that he was playing the game a little bit,' he told the Morris tribunal. He said Frank was still a prisoner, and there was an onus on Gardaí to ensure that he was kept securely. He didn't stop any visitors, but on one occasion Young Frank and Mark McConnell were speaking loudly in the corridor and Detective Garda Martin Anderson told them to be quiet, because there was a terminally ill patient in the next room. Frank also came out and told the two to keep the noise down, Frain said. Visitors were asked their names, but no one was prevented from seeing Frank. Other Guards also pointed out that Frank was technically still under arrest, and they had tried to follow him discreetly. They said they brought him newspapers and magazines to read.

After his return from Blanchardstown, the doctors released Frank back into Garda custody. 'We felt satisfied that he wasn't going to get a coronary or a stroke,' Letterkenny consultant Mr Callaghan explained. However, he said stress could exacerbate Frank's condition, and in a letter at the time he wrote: 'It would not be in his best interest to be inter-rogated at this time.'

'There was uncertainty, he did appear to be stressed,' the consultant explained. He said he had spoken with a Garda in the room where McBrearty was staying, and explained the situation, and 'the officer was very professional and immediately left the room'.

Chapter 17

We Couldn't Understand What Was Happening to Us

While Old Frank McBrearty was in Blanchardstown hospital, Gardaí arrested Sean Crossan, a local electrician who also worked part-time as a doorman at the McBrearty nightclub in Raphoe. Aged forty-seven at the time, the father of six lived in the town, less than five minutes walk from the nightclub. He was working in the car park when a patrol car pulled up, and the detectives inside asked to see him in front of the dance hall. When he got there, Detective Sergeant Sylvie Henry arrested him, shortly before midday.

Crossan had already made two statements to Gardaí, initially saying he saw nothing the night Richie Barron died, and later going to Sergeant Joe Hannigan to make a statement saying he saw three young men coming down the car park. The tribunal established that these were probably Edward McBrearty, Martin Mangan and Martin Nelis arriving at the nightclub. Crossan's statements, in which he mentioned seeing Young Frank McBrearty at critical times, provided Young Frank with an alibi. Crossan's second statement also described how he saw Damien McDaid leaving the nightclub and getting into a row with Old Frank McBrearty for driving too fast. Young Frank was also there, and complained to his father because McDaid was doing work on his house and might not finish it after the row. As a result, Young Frank asked Sean Crossan if he would complete the electrical work if McDaid walked away from the job.

In a statement in early 2002, Detective Sergeant Henry said that he was aware that Crossan, on duty the night Richie Barron died, had made these statements, and 'it was my suspicion at that time that Sean Crossan had identified Frank McBrearty Jnr and Mark McConnell and that he was covering up for them by saying that while he saw men there he could not identify them and was trying to frustrate the criminal investigation . . . It was decided by conference held at Letterkenny Garda station that Sean Crossan should be arrested and questioned and I was given the job of arresting him.'

Both Sean Crossan and the detectives who arrested him agreed that the arrest itself was civilised and went smoothly. The detectives cautioned him and explained his rights, and brought him to Letterkenny Garda station. Sean Crossan was booked in Letterkenny, then spent a quarter hour in the cells before he got to see his solicitor James O'Donnell. They spoke for thirty-five minutes. Later in the day, they would speak again on the telephone for the best part of thirty minutes. O'Donnell had already received a message from Young Frank McBrearty, who told him Sean Crossan had been arrested. He told the solicitor that 'the Gardaí had threatened Sean Crossan that unless he changed his statement by Friday they would get him'.

In his notes, O'Donnell wrote that Crossan complained 'the Gardaí had been harassing him and asking him about his dole'. The solicitor also wrote a letter to Superintendent Fitzgerald complaining that the custody officer was unable to give him a reasonable cause as to why his client was arrested. Because Sean Crossan had voluntarily made two statements, and was willing to cooperate with Gardaí, the solicitor wrote, 'it appears that the arrest of our client today is unwarranted and without cause'.

The electrician said that no notes were taken in his first interview with Detective Sergeant Sylvie Henry and Detective Garda Padraic Scanlan. The second team to interview him was made up of Sergeant John White and Detective Sergeant Mick Keane.

'Sergeant White was coaching me to withdraw the statement. It was him that threatened me,' Crossan recalled. White was very angry. 'I was sitting in a chair with three wheels. He kept pushing me about the place,' Crossan said. Detective Sergeant Mick Keane 'was sitting lying back in a chair with his two feet up on the table' at the time. White 'was shouting abuse', told him he was a menace to society and told him 'the wains would be lifted, he would get in contact with the probation officer the next morning'.

'They hit him in the eye and there are clear marks on his face to show this. They hit him in the mouth, stomach, his genitals and they spat on his face and into his mouth,' solicitor James Sweeney wrote in a memo when he spoke to Sean the following day. He advised Sean Crossan to have the marks around his eye photographed and to see a doctor. Crossan handed a note from his doctor Cyril Quinn (since deceased) to the tribunal, which said he suffered 'superficial lacerations to skin of right ear and his right forehead'.

However, despite the fact that his solicitor noted marks above his eye the next day, and a note from a doctor saying the same thing, the tribunal could not conclude that Crossan had actually been assaulted in custody, save on one occasion when Sergeant White prodded him in the chest. The tribunal had difficulty believing that White would be 'sufficiently reckless' to leave a mark on a prisoner. The solicitor's note from the following day was also not enough to make a finding that Sean Crossan was shown photographs, as several other suspects were. However, the tribunal did find that Sean Crossan was told by Sergeant White that he could be reported for dole fraud, have his children taken away, and have his car seized.

At the Morris tribunal, Sergeant Keane gave evidence that White had abused Sean Crossan during the interview. 'I was of the view that Mr Crossan wasn't a hardened criminal that deserved that type of treatment,' he said. Whether this meant 'that type of treatment' would be acceptable with a hardened criminal was not a question the tribunal pursued. White's barrister challenged Keane's evidence vigorously, and claimed he held a grudge against his client.

The tribunal criticised John White for his conduct, and Mick Keane for his passive role, simply watching instead of intervening. Keane's evidence had 'the ring of someone covering himself, and was not accepted as fully correct'.

Crossan agreed. He'd told the chairman he 'would be as well talking to a bench' as complaining to Detective Sergeant Mick Keane about White, since Keane 'sat back and watched what was going on'. Keane was also criticised for the false statement he made in response to the civil claim from Crossan when he denied that Sean Crossan was improperly treated in any way while he was present, only coming forward at all shortly before he was due to give evidence to the Morris tribunal.

When his wife visited him in the station, Sean Crossan told her he was getting badly treated. She told him: 'Whatever they want, sign it and get to hell out of this place.' Eventually, Sean made a statement to Sergeant White and Detective Sergeant Mick Keane withdrawing the earlier statement he had made describing the sighting of the three people in the car park the night Richie Barron died. He told the tribunal he withdrew his statement because he was 'under pressure', and the dominant reason was 'to keep the children'.

During the twelve hours Crossan spent in custody, Detective Sergeant Sylvie Henry interviewed him twice. Henry took notes in both interviews, but his first afternoon interview was interrupted when the electrician's wife arrived in the Garda station. 'We literally got up and left,' the sergeant said. As a result, he did not follow the usual procedure of reading back the interview notes and having Crossan sign them at the time. Instead, he read the notes of the first interview and asked him to sign all the notes of interview at the end of the second interview. It was not acceptable to amalgamate notes from distinct interviews, the tribunal noted.

Sergeant Marty Moylan was 'kind of puzzled' as to why Sean Crossan changed his statement to John White. He assisted Detective Sergeant John

White in the final interview before Crossan was released. Crossan 'was quiet' and answered any questions put to him by Sergeant White.

Sean Crossan walked out of Letterkenny Garda station at 11.05 p.m., after 11 hours and 55 minutes in Garda custody. The following day, he met James Sweeney, one of the solicitors with VP McMullin, and told him what had happened.

In the years following his arrest, Sean developed an alcohol problem, lost a lot of weight, and separated from his wife for a while. 'I couldn't sleep at night,' he said. 'It just gave me nightmares . . . I spent Christmas day just crying. My family didn't know what was up with me. I couldn't even eat my dinner. I kept it in myself for a year. In the end I had to go to the doctor.'

'I knew Sean was very upset, and he couldn't understand what was happening to him,' Mrs Ann Crossan told the tribunal. 'He was being roared and shouted at, he told me . . . He was crying. He was very upset . . . On the second visit, Sean was more than upset . . . We couldn't understand what was happening to us.' Afterwards, Sean was prescribed anti-depressants and became a heavy drinker, and eventually had to leave the family home. Mrs Crossan was also prescribed anti-depressants, and told how her youngest son was told 'your father is a murdering B-' in the pubs of Raphoe. 'This is going on for ten years,' she explained. 'Raphoe is divided. People don't speak to you any more.'

Chapter 18

Not In His Best Interest

While Sean Crossan met with James Sweeney on 12 December and listed his complaints to the solicitor, Old Frank McBrearty was back in Letterkenny General Hospital after tests in Dublin. Brian Callaghan, the consultant physician in Letterkenny, was still concerned about his patient's condition. He was satisfied that Frank was not in any immediate danger of a heart attack or stroke, but he was worried enough to write a letter listing the range of his symptoms and the medications he had been prescribed.

'It was felt that any stress would certainly exacerbate his condition and he is currently under investigation for an alleged crime,' the consultant concluded. 'It would not be in his best interest to be interrogated at this time. I intend referring him for a further evaluation to a cardiologist in Dublin.'

Callaghan couldn't remember if he gave the letter to a Garda himself, or if he gave it to Frank's solicitor, but he felt he would at least have talked to one of the detectives about Frank's condition. Frank's solicitor, James O'Donnell, recorded in his notes that the doctor 'gave me a letter saying that further interrogation at this stage would exacerbate Frank's present condition. I left with the note at about 12.15 p.m.'

Armed with the note, O'Donnell was confident the Gardaí would now release his client, who had effectively been under arrest for a week. 'It would have crystallised Mr McBrearty's position, his health, for the Guards,' he told the Morris tribunal. 'I mean they couldn't have seen it any plainer. We, as his solicitors, had written to them on the basis of instructions. His doctor had expressed to us that the detention was not assisting his health and was having an effect on it . . . I thought it should have been another very clear indication to the Guards that the detention was having an effect, a certain effect on his condition, on his heart condition.'

Detective Sergeant Sylvie Henry was sent to the hospital to find out the state of play with Frank—was he going to be released from hospital, or did the doctors intend to keep him in? He expected to hear that Frank would be sent for further tests—instead he learned he would be released later that day.

Henry was shown a copy of the consultant's letter at the hospital, but he couldn't recall if it was the doctor or James O'Donnell who showed it to him—he spoke to both men. 'Now, I looked at the letter, but at no stage did Dr Callaghan say to me that Mr McBrearty should not be interviewed. He did not say that this man should not be interviewed. He did not say to me, this man should not be taken back to the Garda station,' Henry said.

Henry added that as Frank was arrested under Section 30 of the Offences Against the State Act, only a superintendent could release him from custody. O'Donnell's note of the conversation put things in stronger terms. He wrote that Henry said Frank would be detained and questioned on his release from hospital 'despite the fact that Detective Sergeant Henry was shown a copy of Mr Callaghan's opinion'.

The Morris tribunal agreed. 'In circumstances where Detective Sergeant Henry acknowledges that he had seen a copy of Dr Callaghan's letter, I am satisfied that he knew of Dr Callaghan's attitude to the further questioning of Mr Frank McBrearty Senior.'

Frank McBrearty was discharged from Letterkenny hospital at 4.35 p.m. on 12 December. He was brought back to Letterkenny Garda station, where Frank said he wanted to talk to his solicitor, and was granted a phone call. He made a second call to his home, and at 5 p.m. he was taken to an interview room by Henry and Detective Garda Jim Frain. Henry left the room within minutes, leaving Frank with Detective Garda Jim Frain and Detective Garda Michael Jennings.

No one told Garda PJ Thornton, the custody officer and member in charge in Letterkenny, about the letter from the hospital consultant. Thornton did not find out about it until he saw a television documentary years later. He would have released McBrearty if he had known about the doctor's opinion, he told the tribunal. The failure to tell Thornton about Dr Callaghan's written opinion was 'disgraceful', Morris found.

Even before his client was discharged from hospital, James O'Donnell had already dictated a covering letter to Superintendent John Fitzgerald, setting out the consultant's opinion on the risks to Frank's health if he was interrogated any more. If his client was not released, he wrote, he would take 'the necessary steps'—'lawyerspeak' for an application to the High Court for a writ of habeas corpus. O'Donnell also prepared a copy of the letter to Superintendent Fitzgerald for Henry. The solicitor took the letter, and a copy of the note from Dr Callaghan, to the station.

O'Donnell arrived at the station just after 6 p.m., and spoke to Frank for twenty minutes. As soon as O'Donnell left, Rosalind McBrearty and her daughter Maria arrived to see Frank. When they left, Frain and Jennings resumed their interview.

Henry checked his internal postbox in the station sometime around 6.30 p.m., he told the tribunal. There, he found a copy of O'Donnell's letter and the note from Callaghan. The solicitor's letter was marked for the attention of the superintendent. Henry said that while the letter in his postbox was a copy, he didn't know if his superintendent had already seen the original or not, so to be on the safe side he took the letter and went looking for a superior officer. He found Detective Superintendent Joe Shelly and Inspector John McGinley. Shelly read the letter, and the senior officers discussed its contents and 'made the decision that [Frank McBrearty] was okay to be interviewed, to keep going ahead with the interviews'.

John McGinley said it was 'a judgement call' whether Frank should be released on health grounds, and the doctor's letter was 'ambiguous' and 'left question marks'.

'It isn't for me to question a medical person, nor would I do it,' Shelly told the tribunal. 'But what I'm saying is, had the letter stated that this person should not be further detained or should not under any circumstances be further interviewed, well that would be the end of the matter. I took it, and I honestly took it, that the letter so to speak, left the door open for us in the circumstances. Whether I was right or wrong in forming that opinion is to be decided. But that's the way I took it.'

Justice Morris was unimpressed. The continued questioning of Frank McBrearty amounted to 'a complete disregard of his right to be treated fairly while in Garda custody,' he decided. The decision to question him 'flew in the face of the medical opinion which had been furnished to them'. Further, the judge was 'astounded that members of An Garda Síochána had such confidence in their own view of Mr McBrearty Senior and his health that they chose to disregard the word of a respected consultant physician'.

Superintendent John Fitzgerald denied vehemently that he knew anything about the meeting where Henry brought the consultant's letter to the attention of Shelly and McGinley. The chairman accepted his word, but criticised the superintendent for negligence in running an office where a letter marked 'urgent' about the health of a prisoner in custody could be acknowledged without his ever seeing it.

Frank's state of health seems to have been a major source of curiosity and speculation in Letterkenny Garda station during his detention. Earlier on the day he was released back into Garda custody, Sergeant John White, who was at his own district HQ in Ballybofey that day, faxed to the station a report on his inquiries into the publican's stay in Blanchardstown hospital. White wrote that Frank was admitted to the hospital for a 'Doppler test' which 'proved negative and no abnormality of any kind showed'. White couldn't remember making the phone call to check up on Frank, or even who asked him to make it. His guess was that he had called one of his own colleagues in Blanchardstown Garda station and asked them to get in touch with any contacts they had in the hospital. Fitzgerald said he didn't know about White's fax until he saw it at the tribunal. Shelly also proclaimed his innocence. McGinley said he had never seen it before when shown it at the tribunal, and had been in Mullingar with the National Drugs Unit that day, only arriving back in Donegal to learn that Frank was released from hospital in the early evening. Apart from White, no other officer admitted knowing anything about the fax.

The chairman was 'highly suspicious' of the fax giving information about the tests on Frank in Dublin which John White had obtained. He was 'shocked' that confidential medical information was 'sought out in such an underhand way' and disturbed by 'the extreme steps that were taken', as well as 'the suggestion that it was not unusual'.

Meanwhile Detective Garda Martin Anderson and Detective Garda Jim Frain were questioning Frank. Anderson sat in on the interview after Detective Garda Michael Jennings left. Frain was reading over notes to Frank, who asked for and initialised several changes. After Frain finished, the detectives asked Frank if he wanted a meal. Anderson supervised the meal, a pot of tea and a chicken sandwich, and tried to make small talk, but Frank wasn't saying much, except to complain that 'this is all rubbish, he shouldn't be here'. After he had eaten, Frank was entitled to a rest period, which Anderson again supervised until 9.30 p.m. Frain and Jennings then interviewed him again. Just before 10 p.m., Frank was taken to another room, where he met with Inspector McGinley and Superintendent Fitzgerald.

Demonstrating a well-honed ability for answers that covered all bases, Fitzgerald described the encounter as 'the most informal formal interview that I could possibly hold' when asked if the meeting with Frank was an interview or an 'informal chat'. McGinley took notes, he said, and at one point Frank got down on his knees and prayed. McGinley added that he 'took a rosary out of his pocket'.

Close to midnight, as the meeting drew to a close, Frank said he was unwell and asked not to be put in the cells overnight. It was at this point that John McGinley mentioned the letter from the doctor, and Superintendent Fitzgerald learned about it for the first time. 'Naturally this was unusual, and I sort of looked at John,' he explained.

'I got a slight *gonc* about it,' he added. 'A little shock.'

'If I had seen that letter, what I would have done, I would have inquired, was it requested by Frank McBrearty Snr, was it requested by his solicitor, or did he write it without,' Fitzgerald told the tribunal. However, he added that Frank's poor health was a constant complaint whenever he met Frank, so he probably would not have taken it seriously at the time. The late night meeting was his only personal involvement in Frank's case, he added. He'd gone to the station after receiving a phone call from

McGinley around 9 p.m. The inspector told him that Frank was in the station, was 'denying everything', wanted to speak to the district superintendent and 'we think it may be a good idea if you talk to him'.

Frank claimed that during the meeting McGinley took no notes, and as a result he believed the entire interview was tape recorded and transcribed afterwards. He also said that he was given a blank sheet of paper by the inspector, and told to 'sign that and you'll have no more bother, you'll be released'. McGinley told him he 'would fill out the rest'. Fitzgerald denied categorically that McGinley had given Frank a blank piece of paper to sign, declaring that 'the only time he was asked to sign his name was when the notes were read over to him, and he refused point blank'. McGinley described the accusation as 'absurd', and pointed out that there was no mention of it in the notes taken by Frank's solicitor during a meeting the following morning. Frank's allegations were dismissed at the Morris tribunal as being without evidence, and made 'very late in the day'.

However, the judge said that Superintendent Fitzgerald should have considered immediately releasing Frank from custody when he learned about the consultant's letter, although he did note the humane decision to allow him to sleep overnight in the interview room rather than in the cells.

Frank was checked several times during the night. At 7.55 a.m. he complained to the custody officer of 'a pain in his chest and stomach' and asked to see his wife and his doctor. The custody officer got no answer when he rang Rosalind McBrearty, and the doctor told him he couldn't come to the station. Frank then rang and spoke to Rosalind, then rang his solicitor. Just after 8.35 a.m., he was taken to the interview room by Detective Sergeant Henry and Detective Garda Michael Jennings.

'I felt at the time that I was speaking to him that he was okay,' Henry told the tribunal. 'He spoke to a solicitor and to his wife prior to us interviewing him. None of them called for a doctor.' Henry said he wasn't sure if he knew that Frank had complained that morning of chest pains, but he was 'given every facility'. He described the interview as 'unproductive' and said Frank was 'very calm' and 'very polite'. 'I don't think he answered any of our questions,' he concluded.

Chapter 19

He Was Told We Had a Statement

When the word came through to the Central Detective Unit that Old Frank might be released from hospital, Detective Sergeant John Melody and Detective Garda John Fitzpatrick travelled back to Donegal.

The two detectives arrived in Donegal late in the evening of 12 December. Melody thought they were briefed by Sergeant Marty Moylan, since he was in charge of the incident room, and he might also have met one or more of the senior officers in Donegal. Either way, they were given the file on alleged intimidation to read up on. Apart from Shelly, Moylan and O'Dowd, the two Dublin detectives were the only officers who knew about the 4 December statement from Noel McBride claiming that Old Frank tried to bribe him.

Melody couldn't explain why the strongest apparent evidence against Frank, the allegation that he offered £500 to Noel McBride for his silence, had not been shown to any detectives in Donegal. He and John Fitzpatrick were among the few people who had seen it. He wasn't sure if he read the statement, but he knew he was briefed on it. He wasn't told about any concerns over Frank's health, or letters from doctors or solicitors. Had he been told there was a problem, he would have approached first the member in charge, and then the senior officers.

'He didn't give any indication to me during our interview that there was a problem,' Melody recalled, and at no point complained he was in pain. 'He gave us no indication that there was anything at all wrong with him at any stage during our interview.'

Frank was 'relatively calm' but 'behaved oddly at one stage as he got down off his chair and asked us to join him in prayer', which the detective thought was 'odd'. The first mention of Frank's condition came around midday on 13 December, when he told the custody officer during a check that he wanted the doctor to check his medication.

Melody took notes, and both detectives questioned Frank. During the interview, the detectives explained that they were in the middle of a serious investigation. 'A man was murdered and your son Frank Junior has admitted his part in this murder,' they told him. 'You're not entitled to intimidate witnesses to influence them not to give evidence against your son.'

'That's lies, all lies,' Frank responded. 'My son wouldn't do anything like that.'

'My son is an innocent man and I'll prove that he's innocent,' he added when the detectives repeated that they had a confession.

That single exchange would cause a row at the Morris tribunal that took weeks to resolve. Frank initially denied he was ever told by the detectives that his son had made a confession. At one point, he agreed to release his solicitor from professional privilege, and the tribunal sought interview notes taken when he met his solicitor in custody. But then Frank withdrew the notes, claiming legal privilege again.

The saga began on 21 November 2006, when Frank handed over a letter to the tribunal allowing them access to the notes taken at the time by the solicitor he met while he was in custody. Frank told the tribunal that he did not answer any questions for Detective Sergeant Melody and Detective Garda Fitzpatrick, as he was unwell at the time. The detectives could not have taken interview notes, because there was no interview. The notes were 'a fabrication', he said, the Dublin Four were 'four black-guards', and any note saying he was told about the confession was 'the biggest load of rubbish'. On 22 November, Frank was questioned by George Bermingham SC, the barrister representing several Gardaí. Bermingham asked him why he had 'a change of heart' about allowing the tribunal to see his solicitor's notes. Frank said he changed his mind because he wanted more documents from the tribunal first, a theme he repeated as the barrister tried to question him. Eventually, Bermingham turned to the chairman, protesting that the right to cross-examine a witness was worthless if the witness refused to answer his questions. The chairman told Frank he had no right to demand any documents or set conditions before he was cross-examined, adding, 'I will not be held to ransom by you or blackmailed by you. You will answer the questions that Mr Bermingham is asking you, and that's the end of that.'

'I will not answer the questions until you agree to release the stuff that you have belonging to us and my lawyers will release my stuff,' Frank responded. 'Now if you don't get that I'm walking out of here. So make up your mind now. I'm not answering no more questions until I get my stuff and until you supply all the stuff that I have asked for here today.'

After a brief exchange, the chairman asked Bermingham to ask his question again. 'I'm not answering any more questions until I get legal advice,' Frank responded. 'That's me finished. I'll see you in the High Court. Now, I will sell the rest of my business and fight my case.' With that, he walked off the stand.

The following day, as the tribunal took submissions from lawyers on what to do next, Bermingham was scathing. McBrearty had used his privilege as a witness to make wild and unfounded allegations, at times using the most flamboyant language, and had described his Garda clients as 'animals', he told the tribunal. Frank McBrearty was 'a volatile and erratic individual', and his actions were not only in contempt of the tribunal, but were calculated to bring the tribunal itself into contempt, using it to make allegations against his clients and then refusing to accept their right to defend their good names. It was time to call a halt. Unless McBrearty returned to finish his evidence, the tribunal should report to the Oireachtas that there was no evidence against his clients, Bermingham concluded.

Frank relented and returned on 30 November. Stung by the accusation from Bermingham that he might have something to hide, Frank began by handing over the notes taken by his solicitor during his arrest. The notes confirmed that Frank had told his solicitor that the detectives said his son confessed. Frank told the tribunal he didn't take the detectives seriously at the time; as far as he was concerned Young Frank was innocent, so why would he confess? This could only have been a trick by the detectives, and he had dismissed it without a second thought. He hadn't remembered it until he had read over the solicitor's notes again. It wasn't until several months after his arrest that he learned the Guards were claiming they had a confession. What the detectives told him just hadn't registered; if it wasn't for the solicitor's note, he wouldn't even know he'd said it.

James O'Donnell later confirmed that on 13 December 1996 'Frank said that two detectives from Dublin, who he called John and John, told him that they had a signed statement from Frank Junior admitting to the murder of Richie Barron.'

Frank thought the idea of his son confessing was 'ridiculous' and 'outrageous', O'Donnell explained. 'He believed that they were saying it to him merely to intimidate him or to get him around to be more malleable I suppose ... He felt actually they were using it as a form of intimidation or harassment. They were using that to break his will ... The impression I got from him was they were using this as an inducement to break his will so that he would say anything to them that they wanted to hear.'

Rosalind McBrearty told the tribunal she'd never heard mention of the 'confession' either, until the day private investigator Billy Flynn phoned her from the High Court in Dublin and told her. 'My son never made no confession,' she told the private eye. 'Frank never took any meaning to it. He knew his son was working with him with 600 people, so how could he go up the road and kill somebody,' she told the tribunal.

Melody said Frank McBrearty showed no reaction when he was told his son had made a confession. 'I thought it was unusual that he didn't react to it,' Melody said. 'He was told we had a statement, he wasn't shown the statement. He said his son wouldn't do anything like that,' was Detective Garda John Fitzpatrick's simple summary of how they told Frank about the confession.

'It would have been of enormous benefit to the tribunal,' Mr Justice Morris concluded, 'had Mr Frank McBrearty Senior told the full truth about being told of the existence of such a statement by the two interviewers, the importance he attached to it in telling his solicitor about it, and the nature and extent of what Mr Frank McBrearty Junior said about it, over the days, weeks and months that followed his arrest. Instead, Mr McBrearty Senior maintained the position that he did not discuss it at all with his son during that period, which is not credible.'

At half past midday, Dr McColgan arrived and examined Frank. When he finished, he told the custody officer he wanted to re-admit Frank to hospital for an ECG test. Frank was in Letterkenny General Hospital from 13 December until 18 December, when he was taken to Dublin again, this time to Beaumont hospital. The following day, still in Beaumont, he was told by Detective Garda PJ Keating at 5.10 p.m. that he was released from the provisions of Section 30 of the Offences Against the State Act. When he was told he was free to go, Frank 'was excited, he jumped up on the bed and shook hands with us and wished us a happy Christmas,' Garda Sean Herraghty later told the tribunal. Frank was discharged from Beaumont hospital the following day, and was collected and driven home to Donegal by his son. His ordeal was over. It was a fortnight since he had last been home.

Summing up, Mr Justice Morris wrote that he was 'satisfied that Mr Frank McBrearty Senior, when making complaints and giving evidence in respect of his arrest and detention, greatly exaggerated some events and told untruths in respect of others. These are documented in the body of the chapter. It must be acknowledged that Mr McBrearty Senior and his family were subjected to numerous wrongs, as documented in this report. Nevertheless, it was wrong and disgraceful on his part to make false allegations from time to time in respect of members of An Garda Síochána who dealt with him at that time. The fact that wrongs were committed against Mr McBrearty Senior does not give him a licence to unfairly and wrongly accuse other Gardaí of transgressions. Mr McBrearty Senior's attitude in this respect was very disappointing to the Tribunal.'

———

On 17 December, the day before Frank was moved to Dublin, Damien McDaid, a local electrical contractor, became the twelfth person arrested

during the Barron investigation. His evidence was perhaps the most sur-
real of all those arrested.

According to Garda records, Damien McDaid was arrested near his
home just after 9 a.m. by four Gardaí, Sergeant Marty Moylan, Detective
Sergeant Hugh Smith, Detective Garda PJ Keating and Garda Sean
Herraghty. He was taken to Letterkenny Garda station where he was held
for almost twelve hours, and questioned first by Smith and Moylan, then
by Herraghty and Keating, before a lunch break. Marty Moylan, the
arresting officer, said the decision to pick up McDaid was made by
Superintendent John Fitzgerald at a case conference a day or two after the
mass arrests on 4 December.

After eating, according to the custody record, Damien McDaid was
questioned by Detective Garda Martin Anderson and Detective Garda
Carroll, then again by Herraghty and Keating, then by Carroll and
Anderson again, followed by Smith and Moylan. The last twenty minutes
or so were spent alone in the interview room with Sergeant Brendan
Roache, who sat with him before his release. During the day, he received
two visits, first from his wife Geraldine and then from his solicitor, Pat
McMyler.

Damien McDaid had spoken to Garda John Harkin and Detective
Garda Keating on 8 November, but was not willing to make a statement.
The memo recorded by Keating is remarkable for the lack of names it
contains. He told how the night Richie Barron died he was in Raphoe and
recalled seeing 'the big fellow that runs the place', and 'the son—the
young boy, the ignorant fellow'. Around 1 a.m., he was in the car park and
saw 'one of the bouncers, a baldy headed boy'. This bouncer was along
with a few women, one of whom was sick. As he left the nightclub, he saw
a 'handling'—a fight—near the main entrance, involving 'two big fellows
causing bother, they were IRA men'.

'They were out for the weekend only,' Keating noted McDaid as saying.
'I saw the big fellow who owns the place and the son—they were dealing
with them. He did not want to let them in. I blew the horn on the van for
them to get out of my way. I came on out and came straight home. I was
home by 1.30 a.m. It was the following day before I heard that a man was
knocked down.' Damien's brief account, as recorded by Keating, matched
what Gardaí already knew from interviews with the McBreartys and Sean
Crossan, the man seen in the car park attending to a girl who was ill.

All of the Gardaí involved with Damien McDaid, from his arrest until
his release, told the Morris tribunal he was not mistreated during his time
in custody. He was questioned about his movements, asked if he had seen
anything, and his answers noted. McDaid told a different story, claiming
he was shouted at and abused, the table in front of him hammered as he
was called scum and told he knew what had happened to Richie Barron.

McDaid claimed that one Garda had spat in his food, stepped on his bare feet, and most seriously of all, placed a gun in his mouth towards the end of the day.

Pat McMyler, the solicitor who visited Damien McDaid in custody, said he advised McDaid to say nothing. 'He was being accused, and despite his innocence as explained to me I felt it would be unsafe to get involved in explaining your innocence without legal advice present.'

Gavin McDaid, who was sixteen at the time, had left school early, and worked for his brother Damien. On their way to work, the Garda cars pulled up in front of and behind his brother's van without warning, and there was a lot of roaring and shouting. Gavin thought there were two or three cars, and initially at least he didn't see any uniforms. 'It was sort of, Go! Go! Go!', he explained at the tribunal.

Not knowing what was happening, he locked the van door, while outside the detectives were shouting to get out of the van, and one Garda held his ID up to the van window. When he got out of the van, the Garda who had held up his ID kicked Gavin, and said, 'Next time I tell you to open the door, you open it you little bastard.'

Damien was told his brother was 'a murdering bastard', and a uniformed Garda moved the van onto the footpath, and gave Gavin the keys, while other detectives placed Damien in an unmarked car. Gavin ran to his parents' home, and told them his brother was under arrest for murder.

After his arrest, Damien seemed 'anxious', Gavin told the Morris tribunal. He started drinking heavily and 'just went to pieces'. The business went downhill. Before his arrest Damien had employed five men in his business, but the firm collapsed. He spent some time in prison. When he drank, or if he saw a Garda on the street, Damien would 'rant' about the Guards and what they had done to him, telling his brother 'you watch yourself with them boys, they'd get you up, they'd do you harm, they tramp on your feet'. When he drank, Damien would also phone Gavin and talk to him about what had happened.

'I just mind the way it was, you know, to his wee brother,' Gavin told the tribunal.

Gavin broke down several times during his evidence at the Morris tribunal, struggling to control his emotions as the memory of his brother's decline overwhelmed him. 'He shouldn't have been telling me, I was his wee brother, you know. I'm not his big brother. It's just hard to watch somebody that is supposed to be your big brother being like that. It's very hard,' he said.

In 1996, Damien and Geraldine had two children—Brian, a toddler, and Danielle, who was eight. Geraldine told the tribunal her husband was a hard worker, and had left early for work that morning. She was still getting her daughter ready for school when she learned he was arrested when two Garda cars arrived at the door of her mobile home in Newtown-cunningham. Damien was just able to tell her 'they're lifting me', and he was taken away. Later in the day, when she was able to get to Letterkenny and see her husband, he looked terrible. 'He was pale, shaken, scared. He was mumbling away,' she told the tribunal. Disturbed by what she had seen, Damien's wife returned home, collected her daughter from school and sat with her children, waiting for her husband.

When Damien got home, he walked in the door carrying his boots in his hand.

'Why are you carrying your boots?' Geraldine asked him. Damien said nothing, walked past his wife and sat down on the sofa.

'Why are you carrying your boots?' Geraldine asked again.

'My feet are sore,' Damien replied.

'Why are your feet sore?'

'They're tramped off me.'

Damien speaks with a pronounced stammer at times, and Geraldine had difficulty getting any sense out of him. She noticed his feet were red and swollen. The toddler had wakened, and began to cry, so she went to attend to him. She felt relieved to have her husband home.

'Damien's not the same fellow now as ten year ago, so he's not,' she told the tribunal. 'This here has wrecked him . . . Damien was a happy fella, Damien would have went to his work, Damien would have come home, Damien worked hard, the men got their wages and Damien would go out then for drinks at the weekend . . . He didn't seem to have a care, he was bringing the money home and he was there for the wains and you know, just happy-go-average man . . . I had a marriage before this. I haven't it now.'

Damien told the Morris tribunal he was shouted at and abused during the first interview. A Garda spat in his breakfast, and stamped on his feet. His most serious claim was that a Garda had put a gun in his mouth. He told the tribunal that a Garda told him he had seen what happened to Richie Barron, and prepared a document for him to sign. When Damien refused to sign, the Garda left the room for a moment. When the Garda returned, his first words were 'Right, on your knees McDaid.' Damien knelt, looked up to the Garda, and before he knew what was happening, the gun was in his mouth.

'I knew I was in bother then,' Damien told the Morris tribunal. 'I was in serious bother.'

'What kind of gun was it?' tribunal barrister Paul McDermott asked him.

'Jesus, I don't know what kind of gun it was. How would I know that?'

'Well it could be a small handgun, it could be larger than that.'

'Aye, the thing was in my mouth, and I was fucking shiteing myself, you know that kind of way.'

With the gun still in his mouth, Damien said he shook his head to show he wouldn't sign anything, and when he opened his eyes, the gun was gone.

Damien McDaid's evidence to the tribunal was hopelessly confused. At times, he appeared to say he was in Raphoe the night Richie Barron died, but was unwilling to admit it because he was with another woman and didn't want his wife to find out. Later, he said he had spoken to the woman in question, and she told him he hadn't been with her that night. Later again, he said he had blanked out the entire night, and could remember nothing after going to the Halfway House, a pub in north Donegal where he drank before going to Raphoe. He was unable to remember any of the Gardaí who had interviewed him, and was able to identify them only by describing them: the nice Guard, the hefty man, the fat Guard, and so on. He pointed out several different people as the Garda who might have driven him home after he was released from custody, and at one stage seemed to identify a member of the Carty team as a witness to the foot-stamping. Another Garda alleged to have driven him home said he was probably in Dublin that day, and another was off duty and at home at the time. The Morris tribunal was unimpressed with much of his evidence. The allegation that a Garda spat in his breakfast 'was mischievous and dishonest', it concluded. His account of the 'horrific and bizarre' placing of a gun in his mouth 'was unconvincing and improbable in the extreme'.

However, the tribunal did accept, in large part because of supporting evidence from Mrs Geraldine McDaid, 'that something happened to Damien McDaid's feet in the station in Letterkenny on that day', although it was not able to say precisely what. But whatever happened, the tribunal did not accept that Garda Seán Herraghty, the man McDaid identified, was responsible.

It was never made entirely clear why Damien McDaid was arrested. The memo recorded by Detective Garda John Harkin in November 1996, as well as statements from Sean Crossan and others, made it possible he had seen something important while in the car park the night Richie Barron died, but as his barrister Jane Murphy pointed out in her closing submission, this made him a potential witness, not a suspect.

The decision to arrest Damien McDaid 'was made haphazardly by an investigation team that had completely lost its capacity to objectively analyse the information before it,' the tribunal decided. The responsibility for the decision to arrest, rather than simply approaching McDaid to clarify any questions they had about what was recorded in the unsigned memo made by Garda John Harkin in November, lay with the senior officers in the investigation team. The chairman also criticised the lack of complete interview notes in the investigation files, not for the first time. McDaid was interviewed seven times, yet in three cases, no notes were available.

Chapter 20

A Town Divided

By January 1997, the rumours in Raphoe were no longer just whispers. The notion of no smoke without fire had its own compelling logic, and to many in the town, the McBreartys were literally getting away with murder. They'd been arrested after all. The Guards must know something.

Paul 'Pip' Roulston recalled that after members of the extended McBrearty family were released without charge after being arrested in December 1996, the town gossip was that they got off because of a lack of evidence. The controversial confession—still not public knowledge—could be used in court as evidence against Young Frank, but not against Mark McConnell. The Morris tribunal was 'satisfied that a group of men in and around Raphoe . . . set about creating such evidence'.

Pip, Stephen Barron and Derrick 'Darcy' Connolly were good friends. Pip worked at the time for Darcy, a farrier and former jockey who had known Richie Barron through his involvement in the horse trade. Darcy was so eager to help solve the Barron case, the Guards had nicknamed him 'The Investigator'. Anything he heard, Darcy passed on to Detective Garda Pat Flynn.

On 14 October 1996, Flynn recorded in his notebook the call from Sergeant Joe Hannigan to investigate the 'fatal hit and run at Townparks, Raphoe (alleged)'. Flynn's next note on the case read 'Information re Richie Barron death, Now looks like foul play.' The entry is undated.

The next entry is titled 'Info from AC'. Flynn couldn't remember who AC was. AC told him that a phone call to Letterkenny hospital the night Richie died didn't come from the cattle dealer's aunt, because she was in Derry and didn't know he died until the following morning.

Flynn's next entry records 'Info from DC'. Flynn told the tribunal DC was Darcy Connolly. In total, Flynn recorded sixteen pieces of information from 'The Investigator'. Darcy told Flynn there was no 'horsey involvement', because Richie didn't owe any money. It wasn't a mugging, because Richie didn't have much money on him.

Darcy also told Flynn about 'Road Sweepers sighting of Mark McConnell outside a pub on Monday morning.' Flynn said he already knew this because Martin Laird had made a statement, but it was not clear how Darcy knew. Laird was adamant at the tribunal that he told nobody what he saw except the Guards, a taxi driver and his parents.

Flynn noted several scraps of information from Darcy. Someone might have seen Mark McConnell crying at 1.30 a.m. at the top of the terrace, while Roisin McConnell walked away angrily. Someone might have seen Roisin McConnell upset the next morning. Two people driving round the town might have seen someone. Mark McConnell went drinking in the Town & Country the next night. Mark was a 'vicious bastard', unlike his brothers, and 'McBrearty's temper is well-known'. Flynn reported all the information he received to the incident room.

When asked about the items in Flynn's notebook marked 'Info from DC', Darcy said he did not recall telling the detective these snippets of information. However, he agreed the notes could have 'reflected his thinking' at the time. Darcy claimed to suffer epilepsy-related amnesia problems, and have difficulty recalling events from 1996 and 1997.

Detective Garda Flynn remembered that on Friday 3 January 1997, he recorded in his notebook that his 'source', Darcy Connolly, told him that 'Kieran Roulston and his friend Roderick Donnelly were sitting in Roulston's car—They saw Frank Jnr and Mark McConnell going together from the Parting Glass towards the car park approx 12.30 a.m.'

'Of course I wanted to speak to Mr Donnelly and Mr Roulston to see was the information correct,' Flynn told the Morris tribunal. Twenty-one-year-old Roderick Donnelly—a friend of the Roulstons—was one of those who heard Richie Barron 'was supposed to have been done in up in Raphoe' by Mark McConnell and Young Frank McBrearty. 'The dogs in the town knew it, everybody knew it,' he remembered.

On the same day that Detective Garda Pat Flynn learned about Roderick Donnelly from Darcy Connolly, the first case conference of the New Year took place. One of the jobs assigned at the conference reads: 'People outside DJ's—statements to be checked', part of the task of verifying the 'Mister X' statement. In his statement of 29 November, Noel McBride had said he was standing outside DJ's for much of the night Richie Barron died—this job would check if anyone else who was there saw him. Sergeant Marty Moylan would eventually check over 500 statements taken during the investigation looking for any sighting of Noel McBride.

The conference notes also contain some brief notes on other jobs to be done by the investigation. A separate file was to be kept on all reports of witness intimidation. John O'Dowd was to get 'Mister X' to identify which bouncer he saw (this is the first mention of the phrase 'Mister X' in any Garda record) and so on. Finally, Detective Garda Pat Flynn was to look into allegations of a previous threat against Richie Barron by Young Frank McBrearty.

———

John White joined An Garda Síochána in 1974, and had a distinguished career which included a spell with the Central Detective Bureau and Blanchardstown Detective Unit. In 1994 the detective was promoted to uniform sergeant rank before transferring to Donegal, his wife's home county. Because of his detective experience, and because Detective Superintendent Joe Shelly knew of his work in Dublin, he was called in to help with the mass arrests on 4 December 1996. In January 1997 he was transferred to Raphoe as uniform sergeant, where he remained until he was assigned to Letterkenny as detective sergeant on 8 August 1997.

On 10 January 1997, the same day that Sergeant John White was transferred from Carrick in west Donegal to Raphoe, Superintendent John Fitzgerald signed an 'Operational Order for the Policing of Letterkenny Urban Area at Weekends with Special Reference to Public Order Issues'.

Among its provisions, the order directed that sergeants were to 'Inspect or cause to be inspected licensed premises where it is known or suspected that blatant breaches of the Liquor Licensing Laws are occurring.' In addition, sergeants were to 'Inspect or cause to be inspected Discos and other venues licensed for Public Dancing and availing of an Exemption under the provisions of the Intoxicating Liquor Acts.'

Sergeants were also to ensure that 'there is a proper and thorough follow-up to all complaints and that the injured party or complainant is kept informed of Garda progress.'

One of the complaints made by the McBrearty family is that they were singled out for special attention by Gardaí enforcing the liquor licensing laws in Donegal. The family claimed that close to 100 summonses served for breaches of these laws were evidence of Garda harassment. The Guards cited the Operational Order at the tribunal as evidence that the McBrearty family were not targeted. However, it is clear that the Operational Order refers to Letterkenny town, and not to the entire district under Superintendent Fitzgerald's control. Duties of Gardaí outlined in the Operational Order include the patrol routes for Gardaí, and these refer specifically to streets in Letterkenny. Discos, bus stops and others details in the order also refer to the town.

Sergeant White said he was sent to Raphoe temporarily to deal with a public order problem in the town, and was given instructions to make sure the liquor licensing laws were enforced. He prepared a policing plan for the town similar to the one Superintendent Fitzgerald had drawn up for Letterkenny. White said he had inspected all the pubs in the town, not just the McBreartys', and served summonses for breaches of the law. The sergeant said he knew a 'get-tough' policy on licensing laws would 'cause problems with politicians', and he kept a diary of all his inspections, which showed his even-handed approach.

Superintendent Kevin Lennon said there was a public order problem

in Raphoe before he arrived in Letterkenny district, and it had been discussed at a meeting in Letterkenny. At the tribunal Sergeant Marty
Moylan agreed that a direction to enforce public order was given at conference in December 1996, two months before Lennon was transferred
from Buncrana to Letterkenny in February 1997.

Sergeant Joe Hannigan, the local sergeant in Raphoe, agreed that the
Guards 'had a problem with public order and I suppose liquor licensing
laws had slipped' and that after Sergeant White arrived 'the level of
enforcement certainly was increased drastically'. Hannigan said the plan
was drawn up with his approval, and that the pubs in Raphoe 'were all getting attention, but Mr McBrearty's premises was getting close attention'.

Superintendent John Fitzgerald said he spoke to Sergeant White after
receiving complaints from Frank McBrearty that he was being singled out
for Garda attention, and the sergeant 'did say he called to all the publicans
and he was treating them fairly'. However, the sergeant's determination to
enforce the law would lead to an escalating confrontation with Frank
McBrearty in the months that followed. There was a serious public order
problem in the town, much of it alcohol related, and White identified
Frankie's nightclub as one of the main sources of the alcohol that fuelled
local aggression and vandalism. Senior officers would later try to dist-
nance themselves from White's zealous policing, but documents supplied
to the Morris tribunal showed that he had kept his superiors briefed
about what was going on, and they approved of his actions.

————

The Barron investigation drifted in January 1997. Inspector John
McGinley spent the first three weeks of the month away from
Letterkenny as Acting District Officer in Glenties, and a fourth week in
Mullingar working on a case with the National Drugs Unit. At the end of
the month, on 27 January, he was appointed to the vacant Detective
Inspector's post in Letterkenny, and took on new responsibilities in
counter-terrorism. At the tribunal, he admitted he 'lost some ground' on
the Barron investigation as a result. 'I wouldn't have been involved in the
nuts and bolts,' was his summation.

The downgrading manifested in other ways. The incident room virtually shut down, and was moved to an obscure office in the Traffic Corps
section known informally in the station as 'the Bunker'. Superintendent
John Fitzgerald, who felt his authority had been undermined for months
by the close working relationship between Chief Superintendent Denis
Fitzpatrick and Superintendent Kevin Lennon, was preparing to transfer
out of the division to a new posting in County Leitrim. When he left,

Fitzgerald would take with him the controversial confession taken from Young Frank, which had been locked securely in his safe since 4 December 1996.

Crime & Security Branch had by now managed to obtain some telephone records officially from Telecom Eireann. There was still no progress on the hoax blackmail calls to the Peoples, but other records were available, including the calls made from the Brollys' phone the night Richie Barron died. One of those calls—made by Mark McConnell—was to Letterkenny hospital. Another was to the Dolan family.

As McGinley himself admitted, the fact that a call was made to Dolans of itself meant nothing. As far as the investigation was concerned on 4 December, what mattered was the call to the hospital. It was not until January that the call to the Dolans became significant, once Sergeant Hannigan spoke to Irene Dolan. The riddle of its meaning would never be resolved. Irene Dolan told the tribunal that Roisin McConnell called looking for Mark. Roisin was adamant she was looking for her brother Gerard, not her husband, who was with her in the Brollys' home. She was looking for Gerard, she said, because she thought there might be a late-night birthday party in the Dolan house. Ultimately, the chairman decided, it didn't matter. Mark might have left the Brolly home in the early hours of the morning, perhaps going for a late night drink with Mark Quinn, explaining how he was seen leaving the pub early in the morning by Martin Laird. Or Irene Dolan might have been mistaken. The incident took place two hours after Richie Barron died, so either way, it was 'not relevant to any suspicion'.

———

On Wednesday 8 January 1997, one week after he learned that Roderick Donnelly might have some information, Detective Garda Pat Flynn spoke to Pip Roulston's brother Kieran, who also told him that Roderick Donnelly 'might have seen something'. He arranged to set up a meeting with Roderick Donnelly.

Pip Roulston remembered that he attended a meeting at Detective Flynn's home. 'I don't remember was it to get my brother to make a statement, or to make a statement myself,' he said. 'Darcy made the arrangement.'

There was no statement from Pip Roulston in the files turned over to the Morris tribunal, but Pip was adamant he made one that day. 'I've been asked this many times before,' he insisted. 'It was a statement on headed Garda paper.' However, the chairman decided that Pip, otherwise an honest witness who admitted to his role in the affair, was somehow confused about this statement. Perhaps he'd simply mistaken the detective taking notes for a statement.

'It may be that because he had made so many statements and complaints to the Gardaí concerning the McBreartys, he could not recall that he had never, in fact, made any statement to Detective Garda Flynn, although he may have intended to do so,' the chairman wrote. 'Alternatively, he could have mistaken the confirming of what Roderick Donnelly had seen, as recorded in Detective Garda Flynn's notes for the 8 January 1997, as the making of a statement. Mr Roulston did his best to be an honest witness. If others had followed his example, the Tribunal would have concluded its work by now.'

The judge's words, written in his second report released in the early summer of 2005, were prophetic. The tribunal would not hear from the last witness until December 2007.

Later Pip Roulston and Detective Garda Pat Flynn approached Roderick Donnelly to make a statement. Donnelly would tell the Morris tribunal he had a drunk driving charge coming up in court at the time. He didn't want to make a statement, but thought there might be something in it for him if he did, some way the drunk driving traffic court case could be taken care of.

Pip also had problems with a traffic case—he was facing a reckless driving charge. He said that while neither he nor Roderick spoke to Flynn about their traffic cases, Darcy Connolly hinted that they might be taken care of.

Whatever anyone else might have told Donnelly about his court case though, he wasn't told anything by Detective Garda Pat Flynn. The truth was much simpler, the tribunal decided. Darcy Connolly 'orchestrated the presentation of these witnesses to the Gardaí in the hope and expectation of bolstering up the case against Mark McConnell'.

———

On Monday 20 January 1997, Roderick Donnelly made a statement to Detective Garda Pat Flynn in Lifford Garda Station. Between first learning that Roderick Donnelly might have something to offer on 3 January, and taking the statement on 20 January, Detective Flynn did not speak with the Barron incident room in Letterkenny about what he had learned from Darcy Connolly and Kieran Roulston.

The Roulstons took Roderick Donnelly to Lifford Garda Station, and introduced him to Detective Garda Flynn. Pip Roulston stayed in the room while Roderick Donnelly spoke to Flynn.

'I honestly tried to find out what Mr Donnelly had seen. I asked him questions in relation to it,' Flynn recalled. 'I didn't put words in his mouth. I asked him afterwards did he want to make a statement in writing about it and I took that statement in writing from him in good faith.'

'I didn't prompt him. I didn't have Mr Roulston prompt him. Mr Donnelly agreed when the statement was read back to him that the state-ment was correct, and he signed it. I have never taken a statement from anybody in which I prompted them.'

Flynn said Roderick Donnelly appeared nervous. He put this down to the young man's unease at being in a Garda station. Donnelly's statement differed significantly from what the detective had been told by Darcy to expect on 3 January. Instead of saying he saw Mark McConnell and Young Frank McBrearty going from the Parting Glass up the car park at 12.30 a.m., Donnelly said he saw 'Mark McConnell and two women coming walking up the street from the Diamond direction' between 1 a.m. and 1.10 a.m.'

'Mark looked very scared looking and his hair was very tossed. His clothes looked to be wet as well. He was staring straight ahead of him.' Mark and the two women walked by the Parting Glass to his car, which was parked in a small car park near the Tech.

Donnelly said that Kieran Roulston was asleep in the car at the time. When Kieran woke up at 1.30 a.m., Donnelly mentioned how Mark McConnell 'looked scared and shook up like he had been fighting'.

When the Carty team interviewed him in March 2000, Roderick Donnelly insisted that words were put in his mouth. Donnelly said he was unhappy with 'the way everything was taken down', he only meant to say in his statement that he had seen Mark McConnell, but 'Paul Roulston was putting words in my mouth to strengthen up the statement against Mark McConnell'.

'Darcy Connolly and Paul Roulston had me set up to believe I had seen more than I did see to set up Mark McConnell,' Donnelly told the Carty detectives. 'I did not know that at the time. I just walked into the station thinking I was telling the truth.'

However, when he gave evidence at the tribunal, Donnelly said that Connolly only told him to make a statement that he had seen McConnell, not that he looked like he'd been in a fight.

Darcy Connolly denied getting anyone to make statements to the Gardaí saying they saw more than they did. 'I never got Paul Roulston or Roderick Donnelly to say anything,' he insisted. Neither did he tell any-one traffic charges could be lessened or dropped. He said Donnelly told him only that he saw Mark McConnell, Roderick never said he saw Young Frank McBrearty.

Pip Roulston said he 'wasn't trying to frame anybody for murder'. 'It was stupid on my behalf at the time. Do you think I don't know it with-out you repeating it over and over,' he told one barrister.

'I've listened to it all day for the last eight years, and it's getting a wee bit sickening. I know I made a mistake, but you're pushing it down my throat. I got rolled up in something I shouldn't have got into,' he protested.

Roderick Donnelly was prosecuted by the Carty team for wasting police time. A Circuit Court jury acquitted him in February 2003. In court he was described as 'having limited education'. Darcy Connolly was also charged with making false statements in claiming that Young Frank McBrearty 'drove in a dangerous manner toward him'. He too was acquitted by a jury, in May 2003. His defence barrister argued that the Gardaí 'plucked two single episodes out of a sequence of events and invite the jury to judge harshly by heavy standards which they do not as yet apply to themselves'. Donegal juries, aware no doubt of the growing controversy over Garda actions during the Barron investigation, were reluctant to convict any civilian involved in the debacle.

Unlike the juries, the tribunal did not accept the various explanations put forward by Donnelly for the extra details he said were wrongly inserted into his statement. 'The Tribunal is satisfied that the statement was a false statement that was told entirely and deliberately by Roderick Donnelly to Detective Garda Flynn,' Mr Justice Morris wrote in his report.

The retired High Court judge went on to write that he was 'of the opinion that somebody must have been feeding information to Darcy Connolly and others which caused the shift in detail between 3 and 8 January 1997 and 20 January 1997. The tribunal does not know who this person was. It would be wrong of the tribunal to speculate as to the identity of such person without evidence in that regard.'

Much was made at the Morris tribunal of the failure by the incident room to cross-check the crucial 29 November 1996 statement from Noel McBride against other statements in the system before arrests were made in December 1996. It was not until the New Year that a job was created to check McBride's statement. In March 1997, after checking over 500 statements, Sergeant Marty Moylan was able to report back to the case conferences that not one single individual had reported seeing McBride in Raphoe the night Richie Barron died.

As the tribunal approached the end of its deliberations, its barristers announced that a similar analysis revealed no one had seen Roderick Donnelly either. Counsel for the tribunal were unable to find any reference to Donnelly in any statement.

Donnelly's statement is sparse on detail, beyond his sighting of Mark McConnell. He outlined how he arrived in Raphoe in Kieran Roulston's car between 10.30 p.m. and 11 p.m. While Roulston slept, Donnelly said he saw McConnell, and told Roulston about him when he woke up at

1.30 a.m. They stayed in the car at the same spot until 2 a.m. Unlike the other young people who spent the night in the town in their cars, Roderick Donnelly doesn't mention talking to anyone, or anyone getting into his car for a chat during the three hours he was in Raphoe. He simply sat in the car. He didn't notice the fight outside the nightclub heading up to St Eunan's Terrace, mentioned by Gareth Friel. He didn't mention seeing Eugene Gamble or Geoffrey Dolan, who were also parked in the area. He didn't mention the ambulance arriving in the Diamond, or leaving. The news of Richie's accident had reached the nightclub by 1.30 a.m. or earlier, but no one came over to his car to tell him; he didn't learn Richie Barron was killed until the next day. And he didn't mention seeing Gazza Gallagher drive from the Diamond at speed and turn at the Tech. Donnelly's omissions might have been a simple oversight because he was focused on the sighting of McConnell when he made his statement, except that he said he 'saw nothing more that was unusual that night'.

The tribunal found Donnelly's evidence 'implausible', and could not accept that 'two young people, who habitually socialised in Raphoe, could drive around the Diamond for forty minutes without seeing anyone they knew', or that while Kieran Roulston slept for a considerable period, 'Roderick Donnelly did not see, or speak to, anyone he knew; that they did not go to the chip shop either for food, or to see if there was anyone there that they knew; and that at the end of the evening they did four further laps of the Diamond without seeing anyone they knew. The evidence was 'simply not credible, even by the standards of behaviour in Raphoe'.

The tribunal had doubts as to whether Kieran Roulston's car was either in Raphoe at all, or was in the place that he said it was on the night Richie Barron died, but in the absence of any firm evidence to the contrary, was unable to make a definite finding that the car was not where Kieran Roulston and Roderick Donnelly said it was.

Justice Morris accepted that Detective Garda Pat Flynn acted in good faith, and recorded 'an accurate record' of what Roderick Donnelly said to him. Neither Detective Garda Flynn nor Pip Roulston prompted Donnelly while he was making the statement in Lifford Garda station, which was told 'entirely and deliberately' by Donnelly.

On Friday 25 February 2000, Pip Roulston began a statement to Detective Garda Hugh Maloney. He told the detective that after Richie Barron's death 'Raphoe split into two factions, one faction blaming the McBreartys for the murder', the other made up of the McBrearty family and their supporters.

'Darcy Connolly was friendly with the Barron family and particularly friendly with Stephen Barron who he ran about with through horses and that,' Pip told the Carty team. 'Darcy blamed the McBreartys for the death of Richy Barron. Darcy Connolly was very friendly with William Doherty

and they were very packed.' Roulston said there was tension between the
camps after Richie Barron died, and 'William Doherty was stuck in the
middle of it, his name always came up.' Pip said Darcy and Doherty asked
him to make false allegations, which he did, mostly against Hugo
McBrearty, Old Frank's twin brother. 'I was made to feel that I had to
make these statements as I was kind of feared of the two boys.'

Pip said that after Darcy told him he could get his driving charges
reduced, he asked his brothers had they seen anything in Raphoe. They said
they hadn't, but Roderick Donnelly was there, and had said he saw Mark
McConnell and Young Frank McBrearty. Pip passed this information to
Darcy. They then arranged for Roderick Donnelly and Kieran Roulston
to make statements.

Pip's problems began in early 1996 when he 'came round a bend on the
wrong side and put an unmarked Garda car in the hedge'.

'I was chatting [to] Darcy Connolly some time after that and I was
telling him about my incident with the Guards,' Pip told the Carty team.
'He knew all about it.' Darcy later told Pip that if he could arrange for
statements to be made against the McBreartys he 'could get the charges
against me dropped or lightened or reduced'.

Pip said he made 'false allegations' against the McBreartys to the
Guards in Raphoe. 'I have trouble remembering what came first but in
total I made ten or eleven statements to Guards in Raphoe against these
people, which all were false,' Pip told the Carty team. In one case, Darcy
asked him to make a statement that Young Frank McBrearty 'swerved at
him in his car.'

On 30 January 1997, ten days after Roderick Donnelly made his statement to Detective Garda Pat Flynn, Darcy Connolly made a complaint to
Garda John O'Dowd at Raphoe Garda station. The former jockey said
that five days earlier he had seen Young Frank McBrearty driving down
the road, and Frank swerved his car at him. As a result Frank McBrearty
was prosecuted on a careless driving charge. This was Darcy's first
complaint against the McBrearty family. There would be several others.
Pip recalled how Darcy kept a diary in which he recorded each of these
complaints, to keep the stories straight.

Pip also told the detectives that he attended Letterkenny court house
several times to give evidence against the McBreartys, as the cases accumulated and because the McBreartys fought them, and the cases were
repeatedly adjourned. During one of his appearances at the court house,
Pip told the detectives, he saw William Doherty printing business cards
in a machine at the nearby shopping centre. The cards read 'the
Murdering McBreartys', or 'Murdering Services'. Pip said that Doherty
distributed the cards around Letterkenny, and Pip saw some of the cards
in Darcy Connolly's van. Kieran Roulston said the cards said something

like 'Contact the McBreartys—for All Your Murdering Needs'. Pip later
heard William Doherty boast that he had painted abusive slogans on the
roads in Raphoe, near the homes of Young Frank McBrearty and Mark
McConnell, which read 'House For Sale, Owner Moving To Mountjoy,
Contact Frank McBrearty'.

At the Morris tribunal, William Doherty denied he had painted
inflammatory slogans on the local roads, or printed defamatory business
cards in a shopping centre. 'That story is concocted,' he protested.

'It's not concocted, I was there,' Kieran Roulston answered. 'And you
were there.'

The business cards (Pip thought the incident happened sometime in
1998) are a virtual carbon copy of another earlier attempt to confound
and bedevil the McBrearty family. This involved pamphlets designed to
look like advertisements for the Parting Glass nightclub, except the main
attraction on offer was 'the Murdering McBreartys. See them live. Father
and son at Frankie's nightclub . . .' There were two versions, both of which
appeared overnight in Raphoe in the first two weeks of March 1997.

Despite Doherty's denials, the tribunal was satisfied he'd created the
business cards, and produced and distributed the leaflets.

Doherty did admit to making abusive phone calls to Old Frank
McBrearty, calling him a 'murdering bastard'. He'd already told the Carty
team he got Frank's ex-directory phone number from Garda John
O'Dowd and Sergeant John White. He withdrew the accusation against
John White at the tribunal.

'Overall, the lives of the McConnell and McBrearty extended family
were made a misery by these crazy actions, by a group of ill-guided
individuals,' the tribunal found. 'The accumulative effect of the actions
should not be overlooked,' the chairman wrote. 'These gestures were
accompanied by the blasphemous abuse of the sign of the cross, on the
part of a number of people where any of the family were seen.'

Chapter 21

A Campaign of Harassment

O n 4 February 1997, Young Frank McBrearty called to the Garda station in Raphoe to renew his car tax and registration. Sergeant Joe Hannigan was on duty. As Frank left the station, a member of the Barron family followed him. To avoid a confrontation Frank went back inside. As he left for the second time, Garda John O'Dowd followed him outside. Sergeant John White appeared with a video camera, and filmed as O'Dowd arrested Frank under Section 18 of the Offences Against the Person Act at 12.52 p.m.

The arrest was made following an alleged assault on Edmond (Ed) Moss, a patron in the Parting Glass nightclub who was injured in the early hours of 30 December 1996. Moss and his girlfriend Pamela McCready, along with their friends Larry and Teresa Harper, had spent the evening at the Parting Glass. As the night drew to a close, Teresa became faint and fell to the floor. As Ed Moss and Larry Harper went to help her, Young Frank and some of the bouncers noticed the commotion.

What happened next is mired in controversy. According to Young Frank, he was the only person in the building with first aid training, and went to administer first aid. According to Moss, Frank pushed Teresa's head between her legs, and was handling her roughly, so that she fainted again. Ed Moss and Larry Harper said they'd bring Teresa outside, and they say that Frank became angry at that point. Moss claimed he was hit in the face by Frank while three bouncers grabbed him, and Frank punched him in the head and body while he was dragged out of the nightclub and thrown on the ground. As he got up from the ground, he said Frank hit him again.

Frank gave a different account. 'I'm the only person was trained in first aid in the nightclub, because of my experience as a doorman in London,' he told the Morris tribunal. 'A girl had collapsed in the nightclub and I attended her, she was fainted, she was along with Edward Moss and another couple and I went over to help and Moss, he said, we'll deal with her and I said that's fine, because I knew he was agitated, he wasn't drunk but he had a good drink taken. I got up to walk away. He grabbed me and actually assaulted me and tore the jumper off me. But it transpired that I was the person and two of the doormen, we were charged with breaking his leg in two places, which never even happened.'

According to the medical report from Tyrone County Hospital, Moss suffered a spiral fracture to the right fibula, bruising below his right eye and around his nose, and a cut nose.

'The circumstances surrounding the incident were that his girlfriend, I think it was his girlfriend, got weak on the floor near the end of the dance and they went to help her and Young Frankie jumped in saying I know all about first aid and there was a bit of an altercation,' was John O'Dowd's recollection.

Moss made a statement of complaint to Garda John O'Dowd at Raphoe Garda station on 31 December. Witness statements were taken in the days that followed. On 6 January, solicitor John Fahy wrote to Garda O'Dowd and asked for copies of any statements that concerned his client, Ed Moss. The same day, Old Frank McBrearty visited Moss at his home in Castlederg in Northern Ireland. Frank told Moss he wanted to make an agreement. He would compensate him for his injuries, and there would be no charges.

On 14 January, at a meeting involving his solicitor and Old Frank McBrearty, Ed Moss signed documents settling his civil claim against the nightclub, and received a large cash payment. After the meeting, John Fahy wrote to Raphoe Garda station telling them his client was withdrawing his statement of complaint. On 21 January, Moss called to the station in person.

'When Mr Moss arrived in Raphoe Garda Station on 21 January 1997 he was certainly in a confused state of mind but was acting on his solicitor's instructions in requesting that he withdraw his statement of complaint,' White wrote in a 1999 report on the case. 'He clearly states in his statement that it was not his personal intention to withdraw it but felt that he was legally compelled to do so after he had accepted the money from Mr McBrearty Snr.'

White explained to Moss that he was not compelled to withdraw a criminal complaint because he'd reached a civil settlement, and Moss agreed that if the DPP took a case against Young Frank and the bouncers and he was summonsed, he would give evidence.

———

Frank was taken from Raphoe to Letterkenny, where he was processed by the custody officer, and brought to the interview rooms. He'd been expecting a second arrest since he was freed on 4 December, but it still came as a shock. Frank asked for a doctor, and to see his solicitor. He was put in the cells, and the member in charge made the phone calls to Dr McFeely and McMullin's firm of solicitors.

Just after 2 p.m., Frank was taken from the cells to an interview room by Garda John O'Dowd and Sergeant John White. He was not aware that the interview was taped. White had set up the same video recorder he had used to tape the arrest to film the question and answer session, in case Frank made any allegations at a later date that he was mistreated.

For Frank, the first interview with O'Dowd and White was 'an absolute nightmare, every bit as bad as the Four Boys from Dublin.'

'I know they had been videoing me at Raphoe Garda station because it's in my complaints. But he was trying to video me to get a confession to the death of Richie Barron, because they knew the one they had would never stand up,' he said.

The first session ended when Frank's solicitor, James Sweeney, arrived at the station at 2.40 p.m. The solicitor told the tribunal that Frank was 'literally terrified' by the time he got to see him. 'It appears that this terror arose as a result of his previous experience in a Garda station,' the chairman wrote. 'The tribunal accepts this as the only logical explanation for the actions that he took on this occasion.'

'I was pleading with James Sweeney, get me out of this fucking place, James. That's the language I was using. You've got to get me out of here James, I can't take the abuse. And he says he couldn't do nothing, he was doing his best. I said, well if you don't get me fucking out of here, I'm going to either bang my head off the fucking wall or I'm going to fucking—I'm going to punch myself three or four times in the face'.

'I was in a hysterical state and I was going at a thousand miles an hour, trying to tell James Sweeney what they were doing to me. James Sweeney could see that I was in an awful state.'

When Garda Martin Leonard told the solicitor his time with his client was up, Sweeney went to see the Superintendent, John Fitzgerald, and O'Dowd and White returned.

'Me and John [White] were in the interview room and John had to leave the interview room,' John O'Dowd recalled. 'He was called out or something. I was in the room on my own with Young Frankie. Young Frank was sitting across. He said "See that wall Dowd. I'm going to go up there and I'm going to bang my head off it and I'm going to blame you." As soon as he said that I took him out of the interview room and I put him into the cell. I brought this matter to the attention of the so [Station Orderly] at the time and I brought it to the attention of his solicitor, who was there.

'Shortly after this, John White was finished whatever he was doing so we took [Frank McBrearty] back to the interview room again and we started questioning him about Eddie Moss. As it happens wasn't John White called out again and as soon as he went out the door, up yer man goes to the wall, bangs his head against the wall as hard as he could and the next thing. This is what he was at, banging . . .

'I opened the door of the interview room and I was blessed that John Rouse was standing at the door. I don't know what he was doing but he was there in the corridor. I said nothing. Just pointed. I said watch that. I didn't say it. I just pointed it because he had his back to us. He went up, banged his head against the wall and started this. That's a fact.'

Young Frank denied he ever banged his head against the wall, but eventually admitted to the tribunal that he did punch his own face.

'I was put back into the interrogation room,' he told the tribunal, 'and I had put my hands on my head on the desk and John O'Dowd pushed my head into the desk, and I got up as if to hit him and I punched myself four times in the face. I started shouting and roaring, he's assaulted me, he's assaulted me. Sergeant White had left the room, I was in the room on my own with him.

'I was desperate to get out of the station. I wasn't going to take that abuse or be accused of murdering Richie Barron when I didn't . . . And I wasn't going to be accused of assaulting Edward Moss when I didn't.

'If I had got a knife, I would have cut my wrists to get out of that station, because I wasn't going to suffer that abuse that I suffered the first time I was arrested.'

Meanwhile, James Sweeney was doing his best to get Young Frank released. He was familiar with the Ed Moss case. He knew a settlement had been reached in the civil case, and in any case he knew Young Frank was on anti-depressants after his first arrest, and was in no state to be questioned. His client was threatening self-harm, and threatening to assault the Gardaí questioning him. Sweeney also handed in a letter from Moss's solicitor, formally withdrawing the complaint. Sweeney was still waiting to see the superintendent when Young Frank punched himself in the face, and he was allowed to see his client again. Young Frank told the solicitor what he had done.

'I then went out of the interrogation room,' James Sweeney recalled. 'And as I was leaving, Garda O'Dowd and Sergeant White went in to continue their questioning. I demanded that the questioning cease until such time as Mr McBrearty had seen a doctor.'

'The bottom line is you don't have to be a genius to know that I had some type of breakdown in that barracks,' Frank told the tribunal. 'I should not have been in that station. I should have been put in a psychiatric ward.'

The tribunal was satisfied that when Sweeney saw Frank 'he found him in an advanced state of emotion and terror. In these circumstances, the

Tribunal is satisfied that Mr Sweeney attempted to address the problem by consulting with the station party. However, he got an unsatisfactory response from them. It should have been obvious to everybody present that Mr McBrearty Junior's condition called for steps to be taken to control the situation. Mr Sweeney got no co-operation in this regard. He is to be commended for his efforts. What followed later is, in the Tribunal's view, a consequence of the lack of co-operation shown by the station party towards Mr Sweeney.'

Frank explained how after his solicitor left he pleaded to be taken to the cells to rest, tried to leave the interview room several times, and 'eventually lay on the floor of the room, saying nothing. He guessed he stayed like that for anywhere between two and four hours, 'receiving severe abuse from all the members of the Garda force that were in the room with me', calling him abusive and insulting names.

Frank also received a visit from his doctor during his detention. 'I pleaded with the doctor to sign me into the psychiatric ward,' he told the tribunal. After 9 hours and 28 minutes, he was released from custody at 10.18 p.m. Two years later, in May 1999, a Circuit Court jury would take thirty-five minutes to acquit Frank of assault charges against Ed Moss. Charges against two bouncers were dismissed earlier on the directions of the trial judge.

Frank refused to be cross-examined by lawyers representing John O'Dowd and John White at the Morris tribunal. The refusal meant that, according to the rules of evidence, the tribunal could make no findings against them based on his testimony. The tribunal, however, decided that it could make findings based on the allegations Frank made, because it had concluded that there was no substance to the allegations. Frank was not assaulted by the Gardaí as he claimed. His injuries were entirely self-inflicted when he banged his head against the wall and punched himself in the face. However, much as one might understand his reasons at the time, Frank was wrong to repeat his allegations in a videotape made by private investigator Billy Flynn and in complaints to the Garda Complaints Board. Giving evidence at his Circuit Court trial in 1999, Frank repeated the allegations again, and did not admit he struck himself in the face until he spoke to tribunal investigators in 2003. Even then, he still maintained that he only hit himself after he was first struck by O'Dowd.

However, the chairman also had harsh words for Sergeant White, who subjected Frank McBrearty to ridicule and called him names as he lay on the floor in the interview room refusing to answer questions. This was 'indicative of an inappropriate zeal, that is entirely at variance with a reasonable and professional approach to the interviewing of suspects'.

Finally, as Frank left Letterkenny Garda station, he was served with two notices of intention to prosecute. These were the false complaints that Darcy Connolly had made a week earlier. The decision to serve the notices during a time when Frank was so vulnerable was 'a mean and vindictive act towards a prisoner who was leaving in a clearly disturbed state'.

_____

The day after Young Frank was arrested and questioned about the Ed Moss case, Old Frank met with Billy Flynn, a private investigator. Ever since the arrests began, Old Frank had been asking friends for the name of someone who could help. Eventually, his inquiries led him to Flynn.

When they met, Frank told the private eye how his son and nephew had been arrested for murder, how he himself was picked up and accused of 'perversion of the course of justice', and of all the other arrests. Frank told Flynn his family were innocent, and asked him to investigate Barron's death and clear his family name. Frank authorised Flynn to offer a £10,000 reward for any information leading to a conviction in the case.

The 52-year-old private detective, a diminutive chain-smoking Meathman, told McBrearty that he would take on his case, but warned him that he would turn any information he found over to the Gardaí, even if it incriminated his client.

The following day, Flynn rang Letterkenny Garda station and spoke to Chief Superintendent Denis Fitzpatrick. He asked for copies of the pathologist's report and witness statements taken by Gardaí investigating the death of Richie Barron. The Chief declined the request, explaining that private citizens were not entitled to internal Garda documents.

Flynn, however, had his own resources, and eventually he and his investigators were able to piece together what happened in Donegal. They interviewed witnesses, collected their own statements, and in some cases managed to track down witnesses the Gardaí had missed.

Kevin Lennon arrived in Letterkenny as district superintendent on 10 February 1997, replacing John Fitzgerald, who transferred to Manorhamilton in County Leitrim. The tribunal felt that Fitzgerald harboured doubts about the statement of admission taken by the Dublin detectives who had interviewed Young Frank McBrearty, and was determined not to let it out of his hands. He took it with him to Manorhamilton.

Lennon claimed that in the first months he spent in Letterkenny, his only part in the Barron investigation was to chair conference meetings on the case. Coincidentally, his appointment as district superintendent took place on 5 February, the same day Frank hired Billy Flynn, although it was a few days before he transferred to his new post.

Kevin Lennon later claimed the Gardaí were receiving complaints from local politicians about public order problems in Letterkenny and Raphoe. Sergeant John White had already been transferred to Raphoe from the Gaeltacht barracks in Carrick on 10 January to deal with the problem there. White was given responsibility for sorting out public order problems in the town.

Lennon said that on his appointment, he quickly became aware of two Raphoe issues he had to work on, the public order problem and allegations that Frank McBrearty was intimidating witnesses.

By the time Lennon arrived, there were already ten cases against the McBreartys for licensing offences. There were also cases pending against other pubs in Raphoe. Public order was an issue in the town. One man had suffered a fractured skull in a fight on New Year's Day, another had suffered 'a serious spinal injury'.

'There was a considerable amount of assaults reported,' Lennon remembered. These weren't peculiar to McBrearty's, or even to Raphoe. Letterkenny also had a problem. 'The local councillors were also kicking up in Letterkenny about it,' he recalled. Lennon also recalled that the then Labour Senator Sean Moloney had complained about the targeting of the McBreartys, and 'at one stage Paddy Harte (a Fine Gael TD) had written to the Chief Superintendent looking for extra manpower in Raphoe'.

Whatever about the ongoing problems in Raphoe, Lennon had a more important matter on his mind: William Doherty. The continued supply of inside information on IRA operations (most of it conveniently unverifiable) attributed to Doherty made Lennon look good and kept his name in lights in Dublin. McGinley and Shelly could deal with the mess in Raphoe—Lennon had his eye on a bigger target, the promotion that would follow more successes against the IRA.

In February 1997, eleven C77 forms detailing intelligence on the IRA went up to Garda HQ, complementing the nine in January and the first three which went to Dublin in November 1996. There were none in December. Kevin Lennon would later claim that he met Doherty in February 1997 and decided that he was an untrustworthy source, laying the blame on John O'Dowd for everything that followed. However, Chief Superintendent Denis Fitzpatrick had no memory of ever being told Lennon had rejected William Doherty. It was another lie, created by Lennon to distance himself from the chaos the Doherty pretence would generate.

———

At 10.20 a.m. on the morning of 24 February the phone rang in the McBrearty family home. The caller was looking for Old Frank. Rosalind McBrearty told him her husband was at work at the Parting Glass. Ten minutes later, the phone rang again. The caller told Rosalind she was the wife of a murderer, and accused her of having an affair with a priest, before hanging up.

Between the two calls to Rosalind, Old Frank received two calls, the first at 10.23 a.m. The caller said his name was 'PJ', called Old Frank a 'fat bastard' and a 'murdering bastard', and told him his money 'would not buy him out of his difficulty this time'. Three minutes later, the phone rang again. One of the barmaids answered, and the caller told her that Old Frank was 'a fat murdering bastard'. There were three more calls in the afternoon, at 2.55 p.m., 3.10 p.m. and 3.33 p.m. The caller said he was 'looking for the fat murdering bastard'.

The McBreartys had told Billy Flynn about the phone calls they'd been receiving. They knew what to do, and immediately wrote down the times of the calls and what was said.

The phone calls were just a single example of the harassment the family had to endure. On two successive Saturdays, 8 and 15 March, flyers were left around Raphoe advertising 'The Murdering McBreartys'. The road outside Frank's house was painted overnight with the slogan 'House for sale. Owner moving to Mountjoy, contact Frank McBrearty.'

The phone calls continued, along with death threats and hoax bomb warnings to the nightclub. In the middle of the chaos, Flynn and his staff continued with their work, interviewing witnesses, working on the phone calls, pressing their contacts to obtain copies of the forensic reports on the Barron case, telephone records to identify the source of the calls, anything to break the case.

Meanwhile, the Garda investigation trundled on, albeit on a reduced scale. At a conference on 20 March, Sergeant Marty Moylan reported that along with Garda John O'Toole, he'd finished a collation exercise on the 'Mister X' statement. He'd examined over 500 Garda statements from people in Raphoe the night Richie Barron died. No one had mentioned seeing Noel McBride in Raphoe that night, 'not even his brother'.

'I remember there was silence around the room,' Moylan recalled. 'The next thing, Superintendent Lennon said "We're not here to test the credibility of witnesses, get on with it."'

Chapter 22
I'm Going To Get You a Big Bunker

On 19 February 1997, Garda John O'Dowd submitted a confidential c77 report to Garda Headquarters. In the report he referred to Jim 'Lofty' Gallagher, who he claimed was minding a dump for the Provisional IRA on Dooish Hill, near Saint Johnstown.

Detective Sergeant Hugh Smith remembered that about a week later, Superintendent Kevin Lennon asked him how things were in 'subversive circles'.

'Everything seems quiet,' Smith told him. 'The Letterkenny IRA seem to be supporting the ceasefire.'

'I'm going to get you a big bunker,' Lennon announced.

'Good luck to you if you can,' the sergeant replied.

Lennon asked Smith for a night-sight, and left the office with it.

On Saturday 1 March 1997 O'Dowd sent in another confidential report. He outlined how the IRA stole an Ifor Williams trailer in Sion Mills and took it to Lofty Gallagher's farm. According to O'Dowd, the IRA spent the previous night preparing the trailer for use as a mortar launcher.

It seems the first c77 from O'Dowd reported that there was an arms dump or bunker near the Gallagher farm, and 'Lofty' was keeping an eye on it. The second report was more urgent. A bomb was in the final stages of preparation on the farm, ready to cross the border.

An emergency meeting was called on the same day. Present were Chief Superintendent Denis Fitzpatrick, Superintendent Kevin Lennon, and Detective Inspector John McGinley. McGinley didn't recall Garda O'Dowd being present. 'It's quite possible he was but from my recall of it he wasn't,' he said later.

McGinley remembered that Lennon had information about a major IRA attack. He told the others an Ifor Williams trailer had been stolen in Sion Mills in Northern Ireland, and brought across the border. He claimed it was hidden on a Saint Johnstown farm belonging to Alfie Gallagher, where a 'Mark 15' bomb would be loaded, creating a 'barrack buster' designed to take out a heavily fortified RUC station. The bomb was in the final stages of assembly, and would go back across the border between 10.30 p.m. and 11.30 p.m. that night.

O'Dowd said his information—that there was an Ifor Williams trailer and a silver and red Mitsubishi jeep in the yard—came from William Doherty, who also told him in February there was a hidden IRA arms bunker in the area.

Saturday 1 March was a busy day for John O'Dowd. It was his partner's birthday, and he had planned a trip to Northern Ireland for the weekend with her. At the tribunal, one of the barristers expressed surprise that he went through with the holiday break in view of the crucial information he claimed he had just received.

'If you spent 'X', you'd avail of it,' O'Dowd answered.

'Not necessarily,' said the barrister.

'You wouldn't? Well I haven't got your wealth,' O'Dowd replied.

John O'Dowd said that after speaking to Doherty he phoned his supervisor, Kevin Lennon. The superintendent instructed him to come in to Letterkenny station. He briefed Chief Superintendent Fitzpatrick, Superintendent Lennon, and Detective Inspector McGinley in the Chief's office. After the briefing, O'Dowd left for his planned trip to Portaferry in County Down. He got back to Donegal the following Tuesday.

Detective Inspector McGinley checked with an RUC contact, who confirmed that an Ifor Williams trailer had indeed been stolen near Sion Mills. However, McGinley was doubtful. He knew the Gallagher family. 'They were known to be a decent, honourable, hard-working, law-abiding family,' he remembered. Alfie Gallagher's father had been one of the first recruits to the Garda Síochána when the force was set up after the War of Independence. Everything McGinley knew said there was some-thing wrong. The Gallagher's just didn't fit the profile of IRA sympathisers.

The detective inspector went to Chief Superintendent Fitzpatrick. 'This information isn't right,' he told the Chief. He asked if Lennon had a track record of producing good intelligence on the IRA. McGinley remembered that Fitzpatrick said he was present when Lennon 'stopped an operation in Bridgend'.

'I don't actually remember saying that to him but I probably did,' Fitzpatrick said.

Fitzpatrick did not know the January 1994 Bridgend operation, where Gardaí intercepted a shipment of home-made explosives on its way to Derry, was a hoax masterminded by Lennon, then an inspector, to impress his superiors and advance his career. Lennon had stage-managed the entire escapade, allowing Denis Fitzpatrick to feel the rush of under-cover work as he watched, wearing a woolly hat and disguised as a drunk, while Lennon's pawn Adrienne McGlinchey dumped three holdall bags of ground fertiliser to be discovered by Gardaí. Fitzpatrick even made the anonymous call that evening reporting suspicious activity in the area which sparked the Garda search that led to the 'discovery'.

The Chief valued McGinley's input. 'John McGinley was the one saying take it easy,' he recalled. 'I regarded him as streetwise. I would value his view.

'If you talk about argument, he was the one arguing against the search. He didn't think the Provos were up to doing that at the time even though the ceasefire was over, and he didn't think that Kevin Lennon had produced any information.'

Fitzpatrick decided to go ahead with the search. If the information was true, and the bomb got through to its target because he did nothing, the result didn't bear thinking about.

As a result of the briefing, a major cross-border security operation was initiated. The RUC was notified of a potential imminent attack against a border station. Cordons were set up. A surveillance team was put in place to keep an eye on the farm. They waited at a hide near the Idle Hour pub, about a quarter of a mile from Gallagher's farm. 'Logically anything leaving his house would have to come that way,' O'Dowd recalled. 'It would be an excellent place to give you cover for a surveillance operation.' The covert surveillance team saw nothing over the weekend.

————

McGinley remembered that Kevin Lennon told the Chief Superintendent 'we'd blown the operation, that some of the people on duty had been seen at the Clady bridge'. According to Lennon, the detectives on stakeout at the Idle Hour pub had been spotted. The IRA hadn't moved the barrack buster as expected. The detectives were unhappy to be told they'd blown the covert surveillance operation. They were convinced no one could have seen them.

The Guards decided to search Gallagher's farm. McGinley still had misgivings. The idea of the Gallaghers as IRA sympathisers just didn't work—something had to be wrong with the information. The worried detective thought the operation was unreasonable, and didn't want to take part when the time came to search the farm.

However, the information could not be ignored. The search warrant, based on the information passed on from William Doherty according to O'Dowd, was signed by Detective Superintendent Joe Shelly.

McGinley had planned to travel to Waterford that evening, but instead he went out with the team to 'do an assessment' on the ground.

'We contacted the Chief Superintendent's office from the scene on Monday evening, and made him aware of the position as we saw it,' McGinley testified at the tribunal. He phoned Superintendent Lennon and told him there was nothing there. By that stage, Detective Super-intendent Shelly had arrived at the scene.

As far as Sergeant Marty Moylan remembered, the information for the search of the Gallagher farm came from Superintendent Kevin Lennon. The sergeant 'organised things', getting a team of Gardaí together, con-tacting the Emergency Response Unit, and later arranging for an army helicopter to take part in the search.

'My understanding was that you were the source of it,' Moylan told Superintendent Kevin Lennon when asked where the information that led to the search of the Gallagher farm had come from.

Asked by Lennon how he understood this, he said he might have been told it by one of the other sergeants. He said he remembered that Superintendent Lennon had given a briefing at the end of the first day of the search. However, Lennon said the information came from O'Dowd and Doherty, and O'Dowd said the same, although Doherty told a different story.

————

Alfie Gallagher's son Jim 'Lofty' Gallagher worked on the family farm in 1997. Lofty arrived home around 6 p.m. on the evening of Monday 3 March 1997. The farmyard was dark and unlit. As he pulled in, four armed men surrounded the van, and one shouted: 'Get out of the vehicle!'

'I was just in a complete state of shock, I couldn't say anything,' Lofty Gallagher remembered. 'I didn't know what was going on. One guy put me up against the van, searched me, spread my legs.' Others tore into the van. Another asked him if he knew of any subversive activity in the area.

'Who are you?' Lofty asked.

'Never mind that for the moment,' one of the men barked in reply.

'No warrant was ever shown to me,' Lofty Gallagher recalled. A 'piece of paper' was shown to his father, but this was in a workshop where there was little light, and his father didn't have his glasses. Lofty thought a sergeant told Alfie Gallagher that Superintendent Kevin Lennon had signed the warrant. In fact, Joe Shelly had signed it. Possibly the Garda assumed that Lennon as district officer would have been the one to issue the warrant.

'Never in the course of the search did any representative approach us to explain what was happening,' Lofty complained. One of the Guards found a hat which was burned by holes from welding, and assumed it to be a balaclava. 'Mum was in deep shock in the house, as was Dad and my younger brother,' Lofty remembered.

'No one told us what was going on. Anyone we asked told us to go to Superintendent Lennon, without the courtesy of contacting him for us.'

————

On Tuesday 4 March, John O'Dowd got back from his trip to Portaferry, Co. Down. While he was away, Lennon had contacted him to let him know the search had proved fruitless. O'Dowd claimed that when he got back, he met with William Doherty, and asked him what went wrong with the information. He said Doherty told him the jeep and trailer had been moved from Gallagher's Farm because Gardaí were spotted on the stakeout near the Idle Hour, and took him to sheds on a neighbouring farm where he claimed the gear was moved, before being transferred elsewhere.

O'Dowd said that Doherty again told him there was an IRA bunker on Dooish mountain, behind the Gallagher farm. Lennon told the Tuesday conference the search was no longer for a barrack buster. The Guards were to look for an arms bunker.

Army airpower, in the form of a helicopter, was called in to assist in the search of the mountain, flying low over the land looking for any sign of a man-made structure. Emergency Response Unit and local detectives also took part in the searches. Despite the intensive effort, no bunker or bomb was found on Tuesday, the second day of searching.

O'Dowd said his faith in Doherty as an informer was not shaken by the debacle. 'I believed him, he was very convincing,' he insisted at the tribunal.

Lofty Gallagher recalled that on Tuesday 4 March, the Guards told his family 'they had reason to believe a bomb had left one of our sheds, and there was another one due to go out in the near future'. The family was 'absolutely devastated' by the news.

'This was a serious and quite vicious invasion of our land,' Lofty remembered. 'I would be aware if anything was happening on the lands, this was lambing season, busy. The shed in the yard made it impossible for us to miss anything.'

The focus of the search widened on Tuesday, away from the farm sheds and yard, as the Guards searched for the bunker. 'The helicopter was present during the search,' Lofty remembered. 'This episode stands out as one of the most horrific parts of the search.' In broad daylight, an army helicopter hovered at low altitude, near heavily pregnant sheep. The animals stampeded, and piled up against a barred gate, 'piled up three high'. Sheep were strangled and suffocated in the pile-up.

Lofty Gallagher said attempts by his solicitor to obtain a copy of the search warrant afterwards were unsuccessful. 'When we tried to get some answers on this, we came up against a brick wall on every occasion.'

———

After the search for the bunker drew a blank, Kevin Lennon claimed he then asked John O'Dowd to have Doherty point out the location of the bunker on Dooish mountain, and place a mark there to guide the searchers.

O'Dowd told the tribunal how he arranged Doherty would bring himself and Kevin Lennon on a tour of Dooish mountain, and mark the location of the bunker. O'Dowd thought that Doherty marked a spot near a white stone in a forest clearing. Lennon remembered it was marked with a stick.

Doherty's version is quite different. He told the inquiry he was brought to a shed in a white transit Garda surveillance van and shown a clear plastic bag of white powder by Kevin Lennon and John O'Dowd. He was then driven to Dooish mountain and walked about half a mile across some fields. Doherty said he was told to bury the bag on the hill 'to fit up the Gallaghers' and mark the spot the weekend before the search took place. He denied giving the Guards any information about a hidden arms bunker on the mountain, or a stolen trailer or barrack buster bomb in a shed on the Gallagher farm. Doherty said he didn't plant the bag of white powder as ordered, but when he returned he told the two Guards he'd done the job.

'The whole incident is so unlikely and bizarre as to lead me to the conclusion that William Doherty must be telling the truth. I confess that I can find no other explanation for the curious circumstances surrounding the Lofty Gallagher search,' Mr Justice Morris eventually concluded.

'I think the purpose was to get at a businessman Mr Gallagher worked for,' Doherty said. 'I was just a petty criminal which I've admitted to. I had no contacts with Sinn Féin or the IRA. It's like a Harry Potter film what you're putting to me,' he told O'Dowd's barrister Tom Creed SC during his cross-examination.

Doherty's evidence portrayed the search as a clear fabrication, a recycling of elements of the hoax explosives finds involving Adrienne McGlinchey and Kevin Lennon some years before.

Lennon denied vehemently that he ever ordered Doherty to plant bags of white powder or anything else on Dooish mountain. 'I went out, not in a sinister attempt, merely in an attempt to establish that there was or wasn't something there, and if there wasn't to get rid of the search, and if there was to deal with it,' he told Gallagher's barrister at the tribunal.

Lennon's protests were to no avail. Justice Morris found that he'd planned the operation with Garda John O'Dowd, but the plan had backfired when Doherty refused to plant incriminating evidence on Dooish mountain.

———

The Wednesday conference was told to look for a stick marking the spot where the arms bunker was concealed on Dooish mountain. But despite another day of intensive searching, no arms bunker was found. Or rather, the searchers found the stick, but no bunker.

'I think Superintendent Lennon was convinced that the information was right,' John McGinley said afterwards. Later he added: 'William Doherty may have hoodwinked them in relation to the Gallaghers.'

The high-profile Gallagher search lasted several days. Lennon trusted Doherty to plant contraband on Dooish mountain, and never verified the job was done.

————

Lennon said that having assessed Doherty's potential as an informant in late 1996, he met him again in February 1997, around the time he was transferred from Buncrana to Letterkenny. He said he decided William Doherty was not trustworthy, because he had lied about a previous conviction for assault. Lennon claimed he told John O'Dowd not to have any further dealings with Doherty, but when Doherty brought in the information on the barrack buster bomb, he felt he could not ignore it no matter what he thought of the informer's credibility. The cost of a mistake was too high.

O'Dowd retorted that this simply wasn't true. Lennon simply invented his late February re-assessment of Doherty as an unreliable liar in an attempt to distance himself from the Gallagher debacle. Chief Superintendent Denis Fitzpatrick also said he was never told of any February re-assessment. Lennon conceded that at the meeting with Fitzpatrick, McGinley and O'Dowd on 1 March to discuss the barrack buster information, he never mentioned that he regarded Doherty as unreliable.

A few days after the search, Lennon met with Chief Superintendent Dermot Jennings of Crime & Security to discuss allegations that a particular Garda was an IRA mole. Again he did not mention his supposed doubts about the informant who had caused a fruitless three-day search involving Army and ERU resources.

O'Dowd pointed out that Lennon, his district superintendent and agent supervisor, was a noted disciplinarian, and would almost certainly find out if he continued to send c77s to headquarters against orders. In those circumstances, it just didn't make sense that he would defy orders as Lennon claimed. Lennon's diary contained no record of any direction to O'Dowd to stop submitting c77 information from Doherty.

Lennon, however, was adamant. 'I went to the Chief after Lofty Gallagher and I said I was having nothing more to do with Doherty,' he told the tribunal. The lies were to no avail. It was simply unbelievable that such a vital assessment of an intelligence source would not have been recorded somewhere at the time.

———

In total, O'Dowd submitted forty-three c77 forms he said came from William Doherty. Nothing on any c77 indicates who the information came from. The only proof that Doherty was the source of any information was O'Dowd's evidence to that effect. Brian Steel Garvie, a Chief Superintendent with the Royal Canadian Mounted Police on secondment to the tribunal as an investigator, said that in the forty cases where information was apparently received from Doherty, 'not one provided tangible evidence of an offence'.

Twelve of the forty-three Doherty c77 forms exist only in the files at Crime & Security in Garda headquarters. No copies of these c77 forms were placed in Chief Superintendent Denis Fitzpatrick's divisional file in Donegal. O'Dowd told the tribunal he gave a copy of every c77 he sent to Crime & Security to either Kevin Lennon or Denis Fitzpatrick. Lennon accepted that he did not pass on some of the c77 forms he got from O'Dowd until Fitzpatrick went looking for them, following enquiries from Crime & Security. The Garda Commissioner's legal team in their closing submission said other c77 forms were found in a locker belonging to Kevin Lennon by the Carty team, although Lennon pointed out that no evidence of this had been presented to the tribunal.

Lennon claimed that after he told O'Dowd to drop Doherty, the Raphoe Garda sent in c77 forms when he was out of the county. He agreed that O'Dowd telephoned him with information from Doherty, but claimed he thought the Garda was 'just telling me things'.

'I'm saying I didn't know there was c77s to back the information he was giving me after March 1997,' Lennon claimed. 'I thought he was telling me the information, but I didn't know there was a considerable amount of c77s in the system.'

'I accepted that information and I did nothing about it, because I didn't believe it.'

In his closing submissions, Lennon argued that Fitzpatrick did not deal with the c77 forms according to Crime & Security regulations then in force. The information on the forms was not sent out for investigation.

A total of three c77 forms were sent to Crime & Security in November 1996. Lennon claimed he saw none of them. Nine c77 forms went up on 18 January 1997. Lennon also claimed he did not see these as he was at the Garda college on a training course between 20 January and 6 February. Five more c77 forms were submitted on 1 February while Lennon was still in Templemore. Further c77s were submitted in April 1997. Lennon said he was in Dublin at a criminal trial between 17 April and 21 April. Lennon was also in Dublin between 19 July and 23 July 1997 when the last of the forms went up.

There were no more c77 forms after July 1997. In the final c77, it was alleged that a 'contract' had been taken out on Young Frank McBrearty, involving an IRA member in County Tyrone. O'Dowd said the c77s stopped because the IRA ceasefire was back in place. Fitzpatrick said it was because the information in the final c77—the alleged 'contract'— demonstrated that Doherty was completely unreliable.

———

The Morris tribunal never did establish exactly what it was the Guards were supposed to find on Gallagher's Farm. Denis Fitzpatrick pointed out at the Morris tribunal that 'Kevin Lennon was very confident there was something there.'

Fitzpatrick thought that Doherty outwitted Kevin Lennon. 'I believe William Doherty was to place something there so that it could be found later,' he explained. 'I think Kevin Lennon was behind that plan,' he elaborated. 'He was so confident that there was something there. That was his information to us.'

Fitzpatrick believed the search parties were looking for a 'bunker', about the size a man could walk into or crawl into, 'the size of a small room, or something of that nature'.

'My theory is that something was going to be found, arms or ammunition,' he said. 'A hide could be small, no bigger than a rabbit hole, something you could put a pipe into. The information was that there was a bunker, but what was going to be found was going to be a smaller size.'

The search was unsuccessful, so it will never be known what it was the Guards searching the hill were supposed to find. Fitzpatrick was the only one to offer a theory, and perhaps came close to the truth with his description of a hole small enough to hide a makeshift pipe bomb, or a handful of rifles and ammunition.

———

After the Gallagher debacle, Detective Inspector McGinley was called to a meeting with Chief Superintendent Fitzpatrick and Superintendent Lennon. He was told that Superintendent Lennon was overstretched as district officer. The Chief asked McGinley if he would take over the supervision of an informant from Lennon.

Lawyers for the Garda Commissioner pointed out that Lennon would
not have tried to pass Doherty off to another officer in March if he had
re-assessed him in February and concluded he was unreliable. He would
simply have dropped him. McGinley said he turned down the advance
because he already has 'a busy portfolio' as detective inspector. He was not
told the informer's name.

'I've thought many times since, Chairman, I'm glad I didn't,' McGinley
told the tribunal.

'Looking back on it, I'd say it was a tentative approach rather than
asking me to take him over.' He agreed the meeting took place 'in the best
of humour'. Chief Superintendent Fitzpatrick and Superintendent Kevin
Lennon did not ask him why he would not deal with Lennon's informer.

'I knew when John McGinley said no it was a bad idea to continue
discussing it,' Chief Superintendent Fitzpatrick recalled.

———

Detective Superintendent Shelly recalled that there were question marks
over O'Dowd's source after the Gallagher debacle. 'There were intelligence
reports that went up in relation to activities in England,' he remembered.
'As a result of what happened in March, there were serious doubts cast
over this intelligence.'

However, the disquiet over O'Dowd's source didn't travel to the top
of the chain of command. Questioned by Kevin Lennon at the Morris
tribunal, Denis Fitzpatrick confirmed that no Garda had approached him
to complain about the search.

Superintendent Kevin Lennon attended a meeting of border superintendents on 10 March 1997, days after the Gallagher search. All border
superintendents and district superintendents in border areas attend these
meetings. Somehow, the fiasco didn't register on the security radar.

———

The contents of only two of the c77 forms are explicitly discussed in the
Morris reports. The first recounts the 'Ivomec scam', where it seems
William Doherty was paid £250 from the secret service fund to buy
Ivomec, a medicine used for treating worms in cattle.

'There was supposed to be an Ivomec scam going on with the Provos
where they were selling cheap Ivomec,' John O'Dowd later told tribunal
investigators. 'This is a drench for cattle. Farmers use it, big farmers that
have maybe a couple of hundred cattle, and it's quite expensive a dose and

they were supposed to be selling it cheaper. It was to find out where this was coming from. Well, initially, Doherty told me that he was to meet these boys in Dublin. I brought this information to the attention of the Chief.

'Now I couldn't go to Dublin so I presumed that it was being dealt with. [William Doherty] went up to Dublin and he told me he met these fellows ... They gave him the stuff. Now I wanted to see it but he only showed me one vial. He said he had given the rest of it to a farmer.'

Denis Fitzpatrick authorised the £250 payment to Doherty. O'Dowd gave him the money. Doherty produced no evidence of conterfeit animal medicine, no charges were ever brought, and no one ever asked for the money back.

The 'Cousins scam' involved a trip to Scotland by William Doherty, again courtesy of the secret service fund. 'I told him on one occasion that I would travel to Scotland to check out the Provo scene in Glasgow. He gave me £400 or £500 to go over and when I returned I gave him information about my two cousins,' Doherty later told the Carty team. 'I told him they were running the Glasgow outfit of the PIRA.' In fact, neither man had anything to do with the IRA, as Doherty later admitted to the Carty team. He'd simply given O'Dowd the only two names he knew in Scotland. At the tribunal, Doherty backed away from this admission, and said he never gave any information about his cousins to O'Dowd.

The information in these C77 forms, and all others sent from Donegal to Garda HQ, was completely bogus. Lennon and O'Dowd were happy to let it go up anyway. Any intelligence was gratefully received in Crime & Security, and rarely questioned. In Donegal, Kevin Lennon was able to control what information Denis Fitzpatrick saw, and anyway the Chief relied on Lennon, who he had regarded as an expert on Border Provos ever since Lennon pulled the wool over his eyes the night Fitzpatrick went undercover in a woolly hat at Burnfoot.

———

After the search, the Gallaghers found they had difficulty running the farm, and Lofty's plant hire business suffered. Many people were unwilling to deal with suspected Provo sympathisers. Lofty Gallagher 'decided because of the collapse of the business to just make a cut, and make a fresh start'.

'At the end of the year I left Ireland,' he told the tribunal. He worked abroad for four years. 'When I went to Australia first I had vowed never to come back. But this thing was always in my head over what happened. My family was still at home, Mam and Dad having to deal with the suspicions. Dad took things extremely bad.'

Lofty pointed out that his mother was a teacher who had taught two generations in the local community, and his father a justice of the peace. His mother's father had been one of the first Gardaí in the State, and served as a sergeant in Donegal. 'We were brought up to respect law and order.' He felt the search should never have taken place solely on the evidence of 'the unreliable informer William Doherty'.

Alfie Gallagher told the tribunal that he saw Superintendent Lennon at the scene of a search, and had asked him to have some Garda cars removed so that he could bring his wife to the doctor. He knew Superintendent Lennon before this, and so recognised him. Lennon, however, said he was not there. 'There is no way I would make a mistake,' Alfie Gallagher insisted.

The Gallagher family sued the State for damages. Their case dragged on for close to a decade, and was settled out of court for an undisclosed sum in late 2007, as the Morris tribunal drew to a close.

Chapter 23

These Phone Calls, That's the Problem

The harassing calls continued. The McBreartys faced open hostility on the streets of Raphoe. Darcy Connolly, William Doherty and others adopted the habit of making the sign of the cross ostentatiously every time they encountered a member of the clan, or crossing to the far side of the street. In extreme cases, they shouted abuse at them. Cries of 'murdering bastard' followed Old Frank wherever he went.

Garda inspections, a routine part of the life of any country publican, expected on average three or four times a year, became a regular part of a night in the Parting Glass. Once, twice, sometimes three times a night, the Gardaí arrived in the nightclub. Frank McBrearty complained that random checkpoints had a habit of appearing on the approach roads to Raphoe. Buses bringing patrons to the nightclub were stopped and searched for drugs. Then there were the phone calls.

The calls came at all hours. Some were simple abuse. 'You fat murdering bastard.' 'Your husband is a murdering bastard.' Some contained threats of violence. Some weren't to the McBreartys at all. Instead, the caller would ring the hospital, or Highland Radio, leaving a bomb warning.

Of all the calls, the one that disturbed Old Frank the most came on 21 April 1997. The phone rang at 9.48 a.m. 'I will get your little daughter, you murdering bastard,' the caller snarled. 'You went up the road and you murdered Richie Barron. See how you get on today in court. You murdered a man in Scotland, you murdered a man outside a pub.'

Frank told the caller his tape recorder was running. 'I don't care about your wee tape,' the caller responded. 'Take it to the Gardaí.' The caller launched into a tirade, and told Frank he would lose his court case.

Beginning with the attempted hoax blackmail call to Old Frank on 5 November 1996, four days before Michael Peoples was the victim of a similar scam, there were a total of twenty-three abusive phone calls and hoax bomb scares. Evacuations at the nightclub became almost routine. It seemed to Frank that the Gardaí seemed more interested in emptying his business than preserving life in the face of a bomb threat. Some of the calls, it was rumoured, involved a UVF codeword, but no one could say for certain if it was a genuine codeword.

The Carty team traced several of the phone calls to public phone boxes in north Donegal, and one to William Doherty's home. 'The overall effect of these hoax bomb calls had a detrimental effect on Frank McBrearty's business,' the Carty report noted. 'On all occasions the town had to be sealed off by the Gardaí and on one occasion it resulted in Frank McBrearty having to cancel a band which he had booked.'

The town split. On one side, McBreartys, McConnells, Quinns, Peoples, Brollys, and those who knew they were innocent. On the other side were lined up people like Darcy Connolly, William Doherty, Stephen Barron and others. Those who remained neutral did their best to avoid both sides. Raphoe became a quiet place. No one wanted to be seen drinking in Frank McBrearty's Tudor Lounge, or in Mark Quinn's Town & Country bar. Business fell away dramatically. Nobody wanted to buy bread from Michael Peoples. Before his arrest, business was going so well, and he'd hired a man to help him with the deliveries. Afterwards, things got so bad he ended up signing on the dole.

Billy Flynn was convinced the phone calls were the key. Michael Peoples and Old Frank had both received blackmail calls within weeks of Richie Barron's death, and in Peoples' case, the call was one of the reasons for his arrest. There were other calls which showed inside knowledge, mentions of court dates. Billy knew he had to get to the bottom of the phone calls.

Meanwhile, on the ground in Raphoe, Billy Flynn's investigator Tom Coffey retraced the investigation. He began by taking statements from everyone arrested, covering the night Barron died and their time in Garda custody, then working outwards from there, questioning the nightclub staff, the patrons at the Town & Country, the staff and patrons in Sarah's Café, the people in the Diamond that night.

Tom Coffey didn't have a Garda badge. Not everyone wanted to talk to him. Even so, he began to piece together what happened on 14 October 1996. The private detectives also got hold of a copy of the completed autopsy report from Dr David Barry.

'Death was due in my opinion to head injuries' was the rather unhelpful conclusion in the autopsy report Dr Barry handed in to the Garda investigation team on 16 April 1997. Under clinical details, the accompanying toxicology report noted 'Fatal RTA (road traffic accident) pedestrian had been drinking'. The Gardaí had no forensic evidence to show that Barron died from an assault. The report made no mention of whether the blow which caused the head injuries was consistent with a blow from a blunt instrument, or a vehicle impact, or anything else to be expected in a forensic pathology report. Billy Flynn checked around, and confirmed what he suspected—the report was what would be expected from a road traffic collision.

It was unlikely that Flynn would solve the case. After six months, the trail had gone cold. But all the information he gathered pointed one way. This was no murder. This was a hit and run, death was caused by a vehicle collision. His clients were innocent. The statements coming in from Tom Coffey made that much clear.

There was still a lot of work to do. Every statement led to two or three more witnesses who had to be interviewed. Meanwhile, both Billy Flynn and McBrearty's lawyers were doing their best to negotiate a 'peace treaty' to stop the excessive inspections. The Tudor Lounge and the Town & Country were bleeding financially. If they could stop the nightly inspections, things might calm down. Raphoe was a town on edge, and it unnerved Billy. In a letter to the Garda Commissioner about his clients, he warned that 'their lives are at risk'.

———

Meanwhile, Sergeant Marty Moylan was working on a report on the allegations that Old Frank McBrearty had intimidated witnesses. Moylan based much of the report, submitted on 2 April 1997, on information he in turn had received in a handwritten report from another Garda.

'I didn't know Frank McBrearty other than he had a pub in Raphoe,' Moylan recalled later. 'I transcribed the issues referred to straight out of that into the report, you can see it is word for word virtually.' Moylan said he accepted the information in the report at 'face value', and checked only one item, how Old Frank won the title of honorary mayor of Raphoe.

When Justice Morris pointed out that Frank had complained that 'there isn't a single good word said about him' in the report, Moylan responded: 'I wasn't given the good words about him, chairman.'

'It is biased,' Moylan conceded. 'I did give the worst side of it. In hindsight I should have balanced it up but I didn't have the balance, I only got one side.'

The Moylan report contained no instance of money offered to a witness, only of people who were approached by Frank and asked what the Guards were asking, following which they apparently felt uneasy and intimidated. Only Noel McBride provided strong support for a case of intimidation or interference with witnesses. In his final report on the intimidation case file, Superintendent Lennon noted the difficulties with McBride, 'a local youth with criminal tendencies'. The DPP decided against a prosecution for intimidation.

———

Frustrated by the effect the constant inspections were having on his nightclub, Old Frank instructed his lawyer to go to the High Court for a remedy, alleging he was the victim of Garda harassment. On 24 April 1997 Kevin Lennon drafted an affidavit for Chief Superintendent Fitzpatrick in reply to the McBrearty High Court case. The final report in the Garda defence files referred to the Garda file being prepared on claims of intimidation against Old Frank McBrearty, and also revealed in public for the first time his son's supposed confession.

'I opposed that statement going into that affidavit,' Kevin Lennon claimed later. He said he argued with his Chief Superintendent against including the document in the Garda defence files, since it breached Young Frank's presumption of innocence, still intact since no charges had been brought in the case, never mind a conviction.

Although the confession was revealed in the affidavit, Lennon never got to see the original document. 'We just worked off the typewritten copy,' he recalled.

When the confession went public, after it was revealed during court hearings, the McBreartys were adamant that it came as a bolt out of the blue, despite the fact that the two Dublin detectives who interviewed Old Frank during his arrest in December 1996 had told him they had a confession. Young Frank was adamant there was no confession. Old Frank told his lawyers to get a copy of the document. He wanted tests to prove it was a forgery. The lawyer sent the copy to a handwriting expert for analysis.

At the Morris tribunal, Mark McConnell recalled there was a meeting in his mother's home discussing the development. Young Frank McBrearty was present. 'I know that Frank was very upset when he found out about the statement, because as far as he was concerned it didn't exist,' he recalled. 'He said that he didn't make any statement to the Guards. That's what he said.'

'It was always my opinion that he was duped into signing the second page of the statement,' Mark said. 'The first time I saw it, I thought it looked like his signature, yes.

'Frank McBrearty had his own opinion on it and I did not want to confront Frank McBrearty about his opinion of what happened to him in the Garda station, and especially over that statement. It was a very sore issue with him. I wasn't going to go up, I was not going to go up to him and say, look Frank, it looks like your signature there . . . Under no circumstances would I have gone up to him and said look Frank, that's your signature, you must have made a statement. I would not have said that to him, even if I thought it in my own head, I wouldn't have went up and said it to him.'

———

The first bomb alert came in the early hours of 3 May 1997. A telephone caller to Letterkenny hospital at 12.50 a.m. claimed there was a bomb in Frank McBrearty's nightclub. A local priest got a similar call five minutes later. The call was a hoax, but the effect was devastating. The nightclub had to be cleared while Gardaí searched and verified it was a hoax.

The following day, Sunday 4 May 1997, Detective Inspector John McGinley met William Doherty for the first time. McGinley hadn't planned to meet Doherty; he really wanted to talk to Noel McBride. Something didn't add up. Even the most uncurious of detectives had to notice that McBride's statements weren't making sense, and McGinley was more than curious.

At the end of McBride's keynote statement on 29 November 1996, the statement which triggered multiple arrests, he claimed he had received a threatening phone call telling him 'don't go to the Guards or else'.

On 4 December 1996, the day of the first arrests, he made another statement claiming Old Frank McBrearty offered him £500 and told him 'you are not to tell the Guards or your family anything about this and everything will be all right'. He claimed he was afraid for his life of the McBreartys, and was too terrified to go into Raphoe.

On 18 March 1997, Noel McBride had made a third statement to John O'Dowd. This time, he claimed he got another threatening call telling him 'I'm going to get you, you touting bastard,' and recognised the caller as Young Frank McBrearty. He then claimed Young Frank drove his car at him on the road (echoing the false claims of Darcy Connolly), as he was walking home from Raphoe, even though McBride had earlier claimed he was afraid to go into the town.

McBride claimed Frank drove past threateningly about four times, then stopped his car and, after shouting insults at him, offered him money to sign into St Conal's, the local psychiatric hospital, and withdraw his statements. When McBride refused the bribe, Frank shouted more abuse at him and chased him.

Detective Inspector John McGinley wasn't quite sure what to make of it all. Despite McBride's claim to be afraid of the McBreartys, he had been seen in their nightclub and pub since making his statements. McGinley found the statement of 18 March particularly hard to understand. He couldn't quite imagine McBride having the courage to call Young Frank a 'big fat bastard' to his face as he refused the offer of a bribe.

Garda John O'Dowd arranged for Detective Inspector McGinley to come to a meeting with Noel McBride in his private home in Letterkenny, but when McGinley arrived, William Doherty was also there. O'Dowd introduced Doherty to McGinley as 'a friend of Noel McBride'. The two men had known each other since they went to school together when they were four years old, O'Dowd told the inspector.

By this time, John McGinley—and most detectives in Letterkenny—suspected William Doherty was the supposed source of the information behind the debacle at Lofty Gallagher's farm.

From that point on, McGinley had 'doubts' about William Doherty. On the day though, he did nothing about his worries. He took down what McBride told him under the watchful eyes of O'Dowd and Doherty.

For all its flaws, it seems the meeting on 4 May was the first time McBride was subjected to anything resembling a critical appraisal. By now John O'Dowd was getting nervous. At one point he went so far as to tape Noel McBride, and repeatedly asked him about the original statement. McBride can be heard on the tape confirming what he said in his very first statement on 29 November 1996, the 'trigger statement' that led to the mass arrests. If McBride was ever uncovered, O'Dowd could use the tape as evidence that he too had been hoodwinked. The tape would prove McBride had lied to him as much as to everyone else, and he could even point to an inspector who had been fooled.

At the meeting in O'Dowd's home, McBride told McGinley that a few weeks earlier, Old Frank had called to his house, and asked him to come in to his pub about 'a wee job'. When he got there, both Old and Young Frank were there. McBride claimed Old Frank quizzed him about his arrest on 29 November 1996, and Young Frank threatened William Doherty.

Noel McBride went on to say the McBreartys tried to get him to meet the private investigator Billy Flynn, and Old Frank gave him £150, asking him to go to the Guards and say he made false allegations about the McBreartys. Old Frank offered to buy him a bicycle, and weeks later, arrived at his house with a new bicycle.

The memo of the interview was signed by Noel McBride, and witnessed by McGinley, O'Dowd and William Doherty.

At the tribunal, McGinley said he wasn't happy after the interview. McBride's stories, alternatively in fear of and threatened by the McBreartys, then given bribes by them, didn't ring true. And what was this William Doherty character doing there? He decided to run a background check on William Doherty.

McGinley's doubts about Noel McBride and William Doherty would harden in the months that followed. Chief Superintendent Denis Fitzpatrick regarded the entire process, as McGinley mulled over Doherty, as an assessment of the informer. What started with the curious meeting at O'Dowd's, and his near-certain knowledge that Doherty was the source of the dud intelligence on Lofty Gallagher, combined with the uncovering of evidence linking Doherty to the hoax extortion calls to the Peoples, would eventually lead to the collapse of the case against the McBreartys based on McBride's statements.

———

On 15 May 1997, eleven days after McGinley met Noel McBride and William Doherty, another Barron case conference was scheduled. The conference notes for that day contain several 'ghost' witnesses. One brief note recorded simply that a man 'saw Michael Peoples jumping over the Tech wall at 1 a.m.'. Of course, the man saw no such thing, and would say so once he was eventually contacted. Michael Peoples was inside the Parting Glass nightclub at the time, and nowhere near the 'Tech'.

John O'Dowd had recorded the same information in his 'Rhino' notebook about a month earlier. The notebook contained information in the pages at the front and at the back, divided into 'subversive' information, such as the Gallagher search, and information on the Barron case. At the Morris tribunal O'Dowd claimed the Barron information came from Noel McBride, and the 'subversive' information from William Doherty. He kept the two separate, recording them at the front and back of the book, to keep track of which source provided the information.

O'Dowd was given the job of taking a statement from the witness who saw Michael Peoples 'jumping over the Tech wall'. Apparently he never did so. The job of taking the statement, job number 307, is marked completed in the Garda files, but either the statement never existed or has since disappeared from the investigation file. In August 1997, O'Dowd wrote a report saying the man denied saying he saw Michael Peoples, and was nowhere near the technical school wall at the relevant time.

Michael Peoples became a suspect early in the investigation, mainly it seems because of the garbled reports that John Patton saw Frank McBrearty with either one or two other men in the car park. This was reinforced when Sean Crossan told Sergeant Joe Hannigan he saw three youths coming down the car park. The trouble was, once the 4 December 'confession' from Young Frank McBrearty was written, there couldn't be a third man. Frank's statement didn't mention Michael Peoples as an accomplice, only Mark McConnell.

O'Dowd claimed the information on the witness who 'saw Michael Peoples jumping over the Tech wall' came from William Doherty. But Doherty should have had no way of knowing a witness had filled in a questionnaire when he was stopped by Guards the Sunday after Richie Barron died, in which he said he was in St Eunan's Terrace, the street opposite the Tech wall. The only people with access to those questionnaires were the Gardaí.

When tribunal investigators interviewed him, the witness told them he was in a friend's house in St Eunan's Terrace the night Richie Barron died. From where he was, there was no way he could have seen the Tech wall, even if Michael Peoples had been there. The sighting was a ghost report.

There were other ghosts. According to the record, there was a report that a local youth 'overheard a conversation in the Parting Glass nightclub, during which Young Frank McBrearty described the injuries to Richie Barron 'graphically'. Again, the job was assigned to John O'Dowd. Again, it would be three months before O'Dowd handed in a report. The report would show that the youth had heard nothing of the sort.

The list of ghosts was growing. The witness who 'saw Michael Peoples jumping over the Tech wall' didn't see what he was supposed to have seen. The youth who heard Young Frank describing Richie Barron's injuries didn't hear what he was supposed to have heard. The witness who supposedly saw Mark McConnell at the spot where Richie Barron died at 7 a.m. the following morning didn't see what she was supposed to have seen. The witness who was supposed to have seen Young Frank in the car park along with Mark McConnell, who was 'covered in dirt and he was wet', hadn't seen what she was supposed to have seen. John Patton didn't see what he was supposed to have seen. But blinded by a conviction that Barron was murdered and McBrearty was responsible, the Guards could see only what they wanted to see. No one questioned why all these ghost sightings came to nothing. If witnesses weren't coming forward with statements, it must be because they were 'got at' by the McBreartys.

Three days after the conference, on 18 May 1997, a telephone caller to Letterkenny hospital claimed there was a bomb in the Parting Glass nightclub. It was a repeat of the hoax of 3 May, and again led to major disruption.

———

Somehow, Billy Flynn got hold of telephone records. The private detective has since told several versions of how he did it. In June 1997, he wrote in a statement that he secretly met 'an acting member of Letterkenny Gardaí who is unhappy with his superiors'. Flynn said the Garda, unhappy with the conduct of the Barron investigation and the treatment of prisoners in Garda custody, met him at a location in Northern Ireland and helped him identify the source of the extortion call to Michael Peoples. In his statement, he said he believed calls made to Old Frank McBrearty and others came from the Adria shirt factory in Strabane, where William Doherty worked.

In an interview with *Village* magazine on 4 May 2005, Flynn gave a different account. 'I was driving home from Dublin to Enfield and I gave a hitchhiker a lift,' he told the magazine. 'He was not a usual hitchhiker, something had happened his car and he was in a hurry to get to a destination before public transport would get him there. On the way I discovered he worked in Eircom and as he was getting out of the car I asked if he could help me. I told him what I had in mind and he said he would.

'Afterwards I would meet him in an agreed location. I would drive up and we would exchange envelopes, his containing the phone logs I needed and I remunerating him.'

However he managed it, by May 1997, Flynn had identified the source of several phone calls, including the hoax blackmail calls to Michael Peoples.

While the Guards were chasing ghosts, Flynn had pieced together what had happened. By late April, he'd tracked down Wilma Laird in Castlederg. Wilma confirmed she'd seen Mark and Roisin McConnell in Sarah's Café around 1.30 a.m. Roisin McConnell had told Detective Sergeant John White the same thing when she was arrested, although she'd given her interrogators Wilma's maiden name, Wilma Barnett. The two women working in the café, Philomena Laird and Carmel Connolly, told Wilma the news about Richie Barron while she waited for her order. She went up to the scene with her husband, and on the way they met the ambulance coming down.

Wilma's account was verified in part by Angela McNulty, who had made a statement to Gardaí back on 26 October 1996, just over a week after Richie Barron died. She remembered seeing Wilma in the café some time after 1 a.m. Angela also remembered being told in the café that there was an accident.

Even more dramatically, Wilma told the private investigator that a couple of weeks after the night Richie died, two detectives had contacted her. She told them what she'd seen, and gave them the times. Billy Flynn passed on the information to the Guards.

There is no Garda record of any detective interviewing Wilma Laird in October 1996. No note or statement exists which refers to it. Lawyers for the Garda Commissioner told the tribunal that they couldn't say the interview never happened, but if it did, the senior officers in Donegal never knew about it. Having listened to the evidence, Justice Morris decided it was 'not surprising' that there was no record in this case. The unknown Guard, or Guards, had 'suppressed' Wilma Laird's statement because it confirmed the wrong version of Mark and Roisin McConnell's movements.

In May 1997, after Billy Flynn had tracked Wilma down, the incident room created job number 285, to interview Wilma. The job is recorded as arising from the memo taken from Roisin McConnell on 4 December 1996, not from information from Billy Flynn. It was assigned to Sergeant John White. It was not until 13 September 1997 that White spoke to Wilma Laird by telephone, and she confirmed what she'd told the private investigator. No reasonable explanation for the delay in contacting Wilma was ever given.

Three days after speaking to Wilma Laird, Flynn's staff went to see Philomena Laird, who was working in the café the night Richie Barron died. Back in October 1996, Philomena had told the Guards that Mark and Roisin were in the café at 12.30 a.m. 'I honestly do not remember what time they were in at,' she told the private investigator. Billy Flynn also forwarded this statement to the Guards. On 22 September 1997, Philomena would make a statement to Detective Garda Joe Foley. She would tell him that she realised she was wrong saying she saw Mark and Roisin at 12.30 a.m., as Wilma was not in the café until after 1 a.m. Two days later, on 24 September 1997, Wilma Laird also made a statement to Joe Foley.

Carmel Connolly, Philomena Laird's co-worker at the café, was not re-interviewed by Gardaí in 1997. At the tribunal, she said she remembered Mark and Roisin came in sometime after midnight. She knew it was after midnight, because at that time she shut down the diner. From then on, they only took take-away orders. She couldn't say how long after she'd closed the dining section she saw Mark and Roisin.

Meanwhile, the hoax security alerts continued. On 7 June 1997, Garda John O'Dowd called to the nightclub and told Andy McBrearty another bomb threat had been received at Highland Radio.

———

For Billy Flynn, what he had discovered about the extortion phone calls was even more shocking than Wilma Laird's alibi evidence. One of the hoax blackmail phone calls to Michael and Charlotte Peoples came from the home of John O'Dowd, a serving Garda. The other four came from the home of Pat Doherty, father of William Doherty.

The Garda investigation into the blackmail calls to Michael Peoples was going nowhere. In early March, the Guards had received a reply from Telecom Eireann saying that no incoming calls had been made to the Peoples from the 01 area, that is from Dublin. After that, nothing more was heard. There was still no word on the records search they were really interested in, the incoming calls from outside Dublin. Until they got the results, there was nothing more they could do.

Billy Flynn had no idea who the Dohertys were. He certainly had no way of knowing that Pat Doherty's son William was working with Garda John O'Dowd. Flynn approached Pat Doherty and asked him why he had made blackmail calls to the Peoples, threatening to go to the Guards accusing them of murder. Pat Doherty was bewildered. He'd made no calls to anybody. He told Flynn he didn't know what he was talking about. Billy Flynn wouldn't give up though, and continued to contact Pat Doherty.

On 27 May, Pat Doherty went to Raphoe Garda station. He asked for advice in dealing with Billy Flynn, who was accusing him of blackmail.

He was told to get a copy of his phone records from Telecom Eireann. With these, he could prove that Billy Flynn's claims weren't true, and that would be the end of it.

A week later, the Fine Gael-led Rainbow Coalition was voted out of office, replaced by a Fianna Fáil/Progressive Democrat government. At the Department of Justice, John O'Donoghue replaced Mrs Nora Owen as Minister. On 10 June, Michael and Charlotte Peoples wrote to Denis Fitzpatrick, the Chief Superintendent in charge of the Donegal division. They told him Billy Flynn had succeeded where the Guards had failed, and identified the threatening calls from the previous November. The Peoples said they'd instructed Billy Flynn to make a report to the new Minister for Justice on his discovery, and intended to sue the State.

At the same time, Billy Flynn wrote to the new Minister for Justice. He said he'd established a blackmail call was made from a Garda's home, and alleged that Gardaí in Letterkenny knew this.

———

On 11 June 1997, Superintendent Joe Shelly applied to Judge Thomas Fitzpatrick at Letterkenny District Court for an order under Section 10 of the Criminal Justice Act 1984 to re-arrest Mark McConnell. Mark's first arrest, like all the others, needed only reasonable cause by the arresting officer to suspect that he had commited a serious offence, but legally he could not be arrested a second time for the same offence without new evidence being presented to a judge. Shelly presented the new evidence to the court—the confession by Young Frank admitting to the attack on Richie Barron and naming Mark as an accomplice. Mark had been released on 4 December 1996 shortly before the confession emerged. He could have been re-arrested at any time in the days and weeks since then on the basis of the confession, particularly after the statement was apparently backed up by Roderick Donnelly in January. In fact, conference records as early as January 1997 contain the note 're-arrest of Mark McConnell'. Yet it was not until June that he was picked up for the second time.

———

On 16 June 1997, Pat Doherty handed over his phone records to the Raphoe Guards. To his dismay, once he got the copy of his bill from Telecom Eireann, he realised Billy Flynn was telling the truth. The bill showed four phone calls to Michael and Charlotte Peoples on 9 November 1996. Detective Sergeant Sylvie Henry also got a copy of the bill.

Henry wasn't sure what to do with the information. He spoke to Billy Flynn, who showed him a handwritten note containing the times of the five telephone calls to the Peoples, four from Doherty and one from O'Dowd. The times on Pat Doherty's bill matched Flynn's information. If he was correct about the first four calls, he might be right about the fifth one too. However, the handwritten note Flynn showed him wasn't going to stand up in court. Even an official printout of the telephone records obtained by the private detective would be legally questionable. Nevertheless, the allegations couldn't be ignored.

On 18 June, Billy Flynn made a statement outlining the thrust of his investigation to date. By then, he had interviewed over 200 witnesses. Flynn said he intended to contact every TD in the new Dáil, asking for a tribunal of inquiry into the treatment of the McBreartys.

Flynn added that his information was that 'senior members of the Gardaí responsible for the investigation into the death of Richard Barron absolutely hate Frank McBrearty Snr because he was responsible for the dismissal from the force of a previously acting Garda Sergeant'.

Billy Flynn had been writing to the Department of Justice since February. He'd also written to the Attorney General, the Director of Public Prosecutions, the Garda Commissioner, and anyone else he could think of. A local politician, Labour Senator Sean Moloney, had also written letters on behalf of the McBreartys, complaining of 'excessive Garda attention' at the nightclub.

The letters flowed in and the allegations became more serious, but the complaints registered with no one in Justice. 'It was being processed as a piece of correspondence, among thousands of pieces of correspondence about the activity of the Gardaí and relatively junior people were forwarding it in a kind of post-box fashion to the Garda Commissioner's office to be looked at,' the Secretary General of the Department of Justice told the Morris tribunal.

But John O'Dowd was in a panic. Flynn had discovered the truth about the phone calls. Worse, when Pat Doherty handed over his phone bill, it confirmed the private detective's information about the first four calls. That alone meant investigators had reasonable grounds for believing his information about the fifth call was also true. If the Guards got their hands on proof from Telecom Eireann about the fifth call, he was in real trouble.

——

As a result of Shelly's application, Mark McConnell was arrested at 9.06 a.m. on 25 June 1997 by Sligo Garda John Nicholson and taken to

Letterkenny Garda Station. In custody, Mark McConnell was interviewed by Nicholson and three Sligo detectives, Paul Casey, Patrick Maguire and John McHale.

'About six months after my first arrest I was again arrested by the Gardaí,' Mark later wrote in a statement to the Garda Complaints Board. 'I was stopped on the road and taken to Letterkenny. I was told it was on a warrant issued by a Judge. They showed me the warrant.'

Mark was held for twelve hours and questioned about the death of Richie Barron. 'I was not questioned at length,' he wrote. 'I was questioned for about one third of the time. About the murder. The rest was small talk and periods in the cell. I was not really questioned.'

Although Mark was unhappy to be arrested a second time, and agreed that there was 'no mental or physical abuse', he asked his solicitor Cathal Quinn to make a complaint on his behalf. In his complaint he singled out Garda Willie Cannon, the custody officer, as a Garda who 'was very good to me'. On his release, Mark made no complaints, but he refused to sign the custody record.

John Nicholson could not explain how interview notes he took during the sessions had gone missing. 'When I discovered it I brought it to the attention of the tribunal. I asked some of the lads that were with me had they got them and had they mislaid them,' he explained. Judge Frederick Morris noted in his report that he was 'asked, once again, to accept that [the notes] have been lost within a system for which nobody has been made accountable or taken responsibility'.

Nicholson said he remembered that because of interruptions, he did not get an opportunity to read Mr McConnell's notes over to him at the end of his first interview, but he did so at the end of a later interview in the evening. He said that 'at all times Mr McConnell was co-operative, and any question he was asked he answered'.

Detective Garda Patrick Maguire said he 'felt the investigation team probably wanted new people to go up there with an open mind, fresh faces, start from scratch', and this was why Gardaí from Sligo were called in for the second arrest.

'We arrived two days before the arrest and we spent those two days familiarising ourselves with the case, reading the files, reading all the statements of witnesses and of other members who had already made statements,' he recalled.

———

John O'Dowd and Kevin Lennon didn't know where to turn at first. Flynn had discovered the phone call from O'Dowd's home. They decided to go to the Chief Superintendent, Denis Fitzpatrick. The Chief was persuaded that O'Dowd knew nothing about the call, and that it had probably been made by William Doherty without his knowledge. The two men convinced him there was no way it could be revealed that a Garda was in any way a party to a blackmail attempt against an innocent family. It would destroy the reputation of the force in Donegal.

Fitzpatrick had a dilemma. As far as he knew, Doherty was an IRA source, a valuable asset. He couldn't be compromised. The reputation of the police in Donegal would suffer if news of the blackmail call from a Garda's home got out. Together with Kevin Lennon, Denis Fitzpatrick authorised a cover-up.

But O'Dowd didn't trust the Chief. Towards the end of June, he secretly taped a conversation with his boss. O'Dowd spent most of the conversation telling Fitzpatrick that William Doherty was tortured by the IRA, who allegedly pulled his teeth and burned his testicles. The Chief advised O'Dowd to send in a c77 form to Crime & Security about the torture of his supposed IRA informer.

O'Dowd also mentioned on tape that Doherty was 'very good friends with [Noel] McBride and he is keeping McBride right'. Without Doherty, McBride 'will fall away like that'. Crucially, the Garda also made sure to mention the phone calls on tape. 'These phone calls, that's the problem you know,' O'Dowd can be heard telling the Chief.

Some time after the botched search of the Gallagher farm, Detective Inspector John McGinley and Detective Superintendent Joe Shelly travelled to Dublin. While they were there, they called in to see Chief Superintendent Dermot Jennings at Crime & Security. Memories of what happened differ.

Joe Shelly was the first to give an account of this meeting. On his first day of evidence at the tribunal, he outlined how he and Detective Inspector McGinley told Dermot Jennings they were worried by the Gallagher search. Jennings, a senior officer in Crime & Security, 'at the time said that they would be reassessing it, and he would be talking to his own people there about it. He certainly took our concerns in relation to him [Doherty] on board,' Shelly explained. He said they told Chief Superintendent Jennings they suspected the source on the botched search was William Doherty.

'Did he say who is William Doherty?' asked tribunal barrister Paul McDermott.

'I'm sure he did, yes,' Shelly answered.

'Were you able to tell him?'

'I think other than Inspector McGinley telling him that he had met him once, and that [he] was doing background information on him, in respect of Mr Doherty and then he goes on to discuss the issue just as background, to see what sort of an individual he was, and basically where he was coming from with all of this, if we could establish that.'

'But Inspector McGinley's involvement with him at this stage had been on 4 May?'

'That is right, yes.'

'We certainly expressed our concern, in relation to, in particular, what happened at Gallaghers', and obviously, he was aware of all of that. And that was totally unreliable. And he went on to discuss it with us, and we with him. There was no doubt in anybody's mind leaving there that day that this source was unreliable,' Shelly said on his first day of evidence.

'Did the Barron death come up?' McDermott asked.

'I'd say we certainly spoke about events in the division. Yes, I have no doubt we discussed it.'

'In the context of William Doherty?'

'I'm not sure because I can't say whether we had, Mr Chairman, the information on the phones at that stage, or not. We may well have had. We certainly would have had mention, mentioned the issue of the phones, and the tracing of the phone calls to him, because we'd had correspondence and several communications in relation to that aspect with Crime & Security.'

'Was Inspector McGinley able to report at that stage that he'd been to the house of Garda John O'Dowd to speak with William Doherty?'

'He was, yes. That connection had been made, yes.'

'What did he tell Chief Superintendent Jennings about that?'

'Well he told him that when he went to speak to Noel McBride by arrangement, that Mr Doherty was there. He wasn't happy about Mr Doherty, and he wasn't happy about his presence there for starters, and it was at that stage he had started to do some background work on Doherty to find out a little more about him. He certainly mentioned that much to him anyway.'

McDermott asked what the significance of this was in terms of the Barron investigation as far as Shelly was concerned.

'In May 1997 Inspector McGinley wanted to speak to McBride, and he wanted to assess him if you like, and to talk to him about things that were happening concerning him and the Barron investigation, particularly in relation to certain claims that he was making. I know that he didn't expect Doherty to be in the house when he got there. I know that he was unhappy about the fact that he was there. I think I'm right in saying, Chairman, that he felt that Doherty had some sort of influence or control over McBride, and from that point on certainly we were taking a more critical look at Doherty to see where he was coming from, what was his possible involvement in all this. Some time later we got the inform-ation on the phones which certainly pointed us in the right direction.'

'The significance in terms of dealing with Chief Superintendent Jennings was that he should understand this involvement of Doherty in the Barron death issue?'

'Yes. As I said I'm not sure whether we had the information to connect him with the phones or not at that stage from Garda O'Dowd's house or indeed from his own home, but it certainly would have been very significant, yes.'

Shelly then, was placing the date of this meeting after 4 May 1996, when McGinley met Doherty and Noel McBride in Garda O'Dowd's home. McGinley, however, placed the brief meeting with Jennings a week earlier when the pair visited the National Forensics Laboratory on 29 April 1997. At that stage of course McGinley had not met Doherty. Shelly later amended his evidence. He said during cross-examination that he had never mentioned Doherty's name to Crime & Security, because at that stage McGinley had not met Doherty.

In his evidence to the tribunal, Dermot Jennings (by then an Assistant Commissioner) said it simply was not true that he'd been told William Doherty's name. He did say that McGinley complained about the delay in obtaining telephone records on the Peoples case, now outstanding for several months. 'This was a regular feature at the time,' he observed, as there were backlogs in processing call requests from all over the country. As far as Jennings was concerned, the encounter was over in 'two or three minutes'.

'I wouldn't describe it as a meeting,' Jennings told the chairman. 'The office door was often open where my office was. They came into the office and in fact I can remember it clearly, they never actually sat down.'

He told the chairman he remembered talking about telephone call traces and 'some reference to Lofty Gallagher's', but added that 'It wasn't a meeting. If it was a meeting we would have been sitting down. They actually never sat down in the office. In fact from my recollection I think Joe Shelly was only ever in my office once.'

'In fact, Chairman,' he added, 'on a matter as serious as this, if he did discuss it with me I would recall it. But I never had any discussion with Joe Shelly about the name Mr Doherty, and I never knew who the source was, if this is the source that we are referring to.'

On his first day of evidence at the Morris tribunal, Shelly believed the meeting happened after 4 May, the day John McGinley met Noel McBride and William Doherty in John O'Dowd's house. Shelly told the tribunal that Chief Superintendent Jennings asked them who was Garda

O'Dowd's source, and McGinley said he thought it might be William Doherty. Shelly said he wasn't sure when the meeting took place, but it was after 4 May 1997, and could have been as late as 10 July.

On his third day of evidence at the tribunal, Shelly changed his evidence. The meeting was before 4 May, he now said, and they were unable to tell Jennings who O'Dowd's source might be. 'The timing of the meeting, I was wrong in that, I accept that,' Shelly said. 'I made a mistake.'

At the close of questioning Dermot Jennings, Paul McDermott noted the existence of the different accounts of the meeting given by Superintendent Shelly. 'That's in a sense a matter for the chairman, to try and disentangle all of that,' the barrister concluded.

In fact, the Morris report made no mention of this curious meeting at all, whichever version of it one believes. The chairman found that 'according to the evidence of Assistant Commissioner Jennings, Crime & Security were not aware that the c77s submitted by Garda John O'Dowd all came from the same source. This was due to the fact that the informant was not identified in any way on the c77 forms used at that time.'

Chapter 24

Long Hot Summer

By July, Noel McBride was close to breaking point. Doherty wouldn't leave him alone—he kept demanding more statements. The Guards hadn't listened when he tried to tell them he wasn't even in Raphoe the night Richie Barron died. McBride couldn't see any way out. At one point, he tried to cut his wrists, but he couldn't take the final step. There had to be a way to escape from Doherty and the Guards.

Detective Sergeant Sylvie Henry was assigned to investigate the phone calls to Michael and Charlotte Peoples. He had learned first from Billy Flynn, and then from Pat Doherty, that the first four calls came from Doherty's home. On 3 July, Henry met William Doherty. He took a statement in which Doherty denied he had anything to do with the phone calls to Michael Peoples. It seems Henry took no statements from the other members of the family. Doherty's parents weren't asked to make a statement about the calls, nor was his sister. Henry had his suspect, he didn't need denials on record from anyone else.

———

Four days later, on 7 July, Detective Sergeant Hugh Smith was on duty in Letterkenny Garda station when Sergeant John White approached him around 6 p.m. in the evening. Noel McBride was coming in to make another statement about the Barron case, White told the detective sergeant, but he couldn't take care of it. Would Smith mind handling it? Smith agreed.

At 9 p.m., McBride arrived, and Smith went out to meet him in the car park. To his astonishment, he found McBride sitting in a car with Sergeant White and William Doherty. Smith was perplexed. He'd assumed White was going off duty and wouldn't be around when McBride came in to make his statement.

'In my own mind I thought, I won't say I was suspicious, he could have taken the statement himself,' Smith recalled. White was a Raphoe-based sergeant, he explained, and the statement covered events on White's beat.

There was no reason for him to pass it on to a detective, he could have taken care of it himself.

Smith took McBride inside the station. William Doherty tried to go with him. A year before, Smith was a member of a team of Guards who had searched Doherty's home and arrested him on suspicion of involvement in a robbery during which a man was kidnapped. No charges were ever brought after Gardaí were able to verify Doherty had an alibi for the crime, but Smith knew William Doherty as a result of the case. The detective sergeant put his foot down. He knew that Doherty had sat in with McBride when Detective Inspector John McGinley met him in May—McGinley had told him of his reservations about the interview afterwards. Any statement he took was going to be done right. He refused to let Doherty into the station. 'I felt he had no function there,' he told the tribunal years later.

'You won't beat him up will you?' Doherty called after Smith as he escorted Noel McBride into the Garda station.

'What kind of people do you think we are? You must have a very low opinion of us,' Smith replied.

Smith was not heavily involved in the Barron investigation, although he was handling a related inquiry; he had been asked to look into the hoax blackmail phone call to Old Frank McBrearty, made a few days before the calls to Peoples, and the harassing and threatening calls the family were receiving. When Pat Doherty handed over his phone bill, proving Flynn's claim that similar calls to the Peoples came from his phone, the detectives naturally wondered if the same person was behind the McBrearty calls. Now William Doherty was in Noel McBride's company for the second time.

Smith wondered what was going on. He knew that Doherty's name had a habit of popping up at odd times and places. 'I knew William Doherty had a close association with John O'Dowd,' he remembered at the tribunal. 'I knew that William Doherty was present when Detective Inspector McGinley interviewed McBride in O'Dowd's house,' he recalled. 'Inspector McGinley wasn't happy with Doherty's presence. He felt he was influencing the interview.'

Smith was adamant that Doherty would not be present when he took McBride's statement. He brought McBride to an interview room, and took his statement there. McBride claimed that a week earlier, on 27 June, he'd gone to the Tudor Lounge and met Old Frank McBrearty. 'I want to ask you something in private,' he claimed Old Frank said. 'I'll make it worth your while.'

McBride said he went into Frank's office above the disco. Frank asked him if he knew anything about Richie Barron's death, and offered him £500 to withdraw his statement. He claimed Frank asked him to make a statement to Billy Flynn, in which he'd say that Garda John O'Dowd had paid him to make his original statement incriminating Young Frank and Mark McConnell. McBride then said he met Young Frank, who asked him 'What did you say to the Guards?'

'Fuck all,' McBride answered.

McBride said that Young Frank responded with 'If I ever hear you did, I'll kill you, you wee cunt ye.'

In earlier statements, McBride said he was afraid to go near Raphoe in case he met the McBreartys, but he now told Detective Sergeant Smith that having been threatened by Young Frank, he went across the road and sat in Sarah's Café for over two hours. He then went back to the McBreartys' disco with his girlfriend Sharon Alexander, where Old Frank plied him with free pints of beer until closing time.

Noel McBride added that he told William Doherty about the offer from Old Frank, and Doherty advised him to go to the Gardaí. Doherty later called him to tell him the Gardaí in Letterkenny wanted to talk to him, and here he was.

The story of alternating threats and bribes didn't quite make sense, but Smith felt that McBride 'sounded very convincing' when making his statement. Smith also noticed Noel McBride had one of his hands bandaged. 'I got the impression it was self-inflicted,' he recalled.

Later, Smith met with Detective Inspector McGinley. The inspector was still mulling over the relationship between McBride and Doherty, and what it could mean. 'He asked me what I thought of McBride. I said he was sort of shifty and I wouldn't trust him, but at the same time, he [McBride] said what he said.'

Smith felt the statement would be cross-checked when it went in to the incident room, and would stand or fall on whether it could be verified. 'In hindsight I could have done a lot more,' he reflected. At the time though, he didn't think to verify the statement. Barron wasn't his case, the incident room could take care of it.

Inspector McGinley added Smith's account of the 7 July statement to his mental file on Doherty and McBride. He knew it was something he would have to address at some point, but it would have to wait. Since his re-assignment as detective inspector, he had less time to devote to the Barron case. His responsibilities now covered not only the Letterkenny district, but the entire Donegal division. There was a Donegal link to a dissident IRA attack in Belfast on 12 May, and the Detective Unit's first priority was State security. 'I'm not making an excuse but there was a lot going on,' McGinley admitted at the tribunal.

McGinley ran a background check on Doherty. He found that Doherty had been arrested by Garda John O'Dowd the year before. The conclusion that Doherty was somehow involved in the search on

Gallagher's farm in March 1997 seemed inescapable. But what else was he up to?

——

The final John O'Dowd C77 attributed to William Doherty went to Dublin in mid-July. It is one of the few about which anything is known in detail. At the end of December 2004, the *Irish Independent* reported that the PSNI were asked to investigate an allegation that £10,000 had been paid to an alleged former member of the Provisional IRA living in Strabane. The Northern Irish police confirmed that they had received a complaint from someone living in Donegal. According to reports, Young Frank McBrearty was to be shot in both legs in return for the payoff.

In a statement to the PSNI, seen by the *Irish Independent*, Young Frank wrote that 'These serious allegations, contained in this C77 document, were never brought to my attention, nor was I ever given protection by the Gardaí. I wish to know if the person in Strabane was paid £10,000 to have me killed and the threat is still there today . . . since I was made aware of this information I am very concerned about my own safety and my young family's safety.

'I go to Northern Ireland a lot because my son plays soccer in Derry. Both my wife, two oldest children and I are British citizens and we now look to the PSNI for this matter to be investigated.'

Crime & Security took no action as a result of the information in the last C77. The second Morris tribunal hints that information was also received at Garda HQ about other alleged operations planned by the IRA against people living in Donegal. No one was warned as a result. Nothing happened. Either HQ knew the threats were bogus, or they were extremely negligent. Justice Morris decided the latter was the case. After this C77, Doherty was dropped as a source of IRA intelligence. He was, quite simply, no longer credible.

——

Detective Sergeant Sylvie Henry investigated Pat Doherty's complaints about Billy Flynn. The case was evolving into an inquiry into the Peoples phone calls. Henry and Detective Sergeant Hugh Smith worked together, since Smith was involved in a similar inquiry into phone calls made to Old Frank McBrearty.

On 3 July, the same day Henry met William Doherty and got from him a statement denying he knew anything about the phone calls, the sergeant also went to see Michael and Charlotte Peoples. Michael Peoples told him he had proof the fifth call came from John O'Dowd. When Henry asked to see it, Michael showed him a note from Billy Flynn. Henry told him the note was no proof. He'd need an official printout from Telecom Eireann. Later that day, he sent off a reminder to Garda HQ about the requests for phone records which had been sent up the previous December. If he was going to make arrests, he wanted confirmation of the fifth call first. Billy Flynn's handwritten note matched Doherty's bill, so the private investigator could be right about O'Dowd too, but it wasn't going to stand up in court.

Michael Peoples gave Henry a letter authorising Telecom Eireann to release any information that would help the detective sergeant uncover the source of the calls he had received. On 11 July, Sylvie Henry sent a second request in to Chief Superindendent Denis Fitzpatrick to forward to Garda HQ, again asking for the details of incoming calls to Michael Peoples' phone on 9 November. He enclosed Michael Peoples' authorisation to access his phone records. He didn't think to ask for the details of outgoing calls made from Doherty and O'Dowd's numbers.

Probably as a result of Sylvie Henry's correspondence, or possibly because of Billy Flynn's constant stream of letters, a reminder went out from Garda HQ to the GPO on 22 July. It was faxed to the Portlaoise call data centre on 30 July.

Pauline Rossiter worked in the Crime Division of the Department of Justice. On 6 August she wrote to the Garda Commissioner about Billy Flynn's letter, requesting an update on the investigation into the allegations that a blackmail call was made from the home of a serving Garda. The following day, she wrote again, requesting a report on the Peoples case 'as a matter of urgency'.

On 7 August, the Portlaoise call data centre ran the computer search for the Peoples calls, and on 11 August the results were sent back to Garda HQ. When Sylvie Henry got the results, he was stunned. The results were negative. As far as Telecom Eireann was concerned, the Peoples had received no phone calls that evening. The detectives couldn't believe it. Henry had already seen the copy of the phone bill from Pat Doherty, and it showed four calls. Whatever about the fifth call Flynn said came from O'Dowd's home, the search should have shown the other four calls.

'I thought my God, this is not possible,' Henry recalled. 'I got a photostat of the phone calls I got from Doherty, and attached it and sent it up again.'

Smith and Henry weren't sure where to go next. All they could do was wait. Maybe Telecom Eireann had made a mistake, and the second check would reveal the calls. They'd only get one chance to make Section 4 arrests in the case. They decided to wait until they had as many cards as possible before playing their hand.

As the senior sergeant in the incident room, Marty Moylan was charged with preparing the report on the Barron investigation for the Director of Public Prosecutions. In August, he got back to Donegal after a break in Galway to find he'd been replaced. John White was taking over the file. White was no longer to work as a uniform sergeant in Raphoe, he'd been reassigned as a detective sergeant, and was now based in Letterkenny.

Moylan told the Morris tribunal that the only reason he could think of for the reassignment was a conversation he'd had with Kevin Lennon some time before. He'd told the superintendent that he'd have to include a paragraph in his report about hoax extortion telephone calls made from Garda John O'Dowd's telephone to Michael Peoples, a prime suspect in the case. 'That's nothing to do with me, don't worry about it,' Lennon had told him at the time.

Moylan said he was 'livid' at being replaced, and spoke to Detective Sergeant Sylvie Henry, Detective Sergeant Hugh Smith and Detective Inspector John McGinley about the reassignment. They told him not to worry, that they would get to the bottom of the calls.

———

With question marks over Noel McBride, Detective Inspector John McGinley and Garda John O'Toole went to see John Patton, the farmer whose account of seeing Young Frank 'looking rise' outside the nightclub 'with one or two others' had been one of the initial pieces of information the case conferences had received back in October 1996. McGinley told the Morris tribunal that the Guards had been wary of taking a statement from Patton at first because he was reluctant to involve himself, and they respected his wish for confidentiality.

At first, only a few Gardaí knew Patton's identity. Detective Garda Pat Tague and Garda Seamus Patton had spoken to him, and they had reported to McGinley on what John Patton said. However, McGinley said that after Garda John O'Toole told him independently that Patton might know something, he figured Patton must have talked about what he saw, and so he was no longer held by the need for confidentiality. On 28 August 1997 McGinley went to speak to the farmer himself and take a statement.

'I took a statement from him outlining how he had arrived in Raphoe at 12.55 a.m. on Monday morning 14 October 1996 and attended the disco in Frankie's Nightclub,' McGinley later wrote. 'He stated that he had observed Frank McBrearty Junior and another man who he did not know walking towards him from the direction of the car park as he approached the entrance to the disco at 1 a.m. Mr Patton was extremely reluctant to make a statement or give any written account on the matter.'

The statement is in marked contrast to the initial report from Patton, as conveyed to McGinley in October 1996 by Detective Garda Tague. Now instead of 'two or three men', there were only two. The man with Young Frank was 'not as well built' as McBrearty, while Mark McConnell was much heavier than Young Frank at the time. Instead of 'running down the car park', the two men were walking 'at a normal pace'. Patton's statement made no mention of being afraid of the McBrearty family.

If alarm bells weren't ringing already, the discrepancies in Patton's statement should have set them off. The Morris tribunal criticised the delay in taking a proper statement from Patton, and the failure of senior officers to react to the discrepancies between Patton's statement and what Tague had reported of Patton to Inspector McGinley in October 1996.

Chapter 25

Going to See a Man About a Bike

On Thursday 11 September 1997, the Barron investigation team held what they intended would be their final case conference. Superintendent Kevin Lennon chaired the meeting. Among those present were Detective Sergeant John White, Sergeant Marty Moylan, Detective Sergeant Sylvie Henry, Detective Sergeant Hugh Smith, Detective Inspector John McGinley and Detective Superintendent Joe Shelly. It appears nobody took any notes of the meeting.

The plan was simple: check through everything, tie up the loose ends and send the file to the DPP. Marty Moylan had the jobs books, and the meeting went through the outstanding jobs. Garda Kevin O'Malley made a statement on this date. He'd been the photographer at the scene on 14 October 1996, and at the autopsy later that day. It appeared no one had bothered to get a statement from him at the time.

There was one major loose end. Noel McBride had claimed several times that he was alternately threatened and offered bribes by the McBreartys. Superintendent Lennon told Detective Sergeant Hugh Smith to put the bribery allegations to the McBreartys. Once that detail was seen to, the file could be closed and sent to the Director of Public Prosecutions.

Smith was a relative stranger to the Barron investigation. He was invited to the conference because of the statement he took from McBride on 7 July, when John White had asked him to help out, but apart from working with Sylvie Henry on the phone calls, he hadn't had much to do with the murder case. Smith looked over the allegations from McBride. According to the statements, Old Frank had given Noel McBride cash, which he'd used to buy clothing, a watch, gifts and jewellery for his girl-friend. He was even supposed to have given McBride a bicycle.

Smith rifled through the file. He was amazed that no one had checked out the allegations in the statement he'd taken in July. Where was the corroboration? The sergeant looked for the routine confirmation of McBride's allegations, a statement from a Garda who'd seen some of the cash, or the gifts the cash had bought, even a receipt. Anything that would back up the claim. There was nothing.

'I'm not going to put unsubstantiated allegations to Frankie,' Smith told the conference. 'He'll go off his head. It has to be backed up with something.'

'How do you back them up?' Lennon asked.

'Well, there's the bicycle,' Smith pointed out.

Shelly asked why the bicycle wasn't in the statement Smith had taken from Noel McBride back in July. Smith told him it was just something McBride had mentioned to him in passing after they'd finished, he'd assumed it was already in a previous statement. The group checked the paperwork. There'd been talk of the bicycle since March or April, but the only mention of it was in the memo John McGinley took on 4 May.

'Nobody had seen the bicycle or checked it out,' Smith recalled. He told the conference he wasn't prepared to go to Old Frank and put the allegations without some back-up. It was basic police work to look for corroboration. He said he'd go back to McBride one last time and double-check everything, then he'd confront the McBreartys.

The following evening, Friday 12 September 1997, Smith went out to see Noel McBride. Sergeant Marty Moylan and Garda John O'Dowd went with him. Smith asked O'Dowd along because he was the local Garda. He knew the area, knew where McBride lived. John McGinley had planned to go out and have another look at McBride too, but wasn't able to make it as he was tied up with other business.

Smith said that when he initially confronted McBride about his statements, he 'basically stuck to his guns', but Smith added: 'We knew that his number was up, he was telling lies.'

'It was hard to believe that he could stay in the system for almost twelve months with the type of lies he was telling, and not be sussed out,' he reflected later at the tribunal.

McBride wasn't at home when the Guards arrived. O'Dowd suggested they might find him at his girlfriend's place. The trio drove to the Alexanders'. Sure enough, Noel McBride was there. 'What do you want now?' he asked them.

'We're here to have a look at this nice bicycle you got from Frankie McBrearty Senior,' Smith answered.

'I can't show it to you now. It's at home in the garage. I can't go now, I'm going out for the night.'

'Right then. I'll call first thing in the morning and see you.'

The three Guards left it at that.

At 10 a.m. on Saturday morning, 13 September 1997, Hugh Smith was back to see Noel McBride again. Detective Inspector McGinley was with him this time. Noel McBride was still in bed when the detectives called. His father woke him for the visitors.

'Can we see this fine bicycle of yours now?' Smith asked.

'I can't. My cousin was here at nine and he took it with him.'

'Where did your cousin go?'

'I don't know.'

The detectives asked McBride if he'd come in the car with them. They wanted to go to one of the nearby stations and take a statement. Noel McBride agreed to go. They hadn't gone far when McBride told them he didn't want to go near any station. Smith and McGinley pulled over into a lay-by, and spoke to him in the car.

Detective Inspector McGinley went through the memo he'd taken back in May at Garda John O'Dowd's house. He put each of the allegations in the memo to McBride again, and McBride confirmed each one in turn. The detectives took down what McBride said, preparing a new statement.

In the statement, McBride essentially repeated all the claims he'd made over the previous nine months. There was one noticeable discrepancy. He changed the amount of money he alleged Old Frank McBrearty gave him from £500 to £300. McBride now claimed Frank gave him £500 but that he counted out £200 and gave it back. As Smith listened, he found the idea that McBride would return £200 laughable.

The detectives took their time. They reminded McBride of the declaration in front of the statement where he swore everything he said was true. 'Whether you like it or not, you're smack bang in the middle of a murder investigation,' Smith told him. 'You're the chief witness, if you're found to be telling lies, you'll be in a lot of difficulty.' McBride stuck to his guns.

The detectives asked McBride to account for the money he'd been given. He told them he'd bought a new watch for £85.

'Where's the watch?'

'I damaged it at work.'

'Show us the broken watch then?'

'I can't. I threw it in the bin.'

'What else did you buy?'

'I bought jewellery for my girlfriend, and clothes.'

'Did you ever show the money to anybody?'

'I showed it to William Doherty. One day we were out drinking in Strabane and I counted it out.'

When the detectives finished taking the statement, McBride asked them to drop him off at Sharon Alexander's house.

McGinley and Smith felt McBride's number was up. He was lying. 'It didn't take brilliant police work to suss McBride out,' Smith recalled. 'I mean he was there for anybody to suss out. It was no brilliant piece of detective work. It was ordinary, everyday, run-of-the-mill checking that you do on a statement.'

Later that day, Detective Sergeant Smith went with Detective Garda Sean Herraghty to see William Doherty. McBride had said he showed Doherty the money he got from McBrearty; they wanted to see what he had to say.

Doherty made a statement backing up Noel McBride's tale. He said he went drinking with his friend in Strabane, and Noel told him 'I got money to keep my mouth shut from Frankie McBrearty Snr.' Doherty said he didn't believe McBride until his friend pulled a roll of banknotes out of his pocket.

'It was unbelievable to see Noel with that amount of money,' Doherty told the detectives. 'The money was made up of £20 and there may have been a £50, I'm not sure. It was all punts. I counted it and there was approximately £450 in it.'

Doherty said he asked Noel McBride where and how he got the money. McBride told him that a few weeks after Richie Barron died, Old Frank stopped on the road and got out of his car, asking him what he saw the night Richie Barron died. 'I saw nothing,' Noel said he replied.

'That's the way to keep it,' Frank said, and handed him the roll of banknotes. 'There's more where that came from.'

McBride got £500 from Old Frank McBrearty, Doherty told the detectives. He told them his friend got another £200 in early 1997, and a bike some time after that. He said his friend had shown him the jeans, shirts, trainers and watch he bought with the money, and that he'd heard that Noel bought jewellery for his girlfriend.

The discrepancy between the two men was on record now. McBride said he only got £300, but Doherty still said he got £500.

——

On Tuesday 16 September, Sylvie Henry sat down to write a progress report for Superintendent Joe Shelly. The chain of events leading to the report had begun when Pauline Rossiter in the Department of Justice requested a report on the Peoples case 'as a matter of urgency' back on 6 August. The request went to Garda HQ, and from there to the Chief Superintendent in Letterkenny, and travelled down the line until it landed on Henry's desk.

Henry laid out the facts of the case to date. He documented the calls to Michael Peoples, the statement Michael made the next day, and Michael's correspondence in an attempt to have the calls traced. He explained how Pat Doherty had turned over a bill showing four calls, but that there remained a fifth unidentified call. In his report, Henry confined himself to the facts he could stand over. He added none of the suspicions, the

The Act had just become law. Shelly asked Lennon if he was sure the provision applied. 'I said, "I'm not wholly sure, but I think that's the position,"' Lennon remembered. He was getting ready for a party in Sligo to mark the 75th anniversary of the formation of An Garda Síochána, but promised to look it up.

Shelly called the DPP's office to make sure of the details. Since the section Lennon quoted came from a new law passed in 1997, he wanted to be sure it applied to an offence committed in 1996.

About two hours later, Shelly called in to Lennon's office again. He wasn't sure how to bring up the relationships he suspected: Doherty as O'Dowd's informer, and Lennon as his supervisor. 'Have you anything to fear from Doherty?' he asked.

'Why would I? I wasn't here when this happened,' Lennon replied, adding, 'But keep the Provo stuff separate,' meaning record any questions relating to intelligence in separate notes, so that if there was a court case, Doherty's role as an informer didn't become public knowledge.

Lennon asked Shelly if he was going to the anniversary party in Sligo. Shelly said no, he was going home to Mullingar, it had been a long week.

At 5 p.m. that evening, Shelly, McGinley and the detectives involved in the case met to plan the details of Doherty's arrest. 'There was really five or six issues going to Milford,' John McGinley recalled. 'There was the phone calls to Peoples, the phone calls to the McBreartys, the information Doherty supplied via Noel McBride, his motivation for all of these issues and then there was the Lofty Gallagher issue in the background also.'

It seemed a long time since they'd first started their investigation of the Peoples blackmail hoax, when Pat Doherty made his complaint about Billy Flynn back in May. That led the detectives to talk to Billy Flynn, and since then they'd known the private investigator was saying there were five blackmail calls, four from Doherty and one from O'Dowd. They had corroboration of the first four calls; Billy Flynn's information matched exactly what was on the phone bill Pat Doherty handed in.

'The obvious knock-on effect of that was that he was probably right in respect of Garda O'Dowd's number as well,' McGinley recalled. But although the detectives had checked twice by now, Telecom Eireann had said there wasn't even a record of the first four calls from Doherty to Peoples.

However, the phone bill from Pat Doherty and the belated admission from Noel McBride provided enough evidence to arrest William Doherty. The detectives made their decision. Doherty would be arrested and taken to Milford Garda station.

Chapter 26

Questions to Answer

At 8.20 a.m. on Saturday morning, 20 September 1997, Detective Sergeant Sylvie Henry, Detective Sergeant Hugh Smith, Sergeant Marty Moylan and Detective Garda Alphie McHale arrived at William Doherty's home in Doorable, Manorhamilton.

William Doherty wasn't home. Pat Doherty told the detectives his son had gone to Northern Ireland with a load of straw, and wouldn't be back until dinnertime. He told Sylvie Henry he'd phone him when William got back. The Guards went back to the station to wait for the call.

Shortly after 10 a.m., as Henry and Smith waited for the telephone call, Superintendent Kevin Lennon arrived. He wasn't in uniform. The sergeants told the superintendent how they'd unsuccessfully gone to arrest Doherty. Lennon mentioned to Smith that he'd met Doherty. 'If anything subversive comes up, record it in separate notes,' he told the pair. 'I met him once to do with all that.' For Smith and Henry, the remark was further confirmation of their suspicion that Doherty, already linked to O'Dowd since the 4 May meeting between McBride and Inspector McGinley, might be the source of the bad information that led to the disastrous Gallagher farm search.

The three men wondered aloud what Doherty's motive might be for putting McBride up to the false statements. Smith mentioned Detective Superintendent Shelly's phone call to the Director of Public Prosecutions to confirm the power of arrest.

'Did Superintendent Shelly not trust my advice?' Lennon asked. Smith wasn't sure what to say. He hadn't known Shelly had asked Lennon about the power of arrest in the case.

———

The morning dragged on. Eventually, at 1 p.m. Pat Doherty rang to say his son was home. He asked Smith not to bring as many Guards as had come in the morning. There was no need to create a scene in front of the neighbours. Henry had gone home for a bite to eat. Smith tried to phone him, but the line was busy. He asked Detective Garda Martin Anderson to run up to his home and give him the message. At 1.40 p.m. Smith, Henry, and

Moylan arrived at Doherty's home. Henry spoke to Pat Doherty at the door, and the Gardaí were invited in. They asked William if they could look in his bedroom. They wanted to check if he owned a computer, which might have printed the 'Murdering McBrearty' fliers.

Henry noticed a notebook beside the bed. The cover had a picture of a rhinoceros, and it would become known as the Rhino notebook. 'Do you mind?' he asked Doherty.

'It's not mine,' William Doherty answered. 'Read away.'

Henry made the arrest. He formally cautioned Doherty, telling him anything he said could be taken down and used in evidence. He asked who owned the notebook. Doherty said nothing.

Henry handed the Rhino notebook to Smith, who flicked through the pages. Smith asked Doherty if he'd made any of the entries.

'That's not my notebook and that's not my writing,' Doherty answered.

Smith was looking at the last page of the Rhino notebook. It laid out the details of one of the statements taken from Noel McBride. Smith handed the notebook back to Henry. They took Doherty to Milford Garda Station as planned.

'We thought it was Doherty's notebook originally,' Henry explained at the tribunal. 'The entries at the back referred to the memo that was taken in John O'Dowd's house in May.' He believed the notebook contained Doherty's record of what McBride was to say to Gardaí. 'As far as I was concerned William Doherty was lying to me. I was convinced he was the person responsible for those calls.'

At the Morris tribunal, William Doherty admitted he stole the notebook from John O'Dowd, because he wanted to see what the Garda was writing about him, taking it opportunistically from O'Dowd's coat pocket which was hanging over the back seat of the car.

'Around the middle of May 1997, I was at a conference in Letterkenny one day and that notebook, I missed it when I left the station that day,' O'Dowd later told tribunal investigators.

'I couldn't report it because I suspected a member took it but I did mention it to two members, did they see a notebook. There was no point in me putting it in the occurrence book that a notebook was taken on Garda O'Dowd so I didn't do anything about it except I watched and kept my ears open to see would I see it appear sometimes.'

———

Jim Gallagher told the tribunal he was 'left out of the loop' and not told Doherty would be taken to his district after the arrest. Gallagher was the superintendent in charge of the Milford district in Donegal at the time (he'd been promoted and transferred in spring 1997) and the acting division duty officer over the entire county on the day William Doherty was arrested.

Gallagher told the inquiry he was at the 75th anniversary celebration of An Garda Síochána in Sligo when he got a phone call from Inspector McGinley telling him 'we got your man'. He said McGinley thought that Shelly had already told him about the plan to arrest Doherty.

Superintendent Gallagher said he assumed Doherty was taken to Milford 'to get him away from the atmosphere in Letterkenny unless there was interference'. He said he 'had no interest in what was going on in Letterkenny. They were running their patch and I was running my patch.'

———

In Milford, Doherty was first processed by the custody officer on duty before being brought to an interview room. About an hour into his detention, he began grasping his chest and rolling on the cell floor in pain. The detectives were sceptical, but a doctor was called anyway. Doherty was taken to Letterkenny hospital for tests, and returned to Milford with a clean bill of health at 6 p.m.

The clock was running. Doherty was arrested under Section 4 of the Criminal Justice Act. He could be held for up to six hours, and for a further six hours if a superintendent extended his detention, but after that, he had to be charged or released. At 6.05 p.m., Smith and Henry began to interview William Doherty, while Marty Moylan took notes.

Doherty denied making any hoax extortion or threatening phone calls, but accepted that a printout of the telephone bill showed the calls 'in black and white'. He also denied making the hoax extortion call to Michael Peoples from John O'Dowd's house. He said he did not know why there were 'nearly one hundred calls' from his house to John O'Dowd's home.

———

Smith was deeply sceptical that Doherty would tell the truth about anything. He knew from the conversation in the morning with Lennon that the superintendent had met Doherty, so at one point he tried a hunch. 'Did you ever speak to Kevin Lennon?' he asked.

'No,' Doherty answered.

'Do you know who Kevin Lennon is?'

'He's a Super in Letterkenny.'

'Did you ever meet or speak to him?'

'No.'

'Are you saying Kevin Lennon is telling lies when he says he met and spoke to you?'

'He must be telling lies.'

Smith knew the lie came from Doherty. Lennon had told him that morning he'd met Doherty. Smith figured there wasn't much chance of getting the truth from Doherty about anything. If he wouldn't admit he'd met the superintendent, he was hardly going to admit to being a blackmailer.

———

Doherty claimed during his interview that 'The Post Office are making out the list and putting the calls in.' He insisted that Noel McBride had told him he was threatened by Frank McBrearty, given £500 and a mountain bike, 'a good one—reddish one'. Even though Noel McBride had admitted the entire string of allegations he'd made were false—from seeing Young Frank and Mark McConnell on 14 October close to the time Richie Barron died to the offers of bribes from Old Frank—Doherty stuck to his story.

———

In the diary he produced to the Morris tribunal, Superintendent Kevin Lennon recorded that he 'spoke to Smith at 10.50 p.m. Doherty was acting up. Asked was extension necessary, did he want me to extend. Told Shelly was going to do it. Shelly is in Mullingar. I learned afterwards the extension already made. If anything doing give me a ring. He agreed. No mention of notebook. I was worried things were not right. I did not sleep all night.'

Lennon said the normal operational procedure would have been for Smith to go to the local superintendent for the extension order, who in this case would have been Lennon. Hugh Smith couldn't see the problem over the extension. A superintendent or higher-ranking officer had to give his authorisation if a prisoner's time in Garda custody was extended beyond the initial six hours, but one superintendent's signature was as good as another as far as Smith was concerned. He agreed that he made no mention of the notebook at that stage, but again, said he didn't think it was important. The notebook showed a link between Doherty and O'Dowd, that was all. As for speculation among the detectives that

Lennon's handwriting was in the notebook found in Doherty's bedroom, if Lennon had written something in the book, it was neither here nor there. As it happened, none of the writing in the book came from Lennon, according to a handwriting analysis. What exactly Lennon was supposed to have written, no one said at the tribunal. Guards referred obliquely to 'an issue of a K', suggesting that a single letter K resembled Lennon's style, and left it at that.

At 11 p.m., Inspector John McGinley phoned Lennon. The superintendent complained he wasn't being kept up to date as the district officer. 'You have some questions to answer about not briefing me,' he growled.

'Perhaps it's not for me to answer them questions,' McGinley shot back.

'John, I'm not being personal with you. It's about the professional operation of a Garda station,' Lennon retorted.

'Fine,' said McGinley.

'What emerges from these incidents was the total breakdown in trust between the officers in the Donegal Division at that time,' Mr Justice Morris later wrote. 'It is, to my mind, totally unacceptable that Detective Superintendent Shelly and Detective Inspector McGinley were required to carry out their duties in the atmosphere where they considered that there was a possibility that Superintendent Lennon was engaged in improper activities with an alleged informer. It is unacceptable, in my view, that the Chief Superintendent should allow such a situation to build up and exist among the officers in his division and, when he became aware of it, to have taken virtually no steps to remedy it.'

———

Doherty's next interview saw some new faces, as McGinley and Detective Garda Alphie McHale took over from Smith and Henry, while Detective Garda Joe Foley took notes. Doherty again denied that he knew anything about the hoax extortion phone calls to Michael Peoples. Shortly before midnight, McGinley asked Doherty if Superintendent Lennon and Garda John O'Dowd were lying, since Doherty denied he had ever met the superintendent.

At midnight, the custody officer told Doherty he was entitled to a night's sleep, and questioning could be stopped until the morning. Doherty told him he wanted to carry on, and asked what time he was due to be released.

The questioning went on. The detectives went through the evidence, and Doherty continued his denials. He didn't deny the phone bills showed the calls he was asked about, but said 'somebody in the exchange could click a few buttons' and forge the phone records. He said he never told McBride to make false statements, and knew nothing about the notebook found in his bedroom. He denied again that he'd ever met Superintendent Kevin Lennon. At 2.20 a.m., the detectives read the notes over, and Doherty signed them.

———

There were two interviewing teams in Milford. First, Smith and Henry as interrogators, with Marty Moylan as note-taker, and second McGinley and McHale, with Detective Garda Joe Foley taking notes.

The two teams got together in the kitchen over a pot of tea to compare notes. Detective Garda Joe Foley was unsure if he should record the questions asked about Lennon. It wasn't exactly standard procedure to ask a suspect if a superintendent was a liar. Foley asked McGinley if he wanted all the questions written down. 'If the question was asked, then write it down,' McGinley told him.

Foley added the questions to his notes, and went back to Doherty in the interview room. He read over the questions about Lennon, and Doherty signed the additions to accept they were correct.

After the kitchen get-together, Detective Sergeants Smith and Henry returned to the interview room along with Sergeant Marty Moylan. Henry played the tape of the telephone call on 9 November 1996 which Michael Peoples had recorded on a dictaphone.

'What have you to say to this tape conversation?' Henry asked.

'It's like two dogs fighting,' Doherty laughed. He denied it was his voice on the tape, and said he'd never seen the 'Rhino' notebook in his bedroom until Henry showed it to him, but said little else. At 4.15 a.m. the notes were read over to him. He refused to sign. There wasn't much else the detectives could do. For most of the day and night, he'd denied knowing anything, and now he wasn't even bothering to deny most of what was put to him, just sitting in silence. It was time to let him go.

Pat Doherty came to the station to collect his son. He was driven by Stephen Barron, Richie's son.

'When I heard that I thought, Oh, the plot thickens,' Marty Moylan told the Morris tribunal. He said he wondered if Stephen Barron was behind William Doherty or 'they were in it together'. He said the Doherty and Barron families 'were very close' and 'the penny dropped with me when I saw Stephen Barron outside'. Stephen Barron told the tribunal he was 'just obliging' Pat Doherty, an old friend of the family who had worked with his father in Scotland. Richie had stood as godfather to one of Pat's children, and Pat had comforted the family after their father's death.

'I didn't think that it was very manly to let him go himself. I just did it to be obliging,' Stephen Barron explained to the tribunal. Pat Doherty had called him at 2 a.m., and he'd gone with him to the station at 4 a.m. to keep him company. The tribunal made no specific finding about the incident, but the chairman did conclude that Stephen Barron 'was caught up on a wave of emotion generated in consequence of the death of his father and the corrupt and negligent Garda investigation'.

'Stephen Barron's other problem was in associating with a vigilante group whom he believed, in good faith, had more information in relation to the death of his father than was, in fact, the case,' the chairman wrote. 'The Tribunal is satisfied that the Barron family have grievously suffered as a result of this situation. They were entitled to expect an objective and competent Garda investigation. Instead the investigation into the death of their husband and father was pursued with unbelievable corruption, sloth and lack of objectivity.'

John McGinley told the Morris tribunal that the detectives 'were hoping that Mr Doherty would come clean with us and tell us what he was doing, why he did it and what his motivation was, and what was as regards his motivation for making the extortion telephone calls to Michael Peoples; for making the calls, a series of calls to Mr McBrearty and his family; for all the false information which McBride alleged came through him and all the information that came in in relation to the Barron investigation, which was false, and all subsequent statements in relation to Mr McBrearty in relation to bribing him, and so on. We hoped to get to the bottom of the Lofty Gallagher affair and we hoped to find out why he was doing these things and what his motivation for it was.'

In the end, however, he had to concede they 'gleaned absolutely nothing, I might say, in relation to the issues which I have described. It threw up other issues and tangents.'

Chapter 27

| Fallout

After a sleepless night, Kevin Lennon arrived in his office around 2.30 p.m. on Sunday. He wasn't there long before Hugh Smith dropped by. They spoke about the Doherty arrest. Lennon later wrote up an account of their exchange in a journal, and read it into the record at the Morris tribunal.

'Was Inspector McGinley on to you?' Smith asked.

'No,' replied Lennon. 'But isn't it about time somebody would get on to me.'

'Well, did you hear we found a notebook in Doherty's house?' said the sergeant.

'Sure nobody told me anything,' the superintendent answered testily. 'I didn't hear. But it's about time somebody would tell me something.'

Smith told the superintendent about the speculation that his handwriting was in the notebook found in Doherty's bedroom.

'Is this a stitching job?' asked Lennon. ' How could that be now?'

'Well, the lads thought that,' said Smith. He told the superintendent they suspected the Rhino notebook belonged to John O'Dowd. 'Did you ever make any entries in O'Dowd's notebook?' he asked.

'Certainly not,' Lennon answered. 'Why would I?'

'Well, some of the writing looks like yours,' Smith answered. 'I'll get a copy for you.'

Lennon waited for the sergeant to fetch a photocopy of the book and examine what everyone seemed to have decided in his absence was his handwriting. The two men went through it page by page. 'That's not my handwriting,' he said, handing back the copies. 'Where's my handwriting in that notebook? I've never seen this before in my life.'

'Well, the lads thought it was your handwriting.'

'Well it's not my handwriting.'

'It must be somebody else's.'

'It's a very logical conclusion for a detective sergeant to reach that, that it must be somebody else's.'

Smith rose to leave. 'Do you want to hold on to these?' he asked, showing Lennon the photocopied pages from the Rhino notebook.

'No, take it with you,' said Lennon.

———

John McGinley comes from the west Donegal parish of Gleann Cholm Cille, a Gaeltacht region. He was heavily involved in promoting the Irish language in An Garda Síochána, and on Monday he travelled to Dublin for a meeting of Conradh na Gaeilge. For Kevin Lennon, the trip left a feeling of foreboding. What if McGinley wasn't simply going to a meeting of Irish language enthusiasts? What if he went to Crime & Security and told them about Doherty? What if Crime & Security looked into it some more? It would open up a can of worms around the Gallagher search, and maybe even lead the intelligence branch to look again at the whole McGlinchey era.

Lennon sat in Donegal, still unsure what was going on. He stewed in his office, imagining McGinley in Garda HQ, getting his side of the story in first. God only knew what he was telling them.

———

Eventually, the detectives in Letterkenny began to put together an accurate picture. Detective Garda Thomas Kilcoyne spoke to Charlotte Peoples' mother, Catherine 'Dolly' Eaton. Dolly told Kilcoyne she'd phoned Letterkenny hospital checking up on her friend Richie Barron when she heard he'd been in an accident.

Kilcoyne also spoke to Geoffrey Dolan. He confirmed that by the time he spoke to Mark McConnell outside Frankie's nightclub, it was after 1 a.m. and the news of Richie Barron's death had already reached the town.

Detective Garda Joe Foley and Detective Garda Alphie McHale spoke to Philomena Laird, who corrected her time to confirm that Mark and Roisin McConnell called to Sarah's Café after 1 a.m., and not at 12.30 a.m. as she'd said originally. She told them she'd realised her mistake after speaking to Wilma Laird. Billy Flynn had found Wilma back in the spring. Detective Garda Joe Foley was sent to take a statement from her confirming that the McConnells were in Sarah's Café after 1 a.m.

———

On Tuesday morning, Lennon marched into McGinley's office, demanding to see the interview notes from Milford. 'I haven't got them,' the inspector answered.

'Where are they?'

'The boys have them.'

'Who are the boys?'

'Joe Foley and those,' said McGinley. He picked up a folder and leafed through it, checking. There was nothing there. Lennon left the office, went to the kitchen for a coffee to calm his nerves, and then headed back to McGinley again. 'What more questions do you want answered now?' asked the inspector, looking up from his work.

'I don't want any. I just want to look at the notes.' He walked out, and found Joe Foley. 'Were you in Milford, Joe?' he asked.

'I was.'

'Well could I have a look at your notes of interview?'

Smith, Henry and Foley were in the detective sergeants' office in Letterkenny, sorting through the paperwork from Doherty's arrests. Smith had just asked Foley to photocopy the interview notes, and get them into a file so they could be typed up when Lennon arrived at the door.

'I'm just going over to have them photocopied,' Foley told the superintendent, holding up the pages.

'I am the superintendent, I want the originals,' Lennon told him.

Lennon took the notes and sat at the table, reading through them. By the time he'd finished, he was furious. 'Why was my name mentioned in questions to a suspect in custody?' he demanded.

Hugh Smith was taken aback. 'I was just testing his credibility,' he told Lennon.

John McGinley arrived. 'Why is your writing in the notebook?' he asked Lennon.

'My handwriting is not there. My handwriting is not in the notebook,' the Super replied.

'Your handwriting *is* in the notebook and you can't deny it,' McGinley said. Turning to Henry he ordered him, 'Show it to him, Sylvie.'

Henry went to fetch the notebook, stored in a locker in a brown envelope. 'Hand it to him,' McGinley said when he returned.

'No,' said Lennon. 'You won't put my fingerprints on an exhibit.' Henry looked from McGinley to Lennon, and opened the notebook himself, leafing through the pages.

'Right,' demanded Lennon. 'Where's my handwriting in that notebook? It's not in it.' Lennon stretched his arms out dramatically. 'Take my fingerprints and my handwriting specimens, I'm willing to give them,' he told the pair.

There was an uneasy silence, until McGinley finally spoke.

'Do you want to know what I really believe?' he asked.

'No, but I would love to, John,' said Lennon.

'That you were involved with Noel McBride.'

Lennon exploded. The shadow boxing was over. The accusation was finally out in the open. 'It's about time,' he growled. 'In other words, you think that I fucked up your fucked-up investigation. Now if you have something to say, caution me now and deal with it now. Here and now.'

'You're paranoid,' said McGinley. 'You're being over-sensitive.'

'I'm suspending all this until the Chief comes back on Thursday,' Lennon announced. 'I have to write a report to the Commissioner on this McBride issue.'

Kevin Lennon went to Denis Fitzpatrick to complain about McGinley. 'I put it to the Chief in the presence of McGinley, very strongly and upfront,' he remembered.

Lennon complained 'that I was being accused of being involved with Noel McBride, that I was accused of having writing in a notebook that was never in it'.

The Chief wasn't impressed. 'John, if you and your lads were working down the town at the bank today, you'd be sacked,' he told Detective Inspector McGinley.

But the Chief went no further than the verbal rebuke to McGinley. There was no disciplinary action against the inspector for accusing his superior in front of junior officers; neither was there an investigation of the inspector's suspicions about Lennon.

'That resolved nothing,' said Lennon. 'It didn't resolve nothing. I carried that then and I moved on. It was over from a point of view of anything being done about it, but it was still in my mind ... Where else could I go? [Chief Superintendent Fitzpatrick] was the boss, he was in charge of discipline, he was in charge of these matters.'

——

Superintendent Shelly recalled at the tribunal that when he spoke to Detective Inspector John McGinley after the Milford arrests, the inspector told him that Superintendent Kevin Lennon was annoyed. The inspector said there was 'a perception' that he had travelled to Dublin after the Milford arrest to report to Garda HQ.

Shelly also remembered that he attended a meeting with Chief Superintendent Denis Fitzpatrick, where he was asked about the arrest at Milford. The Chief asked about the circumstances in which William Doherty was taken to Milford, and told him 'Superintendent Lennon is annoyed he was kept in the dark about Milford.'

'There was an annoyance there, and it was still there, that I hadn't been totally open,' Shelly remembered. 'I tried to be totally open and to tell him that we did what we did to get to the bottom of William Doherty.'

'The chief superintendent said to me, words to the effect of, you should have kept the superintendent up to speed.'

'I felt leaving there he wasn't happy about the way we handled it, that was reprimand enough for me,' Shelly said.

Lennon told the tribunal that, in the aftermath of the unresolved clash with McGinley, he simply put his head down, got on with his job and put it behind him. This was met with some disbelief by the chairman. Judge Morris asked him how he could function in those circumstances. Lennon replied simply 'Bitterness is a degree of something that eats away at your soul like a cancer. I am not a bitter man.' Lennon said that by then, he knew McBrearty and McConnell were innocent. McBride's statement had fallen apart, and there were doubts about the confession. His focus was on how to fix the mess.

———

On Thursday 25 September, Lennon went to meet the State solicitor for Donegal, Ciaran Mac Lochlainn, and spoke to him about the alleged confession from Young Frank McBrearty.

'I was suggesting this statement was a dud. It was manufactured,' Lennon explained afterwards. 'What I said to him was, I wasn't going to have another "Kerry Babies" on my hands.

'What I would say I was conveying was that they certainly had a knowledge that this statement wasn't correct, and they were prepared to stand over it. That's what I was conveying. I felt the statement was wrong.'

However, Lennon said it was not the fallout from the arrest of William Doherty that prompted him to go to Mac Lochlainn. 'I was raising issues about the statement in early September,' he said. 'I told him that [McGinley] had not briefed me, not kept me up to date . . . He had accused me of having my handwriting in the notebook . . . He had accused me of being involved in Robert Noel McBride.'

Mac Lochlainn contacted David Lombard in the DPP's office and passed on what the superintendent told him.

Lennon said that by going to the State solicitor, he was indirectly alerting the DPP to problems with a file. By this sideways mechanism, he could tip off the State prosecutor without putting direct criticisms in his report.

———

The following day, Friday 26 September 1997, Mac Lochlainn wrote up a memo recording what the superintendent had told him. An edited portion of the memo was read into the record at the Morris tribunal on Day 303.

That evening, Lennon set up the 'Second Investigation'. The first investigation into the death of Richie Barron was a mess, Lennon announced. They were starting over. At the tribunal, he denied the second investigation was an attempt to take control and ensure O'Dowd and Doherty were kept low profile because of his links to both men. The first meeting of the second investigation started at 8 p.m. He told the assembled Guards that Nora Barron was questioning the 'bona fides' of the confession. This is the only mention in any conference record of a doubt over the confession. Lennon said he did not want to prejudice the investigators, he wanted them to form their own opinions on the case. They were going to start over, he told them. McBride's key statement was in doubt, everything had to be reviewed.

———

On Monday 29 September 1997, Ciaran Mac Lochlainn phoned the DPP's office and spoke to David Lombard, a senior official. In his diary, the civil servant recorded what he was told about 'the background on this strange case' by Mac Lochlainn.

'The case involves the investigation into the supposed murder of Richie Barron,' Lombard wrote in a memo of the conversation. 'Ciaran Mac Lochlainn told me that he had been speaking to Superintendent Lennon who told him that in the course of the investigation Frank McBrearty Junior made admissions with regard to the murder.

'Superintendent Lennon stated that serious queries had arisen about the statement made by Frank McBrearty Junior, who supposedly admitted involvement in the alleged murder. There were doubts about the account given in the statement. The original statement itself has conveniently disappeared.

'This investigation had been under the supervision of Superintendent Joe Shelly.

'There were in addition doubts as to whether a murder actually took place, and the body may have to be exhumed for a post-mortem. There was an autopsy at the time but this made no reference to the deceased's broken finger, which apparently was invisible from the photograph.

'The Garda investigation is starting again under the supervision of Superintendent Lennon. Apparently the Garda authorities are most unhappy about the earlier investigation, particularly with regard to the statement of Frank McBrearty Junior.

'Superintendent Lennon apparently has doubts about Frank McBrearty Junior's statement. In addition it seems that during the course of the first investigation Gardaí arrested some 13 or 14 people and detained them under Section 4.

'It would seem that these were not suspects and questions around the propriety of these detentions arise. Superintendent Lennon was of the view that the statement of Frank McBrearty does not stand up at all.'

Portions of what David Lombard wrote were not made available on the public record. Instead, only a redacted version of the memo was read at the tribunal.

'Mr Mac Lochlainn [the Donegal State solicitor] was concerned about the fact that there was no file submitted to him or to the Director's office or to anybody else in relation to the so-called investigation,' Lombard wrote.

When Mac Lochlainn phoned Lombard, he told him that Lennon would be in contact shortly and might come up to the office for a meeting with Lombard about the Barron case.

Meanwhile, Kevin Lennon delivered a progress report on the Barron investigation for Chief Superintendent Denis Fitzpatrick.

The report began with a brief mention of Barron's movements the night he died, including the altercation with Mark McConnell, pointing out that the exchange never came to blows. It explained that the crime scene was not preserved because the Gardaí on duty travelled to Letterkenny hospital to collect Barron's clothing. There was no mention of the difficulty in contacting the Garda on duty in Raphoe that night, Padraig Mulligan, or the fact that, having travelled to the hospital, the Guards did not in fact preserve Barron's clothing or remains.

The report gives the impression that 'Gardaí suspected Richard Barron was subjected to a serious assault at the scene where his body was found, resulting in his death' on the morning of 14 October, as a result of which 'the scene was preserved initially from 9.10 a.m. on 14 October 1996'.

There is no mention of the wake house rumour passed on to Chief Superintendent Fitzpatrick by John O'Dowd. It is referred to as 'certain information', which led to the second search of the area on Wednesday 16 October. The worthless autopsy conclusion, that Barron 'died from head injuries', is reported without comment.

The report listed three initial suspects in the Barron investigation, Paul 'Gazza' Gallagher, who was seen speeding in the town, Manny Hegarty, who got into an argument with Richie Barron about a disputed debt, and Mark McConnell. Although it considered the other two men briefly, the report focused in detail on Mark McConnell and Young Frank McBrearty. The initial statements of the staff at Sarah's Café, Carmel Connolly and Philomena Laird, were noted, as was the inconsistency created when Philomena Laird corrected her initial estimate of the time she saw the McConnells after speaking to Wilma Laird, the witness found by Billy Flynn. The statements of several witnesses in the Town & Country bar were analysed.

The statement of Noel McBride was described at length, ending with an acknowledgement that the investigation was 'flattened' when McBride took back his statements. There was no mention of McBride's allegation that he was coerced by William Doherty into making the false statements. Instead, Lennon simply stated that he 'recently had all the facts of this witness's statement pursued as to his "bona fides" and his statements disproved'. There was no mention of the extortion blackmail phone calls to Michael Peoples from the home of William Doherty, the information from Billy Flynn about the source of the calls, or the extortion attempt on Frank McBrearty Senior a few days before.

Lennon then gave an account of the December 1996 arrests. Billy Flynn was criticised for writing letters which 'attempted to discredit individual Gardaí and the Garda investigation'. The report stated that the McBreartys filed papers for wrongful arrest in the High Court on 10 April 1997, and that on 16 April 1997 Dr Barry submitted his written autopsy report to the Garda investigators.

Lennon concluded by noting that because McBride had collapsed as a witness, he was 'conducting a review of the investigation by members who have not been previously involved', and was considering an exhumation.

Chapter 28

The Truth is Lying Under the Ground

Kevin Lennon travelled to Dublin on Thursday 2 October. The following day, he met Professor John Harbison in his offices at Trinity College Dublin. On Saturday 4 October, back in Donegal, he went to see Chief Superintendent Denis Fitzpatrick. He explained that he needed an exhumation order. 'I can't go anywhere with this case because I have no forensic pathology,' he told the Chief. 'I have nothing other than a report saying head injuries were the cause of death.' Fitzpatrick was non-committal.

The following Sunday, Lennon travelled to Dublin again, this time because of a criminal trial. On Monday 6 October, he called to the DPP's office and met David Lombard. Donegal State solicitor Ciaran Mac Lochlainn had already told the civil servant that the superintendent would call at some point. The meeting began at 12.15 p.m. Once again, the dutiful and methodical civil servant recorded a memo outlining what happened.

'In his initial statement Noel McBride says he saw suspect Frank McBrearty Junior and McConnell running away from the area near the scene of the crime. McConnell has an altercation with the deceased about an hour and a half, two hours previously in the pub. At around 12.30 a.m. in the morning in question the deceased was seen walking home and was obviously drunk . . . The deceased found at 12.55 a.m. by Lee Parker and he was dead at this stage. Mr Parker went into the house and told a woman who also knew the deceased. If the deceased was dead at 12.55 a.m. McBride could not have seen McBrearty and McConnell fleeing the scene at 1 a.m. McBride was adamant that 1 a.m. was the time in question given that he said the town hall bell was ringing at the time. This piece of information would clearly undermine McBride's version of events.

'Superintendent Lennon told me that 14 [sic!] persons were arrested including Damien McDaid who was sitting in a van near Frank McBrearty's premises around the time of his death. The basis for the arrest of these people is at the very least suspect and Superintendent

Lennon told me the civil proceedings against the State seemed inevitable arising from same. Frank McBrearty Senior was detained under Section 30 of the Offences Against the State Act, offence under Section 7 of the 1875 Act. Superintendent told me that D/Superintendent Shelly has wanted to send the file up but Superintendent Lennon would not send it up at that stage . . .

'In May 1997 McBride in a statement said that Frank McBrearty Senior took him to his office, offered him £6,000, a bicycle and jewellery to withdraw his story. It is clear McBride never received these. It can now be shown McBride wasn't near the scene of the alleged crime on the night in question as he was at a christening some considerable distance away.

'Frank McBrearty Junior made a statement admitting his involvement in the death. Superintendent Lennon is not at all happy with the statement. It doesn't gel and various points don't add up. He also told me no element from the statement can be corroborated and that, for example, McBrearty Junior refers to a person as being present who can be shown was not present.

'The post-mortem was inadequate, the body was lying in the hospital for over 12 hours without being preserved before the post-mortem commenced. Photographs show an injured finger, which might be a defensive injury on the deceased. Superintendent Lennon has spoken to Dr Harbison and it seems an exhumation may take place.

'The most sinister and serious development in this case surrounds the fact that McBride alleges that William Doherty, a local criminal, told McBride to tell the Gardaí that he saw the suspects running away from the scene of the crime. The question then arose as to what should be done in relation to Doherty.

'An investigation was headed by Detective Superintendent Joe Shelly and Doherty was arrested and detained under Section 4 (somewhat amazingly by liaising with Doherty's father). It seems that Superintendent Lennon was kept out of the picture while this detention was taking place and became seriously uneasy.

'He enquired of the Gardaí would an extension order be required and he was not told at that stage that same had been obtained from Superintendent Shelly at his, Shelly's, home in Mullingar. The normal operational procedure would have been for the Gardaí in question to go to the local superintendent for the extension order.

'The questioning of this particular suspect was conducted by Detective Sergeant Henry and Detective Sergeant Smith, together with Detective Inspector McGinley. They told Superintendent Lennon that a notebook had been found in Doherty's house which contained handwriting made by Superintendent Lennon.

'Detective Inspector McGinley, after some pressure, showed him notes taken of the interview of Doherty and one question put to the detained person by Detective Inspector McGinley was that some of the handwriting in the notebook was in Superintendent Lennon's name. Superintendent Lennon has become seriously unhappy about the manner in which the investigation has been conducted and feels that this may have been part of an attempt by other Gardaí to try and shaft him. He was seriously upset by this sinister development. The Chief Superintendent has now ordered (presumably in directions from headquarters) that the investigation start anew and this is now being done under the auspices of Superintendent Lennon. He assured me that he would try and reach the truth of the matter and he has assembled a team of investigating Gardaí who have had absolutely no involvement with the earlier investigation. The starting point [will] obviously be an exhumation and a proper post-mortem to be carried out by Dr Harbison. He did tell me however that the investigation may take some considerable time, given the complications which had arisen. He assured me that he would endeavour to get to the truth of the matter.'

It is notable that Lennon said Shelly was in charge of the investigation before he took over in late September. Strictly speaking, this was not accurate. As district officer, Lennon took over from Fitzgerald in February 1997. In that post, he was responsible for every major investigation in his district. The reference to 'a person as being present who can be shown was not present' in Young Frank's doubtful confession also shows that Lennon accepted at this point that Mark McConnell was still in the Town & Country when Richie Barron died.

On 8 October the Donegal County Coroner, Dr Fred Kee, wrote to the Secretary of the Department of Justice, requesting authorisation for an exhumation of Richie Barron as legally required by the Coroner's Act, on the grounds that he was informed by Superintendent Kevin Lennon that 'the deceased may have met his death by violent means other than the initial theory of a Hit and Run accident'.

Lennon said that when he first spoke to Kee about the need for an exhumation, the coroner's response was to say to him: 'You're a brave man.' An exhumation was a difficult and trying process.

'Well, I have to establish how he died,' is the reply Lennon remembered giving.

At the Morris tribunal years later, Lennon was at pains to point out that the opinion that 'the deceased may have met his death by violent means' did not reflect his actual view of the case. It was a legal fiction, designed to allow the exhumation and establish how Barron died. Legally, under Section 47 of the Coroner's Act, an exhumation could only be ordered when a Garda of inspector rank or above believed that death 'occurred in a violent or unnatural manner'.

On 9 October 1997 Lennon composed a letter to the Secretary of the
Department of Justice, Equality and Law Reform in support of the
exhumation request by Dr Kee. 'It is my considered opinion that the
deceased met his death by means other than a road traffic, hit and run
accident,' Lennon wrote. 'I am satisfied from consultations with Professor
John Harbison that he may be in a position to establish through further
examination of the remains, the means whereby the deceased met his
death.'

Around 3 p.m. on Monday 13 October, Chief Superintendent Denis
Fitzpatrick called to see Lennon in his office. 'He was aware of what Dr
Harbison and Dr Barry said to me, and he knew that I had made my
applications,' Lennon recalled.

'He came in to my office and asked me, "What's the status of the exhumation order?" and I told him I hadn't got it but the documents are in the
Department and I expect it shortly.'

Lennon said that Fitzpatrick asked him to cancel the autopsy on Richie
Barron. Lennon protested that he couldn't do that. Once a request was
sent to the Department of Justice, there was no way to stop it.

'The truth is lying under the ground in Raphoe,' Lennon told the
Chief. 'Dr Harbison has the view that it should go ahead.' He added that
the State pathologist had assured him he would be able to state definitively how Barron died if he got the chance to examine the remains, and
he couldn't cancel it because he didn't have the power.

'He said, "you cancel it", and I said nothing more and I didn't argue
or fight with him.' Lennon didn't fight with his Chief over the order,
but he didn't do anything else either. He made no move to cancel the
exhumation.

Fitzpatrick said later he reckoned Lennon was moving too fast. The
Barron family hadn't been told about the exhumation yet, and there was
work to do 'above ground' before an autopsy could be done. Besides,
Richie Barron wasn't going anywhere. In fact, with every passing day,
information that an autopsy could reveal was being lost under the
ground. As Richie Barron's remains decayed, the story they could tell
about how he died became less clear.

Lennon said the investigation 'above ground' was stymied until he had
a proper forensic examination. He didn't want to cause the Barron family
any more stress than necessary, and planned to tell them close to the date
of the exhumation. 'I didn't want to have a situation that I had a media
circus around the grave of their dead father,' he explained.

'I had arranged the morgue, and I had arranged the time that we
would do it at, we were going to do it about 4 a.m. in the morning, and
we would have it done before the public would realise that it was done
and I would have had a liaison with the family and all that.'

The following day Orla Kenny, a civil servant in the Department of Justice, drew up the paperwork for the exhumation of Richie Barron, and forwarded it to her boss.

On Thursday 16 October Lennon, Fitzpatrick and Detective Superintendent Joe Shelly travelled together to Sligo to meet the Assistant Commissioner in charge of the Northern Region, Noel Crummey. While Lennon sat outside, Fitzpatrick discussed the exhumation order with Crummy in his office, although the first Lennon would know of this was when he heard Fitzpatrick's evidence at the Morris tribunal seven years later. 'I don't really know what went on at that meeting down there,' he told the tribunal.

As the three officers drove back to Donegal, Fitzpatrick raised the exhumation again.

'I was sitting in the back of the car and Joe Shelly was sitting in the front of the car and as we approached Donegal town [Chief Superintendent Fitzpatrick] asked me, "did you make that cancellation of that exhumation application?"', Lennon remembered.

'I said, "I didn't". So we pulled in at Donegal town and he told me to go in and cancel it. I went into the Garda station, I looked up the number for Department of Justice, I rang the Department of Justice. I looked for the coroner's section. I looked to speak to the secretary of the coroner's section: he wasn't available. This was 4.50 p.m. roughly in the afternoon, and I then spoke to the Assistant Secretary.

'I asked him was the application signed and he said it wasn't at that stage but it was ready. And I asked him to put it on hold. That was the extent of the conversation.'

Legally, no matter what Fitzpatrick's orders were, there was no way to cancel an exhumation order, so Lennon asked the Assistant Secretary to put the order 'on hold'. It was one year to the day since Richard Barron was buried. It would be another four years before his remains were exhumed and finally examined by a professionally qualified forensic pathologist.

Lennon remembered 'an urgency' in stopping the exhumation. The car was only forty minutes drive from home base in Letterkenny, and the call could have been made the next morning, but it had to be that day. 'I was very disappointed, to be honest,' he recalled. 'But I was in his hands. [Fitzpatrick] was my boss. That was it. He was the boss and I complied with his directions. I wasn't happy and I was never happy with it after-wards.'

'I think he cancelled it because he knew the investigation was going 'skyways' . . . If it was a hit and run then everything was in a total heap. If it turned out to be—based on Dr Harbison's views and Dr Barry's views—that it was determined that it was murder, well, that was well and

good. On the other hand, if it turned out to be a hit and run accident that
was a total disaster.

'You had the statement of confession to a murder that never happened,
and you have eleven or twelve people arrested for a murder, an accessory
to murder that never happened. And you had the process of six or eight,
ten months gone by of a total waste of procedures, and you had a process
where an incident room had run the situation on murder. Putting all these
factors together, there certainly would be a big blowout from it.'

At the next conference meeting Lennon reported to the incident room
that there would be no exhumation. It wasn't going to happen.

———

Back in June, Billy Flynn had handed in a statement to his local Garda
station in Enfield, Co. Meath. In the twenty-six-page letter, he laid out
what he'd uncovered so far in Donegal, the Garda negligence in the
initial stages of the Barron investigation, their targeting of the
McBreartys and others, and the phone calls to Michael Peoples from the
homes of Doherty and Garda John O'Dowd. Superintendent Tom
Gallagher from Ballymote Garda Station in County Sligo was sent to
Donegal to investigate. On Friday 24 October, just over a month after
McBride was uncovered as a false witness, casting suspicion on Doherty
as an agent provocateur, Gallagher submitted his report.

Gallagher acknowledged that the crime scene was not preserved, and
laid out the background to the threatening/blackmail calls to Old Frank
McBrearty and Michael Peoples. He outlined hoax bomb alerts caused by
telephone calls to Letterkenny hospital and Highland Radio, allegations
of mistreatment in custody, Frank McBrearty's allegation that his supposed confession was a forgery, and a series of incidents amounting to
harassment of the McBrearty family.

Flynn claimed the McBreartys received up to 150 visits from Garda
John O'Dowd and Sergeant John White in February and March 1997.
Flynn later supplied a seventy-five-page report listing complaints about
visits to the nightclub and pub between 11 January and 28 July.

Flynn claimed he was shown telephone records leading him to suspect
John O'Dowd for one of the hoax blackmail telephone calls to Michael
Peoples by an 'acting Garda' who met him in Northern Ireland and
handed over the printouts. This disgruntled Garda was unimpressed by
the treatment of the McBreartys, the private detective said.

Gallagher recommended that Flynn be interviewed, and asked to disclose his source. If the Garda corroborated the claims, it would help
Flynn's credibility. He acknowledged that the allegation against O'Dowd
was 'most serious' and 'appears well founded'.

Gallagher further recommended that Flynn's claims that he was harassed by Gardaí—made to Chief Superintendent Noel O'Sullivan in the Crime Branch at Garda HQ—should be investigated by the Garda Complaints Board.

Gallagher concluded that 'while some of his claims are legitimate, the majority of his suggestions are based on rumour and innuendo, and are generally of no evidential value'.

'If what Flynn says in his statement was factual,' Gallagher wrote, 'it would reveal a major conspiracy involving officers and Gardaí in the Donegal Division in a bid to pervert the course of justice and harassment of the McBrearty family. This I don't find credible.'

'William Flynn is well known to the Gardaí and has featured in many serious Garda investigations and his agenda is usually to undermine the Gardaí,' Gallagher wrote. He listed a series of convictions Billy Flynn had picked up over the years. Flynn, he concluded, was 'a nuisance and has caused a great deal of annoyance, stress, and hardship to the decent men of An Garda Síochána, in this and other cases.'

———

Around the same time, Detective Sergeant Hugh Smith remembered that John White spoke to him about the Barron case. White told his fellow sergeant he had doubts about the confession Young Frank McBrearty was supposed to have made.

'Are you suggesting to me that two experienced detectives from Dublin concocted a statement and got Frankie to sign it?' Smith asked him.

'All I'm saying is I have grave reservations about the statement of Frank Junior,' White answered. At the Morris tribunal, White said he had raised question marks about the confession as early as August 1997, the month he was transferred from Raphoe to Letterkenny to take over the case file as detective sergeant.

But whatever White may have made of the confession, David Lombard's notes show that at least one officer, Kevin Lennon, was questioning the truthfulness of the confession as early as October 1997.

———

In early November, Telecom Eireann finally confirmed they had records of the four calls William Doherty made from his home to Michael Peoples. However, they had no record of the fifth call. Years later, at the Morris tribunal, an Eircom engineer explained that a series of mishaps combined to create chaos in their records section in the late 1990s. New computers were installed at the time to speed up phone trace requests from Gardaí, but during the testing and changeover phases, data tapes were mishandled. Some data was lost, and other information could only be partially retrieved, depending on which computer was used to run a records search.

―――

By 7 November, Deputy Commissioner Noel Conroy had read the report by Superintendent Tom Gallagher on his inquiry into the allegations made by Billy Flynn. Conroy forwarded the report to the Assistant Commissioner of the C (Crime) Branch, asking for a progress report within one month. Conroy noted that the allegations made by Flynn were 'disturbing to say the least', and should be investigated. He also asked the senior officer to look into any 'criminal action' in how Billy Flynn had obtained telephone records.

On 12 November, Detective Garda Joe Foley tried to interview Roderick Donnelly about his eyewitness statement on 20 January 1997. The attempt was unsuccessful, and Foley submitted a memo on the encounter. 'I was investigating the validity of this sighting as I considered it crucial,' he wrote. He met Donnelly in the yard outside his home, but Donnelly told him he didn't want to speak to him. When Foley asked about Mark McConnell's appearance, in particular his hair and clothing looking wet, Donnelly told him that he'd since seen McConnell, and his hair 'always looks wet'. Donnelly asked the detective to leave, and told Foley that if he 'wanted to know more to go and speak to Darcy Connolly'.

At 8.20 a.m. on 14 November, McBride was arrested under Section 12 of the Criminal Law Act (1976) for making a false statement. McBride was taken to Letterkenny Garda station, and logged in by the custody officer at 8.55 a.m. He was interviewed for several hours, and made a statement after he was cautioned, admitting he had made false allegations against the McBreartys.

McBride told the detectives he thought Doherty's grudge against the McBrearty family stemmed from 'a fight a few years ago with Young Frank', but didn't know why Doherty would have had a grudge against McConnell. Doherty had been a good friend of Richie Barron's. McBride said he saw them 'at a mart in Raphoe, I used to see them together always in the cattle lorry. They used to deal with cattle with Richie's lorry. I would think that they were friends.'

Hugh Caulfield told Detective Garda Alphie McHale that Manny Hegarty, the man who had a row over a disputed debt with Richie Barron the night he died, stayed in his house in St Eunan's Terrace the night Richie Barron died. If he wasn't ruled out already by the Gardaí, this simple statement eliminated Manny Hegarty as a hit and run suspect. In driving from the Diamond to St Eunan's Terrace he would have gone south, and would never have passed the point north of the town where Richie Barron died. McHale also spoke to Manny, who again confirmed he'd been in 'a row' with Richie, and had left the Suile Tavern ten or fifteen minutes later.

Chapter 29

Anomalies Have Occurred

Work continued in the wake of the first Lennon report. Lennon sent in his next report to Chief Superintendent Denis Fitzpatrick on 23 November. The report, titled 'Update on the suspicious death of Richard Barron' carried the subtitle 'Attempt to pervert the course of justice and the provision of false information to the Gardaí'. The report described in detail Noel McBride's statements and subsequent retractions. At the beginning of the report, Lennon stated that he was 'somewhat concerned' with the 'bona fides' of Noel McBride.

The narrative began in mid-November 1996, when Garda John O'Dowd received 'confidential information' from William Doherty that McBride might have information about the death of Richie Barron. Doherty 'had supplied confidential information to Garda O'Dowd in the past'. This information was passed to the incident team in Letterkenny.

Lennon then described the arrest of Noel McBride for the theft of an aerial, and subsequent contacts by William Doherty, who told Garda O'Dowd that McBride had further information to offer. These were McBride's statements in December 1996 and March 1997 claiming variously that he was threatened by the McBreartys, and bribed by them.

'I was querying the bona fides of Noel McBride resulting from the three written statements to date in which he had made very serious allegations against the McBrearty family,' Lennon wrote. 'I instructed Detective Inspector John McGinley to accompany Garda O'Dowd on his next meeting with Noel McBride for the purpose of assessing McBride and the quality of his information.'

Lennon wrote that he instructed McGinley to verify the information in the memo of the 4 May 1997 interview by asking to see the bicycle and other items McBride purchased, and that he repeated this instruction after McBride's 7 July statement to Detective Sergeant Hugh Smith, which 'resulted in Detective Inspector McGinley and Detective Sergeant Smith's visit to Noel McBride on 13 September 1997.' The subsequent visit on 16 September by Detective Sergeants Smith and Henry and Detective

Garda McHale, during which McBride recanted and finally told the truth, was also 'on my directions', the superintendent wrote.

Lennon reported that he planned to recommend prosecuting McBride for the theft of an aerial, and for making false statements. The report enclosed fifteen statements from McBride (the original false accusations, his retractions, and interview notes during his arrest) but it did not contain William Doherty's statement confirming the lie, or any record or mention of Doherty's arrest.

Lennon was eager to claim whatever credit was going for McGinley's partial assessment of McBride in May 1997, and for the final collapse of the web of lies in September. As often as he refers to his 'directions' and 'instructions', however, he makes no mention at all of another fact which was central to the story—nowhere in the report is there any mention of the telephone calls from William Doherty (and from John O'Dowd's home) to Michael Peoples and Old Frank McBrearty, the cases Smith and Henry were investigating. The report minimised any mention of Doherty.

———

On 30 November 1997, Detective Sergeant John White took a detailed statement from Eugene Gamble. The barman told the sergeant he left the Suile Tavern at 12.40 a.m. or so, and headed to Sarah's Café, arriving around 12.45 a.m. There he claimed he saw not only Mark and Roisin McConnell, but also Michael and Charlotte Peoples. 'I will say that Mark McConnell and Michael Peoples came into the café with the others between 12.50 a.m. and 12.55 a.m.,' Gamble said.

Gamble then said he left the café at 1 a.m., and went back to the Suile Tavern, where Stephen McCullagh told him Richie Barron was dead. In his initial statement two days after Richie Barron died, Gamble made no mention of Mark McConnell or Michael Peoples. Now, he insisted that his changed statements were nothing to do with a row he had with the McBreartys in their nightclub in April 1997, which ultimately led to a court case. In a statement on 25 September 1997 to Detective Garda Martin Anderson, Gamble first mentioned seeing Mark McConnell. He hadn't mentioned anything to Sergeant Joe Hannigan in his first statement in October 1996, days after the event when his memory would have been freshest, and said this was because the sergeant only asked him what time Richie Barron left the Suile Tavern, and what time he closed up.

Gamble's statement is inconsistent, not only with Mark McConnell's account, but with the 'Garda version' outlined in the interrogation of Mark and Roisin McConnell when they were arrested. The Garda theory involved Mark arriving in the café around 12.30 a.m. to place his order, then meeting up with Young Frank, assaulting Richie Barron, returning through the car park and entering the nightclub. Gamble's account placed Mark in the café between 12.50 a.m. and 12.55 a.m. Since Richie Barron was seen alive at 12.45, this would have given Mark only five minutes at most to meet up with Frank McBrearty, run up the car park and across 500 yards of rough ground in darkness (crossing a stream in the process), assault Richie Barron, and make his getaway before Lee Parker arrived and raised the alarm. Even if such a superhuman feat was possible, Gamble by his account met Stephen McCullagh at 1.05 a.m. or so, and it is clear from other accounts that it was not until at least 1.15 that Stephen McCullagh learned of the accident, since the first thing he did was to flag down his brother Declan, and they arrived at the scene of the accident at the same time as the ambulance did, between 1.20 a.m. and 1.25 a.m. Clearly, there are problems with Gamble's statement.

Gamble denied the new statement had anything to do with a confrontation with the McBreartys at their nightclub in April 1997, which led to court proceedings. 'The tribunal has heard the evidence of Mr Gamble in this regard and totally rejects it,' Mr Justice Morris concluded. Having regard to the 'discord' arising out of the court case, the judge concluded that the statement 'was calculated to undermine Mr McConnell's credibility, and to implicate Michael Peoples by association'.

––––

On 6 December Martin Quigley, the barman in the Town & Country pub, told Detective Garda Michael Carroll that the time he initially gave for when he left the pub that night was too early. 'I did not want to show the pub to be keeping late hours,' he explained. He said he left 'closer to 12.45 a.m.' than 12.30 a..m, and said he felt the list of people he'd named in a statement to the private investigator as being present when he left— including Mark McConnell—was 'an accurate list'.

––––

The next Lennon report on the Barron investigation, dated 16 December 1997, ran to forty-six pages. The report began with a three-page 'preamble', an account of the investigation since the personnel changes on 29 September, the beginning of the 'second investigation'. Lennon noted that 'circa two hundred new jobs' had been completed since then, and that 'many of these new jobs have emanated from the plethora of statements received from William Flynn', the private investigator Frank McBrearty had hired back in February. Witness accounts in the statements collected by Flynn's investigators didn't match those in the Garda files, and the 'discrepancies' had to be investigated.

Lennon's next step was to conduct house to house inquiries with a questionnaire along the road from Irish Row in Raphoe to the Common, the road Richie Barron was on the night he died. Despite the fact it was over a year since the night Richie Barron died, this would not be done until after the witness statements taken by Flynn's men were re-checked and completed. When all that was done, it was then intended to 'scrutinise the roll [sic!]' played by William Doherty, as his 'behaviour and input [had] resulted in the protraction of this investigation'.

Lennon also noted some 'associated matters on the periphery of the investigation', including a file sent to the DPP about phone calls made by Billy Flynn to Sergeant John White's wife Rosaleen, and how Flynn apparently got hold of telephone records belonging to White, Garda John O'Dowd, and the Raphoe Garda station, possibly in breach of the 1998 Data Protection Act.

Other files in preparation for the DPP covered Noel McBride's 'part in knowingly supplying false information', the theft of the aerial from the Tech in Raphoe, and an arson which destroyed a trailer from an articulated lorry, which was 'first admitted to by Noel McBride who later implicated William Doherty as the sole culprit'.

Having dispensed with the introductions, Lennon then recapped at length the sequence of statements McBride made to Gardaí, from the first false eyewitness statement made under pressure in Letterkenny Garda station on 29 November 1996 ('He agreed to return to an interview room voluntarily'), through further false allegations of threats and bribery by the McBreartys made on 4 December 1996, 18 March 1997, 4 May 1997, 7 July 1997, and 13 September 1997, his retraction on 16 September 1997 to Smith, Henry and McHale, his clarifying statement about the two christenings to Henry the following day, and yet another statement to Smith and Henry on 3 October 1997 about the entire affair.

Having summarised the debacle, Lennon then moved on to Billy Flynn. The superintendent noted that the first he knew of the private detective was when he received a letter from Frank McBrearty on 6 February. Flynn was 'a convicted felon', the superintendent wrote, and his methods left 'an abundance to be desired'. He had 'literally bombarded all sections of An Garda Síochana', including the Commissioner's office, Crime Branch at Garda HQ, and station, district, and divisional offices in County Donegal, with 'a barrage of correspondence' about his clients' plight.

'His prerogative[sic!], it now appears, is to discredit individual members of the force, including high ranking members, whose only concern is to establish the true circumstances surrounding the death of

Richard Barron,' Lennon continued. 'Private citizens had also been contacted,' and 'people have undoubtedly been intimidated.'

Flynn had delivered over 160 statements and interview memos taken
by his investigators to the Gardaí in October 1997, many from people who
had already been interviewed by the Gardaí. 'In some cases,' Lennon
wrote, 'the statements recorded by Flynn were at variance with those
recorded by Gardaí.' Gardaí were now revisiting these people 'to establish
why these anomalies have occurred'.

Lennon also reported Flynn's allegations that one of the people
responsible for defamatory leaflets about the McBreartys was 'a serving
member of an Garda Síochána associated with either Raphoe or
Letterkenny'. Flynn was also alleging that 'blackmail, extortion and death
threat phone calls were made from cattle marts in Donegal'.

Lennon then dealt with some of the 'discrepancies' in statements
collected by Flynn's investigators. Strangely though, he never went into
any detail about the changed statement of Philomena Laird, where she
corrected the time she saw Mark McConnell once Billy Flynn discovered
and interviewed Wilma Laird, seriously challenging any Garda theory
that Mark had left the Town & Country pub by 12.30 a.m.

More seriously, Wilma alleged she was visited by detectives in
Northern Ireland within weeks of Richie Barron's death, and told them
that she saw Mark and Roisin in the café at 1.30 am. There was no record
of this visit in the incident room files, yet no one thought to query how
this could be. Other statements, from witnesses who saw Mark
McConnell in the Town & Country after 12.30 a.m. and even after 1 a.m.,
are also ignored in this report, as they were in the first Lennon report.

Having spent ten pages on the subject of Billy Flynn, Lennon tackled
Noel McBride's confusion over the two christenings in Roper's Lantern Inn,
concluding at the end of his three-page summary that 'it was in fact Noel
McBride who confused the two reception dates causing Garda O'Dowd
and Collins to disbelieve him'. However, he didn't ask why McBride, knowing he wasn't in Raphoe the night Barron died, made a false statement.

A two-page summary and profile of William Doherty concluded he
was 'a very intelligent individual and would be quite capable of manufacturing the false accounts originally given by McBride', but again made no
mention of the evidence linking him to hoax extortion telephone calls, or
to the phone call from Garda John O'Dowd's home.

Lennon then noted that he had met with Dr Barry and Professor John
Harbison, stating that 'from the views expressed by Dr Harbison I am
now satisfied that Richard Barron was murdered'. There was no mention
of the cancelled application for an exhumation order in October.

Finally, Lennon noted that a number of 'simultaneous investigations'
were running in parallel, including 'attempts by Billy Flynn to pervert the

course of justice', 'threatening and abusive phone calls made by Billy Flynn', the extortion calls to the Peoples, 'in excess of thirty summonses' against the McBreartys and their staff 'in relation to breaches of public order', and 'six files in relation to serious assault either within or in the precincts of the premises' owned by Frank. Once again, there was no mention of William Doherty's link to the phone calls to the Peoples, or the suspected link between O'Dowd and the phone calls.

Under the heading of 'current developments', the superintendent wrote that 'a further witness is now being sought that can state that he saw Mark McConnell leaning on a windowsill' outside the Town & Country pub at 7.40 a.m. the morning after Richie died. Not surprisingly, no such witness was ever found.

'It is now beginning to emerge that Mark McConnell may have left the Town & Country public house in the company of Michael Peoples earlier that night around the crucial time', Lennon continued, despite evidence to the contrary. In closing, he noted briefly that Richie Barron 'had an intense interest in horses' and bet large sums at 'flapping' races. This was being looked at 'with a view to establishing if he had acquired any enemies as a result'.

After fourteen months, thousands of Garda work hours, hundreds of statements and several arrests, but with no charges yet brought, Lennon concluded he was 'satisfied with the present pace of the investigation', although he appreciated 'the extraordinary amount of Garda time that has been committed'.

———

The 'second investigation' continued at its sedate pace until the end of the year. On 17 December, Detective Sergeant John White interviewed Liam Sweeney. Sweeney had already spoken to Sergeant Joe Hannigan in November 1996, and told him he left the Suile Tavern along with barman Eugene Gamble 'around 1 a.m.' the night Barron died. He went to Sarah's Café to get some food, then met up with Stephen and Ann McCullagh, who were standing outside the Suile when he got back. They told him Richie Barron was 'knocked down in a hit and run', and they drove up to the scene. Sweeney said he 'didn't see Mark McConnell that night'.

On 20 April 1997, Sweeney's friend Eugene Gamble had a row with the McBreartys, which eventually led to a court case. Gamble made a statement to White on 30 November 1997, which the Morris tribunal concluded 'was calculated to undermine Mr McConnell's credibility'. Now, Sweeney told White he was 'not exactly sure' what time he left the Suile Tavern, and 'did not say to Sergeant Hannigan that I did not see Mark

McConnell that night because I did see him. Mark McConnell was in Sarah's Café when I went into it with Eugene Gamble.' Sweeney told Detective Sergeant White he remembered 'the area of his pants and down the backs of his legs of his pants was wet'.

He said he 'did not mention this to Sergeant Hannigan at the time that he took the statement off me because I did not see any importance in it'. Later, Sweeney told White he 'did not mention to anyone that I saw Mark McConnell in Sarah's Café that morning. I did not ever discuss what we did or what I saw that night with Eugene Gamble in the last months.' Justice Morris rejected Liam Sweeney's second statement because of the 'flat contradictions' with his earlier statement to Sergeant Hannigan.

———

Early in the New Year, on 5 January 1998, Bronagh Laird told Detective Garda Joe Foley she travelled to Raphoe 'after 1 a.m.' the night Richie Barron died, along with her sister-in-law, Wilma Laird. Her brief statement corroborated Wilma Laird, the witness tracked down by Billy Flynn who told Gardaí she saw Mark and Roisin McConnell in Sarah's Café after 1 a.m.

Two days later, on 7 January 1998, the only meeting between the old and new investigation teams took place, to compare notes for the preparation of a defence to the civil cases expected from the McBreartys for wrongful arrest.

The meeting had to address what Lennon by now must have believed was an impossible task. Despite the fact that he'd told David Lombard in the DPP's office in October that he would 'have difficulty sustaining a defence' to the civil cases, he had to justify the arrests of twelve people. Lennon was dealing with the criminal files with his 'second investigation' team, while Detective Superintendent Joe Shelly was handling the civil files.

'The civil team will have to interview members who dealt with any prisoners during arrest and detention. Arising from the civil actions it will have to be fully set out that the arrests were justified and the detentions were also justified,' the meeting was told.

'All members will have to make statements that arrested persons were not abused etc. Every single factor that justified arrest should be outlined in relevant statements. The arresting member should state all the facts on which he could ground his suspicions.'

In his March 1998 report on the Barron case, Lennon would note that nine people 'were arrested for being accessories after the fact to murder. Although no High Court actions have been lodged to date, it is my view we will have difficulty in sustaining a defence should they file claims at a future date, as the grounding suspicions for these arrests appear to be somewhat obscure and lacking in supporting evidence.' Effectively, Lennon acknowledged in his report on the criminal cases that the arrests were probably groundless.

————

On 14 January 1998, John O'Dowd handed over a telephone bill to Detective Inspector John McGinley, showing a telephone call from his home to Michael Peoples on 9 November 1996, just as Billy Flynn had said it would. Telecom Eireann searches still had not produced the same information, despite several Garda requests. In its report, the tribunal would criticise the 'utterly appalling miasma of delay [which] stymied legitimate investigations by An Garda Síochána', which it blamed on a lack of oversight as the company geared up for privatisation.

A week after handing in his phone bill, Garda John O'Dowd submitted a statement in an attempt to deal with the hoax extortion phone call. O'Dowd said the first he became aware of any allegation was when Peoples showed him a letter written to Ms Helen Cullen in the office of the DPP on 24 June 1997. 'I did not make any telephone calls from my home to Mr Peoples and neither am I aware who did this,' O'Dowd claimed. He claimed he had no memory of the night of the calls but had checked Garda station records which showed he was in Raphoe until 10.30 p.m. that night. The forged station records were his alibi.

O'Dowd went on to say that no one else had a key to his home, and claimed that he was threatened by Old Frank McBrearty on 28 October 1998, and afterwards 'noticed interference' on his phone line, including 'clicking noises'. He said he reported the 'interference' to Garda communications centre, and later cancelled his telephone account with Telecom Eireann because of 'persistent calling' by Billy Flynn.

O'Dowd claimed he 'lost faith in the confidentiality' of his phone line, and also that his girlfriend's parents 'received numerous silent phone calls in the middle of the night', and that his own parents in Sligo 'received a call from a man I believe to be Mr William Flynn'. His parents had also received 'a number of silent phone calls'.

'I have on numerous occasions since I received the document from Michael Peoples offered myself for interview to sort this matter out as I feel I am being unfairly left in Limbo and have to suffer derogatory remarks from persons who are presently under investigation in relation to the murder of Richard Barron,' O'Dowd complained.

O'Dowd's statement was designed to waste Garda time, without addressing the key issue, the telephone call that his telephone records plainly showed was made from his home. To process the statement properly, Garda time would be wasted taking statements from O'Dowd's parents, his girlfriend's parents, Billy Flynn, and Letterkenny Garda communications centre, in addition to time spent with Telecom Eireann engineers, investigating complaints of 'interference', 'clicking noises' and 'silent phone calls'. Over the years, O'Dowd would continue to obstruct and prevaricate, frustrating investigations by the Carty team and the Morris tribunal until his Damascan conversion in 2004.

————

Detective Sergeant Sylvie Henry arrested Gazza Gallagher on 11 February 1998 on foot of a series of outstanding bench warrants. On the way to the station, Gazza told him he'd lied about being given £500 by Young Frank the night Richie Barron died. Henry had suspected as much since he'd first heard the story from Gazza when he visited him in Mountjoy prison in November 1996, so it came as no surprise. However, Gazza stuck to his claims that he'd been told to burn his car by Young Frank, and his claims about the billhook. It would take years for the Carty team and Morris tribunal to peel away the layers of lies covering the truth.

————

Superintendent Kevin Lennon sent his final report on the Richie Barron investigation to the DPP on 2 March 1998. Copies were sent to Crime Branch in Garda HQ, the Assistant Commissioner for the Northern Region in Sligo, and Chief Superintendent Denis Fitzpatrick.

Kevin Lennon knew the statement of admission from Young Frank McBrearty was a cockup. Clearly Frank McBrearty Junior and Mark McConnell had been set up for a murder that they didn't commit— indeed a murder that never happened. 'My view was this,' he told the Morris tribunal. 'I had an obligation to those people to be balanced and fair and upfront and up the middle, to investigate properly a position that would clearly, at the end of the day, make them clearly people who did not kill Richard Barron . . . As a senior officer of the Garda Síochána, I was obliged to do this. I have a conscience too and I'm not going to see a man framed for a murder that he didn't commit, under no circum-stances. And I'll go to my maker at the end of a day as an honest broker, knowing that I cleared Frank McBrearty and Mark McConnell of the death of Richard Barron.'

Lennon didn't quite clear McBrearty and McConnell. The one thing missing from the Barron investigation report, the one thing

Superintendent Lennon could not say out loud—even if he believed it as he claimed at the tribunal—was his personal conclusion: Frank McBrearty and Mark McConnell were innocent. Lennon could never go so far as to suggest that Gardaí obtained a false confession or pursued innocent families. But the report to the DPP, while avoiding head-on criticism of the Garda investigation, and going to great lengths to identify them as suspects, highlighted the problems in the Garda case methodically. It is a report designed to make the DPP decide against taking a prosecution. Even so, Lennon's report highlighted the accounts given by Carmel Connolly and Philomena Laird, the workers in Sarah's Café who initially said they saw Mark McConnell around 12.30 a.m. The reports were described as reliable accounts. There was no mention of the fact that the times these two witnesses gave could be unreliable, and Wilma Laird is not even mentioned in the report. Wilma Laird, tracked down by Billy Flynn, established that Mark McConnell was not in the café until after 1 a.m.

Lennon told the Morris tribunal that if he had written what he really thought in his report to the DPP, that his 'second investigation' was stymied from the start by the planned exhumation being cancelled, he 'wouldn't have lasted two hours in Letterkenny Garda Station'.

'I'd have been gone out of it overnight. That's the way the Garda Síochána work. I was not going to condemn the Chief Superintendent in that report as my senior officer who had dictated policy and procedure to me and who had undermined my investigation.'

Chapter 30
The Three Stooges

Bernard Conlon was annoyed. As a late night patron in Frankie's nightclub, he believed he was entitled to a free meal, but there was no food on offer. He complained to one of the bouncers, but got nowhere. The bouncer told him he could go across the road to the café if he was hungry.

Fuming, Bernard stormed out of the nightclub. Standing in the street, he spotted a Garda directing traffic in the Diamond. He went to complain. The Garda was Sergeant John White. The time, the early hours of 20 July 1997.

White took down the details of Conlon's complaint in his notebook. It was a condition of late night licensing laws at the time that meals as well as drinks had to be served to patrons. If Frank was cutting corners on the meals, it was one more piece of official paper the sergeant could serve on the troublesome publican.

Conlon was small-time. Born in Trim, Co. Meath, in 1956, he moved to Sligo in 1992, and lived on the Cartron Bay estate just outside the town. The youngest of seven children, he'd attended a special school for the learning disadvantaged in Navan, and got his first job working as a farmhand on leaving school. Bernard seemed to take well to animal husbandry, but soon the animals under his care fell to a mysterious illness.

James Mulligan hired Bernard Conlon on a month's trial to work on his farm in 1981. Conlon was there about three weeks when one day he came in and told Mulligan a calf wouldn't drink, and 'it was funny the way its tongue was hanging out'.

While Mulligan waited for the vet to arrive, Conlon told him a second animal had also taken ill. 'I found this animal lying out stretched on the ground, lifting up its head, banging its head on the ground,' Mulligan recalled later at the Morris tribunal.

When the vet examined the first calf, he found it had a broken jaw. It had to be put down as it could not feed itself. The vet suspected the second animal had meningitis. That evening, a third animal took ill. Again, the vet suspected meningitis.

Later that week, Mulligan took an animal to Abbotstown central veterinary research laboratory to be examined. The scientists discovered it had been struck on the head. More animals took sick, unable to stand up, and by now the veterinarian was growing suspicious.

The vet told Mulligan 'it's that man of yours', and said he'd seen Conlon on another farm where there were problems too. He was beginnning to suspect the symptoms initially diagnosed as meningitis were due to poisoning. 'If I only knew what he gave them', he told the worried farmer, adding that he suspected the toxin was paraquat.

Conlon was eventually prosecuted and pleaded guilty. He said at his trial he had a grudge against Mulligan because he was underpaid, paid irregularly, underfed and overworked.

Mulligan reacted with indignation to the charges. He produced cancelled cheques which showed Conlon was paid his agreed wage regularly. 'If he was underfed so were we,' said Mulligan. 'We were all sitting at the same table at the same time eating the same food.' He said Conlon's work was 'exactly the same as the rest of us. I never asked anyone to do anything I wasn't doing myself. And he had every second weekend off as agreed.'

'We were very lucky, anything that happened, it was outside in the yard, not inside the house,' Mulligan reflected.

Over the next ten years, Bernard was in and out of trouble with the law, the most serious offence leading to a four-year sentence when he was look-out man on a robbery in Kells. A family of four was tied up while their house was robbed. By the time he moved to Sligo in the early 1990s, he had accumulated thirteen convictions on over 100 charges.

When Bernard Conlon moved to Sligo following his release from prison on the robbery charge, he stayed at first in a local hostel. It wasn't long before he came to the attention of the local law. A wallet belonging to a German student went missing in the hostel, and the Gardaí were called in. The case was easily solved, and on 3 October 1992 Conlon received a suspended sentence, another in his long list of offences.

After his first brush with the law at the hostel, Conlon managed to stay out of trouble in Sligo. He moved to Cartron Bay, where he lived on his Disability Allowance. He made himself useful to his landlord, Ben Maguire, a local building contractor who had built the Cartron Bay estate, and still owned several of the houses there. Bernard did occasional favours for his landlord, collecting rents, doing odd jobs around the place, minding the estate and keeping an eye on some cattle Maguire owned outside the town, acting as an informal caretaker.

Conlon became a familiar face in the local Garda station in Sligo, where he regularly called to report any trouble at the estate, whether it was a spot of vandalism or strange faces hanging around. He got to know several of the Guards there, particularly, it seems, Garda John Nicholson.

Questioned by solicitor Tom Murphy at the tribunal, Nicholson confirmed that Conlon 'gave information to members in Sligo', but that 'things that were passed on turned out to be untrue'. One detective in Sligo described Conlon as a 'police groupie', who 'wanted to get on with Gardaí and impress Gardaí'.

––––

As John White chatted with Bernard Conlon while he took down his complaint over his missing meal in the middle of the Raphoe Diamond, it didn't take long to establish a rapport. Naturally affable, Conlon spoke easily about the Guards he knew in Sligo, and they soon discovered they had a mutual acquaintance in Garda John Nicholson. White had met Nicholson during Mark McConnell's second arrest the previous month.

The same night, John White wrote out thirteen summonses in the Parting Glass for breaches of the Intoxicating Liquor Act and public order offences. By now, the McBreartys were sinking under the weight of summonses from the local Gardaí.

The previous weekend, on 13 July, eight summonses were written up following an inspection of the business. The summonses were added to the growing pile on Old Frank's desk. There were two from 21 June, one for threatening and abusive behavior on 14 June, seven each from 11 May, 27 April, 20 April, and 14 April, one from 17 March, nine from 23 February, two each from 29 January and 25 January, six from 19 January, six from 12 January, six from 6 January, and six on Christmas Day 1996.

Most of the summonses were for various breaches of the Liquor Licensing Act, a few were for alleged Public Order offences (abusive, threatening or insulting behaviour) by members of the family or the bouncers, and there were a handful of careless driving charges made by Darcy Connolly against Young Frank and related applications to have him bound to the peace. In total, Frank and his family and employees had accumulated ninety-one summonses in nine months, including those written on 20 July 1997, many of them multiple summonses under different sections of the Intoxicating Liquor Act from a single inspection at the nightclub.

As Conlon remembered it, Sergeant White contacted him again within a few days of their first late night meeting in the Diamond. They spoke about the McBreartys, and about the Barron case. The stage was set. Bernard would have his revenge on the McBreartys for denying him a feed, and help a powerful Guard into the bargain. The plan was straightforward. Conlon would make sure he had drink in front of him when the Guards inspected the nightclub, and give evidence in court that he was served alcohol after hours.

In early August, White was transferred to the Detective Branch in Letterkenny. However, he still took a keen interest in Raphoe. White by now was also in charge of preparing the prosecution files in the Barron case file, having taken over the task from Sergeant Marty Moylan.

The station party in Raphoe had been beefed up since October 1996, when only Padraig Mulligan was on duty on a fateful weekend night, with a Lifford patrol car scheduled to drop by at 2 a.m. to help clear the crowds when the nightclub closed. Then, the only Guards stationed in the town were O'Dowd, Mulligan, Collins and Sergeant Joe Hannigan. In addition to Sergeant Sarah Hargadon, Garda Shaun Barrett, Garda Noel Keavney and Garda Eamon Doherty had all been transferred to the town since the New Year. Hargadon had transferred to the town in June, her first posting on her promotion. It came as a relief to her to get a local posting, she'd worried that she might be transferred out of the county to the Garda training college in Templemore. Her orders in Raphoe were to police the nightclub strictly.

In the battle of wits between the publican and the Guards, Frank McBrearty had a secret weapon. He had installed an 'early warning system', he admitted at the Morris tribunal a decade later. Closed circuit cameras warned the doormen when the Guards were on the way. A flick of a switch, and a strobe light went off behind the bar. By the time the Guards were inside the building, the shutters were down, the bar closed. By placing a witness—Bernard Conlon—who would testify he was sold drink after legal trading hours on the premises, White could secure a conviction against the nightclub. Also involved in the plan was Sligo Garda John Nicholson, who delivered messages to Conlon from White. Shortly before 3 a.m. on Sunday 31 August 1997 Garda John O'Dowd asked Garda Shaun Barrett and Garda Noel Keavney to make the inspection in the nightclub. As a result, they discovered Bernard Conlon, who told them he had been served drink after hours. The tribunal was also suspicious that Garda John O'Dowd was aware of the plan to create a witness in Bernard Conlon.

———

Bernard Conlon stood out from the crowd. He wore a white cardigan, a white shirt, white corduroy trousers and a loud red tie. Garda Noel Keavney was later asked if Bernard Conlon's distinctive outfit struck him as strange. 'Not necessarily,' he replied drily. 'It's a country and western place.'

When the Guards approached, Conlon helpfully pointed out Eamonn McConnell as the barman he said had served him drink after hours, at about 2.30 a.m. As a result of the inspection, six summonses were served on Old Frank for breaches of the licensing laws. Andy McBrearty and Eamonn McConnell were also written up for aiding and abetting.

The total of summonses written against the McBrearty family and their employees since October 1996 now stood at ninety-nine. By 31 December 1997, there were 117 summonses outstanding against the McBreartys and associated families, their employees and their patrons.

The court cases against the McBrearty family were mounting up. In December 1997, two student Gardaí were sent undercover to the Parting Glass, Hargadon remembered. There was a proposal to mount video surveillance which led to an undercover Garda videotaping the bar serving drink after hours using a camera hidden in her handbag. Near the end of December, Hargadon got back from a patrol in Raphoe one evening to discover Kevin Lennon and John White inside the Garda station, poring over the occurence books. White was no longer stationed in Raphoe, and shouldn't have had a key. The incident bothered Hargadon, and she spoke to Sergeant Joe Hannigan. 'I changed the locks to secure the station, so that I knew then who was coming in and out of the station,' she told the tribunal.

Early in 1998, 'Detective Garda' Bernard Conlon (as he claimed White called him) received his summons to appear in Letterkenny District Court on 9 March as a prosecution witness against Frank McBrearty and the Parting Glass nightclub. Bernard was not called to give evidence—the case was adjourned following legal arguments from the McBrearty legal team. Conlon was called back again on 27 April and 28 April 1998, and again on 25 May 1998 and 26 May 1998, while the legal arguments went on.

By now, the Barron investigation against the McBreartys had disintegrated, and the Letterkenny district was in disarray. The false statement by Noel McBride had been uncovered, and Billy Flynn had discovered witnesses who backed up the McConnells' account of their movements. John O'Dowd had turned over his phone records in January, conceding that a hoax extortion call was made to Michael Peoples from his home, even if he still denied knowing how it was made. Raphoe was divided. Mark McConnell had been assaulted twice, suffering a broken leg and broken jaw. Kevin Lennon's report on the Barron investigation, finally submitted in March 1998, recommended no prosecution.

––––

Letterkenny Court House is a modern building, but even so it can get cramped on court days as Guards, solicitors, barristers, witnesses, defendants and interested members of the press and public move around. By the spring of 1998, the McBreartys were using the court system to fight back against the Guards. As the summonses piled up, their legal team consolidated the apparently unrelated cases of licensing breaches, driving offences, and breaches of the peace into a single tranche of cases, and used their court time to argue that the summonses were symptomatic of a 'wider issue', namely an official campaign of harassment. Conlon attended every hearing as a witness, rewarded each time with inflated expense claims.

The consolidation of the summonses led to even more crowded courts than usual in Letterkenny. Members of the McBrearty, McConnell, Peoples and other families attended to watch the progress of the cases, while the Barrons were joined by William Doherty, Darcy Connolly and other friends who showed support. Clashes were inevitable as emotions boiled over inside and outside the courtrooms.

On 26 May 1998, Garda Eamonn Doherty took a written statement from Bernard Conlon after the lunchtime break. Doherty recorded in a statement afterwards that Conlon alleged that a member of the extended Barron family 'was verbally abused by a man with the goatie and the lilac shirt and tracksuit bottoms'. The man Conlon identified was Mark McConnell. The same day, members of both the McBrearty and Barron families made statements to Garda Doherty and Garda John O'Dowd, each claiming they were on the receiving end of threatening and harassing behaviour by the other side. Faced with a list of accusations and counter-accusations from the warring clans, Garda Doherty wasn't sure what to do. He wrote out the summonses. The judge could sort it out. Doherty went to Superintendent Kevin Lennon, who was in the court, and to Detective Sergeant John White, and told them about the complaints that Conlon had made.

Conlon wasn't called to give evidence in May 1998. The case hearing was postponed once more, and he was called back between 1 June and 4 June, and again from 22 to 24 June. Yet again, the case was postponed.

After his May court appearance, John White arranged for Bernard Conlon to get expenses, sending in a claim for his court appearances in March, April and May. Attached to the paperwork was a certificate confirming that Bernard missed his work as a caretaker because he attended the court as a witness, and lost £40 per day in wages as a result. The signature was a forgery. A few weeks later, a second claim for expenses followed. Again it contained a certificate for lost earnings, covering Bernard Conlon's court appearances on 23 and 24 June as a witness. This too was a forgery.

Sligo Garda John Nicholson would claim he had nothing to do with the forgeries. He told the inquiry that he had tried to reach Conlon's boss to get the certificates to submit for Conlon's claim, but couldn't find him. There was a sense of urgency about the mission, he said, because John White needed the paperwork finished quickly in order to pay Conlon's claim. Nicholson told another Garda, John Keogh, that he was trying to get in touch with Conlon's boss.

A while later, Nicholson claimed, Garda Keogh returned and handed him a certificate. Nicholson told the tribunal he 'didn't ask any questions', yet somehow he was also able to say that 'the other man didn't write it either'.

Garda John Keogh died in 2000. His widow Kathleen travelled to the Morris tribunal in Dublin to defend her husband's reputation in October 2005. 'John was a very honest man, he was honest in his dealings with everybody,' she told the tribunal. 'If he couldn't do you a good turn he wouldn't do you a bad turn.

'He took his job very seriously. He took great pride in his work. He was very honest. If any of the children did anything wrong, if they took 20p off the table, they had to account for it, that was his level of honesty.

'I feel that because my husband is dead, he is being used in the scheme of things to cover up for the wrongdoing of members of the Garda Síochána . . . Because he can't talk, he seems to have been blamed for these documents. I firmly believe he had nothing whatsoever to do with this. He was so honest and treated his profession as a Garda with the highest respect. I want his name cleared and that we his family can leave him to rest in peace.'

After Mrs Keogh made her emotional plea, two handwriting experts gave evidence. Having examined the handwriting and signatures on the forged certificates, they were able to say that Garda Keogh's writing appeared on none of the certificates. Despite his denials, the experts said that Nicholson was the probable forger of at least four signatures, out of a total of seven forgeries they examined. 'In my opinion John Nicholson wrote the four questioned signatures,' said James Nash, an independent expert formerly with the Garda Technical Bureau.

The experts also felt Nicholson was possibly the forger of a fifth certificate, the first forgery submitted in May 1998, but could not give a definitive opinion because they only had access to a photocopy, not the original.

Justice Frederick Morris called Nicholson's attempt to blame the late Garda John Keogh, who could no longer defend his name 'a mean spirited and self-serving pretence with which he persisted in the face of clear evidence contradicting his testimony'.

Just after midnight, as Monday 20 July moved into Tuesday 21 July, Bernard Conlon's flatmate Tony Doyle arrived home to find his friend sitting alone in the dark. Bernard told him he'd just had a visit from two men who called him an informer and threatened his life if he gave evidence against the McBreartys. The men also threatened Detective

Sergeant John White, he claimed, showing him a 'silver coloured bullet' and saying 'There is one for you and one for White.' Conlon would later identify Michael Peoples and Mark McConnell as the men who delivered the threat. The blatant lie would lead to the arrest of both men.

When the Carty team interviewed him later, Bernard Conlon said he met John White in a Donegal District Court that day. According to Conlon, White indicated Mark McConnell and Michael Peoples, and pointed two fingers towards the ground, meaning there was £200 if he made the false allegation. There was no court sitting in Donegal on 20 July 1997.

Doyle called the Garda station, and Detective Garda Michael Reynolds and Detective Sergeant Gerry Connolly called out and spoke to Conlon.

There are oddities in Conlon's statement. The context is clear, Conlon and White are being threatened because of their involvement in the licensing case against Frankie's. He describes the first man as 'a stout lump of a lad with scraggy hair and a goatee whisker, about 5' 7" and aged between 22 and 25.' However, despite telling the detectives he was 'almost certain I saw this lad in the Court House in Letterkenny the last time I attended', Conlon never mentioned the complaint he made to Garda Eamonn Doherty about his previous encounter involving Mark McConnell ('the man with the goatee') on 26 May.

The description of Michael Peoples doesn't quite gel. In fact the initial description of the second man, as recorded by Detective Garda Michael Reynolds is apparently of a 5' 6" tall man. By the time the formal statement was taken the following evening, the second man had grown to 'about 5' 9" having black hair cut tight ... [and] had a stud or an ear ring in one of his ears'.

According to his custody record from 4 December 1996, Michael Peoples is 6' 2" tall. He didn't wear an earring or ear-stud. When Peoples gave evidence to the tribunal about his arrest, he told the inquiry he believed the description was that of one of the bouncers employed at the Parting Glass.

When Detective Sergeant Gerry Connolly contacted Letterkenny to tell them about Conlon's allegation, Superintendent Lennon told him the description of the man with the goatee 'sounded like Mark McConnell'.

Connolly asked Lennon if he could put him in touch with a Guard who could set up some sort of informal ID, and Lennon gave him John White's name. When Connolly got in touch with White and told him Lennon thought Mark McConnell could be a suspect, White agreed that 'it could be him'.

Two and a half months after he made his 'silver bullet' complaint, Bernard Conlon travelled to Donegal with Detective Sergeant Gerry Connolly and Detective Garda Michael Reynolds on 1 October 1998.

Conlon's mission was to identify the man he said threatened him with a silver bullet. The word from Donegal was that the description of one of the men fitted Mark McConnell, and Mark was going to Letterkenny court that day to watch the case arising from one of the assaults he'd suffered earlier in the year. Detective Sergeant John White arranged to meet the Sligo detectives in a restaurant outside Letterkenny, and to guide them to the court house where McConnell was expected.

Mark had been told by Detective Thomas Kilcoyne that his assailants were going to plead guilty, but by now, having been wrongly arrested twice, he was suspicious and wanted to see the outcome himself.

'I stopped to speak to somebody just at the car park at the bottom of Justice Walsh Road and my father went on up to the court,' Mark recalled. 'While I was walking up the hill towards the court house and walking in the door a Guard stopped me from behind, and again he might have asked me my name and I told him. He said that he was arresting me for a firearms offence in Sligo and he named the date. I was completely shocked to tell the truth as well. Another bolt out of the blue.'

Gerry Connolly was the arresting Garda. Because the allegation involved a bullet, the arrest was for an offence under the 1925 Firearms Act. This was a scheduled offence under the 1939 Offences Against The State Act, a law designed to counter the IRA. The special powers of the anti-terrorism legislation meant Mark could be held for up to forty-eight hours, instead of the usual twelve hours allowed under the 1984 Criminal Justice Act.

'I tried to get out of Gerry Connolly what I was being arrested for . . . I pleaded with him that I had nothing to do with it and I asked them had they families of their own, had they children and wives of their own, and how could they not see what was going on here in Donegal, and they just told me to keep quiet and took me to the Garda station.'

Early in the day, Mark McConnell made an allegation of assault against one of the detectives who tapped his shoulder during an interview. 'What I was really doing at that stage was marking the cards of the Guards that were interviewing me,' he told the tribunal. 'Joe Foley just came in and he just went like that to my shoulder and says, "How's it going Mark?" It was really nothing. And what I was doing was marking the ground. Again I didn't want to go through a whole day of being assaulted like I was in the first interview. But I really took nothing out of it to tell you the truth. It wasn't an assault.'

Foley had simply intended to reassure Mark McConnell during the interview. As soon as Mark made the allegation of assault, he contacted Garda Martin Finan, the custody officer. Finan went to the interview room and Mark 'stated he was struck on the shoulder'. Finan asked Mark if he wanted a doctor. Mark told him he was fine. Later, when Dr

McColgan was brought to the room, Mark told him 'it was all a joke'. He told the doctor the only injury he had was the scar on his leg, an old wound. Mark withdrew the assault allegation against Detective Garda Foley the next day, before his release from custody. The tribunal felt that it was motivated as much by his anger at being wrongly arrested for the third time as by any fear that he would be mistreated if he did not lay down a 'marker'.

Either way, with the 'marker' down, Mark had established that he would not tolerate any mistreatment. After his first ordeal, he would make sure his questioning was by the book. The complaint was harsh on Joe Foley, but Mark, arrested for the third time for something he didn't do, was taking no chances.

Mark's leg gave him bother throughout the arrest. It had been broken when he was assaulted several months earlier, and he was still in pain. He'd mentioned the injury to the Guards as early as his first interview. 'You think a man with a metal plate in his leg would go to Sligo and threaten him?' he asked Connolly and Detective Garda PJ Keating.

As time wore on, Mark's leg bothered him more from the long interview sessions. 'I could feel my leg starting to get the pins and needles again that I was being affected with because of the injury and the stiffness and I put my leg up on the chair,' he recalled.

Gerry Connolly and Michael Reynolds were in the room with him at the time. Mark argued with the detectives, pointing out the flaws in their investigation as they put the accusation to him—he'd learned a lot about police procedures since his first arrest. He thought Connolly was giving Bernard Conlon way too much credibility. 'I pointed that out to him in interviews, pointed out the fact that there were no forensics done in the house. There was no roadblock put up to see if we could stop the culprits if they knew who they were. All these led to them getting severely frustrated throughout the interviews.'

Mark told the Morris tribunal that Reynolds had first asked him to put his leg down, and he had refused, explaining the problem with his recent injury. 'He said he didn't care. He took it as maybe arrogance on my behalf, or maybe he didn't believe it.'

Reynolds thought Mark had his leg up on the desk, not on a chair. 'I did request him to take it down and he muttered and reluctantly took it down,' he recalled. The tribunal concluded that Mark had exaggerated what happened, and Reynolds had done no more than ask him to remove his leg.

Mark gave as good as he got during the forty-eight hours he spent in Letterkenny. He pointed out the obvious holes in Conlon's story, and told the Sligo Guards the background to what was going on in Raphoe. He remembered his band had been on tour from 12 July, and played their last

gig in Cookstown on Sunday 19 July. He got home at 7 a.m., woke Dean
to give him some toys he'd bought on the tours, and crashed out. After
that, he couldn't remember. He told them to check with Roisin what he
did on 20 July.

When his frustration at his third trumped-up arrest got to him, he hit
back. He told them it was time they copped themselves on. He told them
they could go with his solicitor to search his home—Conlon said he wore
a leather jacket and a brown T-shirt, and Mark owned neither. He told
them there was no point in sitting in an identity parade—Conlon had
seen him the morning of his arrest, and at the District Court sittings. An
identity parade would be a set-up. 'It must be some of the three stooges
that set him up,' he told Connolly and Reynolds, 'and ye two donkeys
were dragged into this.' The 'three stooges' he had in mind were Kevin
Lennon, John White and John O'Dowd, he said later.

Mark McConnell was arrested at 11.07 a.m. on 1 October. At 11 a.m. on
2 October, Chief Superintendent Denis Fitzpatrick extended his detention for a second day. After forty-eight hours he was finally let go.

After Mark McConnell was released, Conlon got more expenses.
Although he had travelled to Donegal in a Garda car, he was reimbursed
for a bus ticket, and another bogus certificate of earnings was sent in for
the trip.

————

The District Court cases dragged on. In December 1998, Judge O'Donnell
arranged for a special five-day sitting of the court to deal exclusively with
the cases against the McBreartys. The week-long hearing began on
Monday 7 December 1998. For the McBreartys, barrister Martin Giblin
complained that he still had not received various documents he had asked
for six months earlier, including a list of Bernard Conlon's convictions.
Gerry Connolly had faxed the typed list to Kevin Lennon in Letterkenny
back in July, but it had not been passed over to the defence lawyers.

During one of the hearings, Bernard Conlon approached Garda Tom
Ward and tapped him on the shoulder. He pointed out Michael Peoples,
and told the Garda that Peoples was one of the two men who had threatened him six months earlier. Peoples stood out from the crowd. He was
well over 6' tall and had a bandage on his left hand. Ward went over to
Garda Noel Keavney, who was stationed in Raphoe. Keavney told him the
man Conlon had identified was Michael Peoples.

Ward told Conlon to come to the Garda station at lunchtime and
make a statement. That evening, Ward typed up Conlon's statement,
made a statement of his own, and gave the file to the sergeant in charge
to forward to Sligo.

Bernard Conlon hung around the court for most of the week, waiting to give evidence. Martin Giblin had finally got sight of his criminal record, and couldn't wait to cross-examine him. That the Guards were relying on a petty criminal with a string of convictions in a licensing prosecution would show he was right about the 'wider issue' he'd complained to Judge O'Donnell about, particularly once he introduced the 'silver bullet' complaint, and showed how Mark McConnell was arrested in October on the word of the same dubious witness.

Giblin had no idea that Michael Peoples had also been identified by Conlon. There was no arrest after Conlon made his statement to Garda Ward. Meanwhile, Kevin Lennon knew how fragile Conlon might be under cross-examination, and did his best to keep him away from the witness box. When the Garda witnesses finished their evidence, the superintendent told the court he would not be calling Bernard Conlon. The defence lawyers objected immediately. They'd been told he would be called. After hearing legal arguments, Judge O'Donnell invited Kevin Lennon to present Conlon for cross-examination. Giblin and his team told the judge that the focus of their questions would be Conlon's character and credibility.

———

Conlon was scheduled as the first witness on the morning of Friday 11 December 1998. He decided he couldn't go through with it, and headed home to Sligo. Back in his home, Conlon got a phone call from John Nicholson. The Garda asked him about the case. Bernard didn't think it would go ahead, he expected another postponement. 'It's going ahead,' Nicholson told him.

Nicholson called to Conlon's house later in the evening. John White was in town, he told Conlon, and wanted to meet. Nicholson took Bernard to meet White, and they ended up at the back of the Garda station. White had a copy of Conlon's convictions, and the witness statement he'd made.

'McBrearty's Silk will go through you tomorrow morning,' White told him. 'He'll rip through you. You need to stick to your guns, Detective Conlon.' White went through the statement with Conlon, making sure he knew what to say the following morning, and gave him a sample of the kind of questions he'd face, and what to say in answer.

The following morning, Bernard Conlon finally gave evidence against the Parting Glass nightclub, Old Frank McBrearty, Andy McBrearty and Eamonn McConnell. 'Detective Conlon' stuck to his story, but felt under 'a bit of pressure' as Martin Giblin challenged his story. There are no

transcripts in District Courts, but a Garda took notes each day, as did
Frank McBrearty's solicitor Ken Smyth. From those notes, a clear picture
of what happened emerges.

Superintendent Lennon did not ask Conlon any questions about the
night he was 'found on' in the Parting Glass. He simply asked him for his
name, and asked him to 'tell the court of any problems you may have had
with An Garda Síochána in the past, your previous convictions and your
clean sheet for six years'.

Martin Giblin began his cross-examination by going through Conlon's
convictions in more detail, the seven charges of burglary and house breaking, the six cheque fraud charges, false pretences, obtaining credit by
fraud, and larceny, ending with his conviction in Sligo for the hostel theft.

'Didn't you tell blatant lies about Mark McConnell?' Giblin asked.
Conlon said nothing.

'You made an allegation against Mr McConnell,' the barrister said.

'Yes. He called to my house and threatened me,' Conlon replied.

'When was that?'

'The twentieth of July 1998. It was a Monday night, I was watching television, there was a knock to the window, I opened the door and two men
were there.'

Kevin Lennon was on his feet, objecting. 'This matter is under Garda
investigation,' he told the judge.

'You can't ask about any events beyond fixing the date,' the judge told
Martin Giblin.

'What time did this happen?' the barrister asked Conlon.

'A quarter to midnight,' Conlon replied.

Superintendent Lennon again tried to object, and the judge repeated
that the barrister could ask Conlon when the event occurred.

'Mr McConnell was in Letterkenny that evening, he was seen by leading members of the legal profession,' Martin Giblin told Conlon.

'I'm only saying what happened that evening,' Conlon answered. 'I
made a statement.'

'Two leading members of the legal profession saw Mr McConnell
between 9.30 p.m. and 10.20 p.m. and spoke to him plus others,' the barrister persisted. 'Who put you up to making these allegations against Mr
McConnell?'

'No one.'

The barrister moved on, asking Conlon how often he visited Raphoe,
who he knew in the town, who he went to the Parting Glass with. Conlon
repeated his well-rehearsed story, how he'd first met Sergeant White
when he complained that he didn't get any chips, how he'd been 'found
on' several weeks later and gone to the Garda station in Sligo to make his
statement.

'I was approached, I met two Gardaí, they walked in, they approached me, a young uniformed Garda in a yellow jacket, there was another Garda with him. I was drinking at the bar, I saw them, he approached me, asked my name, they were on top of me before I knew where I was. They asked me for my name and address, I got upset and left. One of the barmen followed me out and said to go back in and tell the Gardaí you didn't know who sold the drink,' Conlon told the court.

The judge checked the clock. It was lunchtime. He warned Conlon not to speak to anyone during the break, since he had not completed his evidence. Conlon asked for two Gardaí to go with him over lunch.

After the break, Martin Giblin wanted to know why Conlon asked for the company of two Guards over lunch. 'What playacting are you at, asking for Gardaí to go with you?' he demanded.

'I requested it as I got staring faces at me. I have been abused and threatened since I came here,' Conlon replied.

'I suggest this is all lies,' Giblin countered.

'I'm under oath, I'm telling the truth,' Conlon said.

Giblin asked about the 'found on' again, and Conlon repeated his story. Conlon 'stuck to his guns', and denied he'd spoken to anyone about his statement before making it. Finally, he was done.

During his cross-examination, Bernard Conlon identified Mark McConnell as one of the two men he claimed showed up at his door with a silver bullet in July. Michael Peoples was sitting in the court at the time, but despite having identified Peoples to Garda Tom Ward earlier in the week, Conlon never mentioned that the second man who supposedly terrified him that night was sitting in the court. Giblin, meanwhile, had mentioned that Mark McConnell had a potential alibi from the night of the silver bullet, two 'leading members of the legal profession' who saw him seventy miles away in Letterkenny the same night.

Kevin Lennon and John White were in the court. Sligo was preparing the case file for the DPP at the time, and clearly the news that Mark McConnell had an alibi was relevant to the file. Yet no Garda approached Martin Giblin to ask him who these leading lawyers were, and whether they could make statements for the case file. If Mark McConnell had an alibi and wasn't in Sligo, Michael Peoples could hardly have been with him at the time. Michael Peoples had been identified in court by Conlon, something Lennon and White knew. Garda Ward had sent the statements to Sligo, and Michael Peoples faced imminent arrest. Lennon and White were happy to see more grief heading in the direction of Mark McConnell and Michael Peoples. Sligo was never told about the alibi.

On 25 January 1999, Mark McConnell wrote a letter complaining about his third arrest on the word of Bernard Conlon. He sent the letter to his solicitors, who forwarded it to the Garda Complaints Board.

Mark McConnell's complaint to his solicitor named Garda John O'Dowd, Detective Sergeant John White and Superintendent Kevin Lennon as the men he held responsible for his arrest on 1 October 1998—the 'three stooges' he had mentioned to Connolly and Reynolds while they questioned him.

The Complaints Board sent Chief Superintendent John Carey to take a statement following up on the letter. Mark had already been interviewed by Carey about his first arrest, and nothing had happened. He didn't see any point in going through the same rigmarole again, and told Carey he wouldn't make a statement.

————

On 19 January 1999, Detective Sergeant Gerry Connolly sent a seven-page report on the arrest of Mark McConnell to his superintendent, John Sheridan. Connolly reported that the only evidence against Mark McConnell was the informal identification outside Letterkenny court house, and while Mark McConnell had no previous convictions, Conlon had an armful of convictions. Connolly recommended no further action. On 27 January, Superintendent Sheridan forwarded the file to the Sligo State solicitor, and sent copies to Chief Superintendent Austin McNally and to Crime & Security in Dublin, because the case involved the Offences Against the State Act. The State solicitor forwarded the report to the DPP.

Michael Mooney from the Director's office wrote back on 24 February. Mooney found it 'extraordinary that anybody would go to such lengths to threaten a prosecution witness over a minor prosecution for breach of the licensing acts'. Mooney couldn't understand why the Gardaí needed Conlon as a witness. Since the two Guards who inspected the premises could give evidence in court anyway, threatening Conlon would achieve nothing.

Mooney felt that Conlon's statement read 'somewhat theatrically and has not the ring of reality about it', while Mark McConnell's answers when he was questioned were 'compelling and further call into question Conlon's credibility'.

————

Chief Superintendent Austin McNally was appointed to head up the Sligo Division in January 1999. While he was settling into his new post, what would become known as the Carty Team was put in place. The pressure from the McBreartys was creating ripples on several fronts. Their barristers kept asking awkward questions in the District Court, and the voluminous correspondence from Billy Flynn to the Garda Commissioner and Department of Justice couldn't be ignored. Fine Gael TD and opposition justice spokesman Jim Higgins was taking an interest in the case, and raising questions in the Dáil. Journalists like Frank Connolly were starting to pay attention. Assistant Commissioner Kevin Carty was appointed to head an investigation into what was going on with the Barron case in Donegal, in particular the allegation from Flynn that a hoax extortion phone call came from the home of a serving Garda, John O'Dowd. The Carty Team would be based in Sligo, and on 4 March 1999, Chief Superintendent McNally was put in charge of co-ordinating the Carty investigations into the Barron case and the extortion phone calls to Michael Peoples.

If Conlon's 'silver bullet' claim was extraordinary, his next allegation was simply bizarre. On 27 April 1999, Conlon claimed he got a visit at his home from Billy Flynn. In his statement to Sligo Inspector Michael Barrett and Garda Sergeant PJ Gallagher, he said that Flynn told him that 'one phone call to Frank McBrearty' was all it would take for Bernard to receive £10,000, provided he went to a solicitor and made a statement discrediting John White and John O'Dowd and withdrawing his evidence in the District Court. Conlon said he got a letter from Billy Flynn a few days later.

Flynn's letter made no mention of Frank McBrearty or Donegal. On its face, it related to a traffic accident in County Meath in 1996, which Flynn was investigating for another client. Flynn's letter said he had been given Conlon's name by a colleague, he needed someone 'with Navan connections and local knowledge', and he was willing to pay £5,000 for information that would lead to a conviction in the case.

There was no client in Navan. Flynn knew that Conlon was a witness against the nightclub in a licensing case, and had made a false accusation against Mark McConnell. He wanted to get a closer look at him. If Conlon took the bait, Billy could have someone arrange a meeting, chat to him for a few hours, and get an assessment of the man.

Included with the letter from Billy Flynn that Conlon handed in to Sligo Garda station was a second page, in a different font type and size to the original. Unlike the Flynn letter itself, it was typed on unheaded notepaper. It read in full: 'As I would like if you would agree to that which was discussed down town about White and O'Dowd. If you agree, I will ring Frank McBertie and will arrange for you to get the money. Thanking you, Bernard.'

Chief Superintendent Austin McNally couldn't make sense of the letter when he got it, particularly the second page. There was no mention of the McBreartys, or a bribe to change evidence, or anything else Conlon was claiming. 'I suppose, you know, was it a letter typed out by Bernard Conlon or a proposed reply, or whatever? I certainly had no reason to think otherwise,' he told the Morris tribunal. The letter was 'a mystery' to him.

There was one further oddity. Conlon described the bearded man who visited him and identified himself as 'Flynn from Enfield' as being in his 'late forties, about 5' 9" tall, heavy build, wearing flashy suit and tie, and dark suit'. The description doesn't fit Billy Flynn, who was clean-shaven at the time, and is significantly shorter than 5' 9". Conlon had described Tom Coffey, one of Flynn's investigators.

The 'second letter' is a Conlon invention, a clumsy attempt to bolster the ridiculous story of Flynn's visit that he told the Gardaí. On top of the clumsy construction, the misspelling of McBrearty as 'McBertie' is a give-away. Conlon frequently gets names wrong. Mark McConnell becomes Martin O'Connell, Michael Peoples becomes Michael Pimples, McBreartys become McBerties. The same spelling error appeared in a letter Conlon sent to the Garda Commissioner in 2003.

Superintendent McNally had enough to worry about already with the Carty investigations. The Donegal Gardaí were prosecuting Young Frank McBrearty in the Circuit Court for an alleged assault against Ed Moss. In addition, Sheenagh McMahon had come forward to the Carty team. The estranged wife of Detective Garda Noel McMahon, she told them an incredible story. Her husband, along with Kevin Lennon, had planted bogus home-made explosives in the months before the first IRA ceasefire, then claimed credit for the 'finds'. A series of spectacular finds, which Kevin Lennon claimed came about thanks to intelligence from their informant Adrienne McGlinchey, was nothing more than a hoax. McGlinchey wasn't an informant, she wasn't even a member of the IRA, and the 'finds' were designed simply to boost the two men's careers. The allegations, which Sheenagh was able to back up with documentation and examples of make-shift 'rocket launchers' salvaged from her husband's garden shed, opened up a second avenue of investigation for the Carty inquiry team. Ultimately, it would lead to Kevin Lennon's dismissal from the force.

The scenery was changing in Donegal. Kevin Lennon was transferred to Milford, while the Carty team investigated the allegations against him. John McGinley had been promoted, he was now a superintendent. Conlon's complaint could wait.

———

There was one loose end to the 'silver bullet' complaint. Conlon had identified Michael Peoples as the second man back in December 1998, but Peoples was never questioned. Gerry Connolly had approached Chief

Superintendent McNally about the case in March, but McNally postponed a decision, wanting to get a handle on the whole Donegal investigation with the Carty team first. By May, the detectives were ready to move.

Michael Peoples was arrested early in the morning of 6 May 1999. Chief Superintendent Austin McNally authorised the arrest, and Detective Sergeant Gerry Connolly travelled to Donegal the day before, along with two Detective Gardaí, Eddie McHale and Michael Reynolds.

Detective Garda Sean Herraghty and Detective Garda Noel Jones followed Michael Peoples as he left for work, and from there as he drove to the border town of Lifford. Jones kept in touch with Sligo Detective Sergeant Gerry Connolly by mobile phone, letting him know where Peoples was.

Michael Peoples spotted the red car following him as soon as he left his home that morning. He phoned his boss on his mobile phone and told him he was being followed. The boss called him back a few minutes later. 'Mick,' he told him, 'them two boys are not dole men, they're Guards and they want to speak to you.'

'I just thought, more of the same again,' Michael Peoples said later. 'I was shaking like a leaf with adrenalin. I jumped out of the van and the car just pulled up behind me.'

'We're doing a search,' the detectives told him.

As the detectives searched the van, Gerry Connolly arrived and arrested Michael Peoples under Section 30 of the Offences Against the State Act at 7.50 a.m. Under the provisions of the emergency powers legislation, Michael could be held for up to forty-eight hours. He was taken to Manorhamilton Garda station in Leitrim for questioning, sixty miles away. The tribunal decided that the choice of Manorhamiltion was made for 'sensible operational reasons', and not to intimidate or disorientate Michael.

Michael Peoples knew before Connolly showed up that he was going to be arrested. He was already on the phone to his family, trying to arrange for a solicitor as soon as possible. When he heard Connolly say 'Offences Against the State' and 'possession of ammunition', he realised what was going on. That was the same charge Mark McConnell had been picked up on. 'It's the Bernard Conlon thing,' Michael said into the phone.

'You're well informed, aren't you?' a Garda said to him.

'I need to be well informed with fuckers like you about,' Michael retorted.

Coincidentally, Young Frank McBrearty was due to give evidence the same day in the Ed Moss assault trial in Letterkenny. For some in Raphoe, the coincidence was too much to accept. As far as Michael Peoples was concerned, he was arrested on that date in part to rattle Young Frank before he took the stand in Letterkenny Circuit Court.

The Garda party and Michael Peoples arrived in Manorhamilton Garda station at 9.30 a.m. After processing, he was interviewed by Reynolds and McHale. 'The first interview was fairly straightforward,' Michael said later. 'Just more or less went through my whereabouts on the night, where I was on 20 July and I couldn't remember, I was trying to remember and they believed that I was there. Really that was it.'

The second interviewing team were Detective Garda Richard Caplice and Detective Garda Dominic Hunt. The pair had come up from Monaghan to interview Michael Peoples. Later in the year, they would get to know Donegal very well, when they became part of the 'Carty team'.

'The way the interview started, the two detectives come into the room,' Peoples remembered. 'Detective Hunt, he was sitting at the right-hand side, and Caplice, he was sitting directly in front of me. I don't even know how it started, the two started a shouting and roaring match, an arguing match with one another. It was—he was shouting and I was roaring. I don't even remember what they were shouting about to be quite honest.

'Dominic Hunt, roaring and shouting. I was shouting back. As much as he shouted at me, I shouted back at him. Then I think Caplice says, he says, "look, stop what you are at", he says, "you are impressing nobody". I just calmed down from there, I calmed down then.'

Hunt told the Morris tribunal he hadn't shouted at Michael, he had only raised his voice. As far as the judge was concerned, it was a distinction not worth making. Michael was understandably upset at his arrest, and things got heated for a while, but the heated exchange was not 'symptomatic of his overall treatment by the two Gardaí'.

With everyone calmed down, Caplice and Hunt got on with the interview. While Michael Peoples was questioned, other detectives showed up at his home in Raphoe with a search warrant. Among those present were Detective Sergeant James Fox and Inspector Hugh Coll, members of the Carty team. Michael had once owned a rifle, and still owned a shotgun at the time. At the Morris tribunal, Michael pointed out that if they had examined the gun cabinet, they would have found shotgun cartridges and some old .22 ammunition. Because they had not, this led him to conclude the Gardaí didn't believe Bernard Conlon.

Michael had been trying to remember where he was on 20 July 1998, and thought he might have been on army reserve training with the FCA in Castlebar. He told the two detectives to check it out. If he was there, it would prove he was innocent. In fact, his FCA training had finished on 18 July.

The interviews became a blur to Michael, the same questions and answers over and over. Where were you that night? I don't remember. Conlon says you and Mark McConnell threatened him. He's a liar, someone put him up to it.

The interviews began shortly before 9 a.m. on the second day. Michael was asked if he would take part in an identity parade. 'At this stage I had no belt in my trousers,' he said. 'I had no laces in my shoes and I wasn't shaved. I said, if I go into the ID room, I want the laces back, I want the belt back in my trousers and I want to have a shave and freshen up.

'I was in the ID room with no laces in my shoes, no belt in my trousers and I wasn't shaved. So, no matter what was going to happen I'd be picked out. I don't even know why I didn't protest, I just went ahead with it.

'There was none of them as tall as me. I would have been the tallest person in the room. There was a fella, I think he had red hair, and I walked in and I thought, I'm not standing beside you.

'Conlon, he was brought in. He walked along the line. Pointed to me and says to Detective Flannery: "That's the man who was at my house".

'Detective Garda Flannery, he came over and cautioned me then. I was kind of taken aback by the caution because I didn't really know what was happening. First off I thought it was a charge, the fact that he had picked me out and cautioned me, read out a caution to me. At this stage I wasn't sure what was going on around me and I was taken back then to the interview room.'

Michael's next memory was that as he was led back to the interview room, he was told: 'That's it. You were picked out. You can get seven years for that, boy, you can get seven years in Portlaoise.' The interview notes show that shortly after he arrived back in the interview room, Michael asked the detectives, 'Will I get charged for this? Tell the truth, what will I get?' When he spoke later to his solicitor Ken Smyth, Michael told him he'd been told he would be charged and get seven to ten years. The chairman said that it was likely that Michael was told he would get seven to ten years in response to his question to the detectives.

'I thought at this stage now I'm going up the line. I thought this was it. I was panicking. I was this, that and the other. I was frightened. It was annoying me. I thought I was going away. It worried me.'

Back in the interview room, Caplice and Hunt interviewed Michael Peoples again. 'I was panicking. I thought that was it,' Michael Peoples recalled. 'Seven years just was sitting in my mind at this stage. I was going to do seven years in jail. I just firmly believed it. The fact that he actually picked me out. It was panic stations at that stage, and that's being quite honest.'

Michael begged the detectives to believe him. He'd been nowhere near Conlon's home. Conlon was lying. Finally the Guards had managed to get in touch with Ken Smyth, who was tied up in Letterkenny with Young Frank's court case, and he spoke to the lawyer by phone. As Smyth listened and spoke to him, Michael Peoples calmed down. The solicitor told him the ID parade would be thrown out in court. Michael stood out like a sore thumb, unshaven and without belt or shoe laces, the ID parade would not be admissible. The important thing for Michael was to stay calm and not sign anything.

Michael Peoples got a visit from his mother in the afternoon, and a meal, before his next interview. During the afternoon, he was photographed, fingerprinted and palmprinted and again did his best to protest his innocence. Finally, after over thirty-nine hours in Garda custody, he was released.

In his report to the DPP, Detective Garda Michael Reynolds recommended no prosecution. The DPP agreed. However, the 'silver bullet' affair would ultimately lead to two convictions. Bernard Conlon was charged with three counts of making false statements to Gardaí, and given a three-year suspended sentence. John Nicholson was given the Probation Act after he pleaded guilty to four charges of uttering forged documents. John White was acquitted when the trial judge decided Bernard Conlon was not a credible witness. The Morris tribunal would agree. While it found evidence that White had used Conlon as an agent in a licensing prosecution, it simply couldn't trust his evidence that White also put him up to making the 'silver bullet' allegation.

By the time Michael Peoples was arrested, the McBrearty cases were attracting national attention. The mounting cases in the District Court weren't just getting local coverage in the Donegal newspapers, but in the national press. Frank Connolly, a journalist with the *Sunday Business Post*, had met the McBreartys and was doing everything he could to highlight their case.

The arrest of Michael Peoples in May 1999 would be the last. The tables were turning. On the same day that Michael Peoples was arrested, the *Irish Times* reported under the headline 'Inquiry on claims against Gardaí' that an Assistant Commissioner was appointed to investigate claims made against Gardaí in Donegal, including 'their methods of investigating crime' and attempts to 'frame two members of a Donegal family for the murder of a Donegal man'. In April the DPP had recommended no prosecution against Young Frank McBrearty and Mark McConnell after spending a year considering what to do with the Barron investigation report. But it still would be another year before Kevin Carty would complete his first investigation into Donegal, and send his file to Garda HQ.

Chapter 31

Information from
My Friend

O ld Frank McBrearty was at a low ebb. Despite questions in the Dáil and press coverage of what was happening in Donegal, many people still believed he had covered up a murder. Allegations of Garda corruption sounded like the ravings of a madman. Who would believe a Garda was involved in a harebrained blackmail plot? Or that a Superintendent planted fake bombs which he then 'discovered' to promote his career?

Frank McBrearty knew about those rumours. In the district courts of Donegal, his barristers were fighting several dozen summonses served by Gardaí. The lawyers had agreed what to do with the district court cases: first they would deal with each individual summons, then the lawyers would argue that they were part of a 'wider issue', an abuse of power, the systematic harassment of the family.

Meanwhile, an internal Garda inquiry headed by Assistant Commissioner Kevin Carty was looking into the reports coming from Donegal, and the Garda Complaints Board had received 61 complaints from the family. Finally, the barristers felt, they were getting somewhere in exposing what was going on.

In late June 2000, it all fell apart. The DPP announced that he was dropping all the charges in the District Court. On the one hand, it was a victory in their fight to clear their name. But it also meant that the lawyers couldn't argue the 'wider issue'.

Frank was disheartened. The Carty Inquiry seemed to be going nowhere, and the Garda Complaints Board lacked teeth. He had no faith in the ability of Guards to investigate Guards. Only a public inquiry could uncover the truth.

So it was, the Morris tribunal concluded, that Frank, working along with PJ Togher, a retired Garda, composed a letter which he faxed to Jim Higgins TD and his barrister, Martin Giblin, who contacted Brendan Howlin TD.

As it turned out, the allegations in the document, a mixture of 'half-truths, lies and rumours', were far off the mark. Ironically, having been arrested along with eleven others on the basis of a groundless rumour, Frank himself had used the same kind of baseless rumour in his search for justice.

———

The anonymously authored fax arrived in Jim Higgins' home around 9 p.m. He'd been expecting it—Old Frank McBrearty had called him earlier and told him he was sending something to him. It was Sunday, 25 June 2000 and Higgins, the Fine Gael Opposition spokesman on Justice, had known Frank for some time. The Mayo TD had first met the publican when he arrived at a constituency clinic looking for help. No politician in Donegal wanted to listen to Frank, so he'd travelled to Ballyhaunis.

The information in the fax, if true, was explosive. It claimed that two of the most senior Gardaí in the country, Assistant Commissioners Kevin Carty and Tony Hickey, were corrupt. Hickey had for a time been Assistant Commissioner in charge of the Northern Region, and Carty was at the head of an investigation into corruption claims in Donegal, arising out of complaints from Frank and his family. The fax said both men were compromised, and that Detective Sergeant John White had information on Carty that he could use to avoid being charged.

The allegations were investigated by senior Gardaí, and later by investigators working for the Morris tribunal. Neither investigation found any evidence to support any of the claims made in the anonymous fax.

When Higgins got the fax, he phoned Frank McBrearty and asked where the information had come from. Frank told him it came from 'my friend'—a coded reference to PJ Togher, a retired Garda who worked for him. Frank was convinced his telephone line was bugged by Gardaí, and never referred by name to Togher on the phone.

'I believed that Mr Togher was in fact the source and the author of the document,' Higgins would later tell the Morris tribunal. However, Frank McBrearty disputed his claim and said he never knew the identity of the informant as he'd received the anonymous letter in the post. He retorted that he never used coded language in case his telephone was tapped, and often said during phone calls 'If you're listening, kiss my backside' to show he had nothing to hide.

The same night, Labour Party TD Brendan Howlin received much the same information in a telephone call from Martin Giblin SC, the barrister acting for the McBrearty family. 'In essence I placed my trust in a very senior criminal lawyer whose character I had checked,' Howlin told the tribunal.

'The issue was, my source of information was somebody of substance, whom I trusted and whom I had checked to be trustworthy. And secondly, if the information that was imparted to me resulted in this tribunal, I think the first five reports of it were well justified, justified the establishment of it, so the net result is certainly one I have no regrets about.'

Martin Giblin had also received a fax that evening from Frank, which prompted him to call Brendan Howlin. It was not the first time he had received information in confidence from a Garda source since he had met Frank McBrearty. An anonymous source, who identified himself as 'a Garda based in Donegal', had first contacted him in the autumn of 1997 and told him: 'Your clients are innocent, they had nothing to do with the death of Richie Barron.' The source went on to say that a lot of Guards in Donegal 'were worried about what was going on in Raphoe, and feared that some damage could be done to the Garda force, if it continued'. The source said he would send Giblin some documents, and that he should carefully examine the envelopes in which they came, before destroying the envelope. The source then asked Giblin if he was interested in five-a-side soccer, and if he liked Nike gear, which struck the barrister as odd at the time.

'When the first set of documents arrived I examined the envelope and discovered the Nike symbol on the inside,' Giblin explained later. Over the following years, the barrister received several sets of documents from the mysterious 'Garda Nike', including statements taken by the Carty team and records of a meeting with State pathologist Prof. Dr John Harbison. When Giblin received the fax from Frank McBrearty on 25 June 2000, alleging that the Carty Inquiry was compromised, he 'was intrigued by the contents'. He then spoke to Frank McBrearty, who told him he had received the document anonymously. 'I felt I recognised the author of the document as my anonymous informant from whom I have not heard for a considerable period,' Giblin recalled.

Trusting in Giblin's judgement, Brendan Howlin did not ask the barrister the identity of the source of his information, beyond learning it was 'a Garda based in Donegal'. Howlin recounted how the senior counsel told him that his source had told him that Detective Sergeant John White was being 'looked after', had 'a stash' of stolen property, had planted evidence to secure arrests and convictions, and had done 'dirty work' in the past for Assistant Commissioner Kevin Carty. In a note of the conversation, Howlin wrote that 'Giblin's real concern is that the Carty investigation is compromised.'

Howlin already knew that Jim Higgins had raised the McBrearty case several times in the Dáil. He got in touch with his Fine Gael colleague. They agreed that the information was serious, and should be brought to the Justice Minister, John O'Donoghue. On Tuesday 27 June, Higgins and

Howlin met O'Donoghue in his office in Leinster House. As a result, the minister contacted the Garda Commissioner, who appointed Fachtna Murphy to investigate the allegations.

The two TDs acted 'in good faith' in going to the Minister, the tribunal found, but the 'completely untrue allegations were given an authority to which they were never entitled by the manner in which they were presented to the politicians and ultimately to Mr John O'Donoghue, the Minister for Justice, Equality and Law Reform.'

'It would have been entirely reasonable,' Mr Justice Morris said, 'for the two Teachtaí Dála to say that they were not going to make allegations of such a wild kind about two assistant commissioners and a detective sergeant to the Minister for Justice, Equality and Law Reform and put them under a cloud, without something more than a facsimile and/or a late night phone call.'

Higgins was worried about confidentiality. If people couldn't trust that a TD could keep safe information sent to him, then information would stay hidden, and scandals would never be exposed. The fax led back to Frank, and if Frank was questioned about it, that in turn could lead to PJ Togher. Uncovering the informant would have a chilling effect that would prevent others coming forward to their TDs in future. Higgins removed the top and bottom portions of the fax, which showed the number it was sent from, and had his secretary re-type it. He then destroyed the original fax.

Higgins believed he acted responsibly when he received the anonymous allegations. Rather than going public, contacting a journalist, or broadcasting the allegations from the floor of the Dáil where anything he said was covered by absolute privilege—which could destroy the reputations of two innocent men—he had instead gone to the minister, who could launch an independent investigation. Kevin Carty didn't agree. In a statement in 2001, he said the allegations were made 'with malicious intent with the sole purpose of assassinating my character and good name'.

Minutes of the meeting with John O'Donoghue were taken by Oonagh McPhillips, his private secretary. 'Deputy Higgins seemed to be making the point that he wasn't interested in making it a media issue, he was interested in getting to the truth of the matter,' she recalled. Higgins told the minister his source would co-operate with a Garda investigation, but not with the media. Higgins also told the minister he had been approached by journalist Frank Connolly about the allegations. The source of the information wasn't a huge issue at the time, and the TDs expressed trust in their sources. 'They had no proof of the allegations contained but they had no reason to suspect a malicious motive on the part of their sources,' she remembered.

O'Donoghue was 'highly sceptical' of claims that the Gardaí were corrupt at the highest levels, but the allegations couldn't be ignored. He referred the information to the Garda Commissioner Pat Byrne, and his deputy, Noel Conroy.

As far as O'Donoghue was concerned, the motive behind the allegations was to create a public inquiry into Garda actions in County Donegal. When he questioned Higgins and Howlin, they were neutral on whether there was any evidence to back up the claims. The minister suspected that if the opposition TDs thought there was anything to it, they wouldn't have met him in private, they'd have raised questions in the Dáil to embarrass the government.

For Martin Giblin, the anonymous allegations were a sideshow, a distraction from his main focus, which was to get an investigation into the complaints from the McBrearty family and clear their name. Worse, if the Carty Inquiry—now a year old and drawing to a close—was suspended while the allegations were checked out, the chance that it could clear the McBreartys would be delayed. Giblin's aim was simple: get a declaration of innocence for the family.

Giblin was first hired by the McBrearty family in early 1997, in order to seek an injunction preventing excessive Garda inspections of Frank McBrearty's pub and nightclub. Five days before he saw the anonymous fax, on 20 June 2000, the legal team were told that over 100 District Court prosecutions against the family were being withdrawn by the DPP. Perversely, Giblin saw this apparent victory as a setback. Deprived of access to the courts when the charges were dropped, Giblin lost one of the main avenues he'd been able to use to ask embarrassing questions of the Guards. The barrister had planned to use the hearings on the summonses 'to raise the wider issue, that these were an abuse of process'.

'There was a certain element of bad manners in it, just a telephone call, be in Donegal tomorrow morning, all the summonses are being struck out,' Giblin recalled at the tribunal.

After speaking to Brendan Howlin, Giblin decided he didn't want anything more to do with anonymous allegations. He was 'getting fed up with the whole John le Carré type of thing which was becoming a feature of the case', he explained.

In mid-July 2000, Jim Higgins received a second fax from Old Frank McBrearty. Higgins never forwarded the second fax to the Minister for Justice, or the Garda Commissioner, but came across it later when going through his documents and handed it over to the Morris tribunal. He couldn't explain why exactly he hadn't forwarded this fax, which in some respects contradicted the first. Possibly he'd done nothing with it because it was near illegible. While the June fax painted Kevin Carty as a co-conspirator who had used John White to plant evidence, the July fax painted him as a victim, hampered in his efforts to investigate White by others in high places.

Barrister Martin Giblin said that he did not remember receiving a second document from Frank McBrearty in July 2000. Solicitor Ken Smyth confirmed he received the second fax on 15 July 2000, which he believed came from the same source as the first document, but said it was almost illegible.

Smyth got his copy of the first fax on the morning of 26 June 2000, the day after it was sent to Higgins and Giblin. He said that Frank McBrearty phoned him and asked him to rewrite the document and destroy the fax, but he felt 'uncomfortable' doing this, and held on to the original. He believed the fax was written by PJ Togher, based on conversations he had with the ex-Garda covering similar topics to those in the fax document, but added that Frank McBrearty never told him who the author was. Frank denied he told Smyth to rewrite the fax and destroy the original.

Garda Commissioner Pat Byrne hadn't hesitated after speaking with the Minister for Justice. He appointed Fachtna Murphy to head the investigation into the claims in the anonymous fax.

Hundreds of serving and former Gardaí were interviewed in an attempt to identify the anonymous source of the allegations that the Carty Inquiry into corruption in Donegal was compromised, including thirty detective inspectors working in the Dublin area and forty-six retired Gardaí in County Donegal. The investigators also examined the property books in Blanchardstown Garda station, where John White had worked for several years, because of an allegation that the detective sergeant had a store of stolen property. Firearms records were also examined. Despite this, Murphy's team found nothing to back up the anonymous allegations.

The 'Anonymous Allegations' story broke on 2 July 2000, the Sunday after Higgins received the first fax. Under Frank Connolly's byline, the *Sunday Business Post* reported that the Minister for Justice had asked the Garda Commissioner to investigate allegations of serious corruption brought to him by two senior Opposition politicians.

Frank McBrearty's fax machine had been working overtime. He had also sent a copy of the fax to Connolly. However, the information in the fax was 'unpublishable' as far as the journalist was concerned, until he learned that two politicians had gone to see the Minister for Justice. 'That was the hook that allowed us to publish the story,' he explained. Connolly could not report the allegations in detail, but he could report that two senior politicians had gone to see the Justice Minister after they received information alleging high-level corruption in the force. Connolly said he never considered PJ Togher was the author of the anonymous allegations until his name came up at the tribunal. The fax claimed to contain information from a serving detective inspector in Dublin, and he took it at face value.

Another journalist, John Mooney, also told the tribunal he saw a document containing similar allegations to those outlined to the two TDS. Mooney said that NUJ ethics guidelines would prohibit him from identifying the source of his information, but following consultation with an NUJ representative and his legal counsel, he confirmed that PJ Togher was not the source. Mooney said he thought the document he saw had a Garda stamp, and referred to the Crime & Security branch. What struck him were the allegations detailed in the document, not its appearance. The journalist said that by November 2001, he had come to the conclusion that the document was a forgery, and he did not know who the author was.

That same month, 'absolutely convinced there was an unanswerable case for a tribunal of inquiry at that time', Brendan Howlin introduced a Dáil motion calling for a public inquiry into events in Donegal. The motion was defeated by a single vote, the closest margin in that Dáil term, amid what Howlin described as 'considerable pressure coming on the Donegal deputies obviously to support it'. However, John O'Donoghue agreed to have a senior barrister review the Carty investigation, which had reported to the Garda Commissioner in mid-July, and the resulting report from Shane Murphy SC ultimately led to the establishment of the Morris tribunal in March 2002.

When the Morris tribunal looked into the 'Anonymous Allegations' affair, Assistant Commissioner Kevin Carty was one of the witnesses called. He complained to the Morris tribunal that despite a complete absence of evidence, the allegations still hung over his head like a cloud. 'If you go to the internet, put my name in the internet, you'll get Kevin Carty sensational allegations,' he pointed out. Working with the Organisation for Security and Cooperation in Europe, Carty was aware that people meeting him would check his background. 'I spend a lot of my time visiting ministers of the interior in developing countries, countries in transition in the Caucasus in Central Asia, in relation to policing. And one of the things we are trying to instil into policemen in this part of the world is accountability, rooting out corruption. And it has been actually said to me, "Mr Carty, you have corruption in your country as well, you've been under investigation." You spend the first ten, fifteen minutes of a consultation explaining that there is no substance to these allegations, and you don't know whether these people are actually believing this or not.'

Carty felt the affair had damaged his career, and said he lacked the confidence to apply for a vacancy for Deputy Garda Commissioner in 2006. He was also dismissive of any suggestion that his investigation into corruption in Donegal lacked impartiality. 'The idea that Guards cannot investigate Guards is not true,' he told Frank McBrearty at the tribunal. 'If you look at the Donegal investigation, I would stand behind the Donegal investigation as an example of Guards investigating Guards without fear of any reprisals. I had a dedicated investigation team with me in Donegal and they carried out all of their duties in respect of members of An Garda Síochána in the same manner as they did in respect to the civilian population that we were investigating . . . I accept that the new legislation has been introduced, and I welcome it, but I do not agree the Gardaí were not prepared and incapable of investigating Gardaí.'

Assistant Commissioner Tony Hickey also gave evidence at the Morris tribunal. He said he first learned of the anonymous allegations against him when he was called to a meeting with the Garda Commissioner in June 2000. 'The allegations in it couldn't be any more serious short of murder or rape or robbery or something,' he explained. 'They were pretty horrific and they were very stark . . . I knew it was rubbish and I had faith in the system that we would be exonerated,' he added. 'But I didn't ever foresee that we would be this long.'

John White, already besieged by allegations on several fronts, said the allegations were designed solely to put pressure on the government. 'They were malicious in nature and were designed to pressurise the government into forming a public inquiry into matters relative to the treatment of the McBrearty family and not to rely solely on the Carty report, which was due for submission to the Commissioner within three weeks of these allegations being passed on to the Minister for Justice,' he told the tribunal.

By the time the Morris tribunal was set up, the original Garda investigation into the anonymous allegations had gone as far as it could. Officers named in the fax had been interviewed, and denied the truth of the allegations. Property logs had been checked for evidence of missing contraband that might have been planted on suspects. Expense sheets and overtime logs for Detective Sergeant John White had been checked for evidence of overpayments, and were found to be in order. The author of the allegations was identified as possibly a serving detective inspector in Dublin, or a retired Garda in Donegal. Every retired Garda in Donegal was interviewed, and every serving inspector in Dublin. None could shed any light on the allegations.

In order to take the investigation any further, as required by its terms of reference, the Morris tribunal decided it had to identify the informant. Perhaps if they spoke to him, he could provide further information to back up the corruption claims, or tell them where evidence could be found. Brendan Howlin and Jim Higgins (by now an MEP) decided that they could not reveal their sources. If they did so, it could have a chilling effect on others who wanted to come to them with confidential information.

The battle led to the High Court, and from there to the Supreme Court, as the TDs tried to stop the tribunal gaining access to their phone records, which would reveal who they spoke to and received faxes from on 25 June 2000. The politicians relied on Article 15 of Bunreacht na hÉireann, which promised to protect the private papers of members of the Oireachtas in order to ensure free debate. The courts listened, but decided that since the TDs had gone privately to the minister rather than raising the issue publicly in the Dáil, the information was not privileged.

Following the court decision, Jim Higgins told the tribunal in an October 2006 statement that Frank McBrearty told him the statement came from 'my friend', the shared codephrase for PJ Togher. Howlin could not identify the original source, since he had received the information indirectly from Martin Giblin. Unknown to him, the barrister had already come forward to the tribunal.

Questioned at the tribunal by Michael Durack SC for the Garda Commissioner, Howlin said it was not true that he refused to co-operate with the tribunal, insisting it was his 'proper and correct duty' to protect his source.

'I don't think you'd be standing here without my efforts to pursue the truth, Sir. I don't think we'd have five reports of this tribunal, and I don't think we'd be here discussing this. We wouldn't be here today,' he told the barrister. 'The principle at stake in defending the right of the citizen to contact me remains extremely important to me, and I think it will be important tomorrow, if another citizen who wants to make allegations that should be properly investigated.'

Togher told the tribunal he was not the author of the allegations, and had not even seen the document until it was shown to him by tribunal investigators. Neither did he know anything about a second fax document sent to Jim Higgins concerning the proposed transfer of Detective Sergeant John White to the Special Detective Unit in Dublin following his arrest in the 'silver bullet' affair in March 2000.

'The fact is I never sent or drew up a fax, or had anything to do with the sending of it, nor had absolutely nothing to do with Mr Higgins receiving it,' Togher told the tribunal. 'He got the impression that it was me, and he's entitled to his own opinion on that.'

Togher said he was 'saddened' at allegations of police corruption in Donegal, having faced personal danger in twenty-seven years service with the force. He recounted with pride how he once 'lay in a ditch every night from dark until before dawn from 27 December 1991 to 9 March 1992 on my own watching eleven IRA men building a 4600lb bomb and thwarted their efforts days before the intended outrage. I am sad for the many years I faced danger and uncertainty along the Irish border preventing terrorism.'

However, Cormac Ó Dúlacháin sc, representing John White, went through the fax with Togher, and in a textbook display of forensic cross-examination, identified ten common stylistic features in the anonymous fax and another letter written by Togher around the same time. Despite the analysis, Togher insisted he was not the author of the fax.

Robert Radley, a British document expert, later confirmed several of the items on the checklist outlined by Ó Dúlacháin were also found in documents Togher had typed, including the idiosyncratic use of double spaces and indentation, 'unusual punctuation', and 'almost peppering the document with full stops'. He said there was 'positive limited evidence to support the proposition' that Togher typed the fax document. 'I believe that on the evidence it is more likely that Mr Togher typed it than somebody else who coincidentally has this combination of features,' he concluded.

Frank McBrearty for his part said he had no idea as to the identity of the author of the anonymous allegations, and had received it in the post. Not knowing what else to do with it, he had forwarded it to Jim Higgins. Togher began working for McBrearty after his retirement from An Garda Síochána, and admitted readily to the tribunal that he disliked Billy Flynn, the private investigator. 'I thought he was overdoing his remit, he was annoying people, he was annoying Guards, contacting people at all hours of the night, he wasn't a nice person, and I would not work with him,' he told the tribunal. Before he agreed to work for McBrearty, he said the publican showed him an invoice from Flynn for final payment dating from 1997, and told him that Flynn no longer worked for him.

Togher's animosity towards Flynn may have stemmed from the private investigator's account of a meeting that took place in Flynn's home in Enfield, Co. Meath, on 7 March 2000, three months before Jim Higgins received the anonymous fax. Flynn told how Togher, Old Frank and Young Frank McBrearty and Mark and Roisin McConnell had called to his home on the way home from a debate in Dáil Éireann, where Jim Higgins had spoken about their case.

Everyone was in good spirits, the private eye told the tribunal, and he was delighted to see Old Frank in such good humour. 'He was carrying the weight. The responsibility of all the families rested on his shoulders . . . I considered him a courageous man.' Flynn explained that rumours about Donegal Gardaí were discussed in his home, and Togher spoke of rumours similar to those that eventually appeared in the anonymous allegations fax.

For a long time, it seemed to many that the origin of the anonymous fax lay not with PJ Togher, but with another retired Garda, Jim Madigan. Indeed, Both Old Frank and Young Frank went out of their way on several occasions to praise Jim Madigan for the support he had given them, beginning with a 'Get Well Card' he sent to Old Frank while he was hospitalised during his arrest, lending credence to the idea.

Madigan told the tribunal that after his arrest in December 1996, Old Frank McBrearty often spoke to him about the way he was treated. McBrearty also complained about the large number of inspections of his pub and nightclub business. 'I had never in my experience in the Guards seen any licensed premises get the attention his licensed premises did,' Madigan told the inquiry. 'My opinion was that Mr McBrearty was being harassed in the licensing prosecutions.' Madigan said that after he read about it in the newspapers, Frank McBrearty told him he had faxed the anonymous allegations to Higgins. He said he did not know the identity of McBrearty's source.

The rumours were embellished in the document, created by Frank McBrearty and PJ Togher, which Togher typed, and sent to Jim Higgins and Martin Giblin sc 'in the hope and expectation that they would be used as part of the campaign for a public inquiry in whatever way they thought appropriate.'

'Frank McBrearty Senior was entitled to claim redress for the wrongs committed by agents of the State against him and members of his extended family,' Mr Justice Morris wrote. 'He achieved this when he and others successfully concluded High Court proceedings for damages in 2007. He also sought to have this wrongdoing exposed in the forum of a public inquiry. It was reasonable of him in the circumstances to make representations to have such an inquiry established. However, it was wrong and inexcusable of him to have set about achieving that goal by publishing serious untrue allegations against a serving detective sergeant and two serving assistant commissioners in An Garda Síochána.

'The assistant commissioners, in particular, had exemplary records within An Garda Síochána. These allegations caused them much personal and professional embarrassment. I have no doubt but that their standing was damaged by the publication of such allegations to persons at the highest level in government.'

Chapter 32

How Are the Tapes Going?

The story broke first in the local press, so few noticed it outside Donegal at first. Under the headline 'Solicitor Accuses Gardaí Of Illegal Secret Recordings' on the front page of the 17 May 2001 edition of the *Donegal Democrat*, the paper reported that solicitor Paudge Dorrian claimed Gardaí used secret recording equipment illegally to gather evidence in major investigations.

Connie Duffy, who wrote the story, said at the Morris tribunal that his recall of the meeting with Dorrian which led to the report was vague after six years, but he insisted that he recorded accurately what the solicitor told him. In the story, Dorrian was reported as saying that at least three Gardaí would give evidence to back up the allegation that interviews were secretly recorded. Duffy said the solicitor did not divulge the identity of the three Gardaí in question.

Asked by the tribunal chairman what his criteria were for deciding if someone was a reliable source, he said Dorrian was being quoted directly in the article, and he presumed the solicitor could back up what he was saying. 'I was reasonably happy that being an officer of the court, Mr Dorrian was telling me something which he believed to be true,' Duffy explained. He said that in the six years since the article appeared, no one had contacted him about the allegation until he heard from the Morris tribunal.

The story went national in November 2001, when it was repeated in the Dáil during a debate on an opposition motion calling for a tribunal into the emerging scandals in Donegal.

Solicitor Paudge Dorrian said he learned of the allegations of bugging from his client, John White, and decided to go public with them because White told him senior Gardaí knew it was happening and would not be investigated. He said that he had acted for Gardaí on an unrelated case, and 'the Guards would not discuss anything with me in Letterkenny barracks, they always insisted on going outside'. However, he said no Garda ever told him he was being taped.

Dorrian also said he had concerns that solicitors were being taped, independently of what Mr White told him. He said the decision to go public was made 'with John White stating he was certain there would be no investigation and the only way to get it would be getting it in the press'.

'The information that I had was that everybody in the higher echelons of the Garda Síochána knew about this but they were going to deny it,' Dorrian said. 'He gave me quite clear indications that it was rampant anywhere he served and that there was tape recorders provided and tapes provided in all the stations.'

When Dorrian was approached by senior Garda officers investigating the allegations, he told them that unnamed Gardaí were willing to come forward with evidence of bugging in Letterkenny and other stations. The conditions for their evidence amounted to 'a blanket immunity from prosecution', something the Gardaí could not give. 'The significance of the offer made by Mr Dorrian on Detective Sergeant White's behalf is, in my opinion, that it was an attempt by Detective Sergeant White to avoid the mounting problems with which he was faced at that time; and he was attempting to barter alleged information in exchange for such an immunity. I am of the opinion that there was no truth whatever in the allegation that Gardaí had bugged the interview rooms in Letterkenny Garda Station or taped conversations of the detainees,' Justice Morris decided.

Detective Garda John Dooley told the Morris tribunal he first learned about bugging when he and John White were returning from a tea break on 4 December 1996, the day of the mass arrests in the Barron case, and met Sergeant Joseph Costello in a corridor in Letterkenny Garda station. 'I had never met Sergeant Costello before,' Dooley recalled. White introduced the sergeant as a member of the technical support unit in Garda HQ, and then asked Costello, 'How are the tapes going?' Dooley remembered that Costello replied, 'They're talking very low.'

Dooley said he then went to the station canteen, where the six o'clock news was on. When White joined him, he told him that Roisin McConnell had a visit from her mother, and the room was 'bugged'. Dooley told the Morris tribunal he was '100% that I heard that conversation, and that I have relayed it now the way it is'. White differed on the details—he thought the meeting took place at a different time, for instance, but also claimed the station interview rooms—or one of them at least—were bugged. Costello denied that the incident ever took place.

Justice Morris, however, was satisfied that the reference to tapes did not mean Costello was recording conversations with visitors or solicitors. 'It may be that the comment had its origins in the fact that Detective Sergeant Costello was engaged in video-recording as part of his normal duties from time to time,' he concluded. 'Nonetheless, I am satisfied on the evidence of Mr White and Mr Dooley that such a conversation occurred.'

However, the chairman decided that the later conversation, where White told Dooley that conversations were bugged, was nothing more than the sergeant trying to impress a colleague by 'conveying to him that he had insider knowledge of secret taping'.

Superintendent John Fitzgerald told the Morris tribunal that he first learned that Sergeant Joseph Costello from Garda HQ had been asked to come to Donegal when he met the sergeant at a meeting on 3 December 1996, the night before the mass arrests. Fitzgerald said he understood Sergeant Costello was brought down to do surveillance work on the investigation into alleged intimidation of witnesses, and he had assigned that aspect of the investigation to Detective Superintendent Joe Shelly. No instructions were given to Sergeant Costello at the pre-arrest conference on 3 December 1996, at which tasks were assigned for the following day's arrests. He thought that taping meetings between visitors and prisoners in custody would be unethical.

Garda Tina Fowley told the tribunal she was present when Detective Superintendent Joe Shelly and Inspector John McGinley discussed obtaining support from the Garda technical section to see if any information could be 'gleaned' for the investigation. But the tribunal felt her evidence was 'unreliable', and could not rely on it to support White's allegations.

Retired Detective Sergeant Joe Costello, a member of the telecommunications section in Garda HQ, said he was asked to come to Donegal by Detective Superintendent Joe Shelly. He said he was 'surprised' to learn later that there was no file at Garda HQ recording his visit. Costello said he expected his job in Donegal would be to help with surveillance work as part of an investigation into alleged intimidation of witnesses. The former sergeant said he was not given any instructions when he arrived in Donegal. The lack of paperwork or a clear plan to deploy Costello was typical of the chaos that characterised the Barron investigation, the chairman observed.

Questioned by the chairman, Costello said that although it had not happened, it would be possible using equipment in the Garda technical section to covertly record conversations as White had described. He had only recorded a prisoner's conversation once in his thirty-year career, when he was asked to tape two prisoners in a cell in Ballinasloe during a murder investigation in the early 1990s. One man was convicted, and another vindicated, as a result of the recording, which was disclosed to the legal team for the defence at trial. Costello said he 'was on stand-by duty, waiting for further instructions' while in Donegal, and this was why he had claimed overtime while in Letterkenny, even though he had done no work there.

White also alleged that he saw Inspector John McGinley listening to some of the tapes on the day of the arrests. 'That's ridiculous, Chairman, it just didn't happen,' was McGinley's sharp response.

McGinley said the plan was that Costello could video record or photograph any intimidation by Frank McBrearty if he approached witnesses after his release from custody. But since McBrearty was admitted to hospital shortly after his arrest, the plan was abandoned, and Costello returned to Dublin. McGinley also said it was 'a ridiculous proposition' to suggest that Gardaí would listen in on conversations between solicitors and clients. He pointed out that White had forgotten by the time he made his allegations in 2001 that in December 1996, the detective inspector's office in Letterkenny was used as an interview room, and so he could not have been there listening to a tape recording. McGinley also said he had never heard the expression 'to box', which White said was the practice of placing prisoners together to monitor what they might say to each other. Tribunal barrister Paul McDermott hazarded a guess that the term might be 'a slightly irreverent reference to a confession box'.

White next claimed that he had told Chief Superintendent Austin McNally about the bugging affair at a meeting in a Sligo hotel in November 1999, and the senior officer told him the bugging of interview rooms was 'one of the best kept secrets' in An Garda Síochána. 'That is totally and utterly untrue. He never mentioned anything about recordings,' said Chief Superintendent McNally, who by the time he appeared at the tribunal was working with the Bureau of Fraud Investigation. He said he had 'absolutely no experience and no knowledge' of secret recordings of prisoners' conversations in his Garda career.

'If what Mr White is alleging is correct, to think that I as a senior officer with twenty-six years' service would suddenly turn round and sacrifice my principles that I worked for for so long to engage in this nefarious activity, he is very wrong,' he said. 'And I consider it a terrible slur on all the good people I have served with over the last forty years.' McNally said that when allegations of bugging in Garda stations first emerged in an article in the *Donegal Democrat* on 17 May 2001, he 'knew it was utterly false, utterly false'.

Chief Superintendent Denis Fitzpatrick joined the chorus of disbelievers, describing the bugging allegation as part of a 'pattern of spurious mischievous reports being made, either through the media or directly to the Guards'. The spurious claims absorbed resources, soaking the energy out of investigation teams, and affected public confidence in the force, he complained.

Although an internal Garda inquiry found no evidence to support the allegation, White said two retired Cork Gardaí would give evidence to corroborate his claims that bugging of prisoners' conversations in Garda custody was a widespread practice within the force. 'They sat in a van, outside a Garda station in 1992, saw the equipment being used, and listened to an interview taking place in an interview room in the station, and that that van was driven and the equipment used by members of the National Surveillance Unit,' White told the tribunal on 17 May 2007. 'This will establish that it did happen. Not that it may have happened, or anything else. People who were uninvolved in the Donegal case can say categorically that it did happen. They saw and heard it,' White said.

The tribunal chairman decided he would not hear any evidence from Cork-based Gardaí. 'Even if I accept, as I do for the purposes of this ruling, that all they say is true, this would not in my view entitle me to infer as a matter of probability that what Mr White says, occurred in Letterkenny,' the chairman said in his ruling. 'It would be wrong of me to infer from such evidence that because some other Gardaí in Cork carried out a broadly similar eavesdropping operation to that alleged by Detective Sergeant Costello, that Detective Sergeant Costello did so in Donegal in 1996.'

'Mr White will not be in any way prejudiced in my not calling this evidence and I do not accept that it will in any way assist me in determining the issue as to whether the alleged bugging was carried out by Mr Costello in Letterkenny Garda station in December 1996,' the chairman wrote in his ruling.

Detective Superintendent Joseph Shelly said he had spoken to the Letterkenny district officer, Superintendent John Fitzgerald, about getting help from Garda technical support services in conducting surveillance on Frank McBrearty after his planned release from Garda custody in December 1996. However, Shelly said there was no plan to place listening devices in rooms in the Garda station and listen to conversations between prisoners and visitors.

White claimed the first time he saw secret recording was when, as a young detective working on a case in Wexford, he walked into a conference room where some senior officers were listening to a conversation between a suspect and a priest. White also said he had heard of another case involving Gardaí in County Kilkenny.

Superintendent James Paul Sharpe from the Technical Section said that monitoring conversations was not part of the unit's work, but 'the capability was there' to carry out such work. The thirty-five-year veteran was one of nineteen people with electronics experience recruited to the force in 1972 to advise on technical issues. Sharpe said it would not require sophisticated equipment to bug a room, but he would be surprised if it happened without his knowledge. 'I absolutely and utterly have no knowledge whatsoever of any covert recording carried out by the unit,' he stated.

Assistant Commissioner Nacie Rice, who was a Chief Superintendent at the time, met with solicitor Paudge Dorrian after the article outlining the allegations appeared in the *Donegal Democrat*.

It was at this meeting that Dorrian explained the preconditions his witnesses wanted—effectively a blanket immunity from prosecution. Quite simply, that was not an assurance Rice was prepared to give. Rice carried out an extensive investigation, but found no evidence to back up White's allegations. The solicitor told him the source of the allegations were Gardaí who wanted assurances that there would be no negative repercussions before they came forward. 'What I had was a newspaper article and a solicitor acting on behalf of his clients who declined to cooperate with the investigation,' Rice said. He said there was not enough information to launch a full investigation. It was not until the tribunal was able to investigate the claims, six years after they first appeared in the *Donegal Democrat*, that the truth finally emerged about White's desperate bid to get out of the hole he was in as a result of the Carty Inquiry.

Chapter 33

A Mood in the Air

Jim Higgins never asked John Bruton who had approached him with a suggestion that he should 'ease off' on the McBrearty case, and the Fine Gael leader never volunteered the name. By the time he appeared at the Morris tribunal, the MEP's memory of the conversation was vague, but he was confident the record would show he had never backed off the McBrearty case as a result of anything the former Taoiseach might have said to him.

Bruton told the tribunal that to the best of his memory a member of the Garda Complaints Board, Dermot O'Callaghan, did express concerns about the McBrearty case at a constituency function in County Louth in February 2000, and he recorded in his journal at the time that Justice Spokesman Jim Higgins 'should be careful on the McBrearty case. Dermot O'Callaghan will take a call.'

Bruton said that he spoke to Higgins about the McBrearty case, and the Mayo TD assured him he had 'solid grounds' for the issues he was raising in the Dáil. Bruton added that he was not absolutely certain he had actually met O'Callaghan, or had just been told something O'Callaghan had said.

Bruton's memory was faulty. O'Callaghan, a Fine Gael supporter and businessman, said he never spoke to the then Opposition leader about the McBrearty case, but made no secret of his opinion of the voluminous complaints before the Garda Complaints Board. The Board had received over sixty complaints from the family, and several more from Billy Flynn. No other case had ever generated so many complaints in its history. O'Callaghan had spoken to several people on social occasions about the propriety of politicians commenting on cases the Board had yet to decide, and did 'remember saying to certain members socially that Jim Higgins was offside in what he was doing'.

'While I accept that the views expressed by Mr O'Callaghan were genuinely held ones', Justice Morris later noted, 'I do not regard it as acceptable that individuals appointed by politicians to independent statutory boards proceed to express their personal views in relation to the ongoing work of those boards to members of the political party responsible for their appointment.' Bruton, however, was not to be criticised for speaking to Jim Higgins about the case, 'given the fact that he understood that he was receiving relevant information from an informed source'.

O'Callaghan told the tribunal that a friend of his had checked the diaries, and confirmed that he had not attended the function in Dundalk on 25 February 2000 where Bruton was told about the McBrearty case, but someone else could easily have passed his views on to the Opposition leader.

Roughly two weeks after Bruton approached Higgins, Old Frank McBrearty and several members of his family travelled to Dublin to hear Jim Higgins raise their case during a Dáil debate. On the way home, they stopped in at the Enfield home of private detective Billy Flynn. During the meeting, retired Garda PJ Togher recalled, the talk came around to the conversation between Bruton and Higgins, which Higgins had relayed to the McBreartys. Billy Flynn would later describe the atmosphere at the meeting, at which he said rumours similar to the allegations that later appeared in an anonymous fax sent to Higgins also circulated, as 'paranoid', and likened it to 'Watergate and the Nixon years'.

In June of 2001, Frank McBrearty wrote to complain to the Garda Complaints Board in protest at the approach to Bruton. As a result, Board chairman Seamus McKenna SC asked his senior staff to check if any of the staff had spoken to the Fine Gael leader, while he raised the issue at Board meetings and spoke to each Board member. McKenna also wrote to Frank's solicitors asking if they could name the person alleged to have approached Bruton.

McKenna described O'Callaghan as 'a very admirable, forthright, straight-talking Dundalk gentleman . . . He would never ever betray any confidence of the Board, but he would be forthright in views that perhaps he was better off keeping to himself at times, the same as we all are.'

John Roycroft, a civil servant and member of the Board's staff, was present when McKenna asked O'Callaghan if he had approached Bruton about the McBrearty case. In a memo, Roycroft noted that O'Callaghan said he 'did not at any stage say anything to John Bruton about the case and in fact had not spoken to him in two or three years'.

On 23 July 2001, the Board chairman wrote to Bruton about the claim. The politician's reply was emphatic. 'No member of the Garda Complaints Board asked me to silence members of my party endeavouring to bring the case to the floor of the Dáil,' he wrote on 31 July.

Bruton told the tribunal he did not intend to suggest in his letter that no one from the Garda Complaints Board approached him in 2000 about the McBrearty case. However, tribunal barrister Paul McDermott SC said that the politician's reply to the Board chairman at the time was 'a very direct response, and would appear to suggest that you weren't approached by anybody on the Garda Complaints Board'.

'No, it doesn't suggest that,' Bruton replied. 'It simply suggests that I wasn't asked by any member of the Garda Complaints Board to silence any member of my party in bringing the matter up. I was simply answering the question I was asked.'

Bruton said he 'meant to answer the question I was asked in the terms that it was posed'.

'I felt if I started to expand on the matter that I would be in some way indirectly suggesting by giving additional information that there was a possibility that somebody asked me to silence Mr Higgins. Nobody asked me to silence Mr Higgins, and I didn't want to give any legs to that statement or that suggestion,' he added.

———

As far as the Garda Complaints Board was concerned, the earliest complaints from the McBrearty family dated to shortly after 4 December 1996, the day of the mass arrests. In its view, Deputy Chief Executive Brian O'Brien told the Morris tribunal, any complaint about Garda conduct should be forwarded to the Board to investigate, not only formal complaints. This included complaints in the custody records, letters from solicitors, or any other complaint the Gardaí became aware of.

Superintendent John Fitzgerald had already told the tribunal that he regarded the solicitors' letters he received after 4 December 1996 as place-holders, and expected detailed complaints to follow which he would then send to the Board. No such letters arrived before he left Donegal, and the letters were not forwarded to the Board until after Kevin Lennon took personal charge of the Barron investigation nine months later. The delay in receiving the complaints contained in the solicitors' letters was 'a cause of deep concern', O'Brien told the Morris tribunal.

In October 1997, O'Brien was told by Superintendent Kevin Lennon of eight complaints by the family, six relating to their arrest and detention in December 1996, and two relating to enforcement of the licensing laws at Frankie's. 'Seven of those letters were dated in December 1996, the last one, the eighth one, was undated,' he remembered. 'Word of their coming up was a cause of deep concern in the office because, particularly when we saw the terminology of the letters, they were serious complaints.'

O'Brien spoke to the Chief Executive of the Board, and 'we said that this is unfortunate, these should have been dealt with long ago, we will have to deal with them expeditiously, and we may have to take special measures in relation to them'. Lennon, he explained, learned of the letters from Superintendent Tom Gallagher in Ballymote, who was told about them by Billy Flynn, the private detective. The only copies of the letters were those held by McBrearty's solicitors, which were forwarded to the Complaints Board. Despite a search of Letterkenny Garda station, Lennon was unable to find the originals, and John Fitzgerald, the superintendent to whom they had been sent, was unable to say what had happened to them. O'Brien said that an earlier batch of nine complaints from the extended McBrearty family did not stand out in his mind when they were first received, 'they were fairly normal type of complaints.' What made the McBrearty case so memorable was not the nature of the complaints, but their number.

The Complaints Board would eventually receive sixty-one related complaints from the McBrearty family, and ten more from Billy Flynn. However, the Garda Síochána (Complaints) Act 1986 did not give it the power to investigate on its own. Instead, a senior Garda from outside the district where the complaints were made was appointed to investigate, and reported back to the Board. 'Guards investigating Guards' was Old Frank's cynical dismissal of the process at the Morris tribunal.

Several of the complaints were given to Chief Superintendent John Carey to investigate. O'Brien recalled that when he met with Chief Superintendent Carey to discuss the case in late 1998, the report on the combined cases ran to 1,006 pages, with an additional 1,500 to 2,000 pages of appendices, plus tapes and photographs.

'I had never seen anything the likes of this before,' O'Brien remembered. 'Usually we dealt with individual complaints. Occasionally there might be two or three complaints about the same event or a complainant might have complaints about two or three events that might be related and you might have a fairly big report . . . But nothing of the magnitude of this particular group of complaints and the amount of paper that had been assembled.'

The Garda Complaints Board chairman and an Assistant Commissioner representing the Garda Commissioner were briefed on the complaints on 3 November 1998, an indication of how seriously the Board viewed the affair. It was the only occasion in O'Brien's time at the Board that such a briefing happened.

The Board met in May 1999 to consider Chief Superintendent Carey's reports on the McBrearty affair, but deferred a decision pending developments at ongoing District Court hearings in County Donegal and the internal Garda investigation headed by Assistant Commissioner Kevin Carty. The court cases or the Carty Inquiry might uncover further information that would help it reach a decision, they reasoned.

Carey told the tribunal his covering report on the McBreartys 'didn't set out to create any impression. I gave the facts and I was relying on the facts,' he said. 'I wasn't trying to demonise anybody.' His report covered 'the good and the bad' about members of the extended McBrearty family.

The background information in the report came from investigation files prepared in County Donegal, or from talking to Gardaí there. Tribunal barrister Anthony Barr SC later observed that Carey's covering report to the Board painted a picture of the McBrearty family as 'violent nasty people', referring to alleged assaults, a death in Scotland, and allegations of extra-marital affairs. Carey found himself in an unenviable position investigating the complaints. He did not have the power to cross-examine Garda witnesses, he could only accept their statements. In the words of Justice Morris, he 'was met with the 'Blue Wall' of Garda denial', and given background information by Gardaí in Donegal, many of whom 'had a strong interest in blackening the names of members of the McBrearty family'. Given the information he received, the tribunal found, 'it was little wonder that Mr O'Callaghan reached the views that he did'.

The McBrearty complaints were withdrawn by solicitors acting for the family in October 2001. Solicitor Ken Smyth told the tribunal he was 'embarrassed' by a letter sent in his name withdrawing the complaints. The letter was drafted by Martin Giblin SC, the senior barrister retained to act on behalf of the family, he explained.

'It's not a letter I was happy sending,' Smyth said. The letter, which complained about delays in dealing with the complaints from the family, referred to 'Garda Siochana Grudge Houses' and the 'National Bureau of Underworlders'.

Smyth said the ongoing district court cases and the Carty Inquiry into Garda corruption delayed the Complaints Board reaching a decision, causing the family frustration, particularly when the DPP withdrew prosecutions in the District Court before their lawyers could open up the 'wider issue' of Garda harassment, the 'holy grail' which would keep his clients out of prison and restore their reputations.

Seamus McKenna SC, the chairman of the Garda Complaints Board at the time, was the final witness to give evidence before the Morris tribunal. He said he regretted that the statutory body lacked the power and resources to fully investigate claims of corruption and harassment made by the family. McKenna said he was concerned at the potential for an 'appalling vista' that the Donegal cases presented. 'Not only was there some Guards in Donegal who were corrupt but there was a large conspiracy—if what McBrearty said was true—who were engaged in a conspiracy to pervert the course of justice,' he said.

McKenna said that in hindsight it looked bad that the Complaints Board deferred and didn't take any further action when it met in May 1999 to consider the complaints. He took full responsibility for that decision, but said he was happier to be criticised for postponing the decision than to have reached the wrong decision. Even if he had known the District Court cases would eventually peter out, he explained, he would have done his best to stop the meeting going ahead that day, because he could sense 'a mood in the air that a thing would go a certain way and I certainly would not have been happy to have any or all of those complaints refused or dismissed at that date'.

McKenna's determination to postpone a decision, rather than let the board reach the wrong decision on the most important case ever to come before it 'showed an appreciation of the situation that was quite remarkable', the tribunal found. Justice Morris also noted that in its annual report for the year 2000, the Board recommended that it should be replaced. Legislation to do this was put in place in 2005, and the Garda Complaints Board was replaced on 9 May 2007 by a three-person Garda Síochána Ombudsman Commission staffed with its own investigators, although the Board continued to investigate complaints it received before that date.

Chapter 34

Endgame

Kevin Carty delivered his report to the Garda Commissioner in July 2000. On 26 July, Garda Commissioner Pat Byrne immediately announced five high-profile transfers out of Donegal. Byrne issued a statement saying his action 'should not be seen as an indication of any wrongdoing by those directed on transfer'. Chief Superintendent Denis Fitzpatrick was reassigned to head of the National Traffic Policy Bureau in Dublin. Detective Superintendent John McGinley was sent to a newly created position of detective superintendent in Galway. Superintendent Kevin Lennon was moved to Garda Headquarters in Phoenix Park to take on 'administrative duties'. Two unnamed officers of Garda rank were also transferred.

The Carty report was never published, leading to public speculation about its contents.

John White was arrested by the Carty team in March 2000, as they investigated Bernard Conlon's claim that the sergeant had put him up to the 'silver bullet' claim. On his release, White applied for a transfer to Dublin. It was approved, but White went on sick leave before the transfer took effect. While on leave, he could remain in Donegal. White was arrested again in June 2001, this time following allegations by a fellow detective, Thomas Kilcoyne, that he planted a shotgun at a Traveller encampment in north Donegal, and he was suspended from duty.

Kilcoyne's allegation had an unfortunate fallout. In his statement, he inadvertently named an informant who had provided White with highly sensitive intelligence on dissident republicans. When he saw the name, White immediately contacted Crime & Security. The intelligence branch moved quickly to take the Dublin criminal into protective custody, eventually relocating him in their Witness Protection Programme. The witness gave evidence at the tribunal in late 2006, at a secret Saturday session. White claimed publicly and at his second criminal trial that his troubles stemmed from his decision to speak out about what senior Gardaí knew about dissident republican operations in the day before the Omagh bombing. He was acquitted in his first trial in January 2005 when the trial judge decided that Bernard Conlon was not a credible witness. In July 2006 a jury took just under an hour to return a 'not guilty' verdict on the firearms charge. Three Morris tribunal reports held back to avoid influencing potential jurors were published weeks later. The tribunal found White was responsible for planting a gun at the Travellers' encampment, had used Bernard Conlon as a 'State agent' to prosecute the Parting Glass nightclub for licensing offences, and had caused a hoax bomb to be planted near a telecommunications mast near Ardara in southwest Donegal. No charges were ever brought over the Ardara case. White was dismissed from the force at the end of the year.

Adrienne McGlinchey's evidence to Carty in turn led to the high-profile miscarriage of justice case taken by Frank Shortt, a nightclub owner from Quigley's Point in Inishowen who served twenty-seven months in jail after conviction on drugs charges. After listening to the evidence from Adrienne McGlinchey and from Noel McMahon's estranged wife Sheenagh, the Court of Criminal Appeal found in 2001 that Shortt was the victim of a miscarriage of justice, and that Kevin Lennon and Noel McMahon perjured themselves in his original criminal trial.

Kevin Lennon was suspended after the Court of Criminal Appeal decision. He was fired by the Government in the autumn of 2004 after the first report from the Morris tribunal found that he had planned bogus bomb finds to further his career.

Chief Denis Fitzpatrick had already offered his resignation to the Garda Commissioner after the same report found he was grossly negligent in the performance of his duties. Another Superintendent, John P. O'Connor, also resigned after the report found his handling of the Buncrana district during the early 1990s was negligent.

John McGinley and Joe Shelly offered their resignations to the Garda Commissioner a year later when the second Morris report found that the Barron investigation was 'corrupt in its leadership. It was prejudiced, tendentious and utterly negligent in the highest degree.' John Fitzgerald, having served his forty years in the force, had already retired by the time the report was completed.

In the autumn of 2004, John O'Dowd had an accident and hurt his shoulder. Later, he would tell tribunal investigators that the lies he had told were troubling his conscience, and he had prayed for guidance. When he was injured, he took it as a sign that he should come forward and tell the truth. On 18 October 2004, he sent a statement to the tribunal admitting for the first time that he knew about the hoax extortion phone call William Doherty made from his home to Michael Peoples. Following disciplinary proceedings, O'Dowd and Padraig Mulligan were fired by the Garda Commissioner in December 2004. It is believed that the reason for their dismissal was their failure to give an account of their movements on the night Richie Barron died, when they went to a pub in Lifford while Mulligan was supposed to be on duty in Raphoe.

Phil Collins resigned in October 2004 shortly before giving evidence to the Morris tribunal. He later tried to withdraw his resignation, claiming he acted in haste. The Garda Commissioner refused to entertain the request.

Sergeant Marty Moylan, having reached the thirty-year mark, retired in June 2005, just as the second Morris tribunal report was published. The report found that Moylan had 'allowed himself to be carried along in this disgraceful matter' on the night O'Dowd and Collins coerced a fraudulent statement from Noel McBride. Moylan 'ought to have had enough experience and intelligence not to involve himself in this sorry business. However, he was swept along by the other two.'

'The responsibility for this gross misconduct rests with Garda John O'Dowd and Garda Philip Collins,' the chairman wrote. 'Sergeant Martin Moylan is also responsible for not controlling this misbehaviour and for allowing himself to be dragged into this sorry incident. All three participated in varying degrees. The tribunal is satisfied, however, that the decision to engage in this falsehood was that of the three interviewing Gardaí. The tribunal is satisfied that Garda Collins was brought in on the incident, and brought from his sick bed at that, in order to enhance the threat against McBride so that he could be persuaded to make the statement demanded of him.'

Garda James McDwyer was fired in late 2005, following disciplinary proceedings not related to the Morris tribunal. John Birney, the fourth Garda at the scene the night Richie Barron died, had already retired before he gave evidence to the tribunal.

William Doherty was due to appear in court in September 2001, facing two charges of making false statements and wasting Garda time, but skipped the country and headed for Scotland. From there, he fought against his extradition until December 2003, when his mother died. Doherty then stopped fighting his extradition, and returned to Ireland. On Thursday 11 December, he appeared in Buncrana district court on charges of perjury, making false statements and wasting Garda time on 29 November 1996, the night McBride was arrested over the aerial. More charges were planned, relating to menacing and extortionate phone calls to Old Frank McBrearty. Doherty was remanded until 8 January 2004. A further twenty charges were brought over cheque fraud. The court was told Doherty cashed a total of nineteen cheques drawn on an account in the name of his former partner. No money was ever lodged to the account. Doherty pleaded not guilty to all charges. In June 2004, Doherty changed his plea to guilty, except on one charge, which was dropped. He was remanded in custody, and received one sentence of three years and two sentences of two years, to run concurrently. Doherty had been in custody since his arrest in Scotland at the beginning of his extradition battle. With time served taken into account, he walked free from

Castlerea prison in August 2005. Although he is believed to be living in Britain, his current whereabouts are unknown.

Roderick Donnelly was charged with making a false statement and wasting Garda time. He was found not guilty following a trial in February 2003. Derrick 'Darcy' Connolly was also charged with making a false statement. He was found not guilty following a trial in May 2003. The tribunal found that Donnelly was coached by Darcy Connolly and Paul 'Pip' Roulston before making a false statement to Detective Garda Pat Flynn. It praised Pip Roulston for having the courage to come forward and tell the truth.

The tribunal accepted Paul Roulston's evidence and found 'that there was a campaign mounted by Darcy Connolly, William Doherty, Paul Roulston and others to use a variety of tactics to cause the McBrearty family and Mark McConnell as many problems with the Gardaí as they could. This campaign was also designed to cause the McBreartys considerable difficulty in their home town and ultimately its goal was to drive them out of the town altogether. Probably also, in the warped thinking that gripped a certain section of the town at the time, it was hoped they would break down and confess to "the murder".' The tactics included business cards for the 'Murdering McBreartys' printed by William Doherty, leaflets with similar messages, threatening phone calls to the McBrearty family, and false complaints of dangerous driving.

The chairman went out of his way to praise Paul Roulston, who 'did his best to be an honest witness. If others had followed his example, the tribunal would have concluded its work by now'. He gave his evidence in a 'frank and forthright manner, notwithstanding that this meant admitting to conduct involving himself in this disgraceful campaign'.

However, the tribunal was 'completely unimpressed by the manner in which Darcy Connolly, Kieran Roulston, Roderick Donnelly and William Doherty gave their evidence. The tribunal is of the view that these witnesses have told lies and have deliberately withheld giving information to the tribunal, in an attempt to minimise their role in the vicious campaign which was mounted against the extended McBrearty family, including Mark McConnell. The tribunal is also satisfied that they could have given a much more detailed and coherent account of what went on in Raphoe in the period in question.'

Noel McBride was charged with six counts of making false statements and wasting Garda time. He was found not guilty in June 2004 on direction by the trial judge.

Martin Leonard, the custody Garda during the arrest of Noel McBride and in charge of the welfare of several of those wrongly arrested on 4 December 1996, was fired in early 2005 following disciplinary proceedings. The tribunal described him as 'incorrigible and unbiddable'.

Sligo Garda John Nicholson pleaded guilty to four sample counts of uttering forged documents, and received the Probation Act. The former Sligo Man of the Year has retired from the force, and lives in Sligo. The tribunal found that he 'procured the forged certificates. He forged a number of signatures on these certificates and was furnished with the dates for attendances and the amounts to be included in the certificates by Detective Sergeant White. I am satisfied that both of them were fully aware that the amounts paid on foot of these bogus certificates were not due.'

Another Sligo officer, former Inspector Bernard Lyden, had retired from An Garda Síochána by the time he appeared at the Morris tribunal. The chairman was not satisfied that Lyden 'told the full story of his knowledge of or involvement' in taking Bernard Conlon's statement in September 1997, after he was 'found on' drinking after hours in Frank McBrearty's nightclub. The chairman also found Lyden was 'not candid' about his subsequent dealings with Bernard Conlon.

Bernard Conlon was convicted of making false statements in March 2002, and received a three-year suspended sentence. The tribunal described him as 'a person with previous convictions, living on the margins of society and thought to be untrustworthy and dishonest. He was also somebody of low intellectual ability who was amenable to the promptings and encouragement of Detective Sergeant White and Garda Nicholson' to give evidence against the McBrearty family in a liquor licensing case. 'Garda Nicholson was eager to help the Gardaí in Donegal in their difficulties with the McBreartys, on which he had been briefed by Detective Sergeant White and, perhaps, by other sources whilst in Donegal, during the second arrest of Mark McConnell in June of 1997. He willingly allowed himself to be used as a contact point for, and in the encouragement of, Bernard Conlon in this matter.'

New allegations emerged after the Morris tribunal was set up. It was not until he gave evidence there in the summer of 2004 that Damien McDaid first said that a gun was placed in his mouth. Interviewed by tribunal investigators that same summer, Mark McConnell also claimed for the first time that he saw a detective produce a gun during his third arrest. The lateness of the allegation, given that Mark had made complaints over the years to the Garda Complaints Board, his solicitor, and Billy Flynn, led the tribunal to conclude that his evidence on this point was not credible. More seriously, the multiple and exaggerated claims that both Old Frank McBrearty and Young Frank McBrearty made over the years, and their often confrontational and hostile attitude towards the tribunal, hampered its work considerably. In particular, Young Frank McBrearty's refusal to say clearly what happened on the night he made his false confession, who if anyone he told about it, and when, prevented the chairman reaching a final conclusion.

———

As the Morris tribunal drew close to the finishing line in the autumn of 2007, four and a half years after it first heard evidence, the civil claims by Old Frank McBrearty and others finally came to court. The first, and most contentious, case was the company case. Old Frank, through his company, Frank McBrearty & Co. Ltd, was suing the Garda Commissioner, the State and the Attorney General for the loss of business due to Garda harassment. Since the company had to prove it suffered a loss, the arguments were lengthy and at times technical, as lawyers and accountants argued over projected earnings, and the potential effect of everything from the smoking ban to the rise and fall of the Celtic tiger on the projected profits was debated.

The cases, scheduled for hearing in the court house in Castlebar, Co. Mayo, attracted little attention from the national media. Camera crews and reporters showed up on the first day with one question on their mind—'the number'. How much was Frank looking for? The answer was €7.2 million. With that answer, they had their headlines, and went back to other things rather than cover dry accounting arguments.

A week later, it emerged from the hearings that Old Frank had made use of a tax amnesty in 2004 to reveal to the Revenue Commissioners money he held in an offshore account. Lawyers for the State argued before the Castlebar sitting of the High Court that if the funds held offshore in the 1990s had been kept in Ireland, they could have been invested in the business when it ran into difficulty in 1997. This, in turn, would have reduced the losses suffered by the company, which in turn should reduce the State's liability.

'If the money had been used legitimately by the company, it could have generated a good income for the company,' Paul Burns SC pointed out. But another accountant said that McBrearty could not bring the funds back without incurring penalties before 2004, and they were irrelevant to the losses the company suffered.

The offshore accounts, in the names of Frank and Rosalind McBrearty, held money from 'undeclared sales of the company', the court heard. The accountant said that the company's turnover shrank by 60 per cent in real terms after 1997, when the publican alleged the Garda campaign of harassment began, while the entertainment industry experienced a boom due to the 'Celtic Tiger' economy.

On 25 October 2007, Judge Paul Gilligan awarded the company €1.5 million in compensation for lost profits, €550,000 for lost business opportunities, and €450,000 for a loss in capital value.

The following week, Judge Gilligan began hearings into personal cases brought by Frank and Rosalind McBrearty. Hearings eventually gave way to negotiations, and eventually the case was settled for a reported €2 million. Legal costs incurred by solicitors and barristers defending

District Court prosecutions over the years were also agreed. Settlements were agreed in several cases involving members of the extended McBrearty family and employees of Frank McBrearty over several weeks in Castlebar.

Young Frank McBrearty and his family had already reached an out of court settlement for €1.5 million in 2006.

Roisin McConnell had reached a six figure settlement with the State several years earlier, in 2003, as she was unwilling to face the additional stress of a protracted legal battle. In early 2006, Mark and Roisin celebrated the birth of their second child, Jamie.

In the weeks that followed the first Castlebar settlement, other cases were also settled, although the terms were never made public, save for Mark McConnell, who settled for €1 million plus costs. A Freedom of Information request by the *Irish Independent* in the summer of 2007 revealed that the State had paid out €11.3 million in damages arising out of Garda misconduct in Donegal. Legal costs, which were to be picked up by the taxpayer, would have pushed the final cost of the cases even higher.

In addition to the McBrearty cases, the State settled or lost cases brought by nightclub owner Frank Shortt, who served twenty-seven months in prison and was later declared the victim of a miscarriage of justice by the Court of Criminal Appeal, and was awarded €4.7 million by the Supreme Court in March 2007. Shortt was wrongly convicted in 1995 of allowing the sale of drugs at his Point Inn nightclub at Quigley's Point in north Donegal. His wife and five children settled their cases in October 2006 for a six figure sum. Seven members of the Travelling community, Thomas Collins, Timothy Casey, John Casey, John McCann, Michael McCann, Bernard Power, and David Power, who were arrested at Burnfoot near the border with Derry in May 1998, also settled their cases in 2006. Others who reached settlements included Michael and Charlotte Peoples, Sean Crossan, Eamonn McConnell, Michael McConnell, Liam O'Donnell, Marty McCallion, Willie Logan, Hugo McBrearty, Richard McBrearty, Ann Crossan, Maria McBrearty, and John Mitchell.

———

The Morris reports are a devastating critique of An Garda Síochána, but the retired High Court president is remarkably reluctant to criticise any member of the force outside Donegal. In the first two reports, his condemnation of Crime & Security is withering, but no individual is singled out for responsibility. The only named officer from HQ criticised in the second report into the conduct of the Barron investigation is Detective Inspector Patrick Nyham, who supplied telephone records 'informally' to his brother-in-law John O'Toole in the Letterkenny incident room.

Nyham and O'Toole are censured in only the mildest terms for obtaining records without legal authorisation. In the section of the report dealing with the incident, the word 'illegal' never appears. Nyham wasn't even called to give evidence. In an interview with tribunal investigators, he claimed he'd only bypassed official channels on this one occasion, and had no memory of the person he spoke to in the GPO. No one has ever come forward from An Post or Telecom Eireann to admit helping Nyham. The tribunal conducted no inquiry into this appalling and illegal invasion of privacy, which led to the arrests of twelve people.

Kevin Lennon told the tribunal he sat outside while Chief Superintendent Denis Fitzpatrick and Assistant Commissioner Noel Crummey discussed the Barron affair, and was then ordered to cancel the exhumation of Richie Barron as he drove home from the meeting. Mr Crummey was never called to give evidence.

On the first day he gave evidence, Joe Shelly told the Morris tribunal that Crime & Security branch were told William Doherty's name in the first half of 1997. Three days later, he reversed himself, explaining that the highly detailed evidence he'd given was simply mistaken. The Morris reports make no mention of this remarkable reversal, save a single line finding that Crime & Security were unaware of Doherty's identity.

Even with such reservations, however, the fallout from the tribunal has been earth-shattering for the force, with the resignations, firings and early retirements of officers from Garda to Chief Superintendent rank. The final cost of the Donegal debacle, the thousands of wasted Garda work hours on the Barron investigation and other cases, the diversion of resources away from other operations to the Carty Inquiry, the legal expenses and settlements with the McBreartys and others, and of course, the cost of the tribunal itself, are still being calculated.

On the other side of the balance sheet, the Garda Síochána Act passed into law put the force on a new statutory footing, created a Garda Inspectorate to report and recommend on best policing practices, and created a new body, the Garda Ombudsman Commission, to replace the Garda Complaints Board. The Minister for Justice also published new disciplinary regulations in line with recommendations from the tribunal, and several working groups set up by the Commissioner have led to often unnoticed but crucial reforms in the handling of informants, training, and management oversight. Training programmes don't make for exciting headlines though, so the focus in coverage of the tribunal is usually on the sins of the past.

One significant fact is almost completely overlooked in discussions of the McBrearty case—the system worked. For all that Frank McBrearty complains about the victimisation his family endured at the hands of the State and its agents, the State finally served him well, clearing his name and those of his family, friends and associates beyond reasonable doubt (though not, sadly, beyond unreasonable doubt and prejudice). Frank McBrearty was able to use the legal system, from the humble District Court hearings on liquor law cases to the High Court and Supreme Court, to put his case. He was able to raise his case in Dáil Éireann and the Seanad. An Garda Síochána did respond to the complaints—sending Kevin Carty to find out what was going on in Donegal—albeit sluggishly and reluctantly at first, but with increasing vigour as the Department of Justice demanded answers. A tribunal of inquiry was set up largely at his behest. He may not like all the conclusions it reached, but he can hardly complain he was denied access to justice.

It shouldn't have been so hard though. For most of the time the tribunal sat, Frank had no legal representation. His fight had cost him much of his life's savings, and he could not take the risk of losing before a tribunal, with its astronomical costs. Through the hard work of the legal teams led by Martin Giblin SC, the McBreartys were able to bring pressure on the police force in the courts, obtaining discovery of further evidence in both the District Court and the High Court. But not everyone has the financial resources to hire a senior counsel to fight a three-year battle in a District Court. Frank McBrearty has a truculent warrior's heart, it is not in his nature to back away from a fight, even against the unlimited financial power of the State.

After a fashion then, the system worked. But this provides no grounds for complacency. The system works exceedingly slowly. Nine years passed between the death of Richie Barron and the Morris report, which cleared the names of Young Frank McBrearty, Mark McConnell, Michael Peoples and all the others who fell under suspicion. The McBreartys were blessed in having around them capable and tireless people who worked for their cause. Old Frank had the money first to hire Billy Flynn to investigate his case, and then top-notch barristers like Martin Giblin and others to come to Donegal to fight apparently trivial District Court cases.

There have been other cases like the McBrearty case, where the victims have not had access to the same resources. Dean Lyons, who falsely confessed to two murders in Grangegorman, died a lonely junkie's death in England, and we still don't know exactly how and why he confessed to a murder he didn't commit. Brian Rossiter, a fourteen-year-old boy, died in Clonmel after spending a night in a Garda cell. He was brought from the cell to hospital in a coma, and never recovered consciousness. The limited terms of reference for the inquiry into his death were severely criticised. There have been other questionable convictions, other contested statements of admission. The McBreartys had the financial resources and mental resilience to fight back. Not everyone has been so fortunate.

Legislation on public inquiries introduced by Justice Minister Michael

McDowell was intended to speed up the cumbersome pace of the tribunals of inquiry—yet the minister chose to by-pass his own new law when he set up the inquiry into the Rossiter case, instead relying on an obscure provision of the Dublin Metropolitan Police Act (1924), an eighty-year-old law. The Garda Complaints Board was replaced by the Garda Ombudsman Commission in the Garda Síochána Act (2005), signed into law by the President within weeks of the publication of the second Morris report in June 2005, yet it was not until the end of the year that the names of the three members of the Commission were officially announced. The Commission was not up and running until spring 2007, and in the meantime the people of Ireland had to make do with the largely toothless Garda Complaints Board, which was itself the subject of a module of inquiry by the Morris tribunal for its self-admitted failure to deal with complaints from Raphoe.

The Gardaí need effective oversight—for their own sake and for the sake of the people of Ireland. Models for such oversight exist—the Policing Ombudsman's Office in Northern Ireland is the best known here. Just as important as oversight of ordinary policing, there must be effective oversight of intelligence gathering—Crime & Security Branch. The Offences Against the State Act (OASA)—enacted as a special measure at the outbreak of World War II—gives the police extraordinary powers, which are used more and more in the fight against 'ordinary crime' as feuding gangsters and drug dealers are redefined as a threat to the very existence of the State, a definition happily acceded to by our courts and politicians. OASA and other emergency powers legislation passed in the heat of passion following terrorist atrocities need urgent review. The IRA has effectively gone into retirement, and OASA was never intended as an instrument of everyday policing.

The Morris tribunal has details of the arrests of Old Frank McBrearty, Mark McConnell, Michael Peoples, Bernard Conlon, Hugh and Anthony Diver, Bernard Shovlin, Adrienne McGlinchey and the Burnfoot Seven under the sweeping provisions of Section 30 of OASA. Every one of those arrested could be held for up to forty-eight hours. None of the arrests led to anything substantial. Many of them were illegal arrests. In the wake of the Omagh bombing, the period of detention has been increased from forty-eight to seventy-two hours, and the right to silence weakened. In 2007, the ordinary criminal law was also amended, so that the detention period under 'Section 4' arrests increased from twelve to twenty-four hours. Again, the right to silence was weakened, and in special circumstances, suspects can be held for up to seven days. Senior Garda officers continue to exercise quasi-judicial roles, issuing search warrants, when the role would be better suited to independent judges. Indeed, when the recommendation to do just that, published in the fifth Morris report, was ignored by the Government, the judge took the unusual step of repeating it in full in his sixth report.

The first Morris report was published on Thursday 15 July 2004. The following Tuesday, the *Donegal Democrat* carried a 2,000-word article I wrote summarising its findings, and the entire series of events that made up the 'Explosives module', the allegations by Sheenagh McMahon and Adrienne McGlinchey that Kevin Lennon and Detective Garda Noel McMahon planned bogus explosives finds to further their careers. On the front page that day was a different Garda story. On Sunday 18 July Fergus McGroary, a thirty-three-year-old Garda stationed in Bunbeg in the northwest of the county, received a report that a car had driven over Bunbeg Pier. Garda McGroary ran to the scene, dived in and managed to bring the woman driver to safety. He was later awarded a Silver Scott Medal for his bravery in the line of duty. I spent four years of my life writing about the Morris tribunal. I would rather write about officers like Fergus McGroary.

Corruption means rot, a cancer that eats away at the body. It eats away not just at individuals, but organisations. Every Garda who lied, every Garda who looked the other way, every Garda who stuck by what Freddie Morris called the 'culture of silence', made it more difficult for others to come forward and say what they saw. Every Garda who plants evidence, or lies, or assaults a suspect, or covers up for a colleague's wrongdoing, dishonours the bravery of officers like Fergus McGroary. The State deserves better. The Guards deserve better. You deserve better.

> '*The Garda Síochána will succeed, not by force of arms or numbers, but by their moral authority as servants of the people.*'
> —MICHAEL STAINES, THE FIRST COMMISSIONER OF AN GARDA SÍOCHÁNA (AND TO DATE, THE ONLY CIVILIAN TO HOLD THE POST)

Chapter 35
It Happens

There were always just three possibilities. The first was the Garda version. Young Frank McBrearty made the confession. The way the Guards told it, people sign confessions all the time. It's not their fault that some of them later turn out to be innocent.

The detectives said the confession was made shortly before 8.30 p.m., almost twelve hours after Frank McBrearty was arrested, on two sides of a single sheet of A4 paper. John Melody and John Fitzpatrick were questioning McBrearty at the time. They insist he made the incriminating statement voluntarily.

Questioned by investigators from the Morris tribunal, Fitzpatrick and Melody insisted Frank McBrearty made the statement voluntarily. But following a proper examination of Barron's skull by forensic pathologists from the UK and Ireland, making it clear that the damage he sustained could not be caused by 'a bit of timber', difficult questions arose. McBrearty couldn't have admitted his guilt, because there was no guilt, so why would he confess?

'I don't honestly know why he would consider it,' Fitzpatrick admitted to the tribunal investigators. 'Like, no man would consider admitting something unless there was something wrong with him.' Fitzpatrick went on to say he knew of other situations where innocent people had admitted to crimes as serious as murder. He mentioned a case in Galway, and Dean Lyons, a young Dublin heroin addict who confessed to two murders in Grangegorman.

'You know it's happened. It has happened,' he told Michael Finn, a former detective superintendent hired by the tribunal as an investigator. The interview took place on 27 January 2005, in the presence of Finn and another investigator, retired Assistant Commissioner Patrick Cummins of the Royal Canadian Mounted Police.

There were always just three possibilities.

The second possibility was that Young Frank McBrearty never made the confession. In interviews with tribunal investigators and the press, he was vehement that he would not confess to a crime he didn't commit. Not only that, but he claimed he was verbally and physically abused while under arrest, yet they could not crack his resolve.

Eight years later, the second report of the Morris tribunal found that Barron died as a result of a hit and run, and that McBrearty (and everyone else arrested during the murder investigation) was wrongfully arrested. From that moment, the confession—however it was created—was considered a false confession. Four months later, Young Frank McBrearty settled his claim against the State out of court for a reported €1.5 million. His reaction when the tribunal found that his will crumbled and he made a false confession was to say on RTÉ's *Morning Ireland* programme that he did not regret anything he had done at the tribunal. 'We're going to Europe, we've always been going to Europe, we'll be taking this case to the European Court of Human Rights,' was his final word.

There were always just three possibilities.

So maybe Frank was tricked. According to this third theory, he signed an innocuous statement exonerating his father, and this was later altered. The confession document is a single A4 sheet. The first side contains an account of how Frank McBrearty and his cousin Mark McConnell waylaid Richie Barron on his way home from the pub. Frank then picked up a piece of timber and 'hit him a slap on the back of the head'. On the second page, Frank goes on to say his father never bribed or intimidated anyone.

According to the Trick Theory, Frank never signed the page admitting he attacked Richie Barron. Only the second page, where he declares his father's innocence, is signed. Frank claimed the signature was a forgery, although an English handwriting expert said it matched his signature on a statement he made a month before he was arrested. Frank then said this statement was rewritten, and signed by the same forger who worked on his confession, thus explaining the match. Others suggested that Frank did sign the innocent statement about his father, and that the incriminating statement was added later. But on the basis of forensic tests and expert evidence, the third possibility was easily dismissed by the tribunal.

So where does the truth lie? In a sense, it doesn't matter. No matter what happened, one thing is clear. It's a false confession.

The Morris tribunal was charged with uncovering the truth about what happened during the twelve hours when Frank was in police custody. So what really happened? We may never know. For the detectives, the best-case scenario was that Frank McBrearty was so cowed by their interrogation techniques that he confessed to a crime he knew he didn't commit. In their favour, they could point to the opinion of four respected handwriting experts, and to Frank's own performances at the Morris tribunal, where he frequently clashed with the tribunal chairman, providing ample evidence of an unstable personality.

For the Garda Commissioner, beset with scandals—the Donegal debacle is only the most public—it will come as cold comfort that members of an elite detective unit coerced an innocent man into confessing, even unwittingly. Particularly when one of his detectives argued in his defence that 'it has happened more than once'. This admission casts doubt on confession evidence in every trial in Ireland.

In 1994, a government steering committee recommended that interviews with suspects in Garda custody should be videotaped. The five-year pilot scheme didn't end until 1999. It took several more years to introduce taping in every station designated for interviewing suspects. Had Frank McBrearty been taped, we wouldn't have spent several years arguing the toss over his signature. Ironically, there was a Garda video expert in Donegal the day Frank McBrearty was arrested for the murder that never happened. Detective Sergeant Joseph Costello was told to stand by that day in case his technical assistance was needed. But no one asked him to tape the Garda interview of Frank McBrearty, or of anyone else in custody.

What happened in Room 225 of Letterkenny Garda station on 4 December 1996 remains inside a black box. But ultimately though, it doesn't matter. What matters is what An Garda Síochána and the Department of Justice do to ensure it never happens again.